G.C.S.E.
MATHEMATICS

R. Joinson

**CHECKMATE
GOLD**

© R. JOINSON 1988

First published in Great Britain 1988 by Checkmate Gold Publications,
P.O. Box 36, Ellesmere Port, South Wirral, L66 7PB.

British Library Cataloguing in Publication Data
Joinson, R.
GCSE Mathematics
1. Mathematics ——1961–
I. Title
510   QA39.2

ISBN 1 85313 003 6

Text set in 10/12 pt Univers
by Merseyside Graphics Ltd., 130 The Parade, Meols, Wirral L47 5AZ
Printed by Billing & Sons Limited, Hylton Road, Worcester WR2 5JU.

Cover design by Merseyside Graphics Ltd.

PREFACE

This book has been specifically written for students studying G.C.S.E. Mathematics wishing to acquire the higher grades A, B, C and D of the major examining boards. It will be suitable for students following a one or two year course at school or college. It will also prove a useful text for those students requiring further revision and practice to improve their grade at the higher level. The text follows closely the syllabi of all the major examining bodies and was written when full agreement regarding syllabus structure, design and content had been reached.

The G.C.S.E. higher level has three parts which are:—
1. Two written examination papers at the end of the course.
2. Tests during the course.
3. Investigations during the course.

The book covers the contents of the examination papers and course tests. These are laid out under topic areas for ease of learning and referencing during revision. A separate section of the text has been set aside to deal with investigations. As these cut across topic areas it was felt inappropriate to classify them within the main chapter headings. The answers supplied to this part should only be looked upon as a guide and alternative solutions may be appropriate.

By cutting explanations to a minimum and incorporating hundreds of diagrams I hope that my ideas have been communicated in a clear and concise way. Most readers will be given advice by their teacher as to the appropriate sections to study to fulfil their examination board requirements. It is nevertheless worthwhile for students to obtain a copy of the relevant syllabus and study the contents to ensure they are able to plan and control the study topics and manage their time effectively. In addition to completing the many exercises in the text students should always attempt specimen and past examination questions.

Finally I would like to thank Gareth Roberts and Harry Morton for their advice, my wife Jenny for her help and typing of all manuscripts and Brian Renner and his team at Merseyside Graphics for turning the manuscript into text and for the many splendidly detailed drawings.

R. JOINSON
May 1988.

FORMULAE AND DEFINITIONS

Percentages

$$\text{Simple interest} = \frac{PTR}{100} \quad \text{where} \quad \begin{aligned} P &= \text{Principal} \\ T &= \text{Time} \\ R &= \text{Rate} \end{aligned}$$

Speed and Fuel consumption

$$\text{Average speed or velocity} = \frac{\text{Total distance travelled}}{\text{Total time taken}}$$

$$\text{Average fuel consumption} = \frac{\text{Total distance travelled}}{\text{Fuel used}}$$

Sets notation

$\mathscr{E}$ represents the Universal set

$\in$ means 'is a member of'

$\notin$ means 'is not a member of'

$\subset$ means 'is a subset of'

A' is the complement of set A

$\cap$ represents the intersection of sets

$\cup$ represents the union of sets

$n(A)$ represents the number of elements in set A

Indices

$$a^m \times a^n = a^{m+n}$$
$$a^m \div a^n = a^{m-n}$$
$$(a^m)^n = a^{m \times n}$$
$$(ab)^n = a^n b^n$$
$$a^{-m} = \frac{1}{a^m}$$
$$a^0 = 1$$
$$a^1 = a$$
$$a^{\frac{1}{n}} = \sqrt[n]{a}$$
$$a = \sqrt[n]{a^m} \quad \text{or} \quad \left(\sqrt[n]{a}\right)^m$$

Quadratic equations

If $ax^2 + bx + c = 0$ then

$$x = \frac{-b \pm \sqrt{b^2 - 4ac}}{2a}$$

Inequalities

$>$ means 'is greater than'

$<$ means 'is less than'

$\geqslant$ means 'is greater than or equal to'

$\leqslant$ means 'is less than or equal to'

Variation

If y is directly proportional to x then $y = kx$
i.e. as y increases, x increases.

If y is inversely proportional to x then $y = \dfrac{k}{x}$

i.e. as y increases, x decreases.
If y varies partially with x and z then $y = ax + bz$
i.e. as y increases, x and z increase also.

Graphs

$$\text{Gradient} = \frac{\text{change in } y}{\text{change in } x}$$

Equation of a straight line

$$y = mx + c \qquad \text{where } m = \text{gradient}$$
$$c = \text{y intercept}$$

Trapezoidal rule

$$\text{Area} = w \left(\frac{h_1 + h_n}{2} + h_2 + h_3 + \ldots h_{n-1} \right)$$

where w = width of strip
h = height of ordinates

At a maximum or minimum point the gradient = 0

Rate of change = gradient

$$\text{Acceleration} = \frac{\text{change of speed (velocity)}}{\text{change time}}$$

Geometry

Sum of the interior angles of a polygon
$= (n - 2) \times 180^{\circ}$ where n is the number of sides

Interior angle of a regular polygon

$$= 180^{\circ} - \frac{360^{\circ}}{n} \quad \text{or} \quad \frac{(n - 2)180^{\circ}}{n}$$

Measurement

Area of a triangle	=	½bh
Area of a trapezium	=	½(a+b)h
Area of a circle	=	πr^2
Circumference of a circle	=	πd
Area of a sector	=	$\pi r^2 \times \dfrac{\theta}{360^{\circ}}$
Arc length	=	$\pi d \times \dfrac{\theta}{360^{\circ}}$
Area of a kite	=	½(product of its diagonals)
Area of an annulus	=	$\pi (R + r)t$
Volume of a prism	=	Area of end x length

Cone Volume = $\frac{1}{3} \pi r^2 h$, surface area = $\pi r(r + \ell)$
where r = radius of base   h = height ℓ = slant height
Pyramid Volume = $\frac{1}{3}$ (area of base) h
Sphere Volume = $\frac{4}{3} \pi r^3$, curved surface area = $4\pi r^2$

Ratio

Area ratio	=	(length ratio)^2
Volume ratio	=	(length ratio)^3
(mass ratio)		

Trigonometry

$\text{Sin } x = \dfrac{o}{h}$

$\text{Cos } x = \dfrac{a}{h}$

$\text{Tan } x = \dfrac{o}{a}$

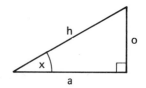

h = hypotenuse
a = adjacent side
o = opposite side

Pythagoras theorem

$$h^2 = a^2 + b^2$$

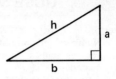

Sine rule

$$\frac{a}{Sin\ A} = \frac{b}{Sin\ B} = \frac{c}{Sin\ C}$$

Cosine rule

$$a^2 = b^2 + c^2 - 2bc\ Cos\ A$$

Area of a triangle = ½ab Sin C

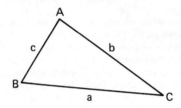

Statistics

Mean $\quad = \quad \dfrac{\text{sum of all values}}{\text{number of values}}$

Median $\quad = \quad$ middle value

Mode $\quad = \quad$ most commonly occurring value

GCSE MATHEMATICS — CONTENTS

NUMBERS AND COMPUTATION

TYPES OF NUMBERS

Many of us tend to call any number without a fractional part a whole number. However, numbers of this kind are defined in different ways according to the use we make of them. The following sets of numbers will be met throughout this book.

Natural numbers
$$\{1,\ 2,\ 3,\ 4\ldots\}$$

Whole numbers   natural numbers including zero
$$\{0,\ 1,\ 2,\ 3,\ 4\ldots\}$$

Even numbers   natural numbers which are divisible by 2
$$\{2,\ 4,\ 6,\ 8\ldots\}$$

Odd numbers   natural numbers which are not divisible by 2
$$\{1,\ 3,\ 5,\ 7,\ 9\ldots\}$$

Prime numbers   natural numbers which have only two factors
$$\{2,\ 3,\ 5,\ 7,\ 11,\ 13\ldots\}$$

Integers   positive integers (natural numbers), zero and negative integers
$$\{\ldots -2,\ -1,\ 0,\ 1,\ 2,\ 3\ldots\}$$
These are also called directed numbers

An example of directed numbers is the temperature scale

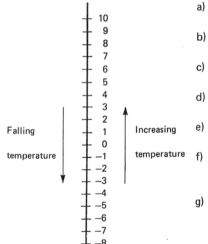

a) Temperature is 8°C and falls by 5°C
New temperature is $8 - 5 = 3$°C

b) Temperature is 8°C and falls by 15°C
New temperature is $8 - 15 = -7$°C

c) Temperature is 1°C and increases by 5°C
New temperature is $1 + 5 = 6$°C

d) Temperature is −9°C and increases by 15°C
New temperature is $-9 + 15 = 6$°C

e) Temperature is −3°C and falls by 7°C
New temperature is $-3\ -7 = -10$°C

f) Temperature is 6°C during the day and −4°C during the night therefore drop of temperature is 10°C

g) Temperature is −12°C during the night and −2°C during the day. Therefore change of temperature is an increase of 10°C

EXERCISE 1.1

By using the temperature scale shown on the previous page answer questions 1 to 20

1) 5°C increased by 9°C
2) 5°C falls by 4°C
3) 9°C falls by 15°C
4) −6°C increases by 4°C
5) −5°C increases by 8°C
6) 9°C − 4°C
7) 8°C − 12°C
8) −4°C + 2°C
9) −7°C + 16°C
10) −6°C − 5°C

11) −17°C + 3°C
12) −1°C + 15°C
13) 0°C − 6°C
14) 12°C − 12°C
15) −6°C + 6°C
16) −17°C − 6°C
17) −43°C + 26°C
18) −17°C + 26°C
19) −7°C − 19°C
20) −31°C + 27°C

In questions 21 to 35 state what the change of temperature is between the two given temperatures.

21) 3°C and 7°C
22) 17°C and 32°C
23) −5°C and 4°C
24) −7°C and 2°C
25) −6°C and −3°C
26) −7°C and 0°C
27) 5°C and 2°C
28) 7°C and −2°C

29) 5°C and −3°C
30) −2°C and −7°C
31) −8°C and −4°C
32) 0°C and −12°C
33) −17°C and −12°C
34) 8°C and −16°C
35) −9°C and −15°C

FACTORS

The factors of a number are all the natural numbers which will divide into it exactly. A number is the product of two or more of its factors.

Example 1.1   The factors of 12 are 1, 2, 3, 4, 6 and 12
Pairs of factors can be multiplied together to make 12
i.e. $1 \times 12 = 12$
$2 \times 6 = 12$
$3 \times 4 = 12$

Prime factors. All factors of a number can be expressed as products of the prime factors of the number.

3

Example 1.2   The prime factors of 12 are 2 and 3. The other factors are

$$2 \times 2 = 4$$
$$3 \times 2 = 6$$
$$2 \times 2 \times 3 = 12$$

To find the prime factors of a number proceed as follows

Example 1.3   Express 360 as a product of its prime factors

2)360	divide by smallest prime factor of 360
2)180	divide by smallest prime factor of 180
2) 90	again divide by 2
3) 45	divide by smallest prime factor of 45
3) 15	again divide by 3
5	stop when a prime number is reached

The prime factors of 360 are 2, 3 and 5.   360 can be written as a product of its prime factors thus

$$2 \times 2 \times 2 \times 3 \times 3 \times 5$$

or $2^3 \times 3^2 \times 5$

Example 1.4   Express 300 as a product of its prime factors and state the smallest number it has to be multiplied by to produce a perfect square
Dividing by primes

2)300
2)150
3) 75
5) 25
5

$$\therefore 300 = 2 \times 2 \times 3 \times 5 \times 5$$
$$= 2^2 \times 3 \times 5^2$$

But $2^2 \times 3^2 \times 5^2 = (2 \times 3 \times 5)^2$ which is a perfect square $(30)^2$
$\therefore$ 300 must be multiplied by 3 to obtain a perfect square

Note all power values must be **even** to make an exact square

4

Example 1.5   What is the largest odd number that is a factor of 540?

$$
\begin{array}{r}
2\ )\underline{540} \\
2\ )\underline{270} \\
3\ )\underline{135}\ ^* \\
3\ )\underline{\ 45} \\
3\ )\underline{\ 15} \\
5
\end{array}
$$

$$\therefore\ 540 = 2^2 \times 3^3 \times 5$$

But the largest odd number which is a factor of 540 is itself a multiple of these prime factors. Since multiplying odd numbers together always yields odd numbers, the largest odd factor is

$$3 \times 3 \times 3 \times 5 = 135 \qquad (^* \text{ which can also be found above})$$

EXERCISE 1.2

Write down all the factors of the following numbers

1)	15	2)	20	3)	24	4)	30	5)	32	6)	40
7)	45	8)	60	9)	71	10)	84	11)	90	12)	100

Express the following numbers as products of their prime factors

13)	150	14)	160	15)	200	16)	210	17)	260	18)	675
19)	945	20)	1715	21)	1155	22)	1035				

Express the following numbers as products of their prime factors and state the smallest whole number it has to be multiplied by to produce a perfect square

23)	12	24)	18	25)	180	26)	80	27)	162	28)	252
29)	275	30)	468	31)	608	32)	980	33)	600	34)	360
35)	540	36)	1452								

What is the largest odd number that is a factor of the following

37)	108	38)	180	39)	200	40)	271	41)	294	42)	504
43)	588	44)	720	45)	780						

VULGAR FRACTIONS

A fraction is part of a whole. There are two types of fraction, the vulgar fraction which is usually referred to as a 'fraction' and the decimal fraction referred to as a 'decimal'.

Vulgar Fractions

Addition and subtraction

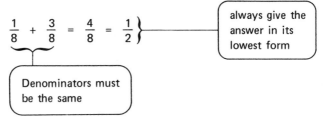

Example 1.6 $\dfrac{1}{8} + \dfrac{3}{8} = \dfrac{4}{8} = \dfrac{1}{2}$ } — always give the answer in its lowest form

Denominators must be the same

Example 1.7 $\dfrac{3}{8} + \dfrac{1}{4}$ L.C.M. of 8 and 4 is 8

$= \dfrac{3}{8} + \dfrac{2}{8} = \dfrac{5}{8}$

Example 1.8 $1\dfrac{3}{4} - \dfrac{7}{8}$

$= \dfrac{7}{4} - \dfrac{7}{8}$

$= \dfrac{14}{8} - \dfrac{7}{8} = \dfrac{7}{8}$

Multiplication and division

Example 1.9 $\dfrac{3}{4} \times \dfrac{1}{2} = \dfrac{3 \times 1}{4 \times 2} = \dfrac{3}{8}$

Example 1.10 $\dfrac{7}{8} \times \dfrac{4}{5}$

$= \dfrac{7}{2} \times \dfrac{1}{5}$ (by dividing the 4 and 8 by their H.C.F.)

$= \dfrac{7 \times 1}{2 \times 5} = \dfrac{7}{10}$

Example 1.11 $\dfrac{3}{8} \div \dfrac{3}{4}$

$= \dfrac{3}{8} \times \dfrac{4}{3}$

$= \dfrac{1}{2} \times \dfrac{1}{1} = \dfrac{1}{2}$ (Dividing the 3's by 3 and the 8 and 4 by 4)

Example 1.12 $1\dfrac{1}{2} \div \dfrac{5}{8}$

$= \dfrac{3}{2} \times \dfrac{8}{5} = \dfrac{3}{1} \times \dfrac{4}{5} = \dfrac{12}{5} = 2\dfrac{2}{5}$

EXERCISE 1.3

1) $\dfrac{1}{2} + \dfrac{1}{4}$

2) $\dfrac{3}{8} + \dfrac{1}{4}$

3) $\dfrac{3}{10} + \dfrac{7}{10}$

4) $\dfrac{1}{4} + \dfrac{7}{8}$

5) $\dfrac{5}{8} + \dfrac{3}{4}$

6) $\dfrac{7}{8} - \dfrac{1}{4}$

7) $1\dfrac{1}{2} - \dfrac{1}{10}$

8) $2\dfrac{1}{4} - \dfrac{7}{8}$

9) $3\dfrac{1}{2} - \dfrac{3}{4}$

10) $3\dfrac{1}{8} - 2\dfrac{1}{2}$

11) $1\dfrac{3}{4} + 1\dfrac{7}{8}$

12) $5\dfrac{1}{2} - 3\dfrac{3}{4}$

13) $7\dfrac{3}{4} - 2\dfrac{1}{2}$

14) $5\dfrac{7}{10} - 2\dfrac{1}{5}$

15) $3\dfrac{1}{2} - 2\dfrac{3}{4}$

16) $5\dfrac{7}{8} - 3\dfrac{3}{4}$

17) $2\dfrac{1}{4} - 1\dfrac{1}{5}$

18) $3\dfrac{1}{2} + 2\dfrac{7}{10}$

19) $4\dfrac{2}{3} - 3\dfrac{1}{8}$

20) $4\dfrac{2}{3} + 3\dfrac{1}{2}$

21) $\dfrac{1}{2} \times \dfrac{1}{3}$

22) $\dfrac{3}{4} \times \dfrac{1}{2}$

23) $\dfrac{7}{8} \times \dfrac{1}{4}$

24) $\dfrac{4}{5} \times \dfrac{1}{2}$

25) $\dfrac{3}{4} \times 1\dfrac{1}{2}$

26) $\dfrac{7}{8} \times \dfrac{2}{3}$

27) $1\dfrac{1}{2} \times 1\dfrac{1}{3}$

28) $2\dfrac{1}{2} \times 1\dfrac{1}{4}$

29) $3\dfrac{1}{2} \times 1\dfrac{7}{8}$

30) $\dfrac{1}{2} \div \dfrac{2}{3}$

31) $\dfrac{5}{8} \div \dfrac{1}{4}$

32) $\dfrac{7}{8} \div \dfrac{3}{4}$

33) $1\dfrac{1}{3} \div \dfrac{5}{6}$

34) $1\frac{1}{2} \div \frac{7}{8}$

35) $2\frac{1}{2} \div 1\frac{1}{4}$

36) $3\frac{1}{2} \div 2\frac{1}{2}$

37) $3\frac{1}{4} \div 2\frac{1}{5}$

38) $2\frac{1}{2} \div \frac{7}{10}$

39) $3\frac{1}{3} \div 1\frac{1}{4}$

40) $1\frac{7}{10} \div 2\frac{1}{2}$

Changing a vulgar fraction into a decimal fraction is done by dividing the numerator by the denominator. It is most easily carried out using a calculator.

Example 1.13   Change $\frac{1}{8}$ into a decimal fraction

On calculator $\boxed{1}$ $\boxed{\div}$ $\boxed{8}$ $\boxed{=}$
Answer is 0.125

EXERCISE 1.4

Change these vulgar fractions into decimal fractions

1) $\frac{3}{8}$

2) $\frac{5}{8}$

3) $\frac{3}{20}$

4) $\frac{7}{20}$

5) $\frac{13}{20}$

6) $\frac{1}{16}$

7) $\frac{5}{16}$

8) $\frac{7}{16}$

9) $\frac{13}{16}$

10) $\frac{3}{25}$

11) $\frac{13}{25}$

12) $\frac{21}{25}$

13) $\frac{13}{40}$

14) $\frac{17}{40}$

15) $\frac{33}{40}$

In questions 16 and 17 arrange the fractions in order, smallest to largest

16) $\frac{7}{27}$ $\frac{106}{409}$ $\frac{239}{922}$ 0.25920

17) $\frac{170}{1043}$ $\frac{7}{43}$ $\frac{387}{2376}$ 0.16280

18)   Change the first two of each of the following fractions into decimals and then predict the rest

a) $\frac{1}{9}$, $\frac{2}{9}$, $\frac{3}{9}$, $\frac{4}{9}$, $\frac{5}{9}$ etc.

b) $\frac{1}{11}$, $\frac{2}{11}$, $\frac{3}{11}$, $\frac{4}{11}$, $\frac{5}{11}$ etc.

SQUARES, CUBES, ROOTS AND RECIPROCALS

The values of each of these can be obtained directly from your calculator so it is important that you have a scientific calculator. Ensure you know which buttons to press by consulting its instruction booklet.

Squares, Cubes, Roots and Reciprocals

SQUARES

Example 1.14

$3 \times 3 = 9$

i.e. $3^2 = 9$

we say three squared equals nine

also $2 \times 2 = 4$ or $2^2 = 4$

$5 \times 5 = 25$ or $5^2 = 25$

etc.

SQUARE ROOTS

Example 1.15

since $3^2 = 9$

we say $\sqrt{9} = 3$ or $9^{\frac{1}{2}} = 3$

or the square root of 9 is 3

but $(-3)^2 = (-3) \times (-3) = 9$

$\therefore \sqrt{9}$ is also -3

so $\sqrt{9}$ has two values, 3 and -3

likewise $\sqrt{100} = 10$ or -10

$\sqrt{25} = 5$ or -5

etc.

Note that the square root of a negative number cannot be found using the above rules, i.e. $\sqrt{-25}$ cannot be found.

CUBES

Example 1.16

$2 \times 2 \times 2 = 8$

i.e. $2^3 = 8$

we say two cubed equals eight

also $3 \times 3 \times 3 = 27$ or $3^3 = 27$

$5 \times 5 \times 5 = 125$ or $5^3 = 125$

CUBE ROOTS

Example 1.17

$2^3 = 8$

we say $\sqrt[3]{8} = 2$ or $8^{\frac{1}{3}} = 2$

or the cube root of eight is two

since $(-2) \times (-2) \times (-2) = -8$

and $2 \times 2 \times 2 = 8$

a cube root has only one value (unlike a square root)

i.e. $\sqrt[3]{8} = 2$

$\sqrt[3]{-8} = -2$

RECIPROCALS

Example 1.18   A reciprocal of a number is 1 divided by that number, i.e. the reciprocal of

5 is $1/5 = 0\cdot2$

we write $5^{-1} = 0\cdot2$

also the reciprocal of 1/5 is $\dfrac{1}{1/5}$ $= 5$

$(1/5)^{-1} = 5$

Estimation

In the case of squares, cubes and reciprocals round off to one significant figure.
In the case of square roots and cube roots, round off to the nearest square or cube number.

Example 1.19   Estimate the following

a) $(6.43)^2$

estimate is $6^2 = 36$

b) $(\cdot474)^3$

estimate is $(\cdot5)^3 = \cdot125$

c) $\dfrac{1}{2\cdot45}$

estimate is $\frac{1}{2} = 0.5$

d) $\sqrt{39}$

estimate is $\sqrt{36} = 6$

e) $\sqrt[3]{80}$

estimate is $\sqrt[3]{64} = 4$

Using a calculator

On most scientific calculators, squares, square roots and reciprocals are straight forward; cubes and cube roots can be more complicated.

Example 1.20

Find the square, square root and reciprocal of 12·5.

a)   Square of 12·5

Calculator sequence is $\boxed{12\cdot5}$ $\boxed{x^2}$

Answer is 156·25

b) Square root of 12·5
    Calculator sequence is ┌─────┐ ┌───┐
                            │ 12·5 │ │ √ │
                            └─────┘ └───┘
    Answer is 3·54 (to 3 significant figures)

c) Reciprocal of 12·5
    Calculator sequence is ┌─────┐ ┌───┐
                            │ 12·5 │ │ 1 │
                            └─────┘ │ ─ │
                                     │ x │
                                     └───┘
    Answer is 0·08

Example 1.21
Find the cube and cube root of 8·5
a) Cube of 8·5
    Calculator sequence ┌─────┐ ┌────┐
                         │ 8·5 │ │ x³ │
                         └─────┘ └────┘
                    or   ┌─────┐ ┌────┐ ┌───┐ ┌───┐
                         │ 8·5 │ │ yˣ │ │ 3 │ │ = │
                         └─────┘ └────┘ └───┘ └───┘
    Answer is 614·125

b) Cube root of 8·5
    Calculator sequence ┌─────┐ ┌──────┐
                         │ 8·5 │ │ ³√   │
                         └─────┘ └──────┘
                    or   ┌─────┐ ┌──────┐ ┌───┐ ┌───┐
                         │ 8·5 │ │ ˣ√y   │ │ 3 │ │ = │
                         └─────┘ └──────┘ └───┘ └───┘
    Answer is 2·04 (correct to 3 sig. figs.)

EXERCISE 1.5

In questions 1 to 10 a calculator should not be used.

1. Write down the square of each of the following

a) 6   b) -60 c) $-0·6$ d) ·05
e) -500 f) -1 g) 0·001   h) 100
i) 20   j) -30 k) $-0·02$ l) 0·3

2. Write down the cube of each of the following
a) 3   b) 0·3   c) -30 d) -5
e) 0·5   f) -50 g) 1   h) $-0·01$
i) -7 j) 0·07   k) -70 l) 70

3. Write down the reciprocal of each of the following
a) 4   b) 2   c) 1   d) $-0·4$
e) 0·2   f) -10 g) 100   h) 40
i) -20 j) -50 k) 0·5   l) $-0·01$

4. Write down the square roots of each of the following
a) 64   b) 100   c) 400   d) 625
e) 0·04   f) 0·01   g) 0·16   h) 0·49
i) 0·25   j) 900   k) 1600   l) 0·64

5. Write down the cube root of each of the following
a) 27 b) −125 c) 1 d) −64
e) 0·064 f) −1000 g) 0·001 h) 8
i) 0·008 j) −0·027 k) 216 l) −8000

6. Estimate the value of the square of each of the following
a) 3·2 b) −5·6 c) 8·7 d) −9·85
e) −18 f) 27·4 g) −0·13 h) 0·756
i) 0·036 j) −0·0753 k) 369 l) −584

7. Estimate the value of the cube of each of the following
a) 2·3 b) 4·1 c) 1·13 d) −5·36
e) −0·31 f) 7·15 g) −10·31 h) −0·241
i) −0·037 j) −0·143 k) 24·1 l) −19·36

8. Estimate the value of the reciprocal of each of the following
a) 5·1 b) 1·7 c) 9·7 d) −0·17
e) 0·475 f) −12·6 g) 127 h) 37
i) −22 j) −43·5 k) 0·557 l) −0·023

9. Estimate the values of the square roots of each of the following
a) 9·7 b) 40 c) 57·6 d) 94
e) 0·8 f) 0·125 g) 0·61 h) 0·413
i) 355 j) 847 k) 1450 l) 2375

10. Estimate the value of the cube root of each of the following
a) 1·45 b) −30 c) 130 d) −7·93
e) 0·007 f) −·002 g) −70 h) ·07
i) −7450 j) −1207 k) 200 l) −·030

Use a calculator for questions 11 to 15

11. Find the square of the following numbers
a) 4·3 b) 5·7 c) −9·4 d) −14·3
e) 0·31 f) −0·031 g) 0·0015 h) −0·076
i) 253 j) 57·6 k) −94·3 l) 128

12. Find the cube of the following numbers
a) 1·32 b) −4·76 c) −5·08 d) 9·21
e) 0·013 f) −0·41 g) −0·073 h) 0·54
i) 73·6 j) 48·09 k) 137·4 l) 256

13. Find the reciprocal of the following numbers
a) 3·41 b) 5·62 c) −8·4 d) −7·2
e) 0·41 f) 0·031 g) −0·056 h) −0·0031
i) 73·6 j) −36 k) −84 l) 163

14. Find the square root of the following numbers

a)	6·48	b)	8·35	c)	19·4	d)	43·61
e)	0·54	f)	0·036	g)	0·019	h)	0·00145
i)	127	j)	256	k)	591	l)	1422

15. Find the cube root of each of the following

a)	2·64	b)	9·75	c)	18·31	d)	24·26
e)	0·415	f)	0·678	g)	0·0145	h)	0·023
i)	57·81	j)	126·43	k)	785·4	l)	9156

STANDARD FORM

Standard form is a method of expressing a number in the form $a \times 10^b$, where 'a' lies between 1 and 10 and 'b' is an integer. It is particularly useful when dealing with very small fractions or very large numbers.

Representing numbers in powers of 10

·00001 or $\dfrac{1}{100\ 000}$		10^{-5}
·0001 or $\dfrac{1}{10\ 000}$		10^{-4}
·001 or $\dfrac{1}{1000}$		10^{-3}
·01 or $\dfrac{1}{100}$		10^{-2}
·1 or $\dfrac{1}{10}$		10^{-1}
1		10^0
10		10^1
100		10^2
1000		10^3
10 000		10^4
100 000		10^5
1000 000		10^6
etc.		

Large numbers are expressed with positive powers

$$27 = 2\cdot7 \times 10 \quad \text{or} \quad 2\cdot7 \times 10^1$$
$$270 = 2\cdot7 \times 100 \quad \text{or} \quad 2\cdot7 \times 10^2$$
$$27\ 000 = 2\cdot7 \times 10\ 000 \quad \text{or} \quad 2\cdot7 \times 10^4$$

etc.

Small numbers are expressed with negative powers

$$\cdot27 = \frac{2\cdot7}{10} = 2\cdot7 \times \cdot1 \text{ or } 2\cdot7 \times 10^{-1}$$

$$\cdot00027 = \frac{2.7}{10\ 000} = 2\cdot7 \times \cdot0001 = 2\cdot7 \times 10^{-4}$$

EXERCISE 1.6

Write down these numbers in standard form

1)	36	2)	426	3)	8300
4)	94 000	5)	562 000	6)	·15
7)	·0314	8)	·0054	9)	·00023
10)	·000015	11)	·00143	12)	157·3
13)	27·41	14)	·0431	15)	357·4

Write down these standard form numbers in the normal way

16)	$1\cdot3 \times 10^1$	17)	$3\cdot4 \times 10^3$	18)	$1\cdot485 \times 10^6$
19)	$2\cdot1 \times 10^{-1}$	20)	$3\cdot41 \times 10^{-4}$	21)	$4\cdot32 \times 10^6$
22)	$2\cdot180 \times 10^{-3}$	23)	$9\cdot36 \times 10^5$	24)	$4\cdot21 \times 10^{-2}$
25)	$5\cdot97 \times 10^4$	26)	$3\cdot26 \times 10^4$	27)	$4\cdot85 \times 10^{-3}$
28)	$7\cdot63 \times 10^{-2}$	29)	$6\cdot215 \times 10^5$	30)	$4\cdot32 \times 10^{-8}$

ORDER OF OPERATIONS

Order of Operation

It is important that when operations involving the four basic rules ($+ - \times \div$) are carried out they are done in the correct order. If order were unimportant then $6 + 2 \times 3$ could give an answer of 24 or 12 depending upon whether the addition or multiplication is carried out first. In fact we must always do multiplication or division before addition or subtraction so $6 + 2 \times 3 = 12$. If we have to do the addition first then it should be enclosed in brackets.

i.e. $(6 + 2) \times 3 = 24$

The order is 1) Brackets
2) Divide or multiply
3) Add or subtract

Example 1.22

$$6 + 4 \div 2$$
$$= 6 + 2 \qquad \text{dividing first}$$
$$= 8$$

Example 1.23

$$3\cdot2 \times (4\cdot3 + 2\cdot2) \div 5$$

$= 3\cdot2 \times 6\cdot5 \div 5$	brackets first
$= 3\cdot2 \times 1\cdot3$	dividing
$= 4\cdot16$	multiplying

multiplying can be carried out before dividing

Example 1.24

$$\frac{6 + 4 \times 3}{7 - 1}$$

In this case the $\div$ sign (the line between the numerator and the denominator) acts as a bracket grouping all the numerator together and all the denominator together

i.e.
$$\frac{(6 + 4 \times 3)}{(7 - 1)}$$

$$= \frac{18}{6} = 3$$

EXERCISE 1.7

1) $3 + 4 \times 2$

2) $7 - 6 \div 2$

3) $3 + 2 \times 2 - 4$

4) $6 \div 2 + 3 \times 2$

5) $(3 + 2) \times 2 - 4$

6) $2\cdot6 + 3\cdot4 \times 3$

7) $5\cdot1 + 4\cdot2 \div 3$

8) $\dfrac{5\cdot1 + 4\cdot2}{3}$

9) $\dfrac{7\cdot4 + 3\cdot1}{1\cdot51 + \cdot49}$

10) $\dfrac{3}{4} + \dfrac{1}{2} \div \dfrac{1}{4}$

11) $\dfrac{7}{8} \div \dfrac{3}{4} + \dfrac{1}{2}$

12) $\dfrac{4}{5} + \dfrac{3}{10} \times 2 + 1\dfrac{1}{2}$

13) $3\left(\dfrac{3}{4} + 1\dfrac{1}{2}\right)$

14) $1\dfrac{1}{2}\left(\dfrac{3}{4} - \dfrac{5}{8}\right)$

15) $\dfrac{5(5 + 2 - 4)}{(3 + 7) \div 2}$

16) $\dfrac{3\cdot4 \times 20}{20\cdot1 - 18\cdot5}$

17) $10 - 12 \div 4 \times (4 - 1)$

18) $\dfrac{1}{4} \div \dfrac{1}{5} \div \dfrac{1}{2}$

19) $6 \div 1\frac{1}{2} + 2 \times 3$

20) $\dfrac{14 + 3\frac{3}{4} - 9\frac{1}{2}}{\dfrac{3}{8} \div \dfrac{1}{4}}$

APPROXIMATION AND ESTIMATION

APPROXIMATIONS

The solutions to many Mathematical problems are given approximate answers when an exact value, containing many digits, can lead to confusion, or when it is a recurring decimal (i.e. some of the digits repeat endlessly). This can be seen on a calculator where there is not always enough room to show all the digits.

Example 2.1

264 to the nearest 10 is 260   (rounded down)
264 to the nearest 100 is 300   (rounded up)
    and so on
When there is a choice of rounding down or rounding up we round up
i.e. 250 to the nearest hundred is 300 not 200

EXERCISE 2.1

In questions 1 to 10 round off to the nearest hundred

1)	206	2)	175	3)	650	4)	3265	5)	2140
6)	3550	7)	35741	8)	68250	9)	31475	10)	24156

In questions 11 to 20 round off to the nearest 10

11)	73	12)	147	13)	83	14)	85	15)	95
16)	183	17)	171	18)	258	19)	3421	20)	5755

Approximate ways of writing down decimal numbers are

a)   to a number of significant figures
b)   to a number of decimal places

a)   **Significant figures**

Example 2.2

9·0175

this is	9·018	correct to 4 significant figures
	9·02	correct to 3 significant figures
	9·0	correct to 2 significant figures
	9	correct to 1 significant figure

Example 2.3

·00315

this is	·0032	correct to 2 significant figures
	·003	correct to 1 significant figure

Notice that the zero's to the right of the decimal point are left in to show the size of the number.

This idea can be extended to whole numbers

Example 2.4		2164	
	this is	2160	correct to 3 significant figures
		2200	correct to 2 significant figures
		2000	correct to 1 significant figure

Again zero's in front of the decimal point are left in

b) **Decimal places**

In this case the number of figures (including zeros) after the decimal point indicates the number of decimal places

Example 2.5		3·156	
	this is	3·16	to 2 decimal places
		3·2	to 1 decimal place

Example 2.6		15·0154	
	this is	15·015	to 3 decimal places
		15·02	to 2 decimal places
		15·0	to 1 decimal place

EXERCISE 2.2

Round off the following numbers correct to the number of significant figures stated

1) 7·4156   to   a) 4 sig. figs.   b) 3 sig. figs.   c) 2 sig. figs.   d) 1 sig. fig.
2) 5·0352   to   a) 4 sig. figs.   b) 3 sig. figs.   c) 2 sig. figs.   d) 1 sig. fig.
3) 526   to   a) 2 sig. figs.   b) 1 sig. fig.
4) 3454   to   a) 3 sig. figs.   b) 2 sig. figs.   c) 1 sig. fig.
5) 0·00545 to   a) 2 sig. figs.   b) 1 sig. fig.

Use your calculator to find

6) $\sqrt{3}$ to 5 sig. figs.
7) $\sqrt{10}$ to 3 sig. figs.
8) $\sqrt{2} \times 5·32$ to 3 sig. figs.

Round off the following numbers correct to the number of decimal places stated

 9) 5·1543   to   a) 3 d.p.   b) 2 d.p.   c) 1 d.p.
10) 5·0135   to   a) 3 d.p.   b) 2 d.p.   c) 1 d.p.
11) 154·304 to   a) 2 d.p.   b) 1 d.p.
12) 256·1005 to   a) 3 d.p.   b) 2 d.p.   c) 1 d.p.

Use your calculator to find

13) 4·23 × 3·64 to 2 d.p.
14) $\sqrt{2} \times \sqrt{3}$ to 2 d.p.

ESTIMATION

An estimation is carried out by rounding off each number to 1 significant figure and then calculating without the aid of a calculator. An estimation is used when a more accurate answer is not required, to check an answer or when the calculation has to be carried out mentally.

Example 2.7

$5 \cdot 24 \times 0 \cdot 76$
Estimation is $5 \times \cdot 8 = \underline{4 \cdot 0}$

Example 2.8

$26 \cdot 5 \div 4 \cdot 3$
Estimation is $30 \div 4 \stackrel{\frown}{=} 7$ ◄────

> Note that for ease of calculation a 1 figure answer is sufficient

Example 2.9

$$\frac{14 \cdot 7 + 28 \cdot 8}{2 \cdot 6 \times 3.2}$$

Estimation is $\dfrac{10 + 30}{3 \times 3} = \dfrac{40}{9} \stackrel{\frown}{=} 4$

Example 2.10

If $x = \sqrt{2\pi \dfrac{3 \cdot 51^2 + 0 \cdot 8^2}{3.51 \times 9 \cdot 81}}$

find an approximate value for x

Estimation is $x = \sqrt{2 \times 3 \times \dfrac{4^2 + 1^2}{4 \times 10}}$

$x = \sqrt{6 \times \dfrac{16 + 1}{40}} = \sqrt{6 \times \dfrac{17}{40}}$

here we must estimate the $\dfrac{17}{40}$ as $\dfrac{20}{40} = \dfrac{1}{2}$

$= \sqrt{6 \times \frac{1}{2}} = \sqrt{3} \stackrel{\frown}{=} \sqrt{4}$ ◄────

> nearest square number

$= +2 \text{ or } -2$

EXERCISE 2.3

Estimate the value of each of the following

1) $6 \cdot 314 \times 2 \cdot 876$
2) $15 \cdot 914 \times 32 \cdot 14$
3) $17 \cdot 68 \times 57 \cdot 58$
4) $9 \cdot 32 \times \cdot 076$
5) $15 \cdot 421 \times \cdot 0034$
6) $\cdot 00234 \times \cdot 0157$
7) $37 \cdot 6 \div 9 \cdot 4$
8) $17 \cdot 73 \div 4 \cdot 65$
9) $14 \cdot 32 \div 2 \cdot 98$

10) $8 \cdot 65 \div 0 \cdot 357$
11) $\cdot 631 \div 0 \cdot 214$
12) $\dfrac{3 \cdot 54 \times 2 \cdot 64}{4 \cdot 31}$
13) $\dfrac{5 \cdot 64 \times 14 \cdot 78}{5 \cdot 74}$
14) $\dfrac{7 \cdot 64 + 3 \cdot 87}{2 \cdot 56}$

15) $\dfrac{5 \cdot 31 + 2 \cdot 64}{3 \cdot 74 - 1 \cdot 68}$
16) $\dfrac{7 \cdot 32 \times 4 \cdot 28}{1 \cdot 64 \times 3 \cdot 17}$
17) $\dfrac{0 \cdot 314 \times 2 \cdot 64}{4 \cdot 13}$
18) $\sqrt{\dfrac{6 \cdot 43 + 4 \cdot 95}{0 \cdot 341}}$

19) $\sqrt{\dfrac{3{\cdot}152 \times 0{\cdot}48}{2{\cdot}63}}$

20) $\sqrt{\dfrac{2{\cdot}31 - 1{\cdot}42}{3{\cdot}64}}$

21) If $v = \sqrt{2 \times 9{\cdot}81 \times 17{\cdot}4}$ estimate the value of v

22) If $c = 2\sqrt{21 \times 13{\cdot}6 \times 5{\cdot}2 - 13{\cdot}6^2}$ estimate c

23) $t = 2\pi \sqrt{\dfrac{37{\cdot}2}{9{\cdot}81}}$ estimate t

24) $D = 3{\cdot}54 \sqrt{\dfrac{6{\cdot}48 + 3{\cdot}21}{6{\cdot}48 - 3{\cdot}21}}$ estimate D

25) Estimate the value of $8 \times 9 \times 10 \times 11 \times 12$

LIMITS OF ACCURACY

Example 2.11

If the attendance at a football match is stated as 22 000 to the nearest thousand, then the actual attendance lies between 21 500 and 22 499 inclusive, i.e. 21 500 and 22 499 are the limits within which the actual value lies.

Example 2.12

A length of metal measures 126 mm to the nearest millimetre. Its actual length is therefore less than 126·5 mm and greater than or equal to 125·5 mm.

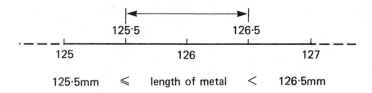

$$125{\cdot}5\text{mm} \quad \leqslant \quad \text{length of metal} \quad < \quad 126{\cdot}5\text{mm}$$

Example 2.13

A value is stated as 2·61 correct to 2 decimal places. Its actual value is greater than or equal to 2·605 and less than 2·615.

EXERCISE 2.4

The following values have been rounded off in the way shown in the brackets. State the limits between which they lie.

1) 240   (to the nearest 10)
2) 750   (to the nearest 50)
3) 1300   (to the nearest 100)
4) 2500   (to the nearest 10)
5) 1350   (to the nearest 10)

6) 56 mm   (to the nearest mm.)
7) 37 metres (to the nearest metre)
8) 5 metres (to the nearest cm)
9) £26   (to the nearest £)
10) 5.7 metres (to the nearest 10 cms)
11) 16·34   (to 2 decimal places)
12) 7·9   (to 2 significant figures)
13) 17·0   (to 1 decimal place)
14) 451   (to 3 significant figures)
15) 5480   (to 3 significant figures)
16) A rectangular lawn is measured as 10 metres by 4 metres, both values being to the nearest metre. Write down the upper and lower limits of (a) the length and (b) the breadth. Use these values to find (c) its maximum area and (d) its minimum area.
17) The gate sizes at a football match on two consecutive weeks are given as 28 000 and 22 000 to the nearest thousand. What is (a) the maximum and (b) the minimum differences between these?

APPLICATION 1 —
PERCENTAGES

PERCENTAGES

A percentage is a third way of expressing a fraction (the other two being vulgar and decimal fractions). A percentage is a fraction written in hundredths ($^1/_{100}$) with the denominator missed out and the percentage sign (%) used.

$$7\% \text{ (seven per cent)} = \frac{7}{100}$$

Converting fractions and decimals into percentages is carried out by multiplying by 100.

Example 3.1   a) $\frac{1}{2} = \frac{1}{2} \times 100\% = 50\%$

   b) $0.351 = 0.351 \times 100\% = 35.1\%$

Converting percentages into decimals and fractions is carried out by dividing by 100.

Example 3.2

a) $75\% = \frac{75}{100} = \frac{3}{4}$

b) $63.8\% = \frac{63.8}{100} = 0.638$

Finding the percentage of a given quantity

Example 3.3   Find 20% of £5·40

$20\% = \frac{20}{100}$ or $\frac{1}{5}$ or 0.2

$\frac{1}{5}$ of £5·40 = 0·2 × 540p = 108p or £1·08

or on a calculator $\boxed{20}\ \boxed{\div}\ \boxed{100}\ \boxed{\times}\ \boxed{5\cdot4}\ \boxed{=}$

To express one quantity as a percentage of another we first express the first as a fraction of the second and change it into a percentage.

Example 3.4   £25 of Paula's total weekly wage of £90 is spent on food. What percentage of her weekly wage is this?

percentage is $\frac{25}{90} \times 100 = \frac{250}{9} = 27.8\%$ to one decimal place.

Example 3.5   What percentage of 2·5 km is 650 metres?

percentage is $\frac{650}{2500} \times 100 = 26\%$

change 2·5 km into 2500 metres

EXERCISE 3.1

1) Change into percentages
   a) 1/4 b) 3/4 c) 1/5 d) 1/8 e) 1/12
   f) 3/8 g) 14/25 h) 1/3 i) 5/8 j) 7/50

2) Change into percentages
   a) 0·4 b) 0·8 c) 0·45 d) 0·31 e) 0·58
   f) 0·715 g) 0·843 h) 0·543 i) 0·594 j) 0·654

3) Change into vulgar fractions
   a) 40% b) 30% c) 65% d) 85% e) 22%
   f) 38% g) 83% h) 36% i) 63% j) 97%

4) Change into decimals
   a) 15% b) 60% c) 75% d) 95% e) 36%
   f) 24% g) 27% h) 61% i) 73% j) 17%

5) Find
   a) 15% of £1·20
   b) 25% of £3·00
   c) 35% of £3·40
   d) 64% of £2·50
   e) 72% of £5.50
   f) 16% of £42
   g) 24% of £24
   h) 57% of £16
   i) 43% of £9
   j) 88% of £12·50
   k) 17% of 5 metres
   l) 52% of 17 metres
   m) 42% of 1km 60m
   n) 12½% of 1km
   o) 65% of 2kg
   p) 55% of 1kg 500g

6) Express the first quantity as a percentage of the second quantity in each of the
   following. Give your answer to 1 decimal place where necessary.
   a) 48 and 120
   b) 40 and 150
   c) 143 and 220
   d) 65 and 250
   e) 700g and 1kg
   f) 850g and 1kg 500g
   g) 24mm and 6cm
   h) 4·2cm and 80mm
   i) 220 miles and 750 miles
   j) 85p and £2·00
   k) £9·40 and £20
   l) 95p and £3·50

7) At a football match the gate was 25 500. If there were 9 500 children what
   percentage were adults?

8) A man pays 30% tax on his annual income of £15 400. How much is this?

9) On any day, a vegetable wholesaler expects to throw away 15% of his cabbages
   due to them being rotten. How many does he throw away if he buys 350?

10) A woman travels 250 miles to London. After 130 miles she stops for lunch.
    What percentage of the journey has she left?

25

PERCENTAGE INCREASE AND DECREASE

Example 3.6   Increase £150 by 12%

£150 + 12% of £150 is 112% of £150

i.e. increased amount is $\frac{112}{100}$ X 150 = 1·12 X 150 = £168

This is called the
multiplying factor

Example 3.7   Decrease £250 by 12%

£250 − 12% of £250 is 88% of £250

i.e. decreased amount is 0·88 X £250 = £220   multiplying factor

EXERCISE 3.2

Write down the multiplying factor for each of these.

1) Increase of 6%

2) Increase of 15%

3) Increase of 75%

4) Increase of 100%

5) Increase of 250%

6) Decrease of 7%

7) Decrease of 27%

8) Decrease of 75%

Increase the following

9) £5·00 by 6%

10) £7·00 by 30%

11) £6·70 by 20%

12) £5·00 by 100%

13) £7·40 by 25%

14) £7·50 by 22%

15) 5 metres by 17%

16) 6¼ metres by 47%

17) 7 metres by 12½%

18) 17 metres by 7½%

Decrease the following

19) £9 by 12%

20) £14·50 by 15%

21) £7·50 by 30%

22) £54 by 23%

23) £9·50 by 34%

24) 7 metres by 13%

25) 18·5 metres by 24%

26) 9 metres by 8½%

27) The premium for a car insurance is £150. A discount of 40% is allowed.
   a)   Find how much is paid
   b)   If the premium is increased by 8% what is the new premium
   c)   If there is a discount of 65% on the new premium how much is paid?

28) Last week shares were quoted at £1·70 each. Today they are worth 5% more
   a)   How much are they worth today?
   b)   If they drop in value by 10% tomorrow, how much will they be worth?

29) A man bought 12 cases of wine for £250 in 1980 and stored it away as an investment. In 1986 it was worth 107% more
   a) How much was it worth in 1986?
   b) If 1 case contains 12 bottles how much was each bottle valued at in 1986 (to the nearest 1p)?

30) The value of the pound against the dollar was £1 = $1·48. If the value of the pound drops by 16% what is its new value correct to 2 decimal places?

TO FIND THE ORIGINAL AMOUNT GIVEN A NEW AMOUNT AND THE PERCENTAGE CHANGE.

Example 3.8   A coat has a discount of 10% in the sale and now costs £76·50. What was its original price?
10% discount means the cost is now 100% − 10% = 90% of the original price

i.e. 90% is £76·50

so   1% is $\dfrac{76·50}{90}$

∴ original price (100%) is $\dfrac{76·50}{90} \times 100 = £85$

Example 3.9   The cost of petrol is increased by 15% to 43·7p per litre. What was its price before the increase?
Price is now 115% of original price
i.e. 115% is 43.7p

so   1% is $\dfrac{43·7}{115}$

∴ 100% is $\dfrac{43·7}{115} \times 100 = 38p$

EXERCISE 3.3

Find the original price for each of the following to the nearest penny where necessary.

1) A coat increased in price by 15% to £92.
2) A house increased in price by 8% to £46 980
3) A bicycle increased in price by 12% to £123·20
4) A watch increased in price by 10% to £72
5) A car increased in price by 7½% to £6 987·50
6) A refrigerator decreased in price by 10% to £198
7) A dress decreased in price by 25% to £36
8) A house plant decreased in price by 30% to £2·10
9) A pair of shoes decreased in price by 18% to £12·30
10) An inclusive holiday decreased in price by 12% to £325·60
11) A gate of 34 686 at a first division football match was 18% down on the previous week. What was the previous week's gate?

12) During a year a tree increases in height by 12·5% to 6m 20cm. What was its height at the beginning of the year to the nearest centimetre?

13) A car is sold for £5400, representing a loss of 40% of the original purchase price. Calculate the original price.

14) The price of a jacket increases by 10% to £60·50. What was the original price?

INTEREST, APPRECIATION AND DEPRECIATION

Interest is the amount by which invested money increases in value over a period of time, or the amount charged for borrowed money. The amount invested or borrowed is called the principal. The annual percentage by which the principal changes or borrowed money is charged is called the rate.

Simple Interest

$$\text{Interest gained} \quad I = \frac{P \times T \times R}{100}$$

where P = Principal
T = Time
R = Rate

Example 3.10   A man invests £100 at a rate of 9% per annum simple interest. How much interest does he earn in 3 years?

$$I = \frac{P \times T \times R}{100}$$

$$I = \frac{100 \times 3 \times 9}{100} = £27$$

Compound Interest   After each year's interest is calculated it is added to the old principal to make a new principal.

Example 3.11   £100 is invested at a rate of 9% per annum compound interest. How much interest is earned in 3 years?

multiplying factor

Original amount is £100
At end of 1st year the amount is £100 × 1·09 = £109
At end of 2nd year the amount is £109 × 1·09 = £118.81
At end of 3rd year the amount is £118·81 × 1·09 = £129·50 (to the nearest penny)
∴ Interest gained = amount at end of 3rd year — original amount
= £129·50 − £100 = £29·50
This can be done very simply on the calculator by multiplying continuously by the multiplying factor.

Example 3.12   For how many years must 50p be invested at a rate of 15% compound interest to gain an interest of £10.
i.e. find when the amount is first greater than £10·50
After 1st year the amount is 50p $\times$ 1·15 = 57·5p
After 2nd year the amount is 57·5p $\times$ 1·15 = 66·125p
            and so on
On the calculator this is done by pressing $\boxed{1\cdot15}$ $\boxed{\times}$ $\boxed{50}$ $\boxed{=}$ and then pressing the $\boxed{=}$ button.   Each press of this button multiplies the previous number by 1·15.   Counting the number of presses gives the number of years invested.
After 22 presses the calculator shows 1082·2372 i.e. £10·82 which is an interest of £10·32
i.e. an interest of £10 is gained in 22 years.

Appreciation and **Depreciation** are terms used to indicate whether the value of an object or commodity **increases** or **decreases** over a period of time.

Example 3.13
A car is bought for £5000 and depreciates in value by 10% the first year and 15% the second year.
a)   Find its value at the end of the second year
b)   What was its overall percentage depreciation?
a)   In the 1st year its value depreciates by 10% of £5000
   ∴ value at the end of 1st year = £5000 $\times$ ·9 = £4500
       value at the end of 2nd year = £4500 $\times$ ·85 = £3825
b)   percentage depreciation = $\dfrac{\text{depreciation}}{\text{original value}} \times 100\%$

$$= \frac{5000 - 3825}{4500} \times 100\% = 23\cdot5\%$$

EXERCISE 3.4

Find the simple interest earned on the amounts in questions 1 to 5.
1)   £30 for 3 years at 5% per annum.
2)   £150 for 3 years at 8% per annum.
3)   £200 for 4 years at 7½% per annum.
4)   £75 for 3 years at 12% per annum.
5)   £110 for 4 years at 11% per annum.
Find the compound interest earned on the amounts in questions 6 to 10, correct to the nearest penny,
6)   £100 for 2 years at 10% per annum.
7)   £150 for 2 years at 12% per annum.
8)   £250 for 3 years at 10% per annum.
9)   £175 for 2 years at 11% per annum.
10) £450 for 3 years at 9½% per annum.
11) A person invests £1500 at a rate of 14½% per annum compound interest. How much is in the person's account after 3 years?

12) How long does it take to make £50 interest when £1 is invested in an account which yields 14% per annum compound interest?

13) How long must £15 be invested at 11% per annum compound interest in order to gain £20 interest?

14) A car was bought at the beginning of 1984 for £6500. During the first year it depreciated in value by 15%, during the second year by 12%, and during the third year by 10%. What was its value at the beginning of 1987? What was the overall percentage depreciation?

15) A town had a population of 25 000 at the beginning of 1980. During that year it decreased by 4% and during 1981 by 2%. What was the population at the beginning of 1982? What was the overall percentage decrease during the two years.

16) An antique is valued at £250 at the beginning of 1980. During 1980 and 1981 it increased in value by 15% each year and in 1982 by 25%. What was its value at the beginning of 1983, correct to the nearest penny? What was the overall percentage increase in value?

17) A firm's profits were £500 000 for 1980. During 1981 they increased by 15%. During 1982 they increased by a further 10% but during 1983 they fell by 3%. What were their profits during 1983?

Value Added Tax (VAT)

This is a tax added to the cost of most goods and services.

Example 3.14

A man and his wife go to a restaurant. The cost of the food is £15·50 but a service charge of 10% is added to that and a further 15% VAT is added. What is the final bill, to the nearest penny?

Cost of food = £15·50

Cost of food + service charge of 10% = £15·50 × 1·10 = £17·05

multiplication factor

Total cost including VAT = £17·05 × 1·15 = £19·6075

= £19·61 to the nearest penny

EXERCISE 3.5

Calculate, to the nearest penny, the selling price of the following if VAT of 15% is added on to their price.

1. £4·50	2. £2·60	3. £3·90	4. £10·40
5. £8·75	6. £18·70	7. £25·45	8. £70·40
9. £113	10. £157	11. £764	12. £1024

13. A restaurant bill amounts to £18·70 plus a service charge of 10% plus VAT of 15%. Find the total charged.

14. A family of 2 adults and 2 children stay at a hotel for one night. Each adult is charged £14·00 and each child £7·00 for the room. They have dinner at £7·50 per adult and £4·50 per child and they all have breakfast at £2·25 each. Calculate the total bill if VAT of 15% is added.

15. The price of a two week holiday in Spain is quoted at £546·25 including VAT of 15%. What was the price before VAT was added?

16. A lady wants a room to be built onto her house. One builder quotes £5700 including VAT at 15% with a reduction of 10% if the quotation is accepted within 1 week. A second builder quotes £4500 excluding VAT. Which is the cheapest quotation and by how much?

APPLICATION 2 — MONEY

WAGES, SALARIES AND INCOME TAX

Whenever anyone works for an employer they are paid a wage or salary. A wage earner is usually paid each week for a set number of hours he or she works. Any extra time is called overtime and paid at a special rate. This is referred to as 'time and a half', 'double time' etc. (meaning the hourly rate is 1½ or 2 times the normal hourly rate). A salaried worker usually earns an annual amount of money which is split into twelve equal parts and paid monthly. Because of this he does not normally receive overtime payment, although there are exceptions to this rule.

Example 4.1

A woman is paid £2·70 per hour for all the hours she works up to 40. Any overtime in the evenings is paid at time and a third, Saturday morning at time and a half and on Sunday double time. How much will she earn if she works 40 basic hours, 5 hours in the evening, 3 hours on Saturday morning and 4 hours on Sunday?

For the basic 40 hours	=	£2·70 × 40	=	£108·00
For 5 hours in the evening at time and a third	=	£2·70 × 1⅓ × 5	=	£18·00
For 3 hours on Saturday at time and a half	=	£2·70 × 1½ × 3	=	£12·15
For 4 hours on Sunday at double time	=	£2·70 × 2 × 4	=	£21·60
		TOTAL WAGES		£159·75

Example 4.2

A manager is paid an annual salary of £19848. How much is this per month? If he has a rise of 5½% what is his new monthly salary?

$$\text{Monthly salary} = \frac{£19848}{12} = £1654$$

multiplication factor

After an increase in pay the new salary is £1654 × 1·055 = £1744·97

INCOME TAX

Most people who have an income have to pay money to the government in the form of a tax. For people employed by someone else this is done using a scheme called PAYE (Pay as you earn) which collects income tax from wages and salaries. Each employer is responsible for deducting the tax that is due and for handing it over to the government.

The rates of tax vary from year to year but for the year April 1986 to April 1987 were as follows

29% on the first £17 200 of taxable income
40% on the next £3 000

45% on the next £5 200
50% on the next £7 900
55% on the next £7 900
60% on anything more

However there are certain allowances which are taken into account enabling one to pay less tax. The main ones are

Single man or woman's personal allowance of £2 335
Married man's personal allowance of £3 655
Wife's earned income allowance of £2 335
Additional personal allowance of £1 320

Example 4.3

Use the above figures to calculate the monthly income, after tax, of a married man earning £11 500 per year.

Taxable income = Annual income − Allowances
$$= £11\ 500 - £3\ 655$$
$$= £7\ 845$$

This is now taxed at 29%

Amount of tax paid = £7845 × 0·29
$$= £2275·05$$

∴ Annual income after tax = £11 500 − £2275·05
$$= £9224·95$$
Monthly income after tax = £9224·95 ÷ 12
$$= £768·75 \text{ (to the nearest penny)}$$

Example 4.4

Calculate the annual tax bill for a single woman who earns £25000 per annum.
Taxable income = £25000 − £2335
$$= £22665$$

Tax paid on first £17200 = £17200 × 0·29 = £4988
Tax paid on next £3000 = £3000 × 0·4 = £1200
Tax paid on remaining £2465 = £2465 × 0·45 = £1109·25

Total amount of tax paid = £4988 + £1200 + £1109·25 = £7297·25

EXERCISE 4.1

1. Ann is paid £1·70 per hour for the first 35 hours she works during the week. After that she is paid at a rate of time and a half. Calculate her gross (before any deductions) wage for a week when she works 46 hours.
2. Gerald is paid a salary of £12 400 and receives an increase of 5·5%. How much increase does he receive per month?

Using the income tax rates for 1986/7 calculate the following

3. The annual tax paid by a single man earning £8 500 per annum.
4. The annual tax paid by a single woman earning £12 300 per annum.
5. The weekly tax paid by a married man earning £220 per week.
   (Hint: find the tax for 1 year and divide by 52)
6. The annual tax paid by a single woman earning £160 per week.
7. A married woman earns £10 500 per year and has an allowance of £2335. How much will she be paid each month?
8. A man works, on average, 48 hours every week. He is paid a rate of £3·10 for each hour up to 38 hours, time and a third for the next 8 hours and time and a half for any remaining hours. Calculate the weekly income after tax has been deducted.
9. A married man earns £14 500 per annum before tax. He is allowed a further deduction of £150 for clothing and equipment necessary for his job. What is his monthly income after tax is deducted?
10. A single woman earns £12 200 per annum when her allowances amount to £3 320 and the rate of tax is 30%. The next year she has a pay rise of 6%. If her allowances are now £3530 and the rate of tax is 29% find the increase in her annual income after tax.
11. A married man earns £27 000 per annum before tax. Calculate the amount of tax paid.
12. A single woman earns £32 500 per annum before tax. What is her monthly pay after tax has been deducted?
13. A company director (a married man) earns £76 000 per annum. Calculate the tax paid per annum and the amount he earns per week.

FOREIGN CURRENCY

In order to travel abroad or buy goods in a foreign country it is necessary to change British currency for the currency of the country concerned. The amount of foreign currency given in exchange for each British pound (sterling) varies from day to day. An example of some exchange rates are shown below.

COUNTRY	MONETARY UNIT		EXCHANGE RATE	
France	100 centimes = 1 franc		Fr 10·65	= £1
Germany	100 pfennig = 1 mark		DM 2·85	= £1
Greece	100 lepta = 1 dracma		DR 189	= £1
Portugal	100 centavos = 1 escudo		ES 206	= £1
Spain	100 centimos = 1 peseta		Ptas 186	= £1
U.S.A.	100 cents = 1 dollar		$ 1.54	= £1

Example 4.5
Using an exchange rate of £1 = Fr 10·65, change £250 into French francs.

£1 = Fr 10·65
£250 = £10·65 × 250 = Fr 2662·5

Example 4.6

In the U.S.A. a camera costs $450. How much is this in pounds sterling to the nearest penny?

$1.54 = £1

$$\therefore \ \$450 = £\frac{450}{1.54} = £292.21$$

Example 4.7

Whilst in France a tourist exchanges £100 of travellers cheques at a rate of £1 = Fr 10·45. She spends F450 and changes the remaining francs back into sterling at a rate of £1 = Fr 10·24. How much sterling does she receive?

$$£100 = 100 \times 10.45 = \text{Fr } 1045$$

Remaining francs after Fr 450 are spent = 1045 − 450 = Fr 595

$$\text{Sterling received} = £\frac{595}{10.45} = £56.94 \text{ (correct to the nearest penny)}$$

EXERCISE 4.2

Using the list of exchange rates shown above find, correct to 2 decimal, the equivalent value of each of the following sterling amounts

1. £56 into French francs
2. £146 into German marks
3. £75·50 into Greek dracmas
4. £126·50 into Portugese escudos
5. £2·56 into Spanish pesetas
6. £27·60 into U.S. dollars

Convert the following into sterling (correct to the nearest penny)

7. 27·34 U.S. dollars
8. 256 French francs
9. 850 Portugese escudos
10. 674 Spanish pesetas
11. 1456 Greek dracmas
12. 97 German marks
13. A bank changes 500 French francs for £46·51. What is the rate of exchange (to 2 decimal places)?
14. Petrol in Britain costs 37p per litre and 4·15 francs per litre in France. If £1 = Fr 10·65 which is the cheaper?
15. A family take a holiday in the U.S.A. They change £650 into U.S. dollars at a rate of £1 = $1·62 and spend $900. When they arrive back they change their remaining dollars at a rate of £1 = $1·76. How much, in sterling, has their holiday cost?
16. Using the table of exchange rates change 100 French francs into German marks.
17. A watch costs $52·50 in the U.S.A. and 370 francs in France. Use the table of exchange rates to calculate which is the cheaper.

HOUSEHOLD RATES

A rate is a tax administered by the local authority on all householders and businesses in their area. Every building is given a rateable value depending on its size, situation and condition. The amount of money collected is based on the rate levied, i.e. the amount collected for every £1 of rateable value.

Annual amount collected = Rate X rateable value

Example 4.8

A house has a rateable value of £450 and the householder has to pay rates of 95p in the pound.

$\therefore$ Annual amount paid = 450 X 95p = £427·50

Example 4.9

A house has a rateable value of £345 and the householder pays £435 per annum. What rate is this?

Since amount paid = rate X rateable value

$$\text{rate} = \frac{\text{amount paid}}{\text{rateable value}}$$

$$= £\frac{435}{345} = £1·26 \text{ (to the nearest penny)}$$

EXERCISE 4.3

1. The rateable value of a house is £375. How much will the householder pay if the rate is £1·35 in the pound?

2. A small business has a rateable value of £3200 and has to pay a rate of £1·73 in the pound. How much is its total annual rate bill?

3. A householder whose house has a rateable value of £486 has to pay £466·56 per annum. What rate is this?

4. A householder whose house has a rateable value of £435 has to pay £535·05 per annum. What rate is this?

5. A householder has to pay £475·02 in rates per year. If the rate is £1·74 in the pound what is the rateable value of the house?

6. If £358·90 is paid per year by a householder and the rate is 97p in the pound, what is the rateable value of his house?

7. In 1985 a householder paid £455·10 rates on a house of rateable value of £370. Calculate this rate. In 1986 the rate was increased by 7p in the pound. How much more would he pay?

8. A householder paid £693 in rates in 1986 and £630 in 1985. If the rateable value of his property was £450 calculate the rise in the rate from 1985 to 1986.

HOUSEHOLD BILLS

Electricity bills
In most cases electricity is paid every quarter of a year. The amount of electricity used is registered on a meter and the total cost is made up from the cost of the units used plus a fixed charge.

Example 4.10
An electricity meter reads 4312 at the beginning of a quarter and 5066 at the end. If the cost of electricity was 5·65p per unit and there was a fixed charge of £7·40 find the total cost for the quarter.

No. of units used = 5066 − 4312 = 754
Cost of units = 754 × 5·65p = 42·60 (to the nearest penny)
  fixed charge = 7·40
∴ total cost = 50·00

Gas bills
Gas is charged for in a similar way to electricity. In this case the number of cubic feet of gas is registered on a meter. This is then converted into Therms (a measure of the amount of energy the gas has). The Gas Board then charge for it at a rate per therm. Again there is a standing (fixed) charge.

No. of therms used $= \dfrac{\text{metered volume} \times \text{Calorific value}}{1000}$

Note that the metered volume is in hundreds of cubic feet.

Example 4.11
The quarterly gas bill for a household stated that the previous meter reading was 5924 and the present meter reading is 6288. Calculate the total cost if the gas has a calorific value of 1040 BTU/cu ft, there is a standing charge of £9·20 and the gas costs 37p per therm.

No. of units used (metered volume) = present meter reading − previous meter reading
  = 6288 − 5924
  = 364 units

No. of therms used $= \dfrac{364 \times 1040}{1000} = 378\text{·}56$ therms

Cost of gas = 378·56 × 37p = £140·07 (to nearest penny)
Total cost = Cost of gas + standing charge = £140·07 + £9·20 = £149·27

Telephone bills

Every time a telephone call is made from a telephone other than a public telephone box, it is metered according to the length of time the call takes, the distance over which the call is made and the rate applicable at the time the call is made. Again there is a standing charge as well as a rental charge for any receiver rented from the telephone company. Bills are sent out every quarter and are subject to VAT.

Example 4.12

Calculate the cost of a quarterly telephone bill of 380 units at 5p per unit if there is a standing charge and rental payment amounting to £16·45 and VAT is charged at 15%.

Cost of calls $= 380 \times 5p = $ £19·00
Total cost before VAT $=$ £19·00 + £16·45 $=$ £35·45
Cost including VAT at 15% $=$ £35·45 $\times$ 1·15 $=$ £40·77 (to the nearest penny)

EXERCISE 4.4

1. Calculate the cost of 352 units of electricity if 1 unit costs 5·3p.
2. Calculate the cost of a quarterly gas bill if 155 therms have been used at 34p per therm and there is a standing charge of £9·40.
3. Calculate the cost of a quarterly telephone bill of 305 units at 4·8p per unit if there is a standing charge and rental of £17·20 and VAT of 15% is added.
4. An electricity meter reads 5126 units in September and 6066 units in December
   — Calculate a. the number of units used in the quarter
                    b. the cost of the units at 5·65p per unit
                    c. the total cost for the quarter if a fixed charge of £7·40 is added.
5. A gas meter reads 9573 units in January and 9774 units in April. If the calorific value of the gas is 1042 BTU/cu ft calculate
   a. the number of therms used
   b. the cost of gas if 1 therm costs 37p
   c. the final cost for the quarter if there is a standing charge of £9·20.
6. Calculate the cost of a quarterly telephone bill of 354 units at 4·7p per unit if there is a standing charge and rental of £16·40 and VAT is charged at 15%.
7. A household is charged for electricity at a standard rate of 5·65p per unit and an economy rate of 1·89p per unit. Calculate the cost of a quarterly bill made up of 910 units at the standard rate, 536 units at the economy rate and a fixed charge of £7·40.
8. I want to pay for my electricity by a budget monthly payment method. This involves paying 12 equal monthly amounts instead of 4 quarterly amounts. The amount I pay is calculated by multiplying the number of units used the previous year by the new rate and adding on four standard charges. This total is then divided by 12. 3243 units were used last year, the cost of units next year is expected to be 5·65p each and the quarterly standard charge is £7·40. Find my monthly payment.

RATIO AND
PROPORTION

RATIO AND PROPORTION

A ratio is a comparison between two or more quantities expressed in the same units.

This is written as   a:b   or $\dfrac{a}{b}$

Ratios must always be given in the simplest form (as with a fraction). The ratio 6:10 is simplified to 3:5. The order is important as 3:5 is not the same as 5:3.

Example 5.1	Express the ratio 25cm to 1½ metres as simply as possible. Ratio is 25cm : 1½ metres $\qquad$ = 25 : 150 $\qquad$ = 1 : 6 or $\dfrac{1}{6}$

Example 5.2   Two prices are in the ratio 2:5. If the first is £1·50, what is the second?

The ratio 2 : 5 = £1·50 : x

$$\frac{2}{5} = \frac{1 \cdot 5}{x}$$

or $\dfrac{2}{5} = \dfrac{150}{x}$ expressed in pence

$$\therefore \quad 2x = 150 \times 5$$
$$2x = 750$$
$$x = 375$$

i.e. the other price is 375p or £3·75

Example 5.3   Divide £110 between Jane and Bill in the ratio of 8:3.

Divide £110 into 11 equal parts giving Jane 8 parts and Bill 3 parts.

i.e.   11 parts = £110
$\qquad$ 1 part = £10
$\qquad$ 8 parts = £80
$\qquad$ 3 parts = £30

∴ Jane gets £80 and Bill gets £30.

Example 5.4   Three local primary schools combine to have a school fair. They decide to share any profit in the same ratio as the number of pupils in the schools. If £1200 profit was made and the number of pupils in each school was 450, 500 and 650 how much did each school get?

ratio of pupils   450:500:650
$\qquad\qquad\qquad$ = 9:10:13

no. of parts = 9+10+13=32

value of 1 part = $\dfrac{£1200}{32}$ = £37·50

$$\therefore \quad \text{1st school gets} \quad 9 \text{ parts} = £37 \cdot 50 \times 9 = £337 \cdot 50$$
$$\text{2nd school gets} \quad 10 \text{ parts} = £37 \cdot 50 \times 10 = £375 \cdot 00$$
$$\text{3rd school gets} \quad 13 \text{ parts} = £37 \cdot 50 \times 13 = £487 \cdot 50$$

EXERCISE 5.1

Write down these ratios in their lowest terms

1) 30 : 20
2) 45 : 30
3) 75 : 65
4) 24 : 36
5) 80 : 35
6) 72 : 18
7) 108 : 48
8) 150 : 65
9) 20cm : 1 metre
10) £4·50 : £3·50
11) £9·20 : £20
12) 1½ metres : 30cm
13) 1kg : 350g
14) 3½ hours : 70 mins
15) Two prices are in the ratio of 3:5. If the lower one is £1·50 what is the other?
16) Two lengths are in the ratio 5:6. If the longer one is 90cm what is the other?
17) £3 is divided between Anna and Beth in the ratio 7:8. How much do they each receive?
18) A school has 450 boys and 495 girls. What is the ratio of the number of boys to the number of girls?
19) Two friends set up a business with investments of £15 000 and £25 000. If they share their first year's profits of £24 000 in the same ratio as their original investments, how much do they each get?
20) £57 is divided between three boys, Adrian, Bob and Christopher in the ratio 3:4:5. How much do they each get?
21) Three sisters Alison, Barbara and Carol inherit £7 500 from their Aunt. It is divided between them in the ratio 3:2:1. How much do they each get?
22) An alloy is made from lead, tin and zinc in the ratio 7:2:1. How much tin will there be in an alloy of mass 250 grams?
23) Three men win £20 000 on the football pools and decide to share it in the same ratio as their original stakes of 40p, 25p, and 15p. Calculate how much they each get.

RATIO AND SCALES

Maps and plans are always drawn to a scale which is usually expressed as a ratio (or representative fraction) of 1:x where x is a whole number.

For example a map can be to the scale of 1:50 000 meaning 1 cm on the map represents 50 000 cm or ½ km.

Or the plans of a house can be drawn to the scale 1:50 meaning that 1 cm on the drawing represents 50 cm or ½ m.

Example 5.5

A map is drawn to the scale 1:25 000. On the map a lake has a perimeter of 18 cm and an area of 20 cm². Find the actual perimeter and area.

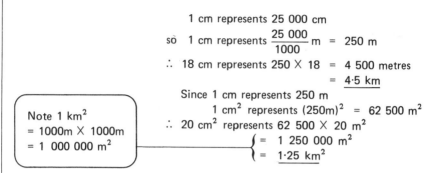

$$1 \text{ cm represents } 25\ 000 \text{ cm}$$
$$\text{so} \quad 1 \text{ cm represents } \frac{25\ 000}{1000} \text{ m} = 250 \text{ m}$$
$$\therefore \quad 18 \text{ cm represents } 250 \times 18 = 4\ 500 \text{ metres}$$
$$= 4 \cdot 5 \text{ km}$$
$$\text{Since } 1 \text{ cm represents } 250 \text{ m}$$
$$1 \text{ cm}^2 \text{ represents } (250\text{m})^2 = 62\ 500 \text{ m}^2$$
$$\therefore \quad 20 \text{ cm}^2 \text{ represents } 62\ 500 \times 20 \text{ m}^2$$
$$\left\{ \begin{array}{l} = 1\ 250\ 000 \text{ m}^2 \\ = 1 \cdot 25 \text{ km}^2 \end{array} \right.$$

Note 1 km²
= 1000m × 1000m
= 1 000 000 m²

EXERCISE 5.2

Questions 1 to 7 are based on a map drawn to the scale of 1:50 000

1. Two villages are 14 cm apart on the map. What is their actual distance apart?
2. The distance between two farms on the map is 1·7 cm. What is the actual distance apart?
3. A straight length of motorway is 64 mm long on the map. What is its actual length?
4. The distance between two railway stations is 2·5 km. What is this represented as on the map?
5. The distance between two churches is 1·7 km. What is this represented as on the map?
6. A forest has an area of 15 cm² on the map. What is its actual area?
7. The area of a town is 2·5 km². What area represents this on the map?
8. The plans of a house are drawn to the scale 1:50. Find a) the length of a room which measures 85 mm on the plan b) the height of the house on the drawing if its actual height is 7 metres c) the area of a window which has an area of 6 cm² on the drawing. d) the area on the drawing of a bathroom floor which has an actual area of 5m².
9. A drawing of an engineering component is to the scale 1:5. Calculate
   a) the length of the component if it measures 8·4 cm on the drawing
   b) its diameter on the drawing if its actual diameter is 10·5 cm.
10. A street map of London is to the scale 1:15 000. Find
    a) the length of the Mall if it measures 7 cm on the map
    b) the area of Battersea Park, in hectares, if it has an area of 35 cm² on the map (1 hectare = 10 000m²)
    If it is known to be 2½ km between Chelsea and Fulham football grounds, what is the distance on the map?

SPEED AND FUEL CONSUMPTION

$$\text{Average speed} \quad = \quad \frac{\text{Total distance travelled}}{\text{Total time taken}}$$

Re-arranging this formula gives

Distance travelled   =   Average speed X time taken

$$\text{Time taken} \quad = \quad \frac{\text{Distance travelled}}{\text{Average speed}}$$

The units of speed are kilometres per hour (km/hr) miles per hour (mph) metres per second (m/s) etc. depending on the units used for distance and time.

$$\text{Average fuel consumption} \quad = \quad \frac{\text{Total distance travelled}}{\text{Fuel used}}$$

Again this can be re-arranged to find the total distance travelled or fuel used.

Example 5.6
A train travels 230 miles in four hours. Find its average speed.

$$\text{Average speed} \quad = \quad \frac{\text{Total distance}}{\text{Total time}}$$
$$= \quad \frac{230}{4} \quad = \quad 57\tfrac{1}{2}\text{mph}$$

Example 5.7
A motorist travels at an average speed of 55 km/hr for 2¼ hours. If his car has an average fuel consumption of 15 km per litre, how much petrol is used?

$$\begin{aligned} \text{Distance travelled} \quad &= \quad \text{Average speed} \times \text{time} \\ &= \quad 55 \times 2 \cdot 25 \\ &= \quad 123 \cdot 75 \text{ kilometres} \end{aligned}$$

15 kilometres requires 1 litre

$$123 \cdot 75 \text{ kilometres require} \quad \frac{123 \cdot 75}{15} \text{ litres}$$
$$= 8 \cdot 25 \text{ litres}$$

Example 5.8
A motorist travels from Aberdeen to Manchester in 7 hours 45 minutes at an average speed of 44 mph. He then travels to London, a further 192·5 miles, at an average speed of 55 mph. Find the average speed of the whole journey.

For the 1st part   Distance travelled   =   speed × time
                                         =   44 × 7·75
                                         =   341 miles

$$7 \text{ hrs } 45 \text{ mins} = 7\tfrac{3}{4} = 7 \cdot 75 \text{ hrs}$$

For the second part   Time taken = $\dfrac{\text{Distance}}{\text{Speed}}$ = $\dfrac{192 \cdot 5}{55}$ = 3·5 hours

For the whole journey   Average speed = $\dfrac{\text{Total distance}}{\text{Total time}}$

$$= \frac{341 + 192 \cdot 5}{7 \cdot 75 + 3 \cdot 5} = \frac{533 \cdot 5}{11 \cdot 25}$$

$$= 47 \cdot 42 \text{ mph} \quad (\text{to 2 d.p.})$$

Example 5.9

A train leaves Exeter at 11.45 and travels to London, a distance of 230 miles.
If its average speed is 67 mph at what time (to the nearest minute) will it arrive in London?

Time taken   = $\dfrac{\text{Distance}}{\text{Speed}}$ = $\dfrac{230}{67}$ =   3·4328 hours

          =   3 hours 0·4328 × 60 minutes
          =   3 hours 25·97 minutes
          =   3 hours 26 minutes

Arrival time in London
          =   11 hours 45 mins + 3 hours 26 mins
          =   15 h 11 mins
          =   15·11 or 3·11 pm

EXERCISE 5.3

1. Find the average speed of a car journey of 135 miles if it takes 2 hrs 40 mins.
2. Find the distance travelled by a motorist who drives at an average speed of 70 km/hr for 1¾ hours.
3. Find the time taken by a train which travels 350 miles at an average speed of 60 mph.
4. Find the average speed of a train which leaves London at 11·05 and arrives in Cardiff, 150 miles away at 13·35.
5. A motorist travels between two service stations on a motorway at an average speed of 64 mph in 36 minutes. Calculate the distance between the stations.
6. A train travels between Edinburgh and Glasgow, a distance of 45 miles at an average speed of 38 mph. If it arrived in Glasgow at 17·04 at what time did it leave Edinburgh (to the nearest minute)?
7. The distance between Calais and Paris is 290 km. If a motorist travels at an average speed of 90 km/hr how long will it take him? If his car consumes petrol at a rate of 13 km per litre, find how much he uses.

8. A car travels for 2½ hours down a motorway at an average speed of 80 km/hr. If the car uses petrol at the rate of 11 kilometres per litre find
   a) the distance travelled b) the amount of petrol used c) the cost of petrol if 1 litre costs 37·4p.

9. A cyclist travels 15 miles between two towns in 1 hr 15 minutes. He then travels to a third town 8 miles away in 50 minutes. Find the average speed of the whole journey.

10. A bus travels between Bristol and Exeter, a distance of 75 miles. It leaves Bristol at 13·43 and arrives in Exeter at 15·23. What is its average speed?

11. A car travels 35 miles on each gallon of petrol (mpg) and the petrol tank holds 9½ gallons. How far will it travel on a full tank? If the car travels at an average speed of 60 mph how long will it take before the tank is empty?

SETS

SETS

A set is a collection of objects or things. Each item in the set is referred to as an **element** or **member**.

Set language and definitions

$A = \{1,2,3,4\}$ means "set A contains the elements 1,2,3,4"

$3 \in A$ means "3 is an element of set A"

$5 \notin A$ means "5 is not an element of set A"

A **subset** is a set which can be found within a larger set.
If $A = \{1,2,3,4\}$ and $B = \{1,2\}$ then B is a subset of A, i.e. $B \subset A$

An **empty** set is a set which contains no members and is written $\emptyset$ or $\{\ \}$

Sets are **equal** when they contain the same elements

$$\{1,2,3,4\} = \{4,3,2,1\}$$

but $\{0,1,2,3\} \neq \{1,2,3,4\}$

The **Universal** set $\mathscr{E}$ is the set which contains all other sets.

Example 6.1

If $\mathscr{E} = \{1,2,3,4,5\}$
and $A = \{1,2,3,4\}$
and $B = \{1,2,3\}$
then $A \subset \mathscr{E}$, $B \subset \mathscr{E}$ and $B \subset A$

Note that A and B **must** be subsets of $\mathscr{E}$

Infinite sets are written $A = \{1,2,3,4 \ldots\}$

Venn diagrams are a method by which sets can be represented diagrammatically.

Example 6.2

If $\mathscr{E} = \{1,2,3,4,5\}$
and $A = \{1,2\}$
and $B = \{2,3,4\}$
then on a Venn diagram they are represented as

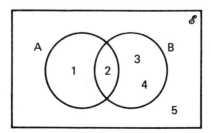

The **Complement** of a set

All the elements in the Universal set which are not in set A are in the complement of set A, written A'. On a Venn diagram this is shown by the shaded area.

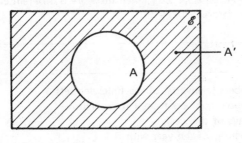

If $\mathscr{E} = \{1,2,3,4,5\}$ and $A = \{1,2,3\}$
then $A' = \{4,5\}$

The **intersection** of sets ($\cap$) is the set containing all elements which are common to the sets

Example 6.3 If $A = \{1,2,3,4,5\}$ and $B = \{3,4,5,6,7\}$ then $A \cap B = \{3,4,5\}$
is the intersection
On a Venn diagram this is represented like this

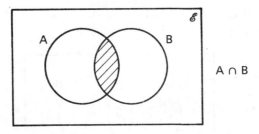

$A \cap B$

The **union of sets** ($\cup$) is the set containing all the elements contained in the individual sets.

Example 6.4 If $A = \{1,2,3,4,5\}$ and $B = \{3,4,5,6,7\}$ then $A \cup B = \{1,2,3,4,5,6,7\}$
is the union of sets A and B.
On a Venn diagram this is represented like this

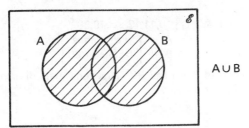

$A \cup B$

The number of elements in a set (n)

Example 6.5

If A = $\{2,3,4,5,6\}$ then there are 5 different elements in the set
therefore n (A) = 5

EXERCISE 6.1

1. List the members (elements) of the following sets
   a) A = $\{$ whole numbers from 1 to 5 inclusive $\}$
   b) B = $\{$ days of the week $\}$
   c) C = $\{$ months of the year with R in $\}$
   d) D = $\{$ Prime numbers between 2 and 10 inclusive $\}$
   e) E = $\{$ Prime numbers $\}$

2. Which of the following are true and which are false?
   a) 6 $\in$ even numbers
   b) 7 $\notin$ odd numbers
   c) Cow $\in$ farm animals
   d) $\{2,3,5\}$ $\subset$ $\{$ prime numbers $\}$
   e) $\{2,4,6\}$ $\subset$ $\{4,6\}$
   f) $\{0,1,2,3\}$ = $\{1,2,3,4\}$
   g) n $\{0,1,2,3,4\}$ = n $\{1,2,3,4\}$
   h) Ø = $\{0\}$

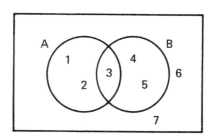

From the above Venn diagram list all the elements in the following sets

(a) A   (b) B   (c) A∩B   (d) A∪B
(e) A′   (f) B′   (g) (A∩B)′   (h) (A∪B)′

4. The Universal set $\mathscr{E}$ = $\{10,11,12 \ldots 19,20\}$
   A = $\{$ even numbers $\}$
   B = $\{$ factors of 60 $\}$

   List the members of P∩B and B′. Draw one Venn diagram to illustrate these
   sets.

5. The Universal set $\mathscr{E}$ = $\{$ 1,2,3. . . . .15,16 $\}$
and P = $\{$ Odd numbers $\}$
Q = $\{$ Prime numbers $\}$
List the elements of P,Q,P ∩ Q,P ∪ Q

6. $\mathscr{E}$ = $\{$ integers from 30 to 39 inclusive $\}$
A = $\{$ square numbers $\}$
B = $\{$ multiples of 3 $\}$
(a) state n(A ∪ B)'
(b) list the elements in (A ∩ B)'

7. The Venn diagram below shows two sets, A and B

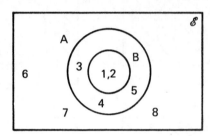

List the elements in sets A,B,A ∪ B,A ∩ B,B'.

8. Describe the shaded areas in the following sets

a)
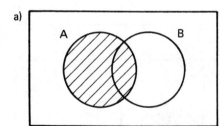

b)
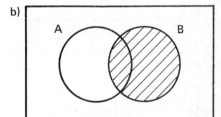

c)
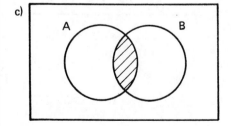

d)
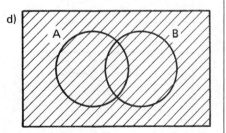

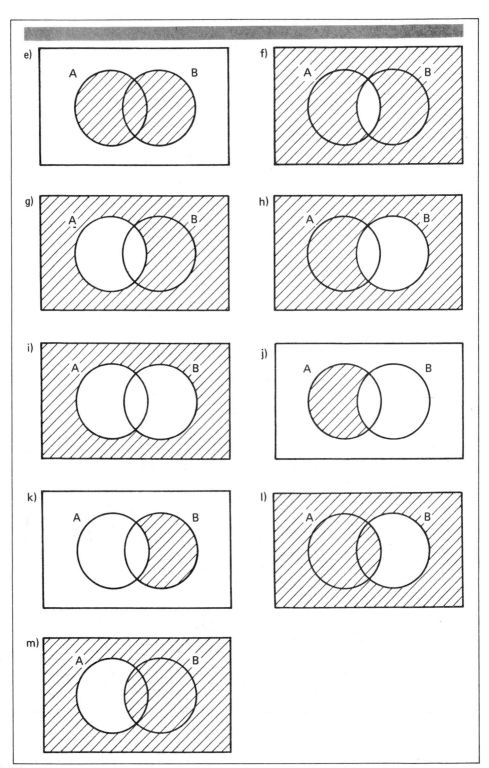

Problems involving three sets

Example 6.6

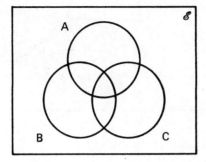

On the Venn diagram above shade in the area representing (a) (A ∪ B) ∩ C
(b) (A ∩ B) ∪ C

(a)   Shade in (A ∪ B) and C with cross hatching going in different directions

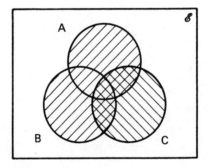

The intersection of (A ∪ B) and C is the area with both cross hatching.

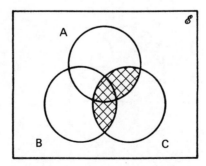

(b)   Shade in (A ∩ B) and C with different cross hatching

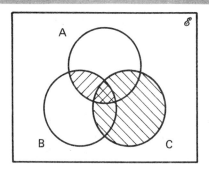

(A ∩ B) ∪ C is the whole of the shaded area.

Example 6.7   If $\mathscr{E}$ = { 1,2,3,4,5,6 }   A = { Odd numbers }
                 B = { Prime numbers }   C = { Multiples of 3 }
                 Find (a) (A ∪ B)′ ∩ C   (b) A ∪ B ∪ C′

(a)   A = { 1,3,5 }   B = { 2,3,5 }   C = { 3,6 }
      A ∪ B = { 1,2,3,5 }
      ∴ (A ∪ B)′ = { 4,6 }
      ∴ (A ∪ B)′ ∩ C = { 4,6 } ∩ { 3,6 } = { 6 }

(b)   A ∪ B = { 1,2,3,5 }
      C′ = { 1,2,4,5 }
      ∴ A ∪ B ∪ C′ = { 1,2,3,5 } ∪ { 1,2,4,5 }
                   = { 1,2,3,4,5 }

EXERCISE 6.2

1.   The Venn diagram below shows the number of students who take Mathematics
     (M) History (H) and Geography (C)

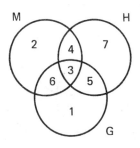

     Find the number of students who take
     (a)   All three subjects

(b)   Mathematics and History but not Geography
(c)   Mathematics and Geography but not History
(d)   Geography only
(e)   History only
(f)   History and Geography but not Mathematics
(g)   Mathematics only

2.   The results of a survey of 60 people are shown on the Venn diagram below

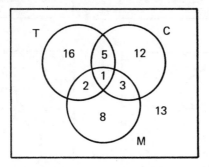

$\mathscr{E}$ = { people questioned in the survey }
T = { people who regularly drink tea }
C = { people who regularly drink coffee }
M = { people who regularly drink milk }
Calculate the number of people
(a)   who drink tea
(b)   who drink none of these
(c)   who drink coffee and milk
(d)   in T ∪ M
(e)   in T ∩ C
(f)   in T ∩ C ∩ M
(g)   in T ∪ C ∪ M

3.   Describe the shaded areas in the following sets

a)
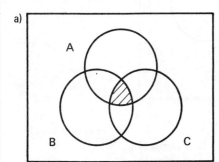

b)
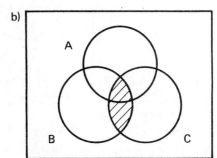

57

c)
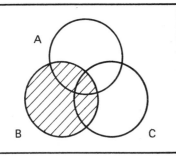

d)
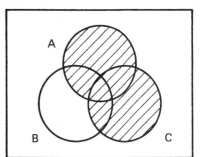

e)
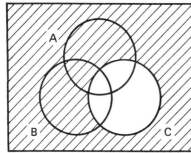

f)
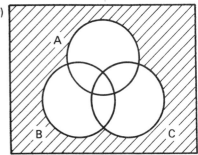

4. $\mathscr{E} = \{ 1,2,3,4 \ldots .19,20 \}$
    $A = \{ 1,2,3,4,5 \}$ $B = \{$ Prime numbers $\}$ $C = \{$ Factors of 20 $\}$
    (a) List sets B and C
    (b) Say whether the following are true or false
    (i) $1 \in C$ (ii) $A \subset$ (iii) $A \subset C$ (iv) $n(C) = 6$
    (c) List the set $B \cap C$ and describe this set
    (d) Copy and complete the following Venn diagram

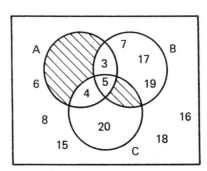

5. If $\mathscr{E} = \{ 1,2,3 \ldots . 9,10 \}$, $A = \{ 1,2,3 \}$, $B = \{$ Prime numbers $\}$,
    $C = \{$ Odd numbers $\}$

List the members of the following sets
(a) A ∩ B ∩ C (b) A ∪ B ∪ C (c) (A ∪ B ∪ C)′
(d) (B ∩ C) ∪ A (e) A ∩ (B ∪ C)′

6.

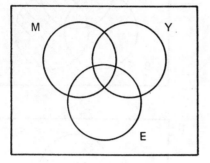

A milkman delivers Milk (M) Yoghurt (Y) and Eggs (E) to houses in a street. He delivers to 70 houses but 5 do not have any of these items.

32 take milk only
 6 take yoghurt only
13 take eggs only
No people take milk and eggs but not yoghurt
 9 take milk and yoghurt but not eggs

Copy the Venn diagram and enter the numbers 5,32,6,13,0 and 9.
If he delivers yoghurt and eggs but not milk to x houses and if one less house has all three delivered, find x and complete the Venn diagram.
State how many (a) have milk
                        (b) do not have yoghurt

7. Describe the shaded areas in the following Venn diagrams

a)
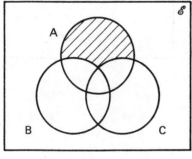

b)
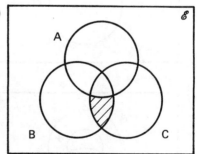

59

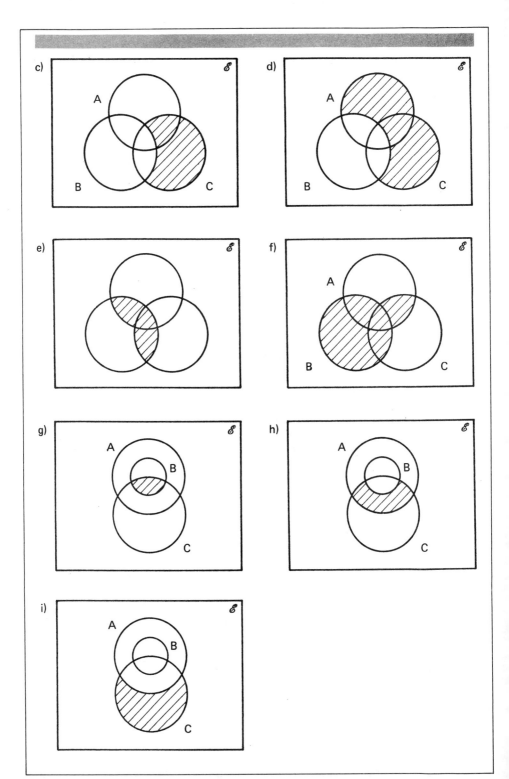

8. Show the following sets on a Venn diagram
   (a) $(A \cap B) \cup (B \cup C)$ (b) $(A \cap B) \cap (B \cap C)$
   (c) $(A \cup B) \cap (B \cap C)$ (d) $(A \cup B) \cup (B \cap C)$
   (e) $B' \cap (A \cup C)$ (f) $B' \cup (A \cup C)$
   Describe (a) (b) (c) and (d) in simpler terms.

ALGEBRA

ALGEBRA

Basic skills

Algebra is used to generalise problems in addition, subtraction, multiplication and division and to solve algebraic equations. This is done by using letters (known as variables) and numbers (known as constants). To be able to do this it is necessary to practice the skills required.

Basic algebraic notation

If x and y stand for two different variables then

$x + y$ means add the value of y to the value of x.

$x + 2$ means add 2 to the value of x.

$x - y$ means subtract the value of y from the value of x.

$x - 2$ means subtract 2 from the value of x.

xy means multiply together the values of x and y.

x^2 means multiply the value of x by itself.

$2x$ means multiply the value of x by 2.

$\dfrac{x}{y}$ means divide the value of x by the value of y.

$\dfrac{x}{2}$ or $\frac{1}{2}x$ means divide the value of x by 2.

also
$$a + a = 2a$$
$$2a + 3a = 5a$$
$$12a - 3a = 9a$$
$$6xy - 2xy = 4xy$$

Example 7.1

Simplify these expressions

a) $6x + 5x + 2y + 3y = 11x + 5y$

b) $7x - 2x + 3y - y = 5x + 2y$

c) $xy + x + 2xy + 3x = xy + 2xy + x + 3x = 3xy + 4x$

d) $5ab - 3a + 4ab + a = 5ab + 4ab - 3a + a = 9ab - 2a$

e) $\dfrac{a}{3} + \dfrac{a}{4} = \dfrac{4a}{12} + \dfrac{3a}{12} = \dfrac{7a}{12}$ $\left(\text{compare this with } \dfrac{1}{3} + \dfrac{1}{4} = \dfrac{4}{12} + \dfrac{3}{12} = \dfrac{7}{12} \right)$

EXERCISE 7.1

Simplify the following expressions

1) $3y + 8y$

2) $9y - 6y$

3) $16y - 18y$

4) $-12y + 3y$

5) $-16a - 7a$

6) $12b + 3b + 2a + 3a$

7) $4b + 5a + 3b + 2a$

8) $6a - 2a + 3b + 4b$

9) $12a + 3b - 4a - b$

10) $16x + 8y - 10x - 9y$

11) $6x + 3y - 8x - 6y$

12) $5xy + 3y^2 - 6xy + 4y^2 - 3xy - 4y^2$

13) $-7ab + 6b - 3ab - 4b - 3ab$

14) $5ab + 3bc - 4ab + 5bc - 6ab - 3bc$

15) $9xy - 4x^2 + 2xy - 5x^2 + 3xy$

16) $\dfrac{x}{2} + \dfrac{x}{3}$

17) $\frac{1}{4} y + \frac{1}{2} y$

18) $\frac{3}{4} x + \frac{1}{6} x$

19) $\dfrac{a}{3} + \dfrac{a}{4} + \dfrac{a}{6}$

20) $\dfrac{3a}{4} - \dfrac{a}{6}$

21) What must be added to $x + y$ to make $3x + 2y$?

22) What must be added to $4x - 2y$ to make $5x + y$?

23) What must be added to $-7x + 2y$ to make $x + y$?

GENERALISED ARITHMETIC

Example 7.2

The diagrams below show square 'holes' surrounded by centimetre squares.

  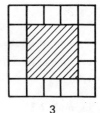

Length of hole side	1	2	3
Number of squares	8	12	16

Find the number of squares needed for holes of side a) 4cm b) 5cm c) n cm
d) Use the generalised rule to find the number of squares needed for a hole of side 20cm.

a) and b) Notice that the series increases by 4 squares each time we increase the hole size.

Hole	No. of squares
1	8
2	12
3	16
4	20
5	24

c) One way to find the generalised form is to break up the squares into corners and sides thus

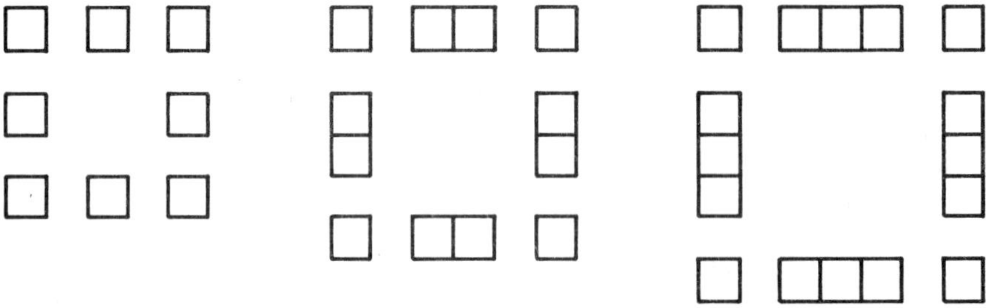

Now we have

Hole size	No. of squares	made from
1	8	4 side squares + 4 corners = 4(1) + 4
2	12	8 .. .. + 4 .. = 4(2) + 4
3	16	12 .. .. + 4 .. = 4(3) + 4

$\therefore$ Number of squares required for an n sided hole is $\underline{4n + 4}$

d) Number of squares required for a 20 sided hole is

$4(20) + 4 = 80 + 4 = \underline{84 \text{ squares}}$

Example 7.3

Windows are made in the form of a grid of square glass panes each surrounded by a wooden frame. A 2 × 3 window is shown below.

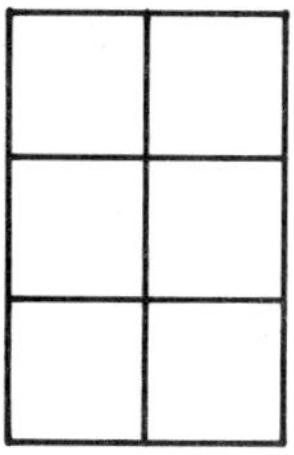

Glass panes cost £1 each and the wood for the frame costs £1 for each side of a pane. Find the cost of a window of size a) 4 × 3 b) h × ℓ and c) 10 × 8 using the formula found in part b.

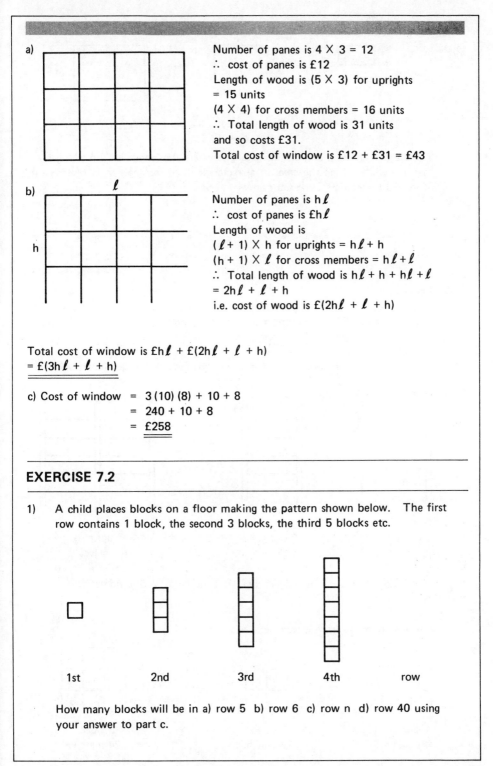

a) Number of panes is 4 × 3 = 12
∴ cost of panes is £12
Length of wood is (5 × 3) for uprights
= 15 units
(4 × 4) for cross members = 16 units
∴ Total length of wood is 31 units
and so costs £31.
Total cost of window is £12 + £31 = £43

b) Number of panes is $h\ell$
∴ cost of panes is £$h\ell$
Length of wood is
$(\ell + 1) \times h$ for uprights = $h\ell + h$
$(h + 1) \times \ell$ for cross members = $h\ell + \ell$
∴ Total length of wood is $h\ell + h + h\ell + \ell$
= $2h\ell + \ell + h$
i.e. cost of wood is £$(2h\ell + \ell + h)$

Total cost of window is £$h\ell$ + £$(2h\ell + \ell + h)$
= £$(3h\ell + \ell + h)$

c) Cost of window = 3 (10) (8) + 10 + 8
= 240 + 10 + 8
= £258

EXERCISE 7.2

1) A child places blocks on a floor making the pattern shown below.   The first
    row contains 1 block, the second 3 blocks, the third 5 blocks etc.

1st   2nd   3rd   4th   row

How many blocks will be in a) row 5 b) row 6 c) row n d) row 40 using
your answer to part c.

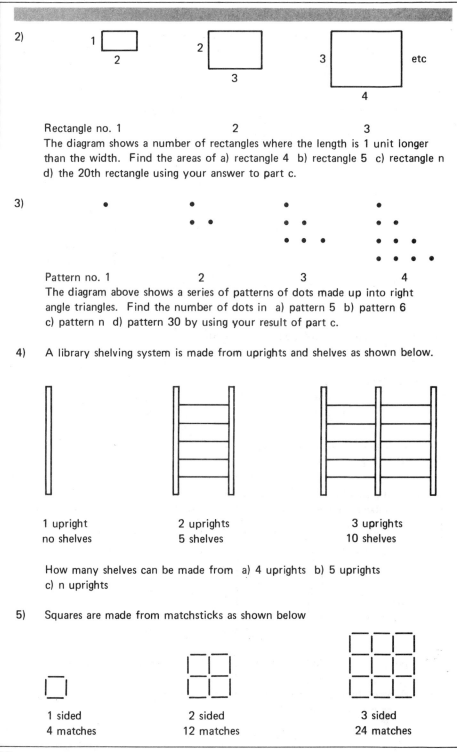

2)

Rectangle no. 1   2   3

The diagram shows a number of rectangles where the length is 1 unit longer than the width. Find the areas of a) rectangle 4 b) rectangle 5 c) rectangle n d) the 20th rectangle using your answer to part c.

3)

Pattern no. 1   2   3   4

The diagram above shows a series of patterns of dots made up into right angle triangles. Find the number of dots in a) pattern 5 b) pattern 6 c) pattern n d) pattern 30 by using your result of part c.

4)   A library shelving system is made from uprights and shelves as shown below.

1 upright   2 uprights   3 uprights

no shelves   5 shelves   10 shelves

How many shelves can be made from a) 4 uprights b) 5 uprights c) n uprights

5)   Squares are made from matchsticks as shown below

1 sided   2 sided   3 sided

4 matches   12 matches   24 matches

Write down the number of matches needed for squares having sides of
a) 4 matches b) 5 matches c) n matches d) 10 matches by using your
result to part c.

6)

1	2	3	4	5	6
7	8	9	10	11	12
13	14	15	16	17	18
19	20	21	22	23	24
25	26	27	28	29	30
31	32	33	34	35	36
—	—	—	—	—	—
—	—	—	—	—	—

The sum of the numbers in the box (shown) beginning with 15 is 74.
Investigate the sum of other boxes and write down the sum of the numbers in
the box beginning with n. Use this to calculate the sum of the numbers in the
box beginning with 242

7) Pens, in which animals are kept are made from posts and cross bars. One pen
requires 4 posts and 8 cross bars, 2 bars along each side.

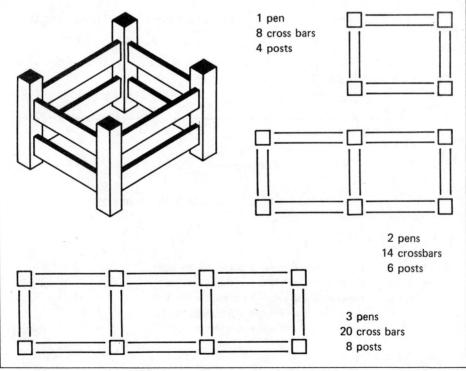

1 pen
8 cross bars
4 posts

2 pens
14 crossbars
6 posts

3 pens
20 cross bars
8 posts

If more pens are made in this way calculate the number of posts and cross bars needed for a) 4 pens b) 5 pens c) n pens. Also d) show a more economical way of making 4 pens.

8)

0	1	2	3	4	5	6	7	8	9
10	11	12	13	14	15	16	17	18	19
20	21	22	23	24	25	26	27	28	29
30	31	32	33	34	35	36	37	38	39
40	41	42	43	44	45	46	47	48	49
50	51	52	53	54	55	56	57	58	59
—	—	—	—	—	—	—	—	—	—

The box shows the numbers centred on number 21. The sum of these numbers is 85. Investigate the sums of other numbers found in the same way and write down an expression to find the sum of the numbers centred on n. Use this expression to find the sum of the numbers centred on 193.

9) The cost of a picture frame is made up of 10p per inch of frame, 1p per square inch of glass plus an assembly charge of £1.
a) Calculate the cost of a picture frame measuring 10 inches by 8 inches.
b) Write down an expression to find the cost of a picture frame measuring
   ℓ inches by w inches.
c) Use this expression to find the cost of a picture frame measuring 20 inches by 10 inches.

DIRECTED NUMBERS

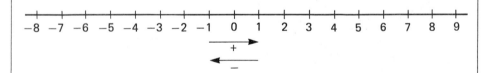

Addition is carried out by moving to the right, subtraction by moving to the left, on the number line above.

Example 7.4

a) 6 + 4   begin at 6 and move 4 places to the right   6 + 4 = 10
b) 6 − 4   begin at 6 and move 4 places to the left   6 − 4 = 2
c) 6 − 11   begin at 6 and move 11 places to the left   6 − 11 = −5
d) −6 + 4   begin at −6 and move 4 places to the right   −6 + 4 = −2
e) −6 − 4   begin at −6 and move 4 places to the left   −6 − 4 = −10

Successive addition and subtraction is carried out by doing it in pairs

f) $- 6 + 7 - 3 + 2$
$= 1 - 3 + 2$
$= -2 + 2 = 0$

EXERCISE 7.3

1) $7 + 4 =$	2) $10 - 5$
3) $12 - 3$	4) $8 - 9$
5) $6 - 9$	6) $7 - 10$
7) $-4 + 8$	8) $-6 + 9$
9) $-4 + 10$	10) $-5 - 3$
11) $-7 - 4$	12) $-9 - 6$
13) $4 - 3 + 2$	14) $6 - 7 + 1$
15) $5 - 9 + 5$	16) $6 - 10 - 2$
17) $-4 + 6 - 3$	18) $-7 + 2 + 4$
19) $8 - 15 + 3$	20) $-5 - 4 + 9$
21) $-5 + 3 - 7 - 3$	22) $-6 + 4 - 9 - 4$
23) $-8 - 6 - 4 + 3$	24) $8 - 10 - 6 + 4$
25) $5 - 6 - 4 + 8$	26) $-9 - 6 + 3 - 4$
27) $-9 - 4 + 2 - 8$	28) $-7 + 2 + 3 - 9$
29) $8 + 6 - 5 + 4$	30) $-6 - 4 + 3 - 8$

Multiplication and division

This is best understood by considering brackets

a)   Consider $3 + 2 (2 + 6)$
This means 3 + twice the contents of the brackets
i.e. $3 + 16 = 19$
This can be written without the brackets as $3 + 4 + 12 = 19$ by multiplying the contents of the bracket by 2

b)   Consider $3 - 2 (2 + 6)$
This means 3 − twice the contents of the brackets
i.e. $3 - 2 (8) = 3 - 16 = - 13$
But when this is written without the brackets it is $3 - 4 - 12 = -13$
So $-2 (2 + 6) = - 4 - 12$
i.e. $- 2 \times 2 = - 4$
and $- 2 \times (+6) = - 12$
This gives the rule that when a positive and a negative number are multiplied together the answer is negative.
i.e. $+ \times - = -$
and $- \times + = -$

c) Consider $16 - 3 (4 - 2)$

This means $16 - 3$ times the contents of the brackets

i.e. $16 - 3 (2) = 16 - 6 = 10$

but without the brackets $16 - 12 + 6 = 10$

so $-3 (4 - 2) = - 12 + 6$

i.e. $- 3 \times 4 = - 12$

and $- 3 \times - 2 = +6$

This gives the rule that when a negative number is multiplied by another negative number the answer is positive.

i.e. $- \times - = +$

Rules

$$+ \times + = +$$
$$- \times - = +$$
$$+ \times - = -$$
$$- \times + = -$$

Division

Since division is the reverse of multiplication the following rules can be obtained

a) $(+2) \times (+3) = +6$
$\therefore (+6) \div (+3) = +2$ i.e. $+ \div + = +$

b) $(-2) \times (+3) = -6$
$\therefore (-6) \div (+3) = -2$ i.e. $- \div + = -$

c) $(-2) \times (+3) = -6$
$\therefore (-6) \div (-2) = +3$ i.e. $- \div - = +$

d) $(-2) \times (-3) = +6$
$\therefore (+6) \div (-3) = -2$ i.e. $+ \div - = -$

Note that the rules for multiplication and division can be remembered in the same way.

Example 7.5

a) $(+6) \times (+3) = + 18$ b) $(-3) \times 4 = - 12$

c) $(-8) \times (-3) = 16$ d) $(-12) \div 6 = -2$

e) $(-72) \div (-12) = + 6$ f) $\dfrac{-12}{2} = - 6$

g) $\dfrac{-14}{-7} = 2$ h) $-3 (6) = -18$

i) $\dfrac{-24}{(-2) \times (-4)} = \dfrac{-24}{+8} = -3$ j) $(-2) \times (-2) \times (-2)$
$= (+4) \times (-2)$
$= -8$

EXERCISE 7.4

1) 8×3

2) $(-9) \times 4$

3) $6 \times (-3)$

4) $(-3) \times (-4)$

5) $-5 (-2)$

6) $+3 (-2)$

7) $\dfrac{-12}{3}$

8) $-12) \div (-4)$

9) $5 - 2(4)$

10) $(-3) - 2(-3)$

11) $-4 + 2 (8)$

12) $\dfrac{-5 - 7}{2}$

13) $\dfrac{-12}{(-2) \times (+3)}$

14) $\dfrac{-18}{(-6) \times (-2)}$

15) $(-1) \times (-1) \times (-1)$

16) $(-1) \times (+1) \times (-1)$

17) $(-3)^3$

18) $(-3)^4$

19) $(-2)^2 \times (+2)$

20) $\dfrac{(-2)^2 \times (+2)^2}{(-2) \times (+2)}$

USING BRACKETS

An expression can sometimes be represented as a product

e.g. $3(x + y) = 3x + 3y$

The 3 in front of the brackets indicates that the contents of the bracket are multiplied by 3.

$3(2a - 4) = 6a - 12$ etc.

Multiplying by negative numbers

a) $12 - (6 + 2)$ means 12 subtract 8

i.e. $12 - (6 + 2) = 12 - 8 = 4$

but writing this down without the brackets means that there is a **sign change**

i.e. $12 - (6 + 2) = 12 - 6 - 2 = 6 - 2 = 4$

so $- (x + y) = -x - y$

sign change

b) $12 - (6 - 2)$ means 12 subtract 4

i.e. $12 - (6 - 2) = 12 - 4 = 8$

Again writing this down without the brackets means that there is a **sign change**

i.e. $12 - (6 - 2) = 12 - 6 + 2 = 6 + 2 = 8$

so $- (x - y) = -x + y$

sign change

Rule

An expression contained in brackets can be subtracted by removing the brackets and changing its signs.

Example 7.6
$$- (2x + 3) = - 2x - 3$$
$$- (2x - 3) = - 2x + 3$$
$$- 3(2x + 3) = - 6x - 9$$
$$- 3(2x - 3) = - 6x + 9$$
$$- 4 (- 2x + 3) = 8x - 12$$
$$- 4 (- 2x - 3) = 8x + 12$$

Simplifying expressions

Example 7.7
$$7x + 8y + 3(2x + 4y)$$
$$= 7x + 8y + 6x + 12y$$
$$= 7x + 6x + 8y + 12y$$
$$= 13x + 20y$$

Example 7.8
$$12x - 3y - 4(2x + y)$$
$$= 12x - 3y - 8x - 4y$$
$$= 12x - 8x - 3y - 4y$$
$$= 4x - 7y$$

Example 7.9
$$14x + 3y - (6x + 4y)$$
$$= 14x + 3y - 6x - 4y$$
$$= 14x - 6x + 3y - 4y$$
$$= 8x - y$$

Example 7.10
$$2(3x + 2x^2) - 3x (2x + 3)$$
$$= 6x + 4x^2 - 6x^2 - 9x$$
$$= 6x - 9x + 4x^2 - 6x^2$$
$$= -3x - 2x^2$$

EXERCISE 7.5

Remove the brackets from the following expressions and simplify them when necessary.

1) $3(x + y)$
2) $6(3x + 4)$
3) $-(2x - 3)$
4) $-(3x + 2)$
5) $-4(2x + 5)$
6) $-7(3x - 4)$
7) $4(-3x - 3)$
8) $-5(-2x + 3)$

9) $-3(-3x - 2)$

10) $7x + 8y + 3(2x + 4y)$

11) $12x - 3y - 2(4x + y)$

12) $14x + 8y - 6(3x - 2y)$

13) $7x - 3y - (5x + 2y)$

14) $12x + 3y - (4x - 2y)$

15) $7x - 3y + (4y - 2x)$

16) $2(3x + 2y) + 3(3x + 3y)$

17) $4(2x + 4y) + 5(6x - 7y)$

18) $5(3x - 2y) - 4(3x + 4y)$

19) $7(3x - 5y) - 4(4x - 5y)$

20) $5x(2x + 3) - 2x(2x - 1)$

21) $3x(3x - 2) - 4x(3x + 4)$

22) $5x(3x + 2) + 3x(4x - 5)$

23) $6x(2x + 1) - x(5x + 3)$

24) $4x(3x - 2) - x(-3x - 2)$

25) $5x(2x + 3) - 3x(-4 - 2x)$

Multiplying two brackets together

Example 7.11
$(3x + 2)(2x - 3)$
means multiply $(2x - 3)$ by $(3x + 2)$
or multiply $(2x - 3)$ by $3x$
and multiply $(2x - 3)$ by 2
i.e. $(3x + 2)(2x - 3) = 3x(2x - 3) + 2(2x - 3)$
$= 6x^2 - 9x + 4x - 6$
$= 6x^2 - 5x - 6$

Example 7.12
$(4x - 3)(2x - 4)$
$= 4x(2x - 4) - 3(2x - 4)$
$= 8x^2 - 16x - 6x + 12$
$= 8x - 22x + 12$

EXERCISE 7.6

Multiply the following pairs of brackets together.

1) $(x + 2)(x + 3)$

2) $(2x + 1)(x + 2)$

3) $(3x + 2)(x + 4)$

4) $(5x + 2)(6x + 7)$

5) $(3x + 4)(2x - 3)$

6) $(4x + 5)(3x - 5)$

7) $(6x + 3)(4x - 6)$

8) $(3x + 2) (5x - 3)$

9) $(4x - 3) (2x + 1)$

10) $(3x - 4) (x + 2)$

11) $(6x - 5) (4x + 3)$

12) $(3x - 7) (2x - 8)$

13) $(6x - 4) (7x - 5)$

14) $(3x - 6) (4x - 5)$

15) $(8x - 6) (9x - 2)$

16) $(3x + 2)^2 \longrightarrow$ written as $(3x + 2) (3x + 2)$

17) $(5x + 3)^2$

18) $(6x - 2)^2$

19) $(4x - 5)^2$

20) $(4x - 9)^2$

FACTORISING

A factor of a number or expression is a number or expression which will divide into it exactly.

for example
$$16 = 16 \times 1$$
$$16 = 8 \times 2$$
$$16 = 4 \times 4$$

Therefore the factors of 16 are 1, 2, 4, 8 and 16

also
$$4m^2 = 1 \times 4m^2$$
$$4m^2 = 2 \times 2m^2$$
$$4m^2 = 4 \times m^2$$
$$4m^2 = m \times 4m$$
$$4m^2 = 2m \times 2m$$

$\therefore$ the factors of $4m^2$ are 1, 2, 4, m, 2m, 4m, m^2, $2m^2$, and $4m^2$.

Highest Common Factor (H.C.F.)

The H.C.F. of a set of numbers or expressions is the biggest number or expression which is a factor of each of the given expressions.

i.e.
H.C.F. of 8 and $4x^2$ is 4

H.C.F. of $9x^2$ and $3x$ is $3x$

H.C.F. of $12xy^2$ and $8y$ is $4y$

H.C.F. of $\frac{1}{2}x$ and $\frac{1}{4}x^2$ is $\frac{1}{4}x$

The H.C.F. is made up of the largest number which will divide into the given expressions and the smallest power of each of the letters which appear in the expression.

Example 7.13	Find the H.C.F. of $4x^2$, $8xy$ and $6xy^2$.
	The largest number factor is 2
	The smallest power of x in all expressions is x
	y does not appear in all expressions
	$\therefore$ H.C.F. is 2x

Factorising using common factors

To factorise an expression made up of more than one part first find the H.C.F. of each of the parts. The remaining factor of each part is written down inside a bracket with the H.C.F. outside.

Example 7.14	Factorise $4x^2 + 3x$
	H.C.F. of $4x^2$ and $3x$ is x
	$\therefore 4x^2 + 3x$ factorised is $x(4x + 3)$
	(because $4x \times x = 4x^2$ and $3 \times x = 3x$)

Example 7.15	Factorise $12x^2y - 3xy^2$
	H.C.F. of $12x^2y$ and $3xy^2$ is 3xy
	$\therefore 12x^2y - 3xy^2 = 3xy(4x - y)$
	(because $3xy \times 4x = 12x^2y$ and $3xy \times y = 3xy^2$)

Example 7.16	$\frac{1}{2}a^2b - \frac{1}{4}ab^2$
	H.C.F. of $\frac{1}{2}a^2b$ and $\frac{1}{4}ab^2$ is $\frac{1}{4}ab$
	$\therefore \frac{1}{2}a^2b - \frac{1}{4}ab^2 = \frac{1}{4}ab(2a - b)$
	(because $\frac{1}{4}ab \times 2a = \frac{1}{2}a^2b$ and $\frac{1}{4}ab \times b = \frac{1}{4}ab^2$)

EXERCISE 7.7

Find the H.C.F. of the expressions in questions 1 to 5.

1) $4x^2y$, $2xy$, $6x$
2) a^2b, ab, a^2b^2.
3) $6a^2b$, $4a^2b^2$, $2ab$.
4) $7xy$, $5x$, $12x^2y^2$.
5) $9x^2y^2$, $6xy$, $12xy^2$.

Factorise the following expressions

6) $3a + 6$

7) $4x + 6$

8) $3ab - 6b$

9) $5ab - 10c$

10) $10xy - 5x^2$

11) $6a^2 - 9ab$

12) $4ab + 6a^2b^2$

13) $\frac{1}{2}ab + \frac{1}{8}a$

14) $a + ab - a^2$

15) $6ab - ac + abc$

16) $7a^2b^2 - 4a^3b$

17) $6xy - 4x^2y$

18) $\frac{a^2}{2} - \frac{a}{4}$

19) $4x^2y + 6xy - 12x^3$

20) $5x^3 - x^2 + x$

22) $5xy + 6x^2 y - 4xy^2 + 3x^3 y$

24) $\dfrac{a^2 b^2}{4} - \dfrac{ab}{2}$

21) $6a^3 - 4ab + 10b$

23) $4a^2 b^2 + 8ab^2 - 12a^2 b$

25) $\dfrac{4n}{3} + \dfrac{2n^2}{3}$

Difference of two squares rule

$$\text{Consider } (a + b)\,(a - b)$$
$$\text{Expanding this gives } \quad a(a - b) + b(a - b)$$
$$= a^2 - b^2$$

This gives a general rule for expressions of the form $a^2 - b^2$

$$a^2 - b^2 = (a + b)\,(a - b)$$

Note $a^2 - b^2$ is known as the difference of two squares.

Example 7.17

Factorise

a) $x^2 - y^2$ b) $a^2 b^2 - c^2$ c) $4a^2 - 9b^2$ d) $8a^2 - 18b^2$ e) $a^4 - b^4$

a) $x^2 - y^2 = (x + y)\,(x - y)$

b) $a^2 b^2 - c^2 = (ab)^2 - c^2 = (ab + c)\,(ab - c)$

c) $4a^2 - 9b^2 = (2a)^2 - (3b)^2 = (2a + 3b)\,(2a - 3b)$

d) $8a^2 - 18b^2 = 2(4a^2 - 9b^2) = 2[(2a)^2 - (3b)^2] = 2(2a + 3b)\,(2a - 3b)$

e) $a^4 - b^4 = (a^2)^2 - (b^2)^2 = (a^2 - b^2)\,(a^2 + b^2) = (a + b)\,(a - b)\,(a^2 + b^2)$

EXERCISE 7.8

Factorise the following

1) $m^2 - n^2$

3) $x^2 y^2 - z^2$

5) $a^2 b^2 - 9c^2$

7) $b^2 - 1$

9) $12x^2 - 27y^2$

11) $x^4 - y^4$

13) $9x^4 - y^4$

2) $a^2 - 4$

4) $a^2 b^2 - 9$

6) $25a^2 - 9b^2$

8) $8a^2 - 50$

10) $x^4 - y^2$

12) $4a^4 - b^2$

14) $2xy^2 - 8x^3$

Factorising trinomials (quadratics)

A trinomial has a (variable)^2 part, a variable part and a constant part.

i.e. $x^2 + 3x + 2$ is a trinomial

or $6a^2 + 4a + 2$ is a trinomial

Consider $(x + 2)(x - 3)$

Expanding this $\quad x(x - 3) + 2(x - 3)$
$$= x^2 - x - 6$$

$\therefore x^2 - x - 6$ is $(x + 2)(x - 3)$ in factorised form.

Factorising trinomials when the coefficient of x^2 is 1

From the above example we see that $+2$ and -3 in the brackets are the factors of -6 and $+2 \, -3$ gives the coefficient of x

Example 7.18   Factorise $x^2 + 6x + 5$
The factors of 5 are 5 and 1
The sum of 5 and 1 is 6, the coefficient of x
$\therefore x^2 + 6x + 5 = (x + 5)(x + 1)$

Rule   Find the factors of the constant part
These factors should sum to give the coefficient of x.

Example 7.19   Factorise $\quad x^2 - 7x + 12$
The factors of $+12$ are -1 and -12 or $+1$ and $+12$
or -2 and -6 or $+2$ and $+6$ or -3 and -4 or $+3$ and $+4$
However the factors which sum to give -7 are -3 and -4
$\therefore x^2 - 7x + 12 = (x - 3)(x - 4)$

Example 7.20   Factorise $\quad x^2 - 2x - 15$
The factors of -15 which give a sum of -2 are -5 and 3
$\therefore x^2 - 2x - 15 = (x - 5)(x + 3)$

Example 7.21   Factorise $\quad x^2 + 7x + 12$
The factors of $+12$ which give a sum of $+7$ are $+4$ and $+3$
$\therefore x^2 + 7x + 12 = (x + 4)(x + 3)$

EXERCISE 7.9

Factorise the following

1) $x^2 + 9x + 20$

2) $x^2 - 3x + 2$

3) $x^2 + 2x - 2$

4) $x^2 - 2x - 8$

5) $x^2 + 11x + 30$

6) $x^2 - 10x + 24$

7) $x^2 + 4x - 21$

8) $x^2 + 5x - 14$

9) $x^2 + 13x + 42$

10) $x^2 - 13x + 42$

11) $x^2 - 8x - 20$

12) $x^2 - 15x + 36$

13) $x^2 - 7x - 44$

14) $x^2 + 4x - 60$

Factorising trinomials when the coefficient of x^2 is not unity

This is done by   finding the factors of the x^2 coefficient
finding the factors of the number (constant) part
trying different combinations of these to find which give the
middle (x) term

Example 7.22   Factorise $2x^2 - 7x - 4$
Factors of $2x^2$ are x and $2x$
Factors of -4 are -4 and $+1$
$+4$ and -1
-2 and $+2$

Trying all these combinations gives
$(2x - 4)(x + 1) = 2x^2 - 2x - 4$
$(2x + 1)(x - 4) = 2x^2 - 7x - 4$
$(2x + 4)(x - 1) = 2x^2 + 2x - 4$
$(2x - 1)(x + 4) = 2x^2 + 7x - 4$
$(2x - 2)(x + 2) = 2x^2 + 2x - 4$
$(2x + 2)(x - 2) = 2x^2 - 2x - 4$
Clearly $2x^2 - 7x - 4 = (2x + 1)(x - 4)$ is the required solution.

EXERCISE 7.10

Factorise the following

1)	$2x^2 + 3x + 1$	2)	$2x^2 + 9x + 4$
3)	$2x^2 + 7x + 3$	4)	$2x^2 + 8x + 6$
5)	$2x^2 + x - 6$	6)	$3x^2 - 7x - 6$
7)	$2x^2 - 9x + 4$	8)	$3x^2 - 10x + 3$
9)	$3x^2 - 14x + 8$	10)	$3x^2 + x - 14$
11)	$3x^2 + 19x + 20$	12)	$3x^2 - 12x + 12$
13)	$4x^2 + 10x + 6$	14)	$4x^2 - 10x + 6$
15)	$4x^2 + 13x + 3$	16)	$4x^2 - 21x + 5$
17)	$5x^2 + 13x - 6$	18)	$4x^2 + 21x + 5$
19)	$6x^2 + 5x + 1$	20)	$9x^2 + 12x + 4$
21)	$8x^2 + 11x + 3$	22)	$4x^2 - 23x + 15$
23)	$5x^2 - 13x - 6$	24)	$12x^2 - 13x + 3$

ALGEBRAIC FRACTIONS

Multiplication and division

Example 7.23

Consider each of the following

a) $\dfrac{2}{3} \times \dfrac{1}{3} = \dfrac{2 \times 1}{3 \times 3} = \dfrac{2}{9}$

b) $\dfrac{2}{\cancel{3}_1} \times \dfrac{\cancel{9}^3}{11} = \dfrac{2 \times 3}{1 \times 11} = \dfrac{6}{11}$

Divide numerator and denominator by the same number i.e. cancel down

c) $\dfrac{1}{6} \div \dfrac{1}{3} = \dfrac{1 \times \cancel{3}^1}{\cancel{6}_2 \times 1} = \dfrac{1}{2}$

d) $\dfrac{a}{b} \times \dfrac{x}{y} = \dfrac{a \times x}{b \times y} = \dfrac{ax}{by}$

e) $\dfrac{\cancel{a}^1}{b} \times \dfrac{x}{\cancel{a}_1} = \dfrac{1 \times x}{b \times 1} = \dfrac{x}{b}$

f) $\dfrac{5a}{\cancel{6}_2} \times \dfrac{\cancel{3}^1 b}{4} = \dfrac{5a \times 1b}{2 \times 4} = \dfrac{5ab}{8}$

g) $\dfrac{5x}{6} \div \dfrac{10x}{21} = \dfrac{\cancel{5}^1 \cancel{x}^1}{\cancel{6}_2} \times \dfrac{\cancel{21}^7}{\cancel{10}\cancel{x}_{2\,1}} = \dfrac{1 \times 7}{2 \times 2} = \dfrac{7}{4} = 1\dfrac{3}{4}$

h) $\dfrac{3}{x-1} \times \dfrac{3 - 2x}{4} = \dfrac{3(3 - 2x)}{(x-1) \times 4} = \dfrac{3(3 - 2x)}{4(x-1)}$

Leave in factorised form

i) $\dfrac{2}{2x + 3} \div \dfrac{4}{x-1} = \dfrac{\cancel{2}^1}{2x + 3} \times \dfrac{x - 1}{\cancel{4}_2} = \dfrac{1 \times (x - 1)}{2 \times (2x + 3)} = \dfrac{x - 1}{2(2x + 3)}$

J) $\dfrac{3}{2(x-1)} \div \dfrac{4}{x-1} = \dfrac{3}{2\cancel{(x-1)}_1} \times \dfrac{\cancel{(x - 1)}^1}{4} = \dfrac{3 \times 1}{2 \times 4} = \dfrac{3}{8}$

EXERCISE 7.11

Simplify each of the following

1) $\dfrac{1}{2} \times \dfrac{1}{3}$

2) $\dfrac{2}{3} \times \dfrac{1}{4}$

3) $\dfrac{3}{8} \div \dfrac{1}{2}$

4) $\dfrac{x}{y} \times \dfrac{v}{w}$

5) $\dfrac{2}{3} \times \dfrac{a}{b}$

6) $\dfrac{x}{y} \times \dfrac{v}{x}$

7) $\dfrac{3x}{y} \times \dfrac{2x}{3}$

8) $\dfrac{2a}{3} \div \dfrac{3a}{4}$

9) $\dfrac{5a}{6} \div \dfrac{10a}{21}$

10) $\dfrac{3x}{2y} \div \dfrac{4x}{y}$

11) $\dfrac{3ab}{5} \times \dfrac{2b}{7a}$

12) $\dfrac{9a}{4} \div \dfrac{15b}{8}$

13) $\dfrac{2}{x-1} \times \dfrac{3}{4}$

14) $\dfrac{3}{2x+1} \div \dfrac{3}{4}$

15) $\dfrac{x+3}{4} \times \dfrac{5}{x-1}$

16) $\dfrac{5}{x+1} \div \dfrac{3}{x+2}$

17) $\dfrac{3}{x-1} \div \dfrac{9}{x+3}$

18) $\dfrac{3x+1}{4} \times \dfrac{5}{x+2}$

19) $\dfrac{3(x-1)}{4} \times \dfrac{x-1}{5}$

20) $\dfrac{2(x+3)}{7} \div \dfrac{x+3}{4}$

Addition and Subtraction

Example 7.24

Consider each of the following

a) $\dfrac{1}{3} + \dfrac{1}{2}$ L.C.M. of 3 and 2 is 6

$= \dfrac{2}{6} + \dfrac{3}{6} = \dfrac{5}{6}$

b) $\dfrac{1}{a} + \dfrac{1}{b}$ L.C.M. of a and b is ab

$= \dfrac{a}{ab} + \dfrac{b}{ab}$ $\left(\text{because } \dfrac{1}{a} = \dfrac{a}{ab} \quad \text{and } \dfrac{1}{b} = \dfrac{b}{ab} \right)$

$= \dfrac{a+b}{ab}$

c) $\dfrac{a}{3} + \dfrac{b}{2} - \dfrac{c}{6}$ L.C.M. of 3, 2 and 6 is 6

$= \dfrac{2a}{6} + \dfrac{3b}{6} - \dfrac{c}{6}$

$= \dfrac{2a}{6} + \dfrac{3b}{6} - \dfrac{c}{6} = \dfrac{2a + 3b - c}{6}$

d) $\dfrac{2}{3} - \dfrac{3}{b+1}$ L.C.M. of 3 and (b+1) is 3(b+1)

$= \dfrac{2(b+1)}{3(b+1)} - \dfrac{9}{3(b+1)} = \dfrac{2(b+1) - 9}{3(b+1)}$

$= \dfrac{2b + 2 - 9}{3(b+1)} = \dfrac{2b - 7}{3(b+1)}$

e) $\dfrac{x}{2} + \dfrac{x - 1}{3}$ L.C.M. is 6

$= \dfrac{3x}{6} + \dfrac{2(x-1)}{6} = \dfrac{3x + 2(x-1)}{6}$

$= \dfrac{3x + 2x - 2}{6} = \dfrac{5x - 2}{6}$

f) $4x - \dfrac{3(x + 2)}{5}$ L.C.M. is 5

$= \dfrac{5(4x)}{5} - \dfrac{3(x + 2)}{5}$

$= \dfrac{20x}{5} - \dfrac{(3x + 6)}{5} = \dfrac{20x - 3x - 6}{5}$

$= \dfrac{17x - 6}{5}$

EXERCISE 7.12

Simplify each of the following

1) $\dfrac{1}{2} - \dfrac{1}{3}$ 2) $\dfrac{3}{4} - \dfrac{1}{6}$ 3) $\dfrac{7}{8} - \dfrac{5}{6}$

4) $\dfrac{1}{x} + \dfrac{1}{y}$

5) $\dfrac{3}{x} - \dfrac{2}{y}$

6) $\dfrac{5}{a} - \dfrac{2}{a}$

7) $\dfrac{x}{3} + \dfrac{x}{2}$

8) $\dfrac{a}{5} - \dfrac{a}{10}$

9) $\dfrac{2a}{3} - \dfrac{a}{6}$

10) $\dfrac{x}{2} - \dfrac{y}{3}$

11) $\dfrac{2a}{3} + \dfrac{b}{4}$

12) $\dfrac{3a}{2} - \dfrac{b}{6}$

13) $\dfrac{a}{3} + \dfrac{b}{4} - \dfrac{c}{8}$

14) $\dfrac{2a}{3} + \dfrac{b}{6} + \dfrac{2c}{9}$

15) $\dfrac{3}{4} + \dfrac{2}{a+1}$

16) $\dfrac{4}{5} - \dfrac{3}{x+1}$

17) $\dfrac{2}{x-1} + \dfrac{3}{5}$

18) $\dfrac{x}{3} + \dfrac{2x - 1}{4}$

19) $\dfrac{x - 3}{4} - \dfrac{x}{2}$

20) $\dfrac{4x + 3}{9} + \dfrac{5x}{2}$

21) $\dfrac{x}{2} - \dfrac{3(x-2)}{4}$

22) $x + \dfrac{2(x-3)}{5}$

23) $4x - \dfrac{5(x-1)}{3}$

24) $\dfrac{3x + 2}{4} - \dfrac{5(x+2)}{6}$

25) $\dfrac{3(x + 3)}{8} - \dfrac{3(x - 3)}{4}$

INDICES

$a^4 = a \times a \times a \times a$

$a^n = a \times a \times a \ldots\ldots n$ times   where n is an integer

Example 7.25

$a^4 \times a^3 = \underbrace{a \times a \times a \times a}_{a^4} \times \underbrace{a \times a \times a}_{a^3} = a^7$

so $a^4 \times a^3 = a^{4+3} = a^7$

Example 7.26

$a^5 \div a^3 = \dfrac{a \times a \times a \times a \times a}{a \times a \times a} = a^2$

so $a^5 \div a^3 = a^{5-3} = a^2$

Example 7.27

$$(a^2)^3 = a^2 \times a^2 \times a^2$$

$$= \underbrace{a \times a}_{a^2} \times \underbrace{a \times a}_{a^2} \times \underbrace{a \times a}_{a^2} = a^6$$

so $(a^2)^3 = a^{2 \times 3} = a^6$

Example 7.28

$$(ab)^3 = ab \times ab \times ab$$
$$= a \times b \times a \times b \times a \times b$$
$$= a \times a \times a \times b \times b \times b$$
$$= a^3 \times b^3$$
so $(ab)^3 = a^3 \times b^3$

General Rules
(1) $a^m \times a^n = a^{m+n}$
(2) $a^m \div a^n = a^{m-n}$
(3) $(a^m)^n = a^{m \times n}$
(4) $(ab^n) = a^n b^n$

Example 7.29

By using the above rules, simplify the following

(a) $2x^3 \times 4x^6$ (b) $\dfrac{x^8}{x^2}$ (c) $(b^3)^2$

(d) $(xy)^6 \times x^5$ (e) $(2x)^4$ (f) $9a^4 \div 3a^2$

(a) $2x^3 \times 4x^6 = (2 \times 4)x^{3+6} = 8x^9$

(b) $\dfrac{x^8}{x^2} = x^{8-2} = x^6$

(c) $(b^3)^2 = b^{3 \times 2} = b^6$

(d) $(xy)^6 \times x^5 = x^6 \times y^6 \times x^5 = x^{6+5} \times y^6 = x^{11}y^6$

(e) $(2x)^4 = 2^4 x^4 = 16x^4$

(f) $9a^4 \div 3a^2 = (9 \div 3)a^{4-2} = 3a^2$

EXERCISE 7.13

Simplify each of the following

(1) (a) $x^2 \times x^3$ (b) $x^5 \times x^6$ (c) $a^4 \times a^8$ (d) $y^2 \times y^{11}$

(2) (a) $a^4 \div a^2$ (b) $a^6 \div a^3$ (c) $x^5 \div x^3$ (d) $2^{10} \div 2^4$

(3) (a) $(a^6)^4$ (b) $(x^3)^6$ (c) $(y^2)^4$ (d) $(b^3)^6$

(4) (a) $(xy)^2 \times x^2$ (b) $(ab)^3 \times a^2$ (c) $(xy)^4 \times y^2$ (d) $(ab)^3 \times b^3$

(5) (a) $(3x)^2$ (b) $(2x)^3$ (c) $(3x)^3$ (d) $(5a)^2$

(6) (a) $12a^2 \div 4a^2$ (b) $21x^5 \div 7x^2$ (c) $\dfrac{50b^5}{10b^2}$ (d) $\dfrac{100x^7}{20x^2}$

(7) (a) $3x^2 \times 4x^3$ (b) $9a^4 \times 12a^3$ (c) $6y^5 \times 5y^4$

(8) (a) $x^5 \times x^3 \div x^2$ (b) $\tfrac{1}{2}x \times \tfrac{1}{4}x \times \tfrac{3}{4}x$

    (c) $\dfrac{x^2 \times x^3 \times x^4}{x^5}$ (d) $\dfrac{x^7}{4} \times \dfrac{x^6}{3}$

Example 7.30 $a^3 \times a^{-3} = a^{3+(-3)} = a^0 = 1$
         i.e. $a^3 \times a^{-3} = 1$
         by dividing both sides by a^3
         $a^{-3} = \dfrac{1}{a^3}$

Example 7.31 $a^3 \div a^3 = \dfrac{\cancel{a} \times \cancel{a} \times \cancel{a}}{\cancel{a} \times \cancel{a} \times \cancel{a}} = \dfrac{1}{1} = 1$
         also $a^3 \div a^3 = a^{3-3} = a^0$
         $\therefore a^0 = 1$

Example 7.32 $x^{1/2} \times x^{1/2} = x^{1/2+1/2} = x^1$
         $\therefore x^{1/2} = \sqrt{x}$
         also $x^{1/3} \times x^{1/3} \times x^{1/3} = x^{1/3+1/3+1/3} = x^1$
         $\therefore x^{1/3} = \sqrt[3]{x}$

Example 7.33 $a^{3/2} = a^{\frac{1}{2}\times 3} = (a^{\frac{1}{2}})^3$

$\therefore \ a^{3/2} = (\sqrt{a})^3 \quad \text{or} \quad \sqrt{a^3}$

General Rules

$$a^0 = 1$$

$$a^{-n} = \frac{1}{a^n}$$

$$a^{\frac{1}{n}} = \sqrt[n]{a}$$

$$a^{\frac{m}{n}} = (\sqrt[n]{a})^m \quad \text{or} \quad \sqrt[n]{a^m}$$

Example 7.34

Simplify each of the following

(a) $2x^5 \div 3x^5$ (b) $3a^3 \times 5a^{-4}$ (c) $(4a)^{\frac{1}{2}}$

(d) $(2a)^{-3}$ (e) $3a^{-3}$ (f) $16^{\frac{1}{4}}$

(g) $16x^0$ (h) $27^{2/3}$ (i) $\sqrt[4]{x^{16}}$

(j) $(\frac{1}{16})^{-\frac{1}{4}}$ (k) $(2\frac{1}{4})^{-\frac{1}{2}}$

(a) $\dfrac{2x^5}{3x^5} = \dfrac{2x^{5-5}}{3} = \dfrac{2x^0}{3} = \dfrac{2}{3}$

(b) $3a^3 \times 5a^{-4} = (3 \times 5)\ \dfrac{a^3}{a^4} = \dfrac{15}{a}$

(c) $(4a)^{\frac{1}{2}} = \sqrt{4a} = 2\sqrt{a} \quad \text{or} \quad 2a^{\frac{1}{2}}$

(d) $(2a)^{-3} = \dfrac{1}{(2a)^3} = \dfrac{1}{8a^3}$

(e) $3a^{-3} = \dfrac{3}{a^3}$

(f) $16^{\frac{1}{4}} = \sqrt[4]{16} = 2$

(g) $16x^0 = 16 \times 1 = 16$

(h) $27^{2/3} = (\sqrt[3]{27})^2 = 3^2 = 9$

(i) $\sqrt[4]{x^{16}} = (x^{16})^{\frac{1}{4}} = x^{16 \times \frac{1}{4}} = x^4$

(j) $\left(\frac{1}{16}\right)^{-\frac{1}{4}} = \frac{1}{\left(\frac{1}{16}\right)^{\frac{1}{4}}} = \frac{1}{\frac{1}{2}} = \frac{2}{1} = 2$

(k) $\left(2\frac{1}{4}\right)^{-\frac{1}{2}} = \left(\frac{9}{4}\right)^{-\frac{1}{2}} + \frac{1}{\left(\frac{9}{4}\right)^{\frac{1}{2}}} = \frac{1}{\frac{3}{2}} = \frac{2}{3}$

EXERCISE 7.14

Simplify the following

1. (a) $2a^2 \times a^{-3}$ (b) $3x \times 4x^{-2}$ (c) $2x^2 \times \dfrac{3}{4x^3}$

    (d) $4a^2 b \times 3a^{-1}$

2. (a) $8^{\frac{1}{3}}$ (b) $25^{\frac{1}{2}}$ (c) $81^{\frac{1}{4}}$ (d) $16^{-\frac{1}{2}}$ (e) $27^{-\frac{1}{3}}$

    (f) $(125a)^{-\frac{1}{3}}$ (g) $125^{-\frac{1}{3}}a$ (h) $\left(\frac{1}{4}\right)^{\frac{1}{2}}$ (i) $\left(\frac{1}{9}\right)^{-\frac{1}{2}}$

3. (a) $4^{\frac{3}{2}}$ (b) $8^{\frac{2}{3}}$ (c) $(9)^{1\frac{1}{2}}$ (d) $(81)^{\frac{3}{4}}$ (e) $(64)^{\frac{2}{3}}$

    (f) $(32)^{\frac{3}{5}}$ (g) $(25)^{\frac{3}{2}}$ (h) $(25)^{-\frac{3}{2}}$ (i) $(64)^{-\frac{5}{6}}$

4. (a) $\left(6\frac{1}{4}\right)^{\frac{1}{2}}$ (b) $\left(3\frac{3}{8}\right)^{\frac{1}{3}}$ (c) $\left(1\frac{7}{9}\right)^{-\frac{1}{2}}$ (d) $\left(\frac{125}{8}\right)^{\frac{2}{3}}$ (e) $\left(3\frac{3}{8}\right)^{\frac{2}{3}}$

EQUATIONS AND
FUNCTIONS 1

EQUATIONS

An equation is used to show that two mathematical quantities are equal.

$$4 + 6 = 10$$
$$x + 3 = 4$$
$$3x^2 + 2x + 1 = 5x + 3$$

Linear equations

These are equations in which the variable (x) is raised to the power 1 only.

i.e. $$3x + 2 = 5$$

$$\frac{2(x + 3)}{5} = 3x + 2$$

Solving linear equations

Linear equations are solved by using the following methods.

a) Adding the same amount to both sides of the equation.

b) Subtracting the same amount from both sides of the equation.

c) Multiplying both sides of the equation by the same amount.

d) Dividing both sides of the equation by the same amount.

Example 8.1

$3x + 2 = 8$		
$3x = 6$	by subtracting 2 from both sides
$x = 2$	by dividing both sides by 3
check	$3(2) + 2 = 6 + 2 = 8$	

Example 8.2

always subtract smaller x value

$4x + 3 = 7x - 6$		
$3 = 3x - 6$	subtracting 4x from both sides
$9 = 3x$	adding 6 to both sides
$3 = x$	dividing both sides by 3
check	$4(3) + 3 = 15$	L.H.S.
	$7(3) - 6 = 15$	R.H.S.

Example 8.3

$4(x + 3) = 7x + 18$		
$4x + 12 = 7x + 18$	multiplying bracket
$12 = 3x + 18$	subtract 4x from both sides
$-6 = 3x$	subtract 18 from both sides
$-2 = x$	divide by 3
check	$4(-2 + 3) = 4$	L.H.S.
	$7(-2 + 18) = 4$	R.H.S.

Example 8.4

$$\frac{2}{x + 1} = 4$$

$2 = 4(x + 1)$ multiplying by $(x + 1)$

$2 = 4x + 4$

$-2 = 4x$ subtracting 4

$-\frac{1}{2} = x$ dividing by 4

i.e. $x = -\frac{1}{2}$

check $\dfrac{2}{-\frac{1}{2} + 1} = \dfrac{2}{\frac{1}{2}} = 4$ R.H.S.

Example 8.5

$$\frac{3x + 2}{2} - \frac{x - 6}{4} = 10$$

L.C.M. of denominator is 4

$$\frac{4(3x + 2)}{2} - \frac{4(x - 6)}{4} = 40 \quad \text{multiplying by 4}$$

$2(3x + 2) - (x - 6) = 40$

$6x + 4 - x + 6 = 40$

$5x + 10 = 40$

$5x = 30$ subtracting 10

$x = 6$ dividing by 5

check $\dfrac{3(6) + 2}{2} - \dfrac{(6 - 6)}{4} = 10 - 0 = 10$

Example 8.6

$$\frac{1}{x + 2} = \frac{2}{x + 3}$$

Multiplying throughout by the L.C.M. of the denominators, i.e.

$$(x + 2)(x + 3)$$

$$\frac{(x + 2)(x + 3)}{(x + 2)} = \frac{2(x + 2)(x + 3)}{x + 3}$$

$x + 3 = 2(x + 2)$

$x + 3 = 2x + 4$

$3 = x + 4$ subtracting x

$-1 = x$ subtracting 4

check $\dfrac{1}{-1 + 2} = \dfrac{1}{1} = 1$ L.H.S.

$\dfrac{2}{-1 + 3} = \dfrac{2}{2} = 1$ R.H.S.

EXERCISE 8.1

Find the value of x in each of these equations

1) $x - 4 = 6$

2) $x + 6 = 10$

3) $x - 5 = 16$

4) $5 - x = 2$

5) $9 + x = 17$

6) $12 - x = 14$

7) $4x = 20$

8) $6x = 28$

9) $6x = -36$

10) $2x + 1 = 7$

11) $7x - 3 = 60$

12) $12x - 14 = 130$

13) $24 - 3x = 6$

14) $7 - 2x = -1$

15) $\dfrac{1x}{4} = 30$

16) $\dfrac{x}{6} = 25$

17) $\dfrac{2x}{3} = 8$

18) $\dfrac{2}{x} = 4$

19) $\dfrac{3}{x + 2} = 1$

20) $\dfrac{4}{x - 1} = 4$

21) $\dfrac{2}{2x - 1} = 5$

22) $2x + 3 = 3x + 2$

23) $4x + 3 = 3x + 5$

24) $4x - 5 = 3x + 3$

25) $7x + 3 = 10x - 6$

26) $5(x + 3) = 7x + 5$

27) $3(2x + 4) = 5x + 17$

28) $2(x + 3) = 4(2x - 9)$

29) $3(2x - 1) = 5(3x - 15)$

30) $3(x + 2) - 2(3x - 5) = 10$

31) $4(2x - 3) - 3(3x - 10) = 11$

32) $\dfrac{x}{3} + \dfrac{x}{4} = 14$

33) $\dfrac{2x}{5} + \dfrac{x}{4} = 13$

34) $\dfrac{x}{3} - \dfrac{x}{7} = 12$

35) $\dfrac{x - 2}{3} + \dfrac{x + 2}{2} = 25$

36) $\dfrac{2x - 1}{3} - \dfrac{x + 1}{4} = 4$

37) $\dfrac{3(x + 2)}{5} = 6$

38) $\dfrac{3x}{2} = \dfrac{5}{3}$

39) $\dfrac{3}{x} = \dfrac{4}{x + 2}$

40) $\dfrac{2}{x - 1} = \dfrac{3}{2x+4}$

CONSTRUCTING LINEAR EQUATIONS

In order to construct a linear equation the following steps must be followed

a)   Any unknown value must be represented by a letter.

b)   All parts of the equation must be in the same units, e.g. (metres not centimetres and metres).

c)   When the equation has been solved the original problem must be checked with the answer to ensure it makes sense.

Example 8.7

A rectangle has a perimeter of 50cm. If one side is 6cm longer than the other side, find the lengths of the two sides.

Let the smaller side be x cm and the larger side be (x + 6) cm.

$$\text{Then} \quad x + (x + 6) + x + (x + 6) = 50$$
$$4x + 12 = 50$$
$$4x = 38$$
$$x = 9\tfrac{1}{2} \text{ cm}$$

i.e.   smaller side is 9½ cm

larger side is 9½ + 6 = 15½ cm

check   Perimeter = 9½ + 15½ + 9½ + 15½ = 50 cm

Example 8.8

A woman is 6 times older than her son. In 4 years time she will be 4 times older than him. Find the age of the woman and son now.

Now   son is x years old

woman is 6x years old

In 4 years time   son is x + 4 years old

woman is 6x + 4 years old

But the woman is also 4 times older than her son, i.e. 4(x + 4) years old

∴ we have two expressions for the woman's age in 4 years time

$$\text{so} \quad 6x + 4 = 4(x + 4)$$
$$6x + 4 = 4x + 16$$
$$2x + 4 = 16$$
$$2x = 12$$
$$x = 6$$

∴ son's age now is 6 years

woman's age now is 6 × 6 years = 36 years

check   In 4 years time son is 6 + 4 = 10

woman is 36 + 4 = 40

So woman is 4 times older than her son.

EXERCISE 8.2

1) A rectangle has a perimeter of 40 cm and one side is 3 cm longer than the other. Find the lengths of the sides.

2) A triangle has one side twice as long as the first side and a third side 3 cm longer than the first side. If the perimeter is 28 cm, find the lengths of the three sides.

3) Three consecutive numbers add up to 81. What are the numbers?

4) A man walks a certain distance from his place of work to his car and then drives home 8 times this distance. If his total journey is 3·6 km find the length of his car journey.

5) Find four consecutive even numbers which add up to 126.

6) A man is 4 times as old as his daughter. In 4 years time he will be three times as old as her. Find their ages now.

7) The total age of three children is 33 years. If each is 3 years older than the next how old are they?

8) Three sisters are left an amount of money by their Aunt. Annabel receives £400 more than Bethan who receives twice as much as Cathy. If Cathy receives £x write down an expression for the amount Annabel receives. If Annabel receives £1000, how much does Cathy receive?

9) A box contains 10p and 50p coins. There are 3 times as many 10p coins as 50p coins. If their total value is £8 how many of each are there?

10) Twenty articles are bought for a total cost of 82p. If some cost 5p each and others 3p each how many of each were bought?

11) A school minibus can carry 2 more passengers than a hired one. When they have both carried the same number of pupils, the school bus has made 3 journeys and the hired bus 4 journeys. How many pupils can each carry?

12) A woman has two bank accounts, both with the same amount of money in. She transfers £300 from one account to the other. One account now has twice as much money in as the other. How much money has she in total?

13) A bus costs £200 to hire for a day. A social club charges £10 for each non-member (n) and £6 for each member (m) to go on an outing.
    a) Write down an equation linking m, n and the cost of hiring the bus if the club is not to lose money.
    b) If twenty members go on the outing how many non-members need to go?

14) A man's wages are made up of a basic wage (for 40 hours) and overtime, as shown below.
    First 40 hours at £5 per hour = £200
    Next 10 hours at time and a half.
    Any remaining hours at double time.
    a) Write down an equation showing how his total wage T is calculated if he works x hours overtime and $x > 10$.
    b) If his total wage for a week is £375 how many hours overtime does he work?

LINEAR INEQUALITIES

$>$ means 'is greater than'
$<$ means 'is less than'
$\geqslant$ means 'is greater than or equal to'
$\leqslant$ means 'is less than or equal to'

Example 8.9

a) If $x > 6$ and x is a whole number then x can have the value of 7 or 8 or 9 etc. i.e. its solution set is
$$\{ 7, 8, 9, 10 \ldots \}$$

b) If $x < 4$ and x is an integer then its solution set is
$$\{ 3, 2, 1, 0, -1 \ldots \}$$

c) If $x \geqslant -3$ and x is an integer then its solution set is
$$\{ -3, -2, -1, 0, 1 \ldots \}$$

d) If $x \leqslant 5$ and x is whole then its solution set is
$$\{ 5, 4, 3, 2, 1, 0 \}$$

Example 8.10

Find suitable values of x if $2x > 5$ and x is a whole number.

> use the rules
> for solving
> linear equations

If $2x > 5$
then $x > 2\frac{1}{2}$ by dividing throughout by 2
$\therefore$ the solution set is
$$\{ 3, 4, 5 \ldots \}$$

Example 8.11

Find suitable values of x if $2x + 4 \leqslant 18$ and x is an integer

$$2x + 4 \leqslant 18$$
$$2x \leqslant 14 \quad \text{by subtracting 4}$$
$$x \leqslant 7 \quad \text{by dividing by 2}$$
$\therefore$ solution set is
$$\{ 7, 6, 5, 4 \ldots \}$$

Example 8.12

Find suitable values of x if $x + 4 < 2x + 3$

$$x + 4 < 2x + 3$$
$$4 < x + 3 \quad \text{by subtracting x}$$
$$1 < x \quad \text{by subtracting 3}$$
This reads 1 is less than x or x is greater than 1
$\therefore$ solution set is
$$\{ 2, 3, 4 \ldots \}$$

EXERCISE 8.3

Find solution sets for the following inequalities, where x is an integer

1) $x > 4$

2) $x < 2$

3) $x \geqslant 4$

4) $x \leqslant 7$

5) $2x > 4$

6) $3x < 12$

7) $3x \geqslant 21$

8) $4x \leqslant 4$

9) $x + 2 \leqslant 7$

10) $x + 4 < 7$

11) $x - 7 < 12$

12) $x - 3 \geqslant 6$

13) $2x + 3 > 7$

14) $2x - 4 < 6$

15) $2x + 9 \geqslant 13$

16) $2x + 4 \leqslant 16$

17) $3x + 2 > 14$

18) $5x - 2 < 8$

19) $x + 3 < 2x + 1$

20) $2x + 1 > x - 3$

21) $3x - 2 > 2x + 1$

22) $2x + 1 < 3x - 2$

23) $4x + 5 \leqslant 3x + 3$

24) $2(x + 3) > 5$

25) $3(x - 2) \geqslant 3$

26) $2(x - 4) \leqslant 6$

27) $2(x - 3) < 4$

28) $3(2x - 1) \leqslant 3x$

29) $4(x + 3) > 2x$

30) $3(2x + 1) \leqslant 5x$

CHANGING THE SUBJECT OF A FORMULA

The rules used are the same as those for solving an equation, where the variable x became the subject.

Example 8.13

If $A = \ell b$ make b the subject

$$\frac{A}{\ell} = b \qquad \text{by dividing both sides by } \ell$$

$$\text{i.e.} \quad b = \frac{A}{\ell}$$

Example 8.14

If $\pi = \frac{C}{D}$ make C the subject

$$\pi D = C \qquad \text{by multiplying both sides by D}$$

$$\text{i.e.} \quad C = \pi D$$

Example 8.15

If $y = \frac{x}{a}$ make a the subject

$$ay = x \qquad \text{by multiplying by a}$$

$$a = \frac{x}{y} \qquad \text{by dividing by y}$$

Example 8.16

If $v = u + at$ make u the subject

$v - at = u$ by subtracting (at)

i.e. $u = v - at$

Example 8.17

If $v = u + at$ make a the subject

$v - u = at$ by subtracting u

$\dfrac{v - u}{t} = a$ by dividing both sides by t

i.e. $a = \dfrac{v - u}{t}$

Example 8.18

If $x(a + b) = y$ make x the subject

$x = \dfrac{y}{a + b}$ by dividing by $(a + b)$

Example 8.19

If $x(a + b) = y$ make a the subject

$a + b = \dfrac{y}{x}$ by dividing by x

i.e. $a = \dfrac{y}{x} - b$ by subtracting b

Example 8.20

If $A = \pi r^2$ make r the subject

$\dfrac{A}{\pi} = r^2$ by dividing by π

$\sqrt{\dfrac{A}{\pi}} = r$ by square rooting both sides of the formula

i.e. $r = \sqrt{\dfrac{A}{\pi}}$

$$\boxed{\text{Note } \sqrt{a^2} = a \quad \left(\sqrt{a}\right)^2 = a}$$

Example 8.21

If $I = \dfrac{x}{y} \sqrt{w}$ make w the subject

$Iy = x \sqrt{w}$ by multiplying by y

$\dfrac{Iy}{x} = \sqrt{w}$ by dividing by x

$\left(\dfrac{Iy}{x}\right)^2 = w$ by squaring both sides

Example 8.22

If $\dfrac{1}{a} + \dfrac{1}{b} = \dfrac{1}{3}$ make a the subject

$$\left. \begin{array}{l} \dfrac{3ab}{a} + \dfrac{3ab}{b} = \dfrac{3ab}{3} \\[2mm] 3b + 3a = ab \end{array} \right\} \quad \text{by multiplying by the L.C.M. of the denominators (3ab)}$$

$$3b = ab - 3a \qquad \text{by subtracting } 3a$$

$$3b = a(b-3) \qquad \text{by factorising for a}$$

$$\dfrac{3b}{b-3} = a \qquad \text{by dividing by } (b-3)$$

i.e. $\quad a = \dfrac{3b}{b-3}$

EXERCISE 8.4

Rearrange each of the following formulae to make its subject the letter indicated

1) $C = \pi D$ (D)   2) $C = 2\pi r$ (r)   3) $F = ma$ (m)

4) $A = \frac{1}{2}bh$ (h)   5) $V = \ell bh$ (h)   6) $V = \frac{1}{3}\pi r^2 h$ (h)

7) $y = mx + c$ (c)   8) $y = mx + c$ (m)   9) $v = \pi r^2 h$ (h)

10) $v = \pi r^2 h$ (r)   11) $C = \frac{5}{9}(F - 32)$ (F)   12) $I = \dfrac{PTR}{100}$ (R)

13) $v^2 = 2gh$ (h)   14) $v^2 = u^2 + 2as$ (s)   15) $s = ut + \frac{1}{2}at^2$ (a)

16) $s = \frac{1}{2}(u+v)t$ (v)   17) $T = 2\pi\sqrt{\dfrac{\ell}{g}}$ (ℓ)

18) $\dfrac{1}{x} + \dfrac{1}{y} = 1$ (x)   19) $A = \dfrac{2x + y}{3}$ (x)

20) $P = \dfrac{3(x - y)}{6}$ (x)   21) $P = \dfrac{Rx^2}{2y}$ (x)

22) $C = \dfrac{Dx^2}{zy}$ (y)   23) $x = \dfrac{ab}{a-b}$ (a)

24) $x = \sqrt{\dfrac{a}{a+b}}$ (b)   25) $x = \sqrt{\dfrac{a}{a+b}}$ (a)

26) $A = \pi(R^2 - r^2)$ (R)   27) $A = \pi(R^2 - r^2)$ (r)

28) $C = d + t\sqrt{x}$ (x)   29) $a = \sqrt{\dfrac{C(x - c)}{b}}$ (x)

SUBSTITUTION

Example 8.23

Given that $t = 2\pi \sqrt{\dfrac{\ell}{g}}$ find the value of t, correct to 3 significant figures

when $\ell = 4.6$, $g = 9.8$ and $\pi = 3.142$

$$t = 2 \times 3.142 \times \sqrt{\dfrac{4.6}{9.8}}$$

$$t = 6.284 \times \sqrt{0.4694}$$

$$t = 6.284 \times 0.685$$

$$t = 4.31 \quad \text{correct to 3 significant figures}$$

Example 8.24

If $y = 3x^2 + 2x - 4$ find the value of y when $x = -3$

$$
\begin{aligned}
y &= 3(-3)^2 + 2(-3) - 4 \\
&= 3(9) - 6 - 4 \\
&= 27 - 6 - 4 \\
&= 17
\end{aligned}
$$

EXERCISE 8.5

Find the values of the expressions in questions 1 to 6 given that $a = 3$, $b = 4$ and $c = 5$.

1) $3a + 4b$ 2) $5a - b$ 3) $a - b - c$

4) $3a + 2b - 4c$ 5) $5c - 7a$ 6) $3a - 2b + 6$

Find the values of the expressions in questions 7 to 12 given that $a = 1$, $b = -2$ and $c = 3$.

7) $4a + 2b - c$ 8) $3a + 2b - 4c$ 9) $6a - 7b$

10) $a + b - c$ 11) $3a - 3b - c$ 12) $4a + 2b - c$

13) If $v = u + at$, find v when $u = 2$, $a = 0.25$ and $t = 6$.

14) Find the area of a circle of radius 2.54cm if $A = \pi r^2$ and $\pi = 3.142$.

15) Find the circumference of a circle of diameter 6.5cm if $C = \pi D$.

16) If $y = mx + c$ find the value of y when $m = 6$, $x = 2$ and $c = 1$.

17) The volume of a cone is given by $V = \frac{1}{3}\pi r^2 h$. Find its volume when $r = 3$cm, and $h = 2.5$cm.

18) The temperature F ($^\circ$ Fahrenheit) is connected to the temperature C ($^\circ$ Celsius)

by the formula $C = \frac{5}{9}(F - 32)$. Find, to the nearest degree, the value of C when $F = 82^\circ$.

19) Find the simple interest paid if the principal (P) is £250, the time (T) is 3 years and the rate of interest (R) is 9·5% using the formula $I = \frac{PTR}{100}$

20) If $v^2 = u^2 + 2as$ find v when $u = 7\cdot3$, $a = 1\cdot1$ and $s = 150$.

21) If $v^2 = 2gh$ find v when $g = 9\cdot8$ and $h = 12$.

22) If $S = \frac{1}{2}(u + v)t$ find S when $u = 20$ and $v = 57\cdot5$ and $t = 2\cdot5$.

23) If $A = \frac{2x + y}{3}$ find A when $x = 6$ and $y = 19$.

24) If $P = \frac{Rx^2}{2y}$ find P when   (a) $R = 6$, $x = 7$ and $y = 4$
                      (b) $R = -3$, $x = -2$ and $y = 5$

25) If $x = \frac{bc}{b-c}$ find x when $b = 13$ and $c = 9$

26) If $y = 4x^2 + 3x - 2$ find y when x is (a) 3   (b) -2

27) If $y = 3x^2 - 2x + 1$ find y when x is (a) 5   (b) -1

28) If $y = (x + 3)(x - 4)$ find y when x is (a) 3   (b) -3.

29) If $y = (3x - 2)(x + 1)$ find y when x is (a) 7   (b) -3.

30) If $y = 2x^2 + \frac{1}{x}$ find y when $x = -2$.

EQUATIONS AND FUNCTIONS 2

QUADRATIC EQUATIONS

A quadratic equation takes the form $ax^2 + bx + c = 0$ where a, b, and c can have any numerical value.

A quadratic equation **must** contain the square term but does not have to have the other terms.

Examples

$6x^2 + 2 = 0$ where a = 6, b = 0, c = 2

$x^2 + 5x = 0$ where a = 1, b = 5, c = 0

$6x^2 = 0$ where a = 6, b = 0, c = 0

$9x^2 + 3x + 2 = 0$ where a = 9, b = 3, c = 2

Type 1   **Equations of the type $ax^2 - c = 0$**

Example 9.1

$$x^2 - 9 = 0$$
$$x^2 = 9$$
$$x = \pm \sqrt{9}$$
$$\therefore x = +3 \text{ or } -3$$

Example 9.2

$$4x^2 - 100 = 0$$
$$4x^2 = 100$$
$$x^2 = \frac{100}{4} = 25$$
$$x = \pm \sqrt{25}$$
$$\therefore x = 5 \text{ or } -5$$

Type 2   **Factorised equations**

If $(dx - e)(fx - g) = 0$ (where d, e, f and g are numerals) then since the product of the two brackets gives zero, either one of the two brackets can take the value zero.

Example 9.3

If $(x - 2)(x + 3) = 0$

then either $x - 2 = 0$ in which case x = 2

or $x + 3 = 0$ in which case x = −3

$\therefore$ solution is x = 2 or x = −3

Example 9.4

If $3x(2x + 5) = 0$
then either $3x = 0$ in which case $x = 0$
    or $2x + 5 = 0$
              so $2x = 5$ $\therefore x = -5/2$ or $-2\frac{1}{2}$
$\therefore$ solutions are $x = 0$ or $x = -2\frac{1}{2}$

Type 3   **Where the equation needs to be factorised first**

Example 9.5

If $2x^2 + 3x = 0$
factorising gives $x(2x + 3) = 0$
            $\therefore$ either $x = 0$
            or $2x + 3 = 0$ $\therefore 2x = -3$ $x = -3/2$
$\therefore$ solutions are $x = 0$ or $x = -1\frac{1}{2}$

Example 9.6

If $2x^2 - 5x - 3 = 0$
factorising into two brackets gives
$(2x + 1)(x - 3) = 0$
    either $2x + 1 = 0$ from which $2x = -1$ $x = -1/2$
    or $x - 3 = 0$ from which $x = 3$
$\therefore$ solutions are $x = -1/2$ or $x = 3$

EXERCISE 9.1

Solve the following equations

1) $x^2 - 25 = 0$ 2) $x^2 - 81 = 0$
3) $2x^2 - 72 = 0$ 4) $3x^2 - 27 = 0$
5) $(x + 2)(x - 3) = 0$ 6) $(x - 6)(x + 5) = 0$
7) $(3x + 4)(2x - 1) = 0$ 8) $(2x - 3)(4x - 3) = 0$
9) $x(3x - 2) = 0$ 10) $x(4x + 3) = 0$
11) $2x(x - 4) = 0$ 12) $4x(x - 3) = 0$
13) $4x^2 + 3x = 0$ 14) $6x^2 - 4x = 0$
15) $5x^2 - 3x = 0$ 16) $4x^2 - x = 0$
17) $x^2 - x - 6 = 0$ 18) $x^2 + x - 2 = 0$
19) $2x^2 - x - 3 = 0$ 20) $6x^2 + 4x - 2 = 0$
21) $x^2 - 3x - 10 = 0$ 22) $x^2 - 7x + 12 = 0$

23) $3x^2 + 6x = 24$ 24) $3x^2 + 10x = 8$

25) $5(x + 3)(2x - 1) = 0$ 26) $4x^2 - 25 = 0$

27) $8x^2 = 2x + 15$ 28) $5x(4x - 3) = 0$

SOLUTIONS OF QUADRATIC EQUATIONS BY FORMULA

When a quadratic equation of the form $ax^2 + bx + c$ cannot be solved by factorisation it is solved by the formula

$$x = \frac{-b \pm \sqrt{b^2 - 4ac}}{2a}$$

Example 9.7   solve the equation $3x^2 - 4x - 2 = 0$ correct to two decimal places

here $a = 3$, $b = -4$ and $c = -2$

using $x = \dfrac{-b \pm \sqrt{b^2 - 4ac}}{2a}$

then $x = \dfrac{-(-4) \pm \sqrt{(-4)^2 - 4(3)(-2)}}{2(3)}$

$x = \dfrac{4 \pm \sqrt{16 + 24}}{6}$

$x = \dfrac{4 \pm \sqrt{40}}{6}$

$x = \dfrac{4 \pm 6.325}{6}$ ⟵ *Round off to 1 more decimal place than the question asks for at this point*

Always leave the division until this point $x = \dfrac{10.325}{6}$ or $\dfrac{-2.325}{6}$

$x = 1.72$ or $-.39$ correct to 2 d.p.

Example 9.8   solve the equation $-x^2 - 3x + 2 = 0$ correct to two decimal places.

When the coefficient of x^2 is negative then the problem is easier to solve if both sides of the equation are pre-multiplied by (-1)

i.e. $x^2 + 3x - 2 = 0$

here $a = 1$, $b = 3$ and $c = -2$

$\therefore \; x = \dfrac{-3 \pm \sqrt{3^2 - 4 \times (1) \times (-2)}}{2 \times 1}$

$$x = \frac{-3 \pm \sqrt{9 + 8}}{2}$$

$$x = \frac{-3 \pm \sqrt{17}}{2}$$

$$x = \frac{-3 \pm 4.123}{2}$$

$$x = \frac{1.123}{2} \quad \text{or} \quad \frac{-7.123}{2}$$

$$x = 0.56 \quad \text{or} \quad -3.56 \quad \text{correct to 2 d.p.}$$

EXERCISE 9.2

Solve the following equations correct to two decimal places

1) $x^2 + 4x - 6 = 0$
2) $x^2 - 3x + 1 = 0$
3) $x^2 - 4x - 3 = 0$
4) $x^2 + 6x - 4 = 0$
5) $x^2 + x - 1 = 0$
6) $4x^2 - 7x + 1 = 0$
7) $6x^2 + 3x - 1 = 0$
8) $10x^2 + 2x - 7 = 0$
9) $4x^2 + 5x - 10 = 0$
10) $-x^2 + 5x - 1 = 0$
11) $-x^2 + 7x - 3 = 0$
12) $-2x^2 + 4x + 3 = 0$
13) $-2x^2 - 3x + 1 = 0$
14) $-3x^2 + 4x + 1 = 0$
15) $-3x^2 - x + 1 = 0$

SIMULTANEOUS EQUATIONS (1)

Simultaneous equations are two equations containing two unknown values (usually x and y). These can be found by combining the equations in some way.

ELIMINATION METHOD

Example 9.9   Solve the simultaneous equations

$$2x + 2y = 10 \ldots\ldots(1)$$
$$2x + y = 7 \ldots\ldots(2)$$

Subtracting (2) from (1) to eliminate x

$$0 + y = 3$$
$$\therefore y = 3$$

Substituting for y into (1)

$$2x + 2(3) = 10$$
$$2x + 6 = 10$$
$$2x = 4$$
$$\therefore x = 2$$

Example 9.10   Solve the simultaneous equations

$$3x + 2y = 10 \ldots\ldots\ldots(1)$$
$$x - 2y = 6 \ldots\ldots\ldots(2)$$

Adding (1) and (2) to eliminate y

$$4x + 0 = 16$$
$$4x = 16$$
$$\therefore x = 4$$

> NOTE $+2y + (-2y)$
> $= 2y - 2y = 0$

Substituting for x into (1)

$$3(4) + 2y = 10$$
$$2y = 10 - 12$$
$$2y = -2$$
$$\therefore y = -1$$

Example 9.11   Solve the simultaneous equations

$$4x + 3y = -2 \ldots\ldots\ldots(1)$$
$$2x + y = 0 \ldots\ldots\ldots(2)$$

Multiplying (2) by 2 gives $4x + 2y = 0 \ldots\ldots\ldots(3)$

Comparing (1) and (3) $4x + 3y = -2 \ldots\ldots\ldots(1)$
$$4x + 2y = 0 \ldots\ldots\ldots(3)$$

Subtracting (3) from (1) gives

$$0 + y = -2$$
$$\therefore y = -2$$

> NOTICE
> We must make either the
> x or y coefficients equal
> in both equations

Substituting for y into (2)

$$2x - 2 = 0$$
$$2x = 2$$
$$\therefore x = 1$$

Example 9.12   Solve the simultaneous equations

$$3x + 2y = -3 \ldots\ldots\ldots(1)$$
$$2x - 3y = -15 \ldots\ldots\ldots(2)$$

Multiplying (1) by 2 gives

$$6x + 4y = -6 \ldots\ldots\ldots(3)$$

Multiplying (2) by 3 gives
$$6x - 9y = -45 \ldots \ldots (4)$$
Subtracting equation (4) from (3) gives
$$13y = +39$$
$$y = +3$$

NOTE
$-6-(-45) = +39$
and
$4y - (-9y) = 13y$

Substituting for $y = +3$ into (1) gives
$$3x + 2(+3) = -3$$
$$3x + 6 = -3$$
$$3x = -9$$
$$x = -3$$

EXERCISE 9.3

1) $2x + 2y = 10$
    $x + 2y = 6$

2) $3x + y = 18$
    $2x + y = 13$

3) $4x + 2y = 2$
    $2x + 2y = 0$

4) $5x + 3y = 18$
    $5x + y = 16$

5) $x + y = 1$
    $x - y = 5$

6) $3x + 4y = 29$
    $x - 4y = -17$

7) $3x - 2y = 10$
    $-3x + y = -11$

8) $2x + 4y = 18$
    $3x - 4y = -3$

9) $4x + 3y = 11$
    $2x + y = 7$

10) $5x + 2y = -16$
    $2x + y = -6$

11) $6x + 2y = -18$
    $4x + y = -11$

12) $3x - 2y = -16$
    $x - y = -7$

13) $2x + 3y = 28$
    $3x - y = 9$

14) $2x + 3y = 15$
    $5x - y = 46$

15) $4x + 3y = 13$
    $6x - 2y = 13$

16) $5x + 3y = 14$
    $2x + 2y = 4$

17) $6x - 2y = 10$
    $-4x + 3y = -5$

18) $-7x - 2y = 20$
    $3x + 2y = -12$

19) $7x + 2y = 5$
    $-3x - 5y = -27$

20) $5x - 2y = -23$
    $-6x + 3y = 30$

SIMULTANEOUS EQUATIONS (2)

Problems

Example 9.13

A shopkeeper sells Mrs Jones 3 tins of beans and two tins of peas for £1·37 and he sells Mrs Patel 4 tins of beans and 1 tin of peas for £1·31. Find the cost of 1 tin of each.

Let the cost of the beans be x and the cost of the peas be y

$$\therefore \quad 3x + 2y = 137 \ldots \ldots \ldots (1)$$
$$4x + 1y = 131 \ldots \ldots \ldots (2)$$

Multiplying
(2) by 2

$$8x + 2y = 262 \ldots \ldots \ldots (3)$$

Subtracting
(1) from (3)

$$5x = 125$$
$$x = 25$$

Substituting into (2)

$$4(25) + y = 131$$
$$100 + y = 131$$
$$y = 31$$

i.e.   the cost of 1 tin of beans was 25p and 1 tin of peas was 31p.

EXERCISE 9.4

1.   A family of 2 adults and 2 children go to the cinema. Their tickets cost a total of £7·00. Another family of 1 adult and 4 children go to the same cinema and their total bill is £6·80. Find the cost of 1 adult ticket and 1 child's ticket.

2.   The sum of two numbers is 39 and their difference is 9. Find the numbers.

3.   A rectangle has a perimeter of 42 cm. Another rectangle has a length double that of the first and a width one third of that of the first. If its perimeter is 57 cm, find the length and breadth of the first.

4.   4 oranges and 3 apples weigh 720 g. 3 oranges and 4 apples weigh 750 g. Find the weight of 1 apple and 1 orange.

5.   3 mugs and 2 plates cost £3·60 but 4 mugs and 1 plate costs £3·95. Find the cost of a mug and a plate.

6.   A man finds that with £3 he can either buy 6 second class and 12 first class stamps and have 6p change or 10 second class and 9 first class stamps and have 8p change. Find the cost of both a first and a second class stamp.

7. Mrs Smith withdrew £200 from the bank. She was given £10 and £5 notes, a total of 23 altogether. How many notes of each type was she given?

8. A quiz game has two types of question, hard and easy. Team A answers 7 hard questions and 13 easy questions whereas team B answers 13 hard questions and 3 easy questions. If they both score 74 points find how many points were given for each of the two types of question.

9. A man stays at a hotel. He has Bed and Breakfast for 3 nights and two dinners. A second man has 4 nights B and B and 3 dinners. If the first man's bill is £45 and the second man's bill is £62 find the cost of a dinner.

10. Four large buckets and two small buckets hold 58 litres. Three large buckets and five small buckets hold 68 litres. How much does each bucket hold?

SIMULTANEOUS EQUATIONS (3)

Substitution method (One linear and one quadratic equation)

Example 9.14 Solve the simultaneous equations

$$y - 2x = 3 \ldots\ldots\ldots (1)$$
$$x^2 + y^2 - 2xy - 5x = 15 \ldots\ldots (2)$$
$$\text{from (1)} \quad y = 3 + 2x \ldots (3)$$

> Always substitute the linear equation into the quadratic

substitute for y in equation (2)
$$x^2 + (3 + 2x)^2 - 2x (3 + 2x) - 5x = 15$$
$$x^2 + (9 + 12x + 4x^2) - (6x + 4x^2) - 5x - 15 = 0$$
$$x^2 + 9 + 12x + 4x^2 - 6x - 4x^2 - 5x - 15 = 0$$
$$x^2 + x - 6 = 0$$
$$(x + 3)(x - 2) = 0$$
$$\therefore x = -3 \text{ or } x = 2$$

Substituting into (3)
when $x = -3$ $y = 3 + 2(-3) = 3 - 6 = -3$
when $x = 2$ $y = 3 + 2(2) = 3 + 4 = 7$
$\therefore$ solutions are $\underline{x = -3, \quad y = -3}$
and $\underline{x = 2, \quad y = 7}$

EXERCISE 9.5

Solve the following simultaneous equations

(1)
$$y - x - 1 = 0$$
$$2x^2 + 3y^2 - xy + 5y + 3 = 0$$

(2) $3x - y + 1 = 0$

         $x^2 + 2y^2 - 3xy + 11x + 4 = 0$

(3) $y = \dfrac{x + 1}{2}$

         $x^2 + 4y^2 - 2xy - 7 = 0$

(4) $2x^2 + y^2 + 3xy = 0$

         $y = 2 - 3x$

(5) $2x + y = 4$

         $y^2 + xy + 7x - 19 = 0$

(6) $x^2 + 2xy + 3y - 6 = 0$

         $y = x + 4$

(7) $2y^2 - xy + 2x - 3 = 0$

         $2x + y = 3$

(8) $y = 2x + 3$

         $2x^2 + y^2 - 2xy - 5 = 0$

(9) $y = x + 5$

         $x^2 - y^2 + xy + x + 20 = 0$

(10) $y = 3x + 1$

         $x^2 + y^2 - 3xy - 5x - 4 = 0$

ITERATION

An iterative process is one which is repeated in order to improve a result. The iteration method can be used to solve equations and find square roots. It is often used in computing where it is simple to program a loop to do the repeated operation.

Example 9.15

Show that the equation $x^2 - 5x + 1 = 0$ can be written as $x = 5 - \dfrac{1}{x}$. Use the iteration $x_{n+1} = 5 - \dfrac{1}{x_n}$, where $x_1 = 5$, to calculate a solution to the equation $x^2 - 5x + 1 = 0$ correct to 3 decimal places.

Solution $x^2 - 5x + 1 = 0$

    dividing by x $x - 5 + \dfrac{1}{x} = 0$

    re-arranging $x = 5 - \dfrac{1}{x}$

By substituting x = 5 into the iteration, we can find a better value for x.

$$\text{i.e.} \quad x = 5 - \frac{1}{5} = 4 \cdot 8$$

By using this value of x we can find a better value for x.

$$x = 5 - \frac{1}{4.8} = \underline{4 \cdot 7916667}$$

from the calculator

keep the former answer on your calculator to find its inverse

Iterating again
$$x = 5 - \frac{1}{4 \cdot 7916 \ldots} = 4 \cdot 7913044$$

again
$$x = 5 - \frac{1}{4 \cdot 7913 \ldots} = 4 \cdot 7912886$$

Since the answer has been 4·791 (to 3 d.p.) for 2 iterations we now stop

$$\therefore \text{ a solution of } x^2 - 5x + 1 = 0 \text{ is}$$
$$\underline{x = 4 \cdot 791 \text{ (to 3 d.p.)}}$$

Example 9.16

Find $\sqrt{20}$ using the iteration $x_{n+1} = \frac{1}{2}\left[x_n + \frac{s}{x_n}\right]$ where s is the number whose square root is to be found.

Since $\sqrt{20}$ lies between 4 and 5 let x = 4

$$\therefore \quad x = \frac{1}{2}\left[4 + \frac{20}{4}\right] = \frac{1}{2}\left[4 + 5\right] = 4 \cdot 5$$

$$x = \frac{1}{2}\left[4 \cdot 5 + \frac{20}{4 \cdot 5}\right] = 4 \cdot 472222$$

$$x = \frac{1}{2}\left[4 \cdot 47 + \frac{20}{4 \cdot 47 \ldots}\right] = 4 \cdot 472136$$

This is the same value which is obtained by pressing the $\sqrt{}$ button on the calculator.

EXERCISE 9.6

1. Starting with x = 4 and using the iteration $x_{n+1} = 4 - \frac{1}{x_n}$ find a solution of $x = 4 - \frac{1}{x}$ correct to two decimal places.

2. Starting with x = 5 and using the iteration $x_{n+1} = 7 - \frac{9}{x_n}$ find a solution of $x = 7 - \frac{9}{x}$ correct to 2 decimal places.

3. Starting with $x = 4$ and using the iteration $x_{n+1} = 3 + \dfrac{3}{x_n}$ find a solution of $x = 3 + \dfrac{3}{x}$ correct to 2 decimal places.

In questions 4, 5 and 6 re-arrange the equations to form an iteration and use it to find one solution in each case.

4. $3x^2 - 4x - 2 = 0$ starting with $x = 2$
5. $2x^2 - 7x = 3$ starting with $x = 4$
6. $x^2 - 9x - 2 = 0$ starting with $x = 9$

7. Use the iteration $x_{n+1} = \frac{1}{2}\left[x_n + \dfrac{S}{x_n} \right]$ to find

     a) $\sqrt{10}$ b) $\sqrt{30}$ c) $\sqrt{40}$

     giving your answers correct to 3 d.p. each time.

FUNCTIONS AND MAPPINGS

A **function** is a process which changes (or **maps**) one set of objects or numbers into another set of objects or numbers. The first set is called the **domain** of the function and the second set (its image) is called the **range** of the function.

Furthermore, each element of the domain will map onto only one element of the range (although one element in the range can have more than one element in the domain mapping onto it). This is shown in the diagram below.

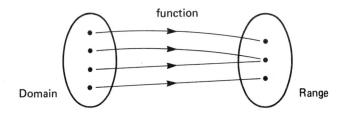

The symbol $\mapsto$ is used to indicate the relationship between an object and its image and the letters f and g are usually used to indicate the function. If f is some function which maps values of x onto some image then we represent the image by f(x).

Example 9.17

If f maps x onto 3x + 2 then we can write f:x ↦ 3x + 2 and this function maps individual values in the following way

$$f\ (1) = 3\ (1) + 2 = 3 + 2 = 5$$
$$f\ (2) = 3\ (2) + 2 = 6 + 2 = 8$$
$$f\ (3) = 3\ (3) + 2 = 9 + 2 = 11 \qquad \text{etc.}$$

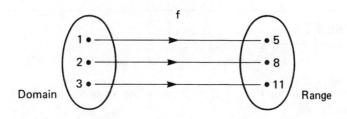

Domain   Range

Example 9.18

The function f maps x onto 3x + 1

(a)   if A is the set $\left\{ -2, 2 \right\}$ find onto what set A is mapped by f

(b)   find the value of x if f maps x onto 10

(c)   find f(f(0))

(a) $f\ (-2) = 3\ (-2) + 1 = -6 + 1 = -5$

      $f\ (2) \ = 3\ (2) \ + 1 = 6 \ + 1 = 7$

      ∴ Range of set A is $\left\{ -5, 7 \right\}$

> f:x ↦ 3x +2 and
> f(x) = 3x +2 are both
> ways of expressing a
> function

(b) $f(x) = 10$

    ∴ $3x + 1 = 10$

        $3x = 9$

    ∴ $x = 3$

(c). $f\ (0) = 3\ (0) + 1 = 1$

    ∴ $f\ (f(0)) = f\ (1) = 3\ (1) + 1 = 5$

Composite function — this is a function which is built up from other functions.

Example 9.19

$f\ (x) = 3x + 2$ and $g\ (x) = \dfrac{x^2}{2}$

then the composite function

$$f\ (g(x)) = 3 \left(\frac{x^2}{2} \right) + 2 = \frac{3x^2}{2} + 2$$

also the composite function

$$g(f(x)) = \frac{(3x + 2)^2}{2} = \frac{9x^2 + 12x + 4}{2} \qquad \text{or} \qquad \frac{9x^2}{2} + 6x + 2$$

The composite function f(g(x)) can be written as f o g
Similarly g(f(x)) can be written as g o f.

EXERCISE 9.7

1) If f : x ↦ x + 2 write down the values of   (a) f(1)   (b) f(2)   (c) f(20)
   (d) f(n)

2) Find the range for f : x ↦ 2x + 2 having the set of integers $\{1, 2, 3, 4, 5\}$
as its domain.

3) The function f maps x onto f(x) where $f(x) = 3x^2 - 6$
   (a)   If A is the set $\{1, -1\}$ find onto what set A is mapped by f.
   (b)   Find the values of x if x maps f onto 21.
   (c)   Find f(f(0))

4) If f:x ↦ 4 − 3x find
   (a)   f(−3)
   (b)   the value of x if f(x) = 0
   (c)   f(f(1))

5) f(x) is defined as $f(x) = \dfrac{3x + 2}{x + 3}$
   Evaluate   (a) f(6)   (b) f(f(6))   (c) the value of x if f(x) = 10

6) f(x) and g(x) are defined as
   f(x) = 4x − 5 and g(x) = 4 − 3x
   Calculate   (a) f(2)   (b) g(4)   (c) f(g(4))   (d) g(f(3))
                (e) the value of x if f(x) = 30
   Also determine the functions f(g(x)) and g(f(x))

7) The function f maps x onto f(x) where $f(x) = x^2 - 4x + 3$ and the function g
maps x onto g(x) where g(x) = x − 3
   Find   (a) f(−3))   (b) g(6)   (c) f(g(6))
           (d) the values of x if f maps x onto 0
           (e) the values of x if f(x) = g(x)

8) If f:x ↦ $x^2 + 2x - 1$ find   (a) f(−3)   (b) f(5)
   (c) the values of x, correct to two decimal places if f(x) = 0

9) A function f is defined by f:x ↦ (x−1) (x−5)
   Find   (a) the value of f (−3)
          (b) the values of x for which f(x) = 0
          (c) the values of x for which f(x) = 14

A second function g is defined by $g:x \mapsto 2x + 2$

      (d) express fog in terms of x.

      (e) find x when fog = 0

10) A function f is defined by $f(x) = 4x + 3$ and a function g is defined by $g(x) = mx + 3$

    Find   (a) $f(-3)$ (b) the value of m if $f(-3) = g(-3)$

    Express gof in terms of x

11) A function f is defined by $f(x) = mx + c$. If the set $A = \left\{ 1, 2 \right\}$ represents its domain when the set $B = \left\{ 5, 8 \right\}$ represents its corresponding range, find the values of m and c.

VARIATION

If y is proportional to x $(y \propto x)$ then the graph of y against x is a straight line going through the origin.

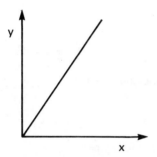

If the gradient of this line is k then $y = kx$

This is called direct variation and means that if x is doubled then y is doubled; if c is halved then y is halved, etc.

Example 9.20

If y varies directly as x and y = 4 when x = 6 find the value of y when x = 8.

      because $y \propto x$

      then $y = kx$

      when $y = 4$, $x = 6$

      then $4 = k \times 6$

      $\therefore k = \frac{2}{3}$

$$\therefore \text{ relationship is } y = \frac{2}{3}x$$
$$\text{when } x = 8$$
$$y = \frac{2}{3} \times 8$$
$$y = \frac{16}{3} \text{ or } 5\frac{1}{3}$$

Example 9.21

If v varies directly as r^3 and v = 24 when r = 2 find the value of v when r = 3.

$$v \propto r^3$$
$$v = kr^3$$
$$24 = k(2)^3$$
$$24 = k \times 8$$
$$k = 3$$

$$\therefore \text{ relationship is } v = 3r^3$$
$$\text{when } r = 3 \quad v = 3(3^3)$$
$$v = 81$$

If y is inversely proportional to x then $y \propto \frac{1}{x}$ and $y = k\frac{1}{x}$ or $y = \frac{k}{x}$

This means that as y increases then x decreases and vice versa.

Example 9.22

y varies inversely as x^2. Copy and complete the following table.

x	1	2	3	4
y		3/4		

$$y \propto \frac{1}{x^2} \qquad y = \frac{k}{x^2}$$
$$\text{when } x = 2 \qquad y = 3/4$$
$$3/4 = k/2^2$$
$$\therefore k = 3$$
$$\therefore \text{ relationship is } y = \frac{3}{x^2}$$
$$\text{when } x = 1 \quad y = \frac{3}{(1)^2} = 3$$
$$\text{when } x = 3 \quad y = \frac{3}{3^2} = \frac{3}{9} = \frac{1}{3}$$
$$\text{when } x = 4 \quad y = \frac{3}{4^2} = \frac{3}{16}$$

The completed table is

x	1	2	3	4
y	3	3/4	$\frac{1}{3}$	3/16

Joint variation   If c varies directly as x and inversely as y then

$$c \propto \frac{x}{y} \qquad \text{or} \qquad c = \frac{kx}{y}$$

Example 9.23

If A varies directly as b and inversely as the root of c, and A = 12 when b = 6 and c = 4, find the value of A when b = 3 and c = 9.

$$A \propto \frac{b}{\sqrt{c}}$$

$$A = \frac{kb}{\sqrt{c}}$$

when A = 12, b = 6 and c = 4

$$\therefore 12 = \frac{k(6)}{\sqrt{4}} = \frac{6k}{2}$$

$$\therefore k = 4$$

$$\therefore \text{formula is } A = \frac{4b}{\sqrt{c}}$$

when b = 3 and c = 9

$$A = \frac{4(3)}{\sqrt{9}} = 4$$

Partial variation   If $y = px + qx^2$ then y varies partially with x and partially with x^2.

Example 9.24

y is the sum of two terms one of which varies directly as x and the second directly as x^2. If y = 5 when x = 1 and y = 12 when x = 2 find the value of y when x = 3.

$$y = ax + bx^2$$

when x = 1 and y = 5 $5 = a + b$ . . . . (1)

when x = 2 and y = 12 $12 = 2a + 4b$ . . . . (2)

multiplying (1) by 2 $10 = 2a + 2b$ . . . . (3)

subtracting (3) from (2) gives $2 = 2b$

$$\therefore \quad b = 1$$

substituting b = 1 into equation (1) gives

$$5 = a + b$$
$$\therefore \quad a = 4$$

relationship is therefore

$$y = 4x + x^2$$

when x = 3

$$y = 4(3) + 3^2$$
$$= 12 + 9$$
$$= \underline{\underline{21}}$$

EXERCISE 9.8

1) Y varies directly as $\sqrt{x}$. If x = 9 when Y = 2 find the value of Y when x = 4.

2) a varies directly as b^3. If a = 32 when b = 2 find a when b = 4.

3) y varies inversely as x. If y = 1.5 when x = 2 find y when x = 4.

4) a varies inversely as the square root of b. If a = 1 when b = 9 find a when b = 4.

5) y varies directly as the cube root of x. Copy and complete the following table.

x	1/8	1	8	64
y			1.5	

6) The table below shows values of y for values of the variable x, which are linked by the equation $y = 8x^n$.

x	½	1	2
y	1	8	64

Find   (a) n
        (b) y when x = ¼

7) If $y \propto \dfrac{1}{x+1}$ and x = 2 when y = 1 find y when x = 5.

8) y varies directly as x and inversely as the square of z. If y = 3 when x = 4 and z = 2, find y when x = 5 and z = 3.

9) W is the sum of two parts. The first part varies directly as the cube of x and the second part varies inversely as the square of x. Given that W = 74 when x = 1 and W = 34 when x = 2 find the value of W when x = 3.

10) y varies inversely as the square of x. Copy and complete the table below. On graph paper plot $\frac{1}{x^2}$ horizontally and y vertically. From your graph calculate its gradient and using this value write down the relationship between x and y.

x	1/2	3/4	1	1½
y	6			
$1/x^2$	4	8/3		

11) A, B and C are related such that A varies directly as C and inversely as the square root of B. If A = 5 when C = 10 and B = 16 find the value of B when A = 20 and C = 4.

12) Y is the sum of two numbers, one varying inversely as x and the other directly as x. Write down Y in terms of x in a formula containing two constants p and q.
Given that Y = 10 when x = 2 and Y = 14 when x = 4, form two equations involving p and q and hence show that Y = 8/x + 3x.

GRAPHS 1

CARTESIAN CO-ORDINATES

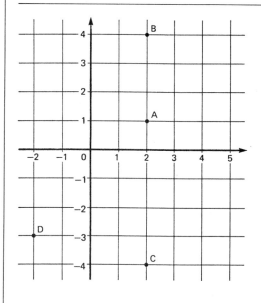

Point A has co-ordinates (2,1)

Point B has co-ordinates (2,4)

Point C has co-ordinates (2,−4)

Point D has co-ordinates (−2,−3)

To find the distance between two co-ordinates use Pythagoras' theorem.

Example 10.1

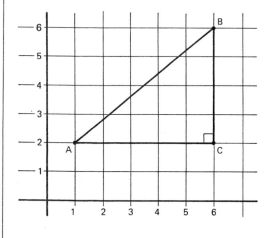

a) Find the distance between the points A(1,2) and B(6,6)

b) Find the area of the triangle ABC where point C is (6,2)

Using Pythagoras' theorem on the right angled triangle ABC

$AB^2 = AC^2 + BC^2$

$AB^2 = 5^2 + 4^2$

$AB^2 = 41$

$AB = \sqrt{41} = \underline{6.40}$ to 2 d.p.

Area of △ ABC = ½ base × height

= ½ × 5 × 4

= <u>10 sq. units</u>

Co-ordinates of the mid-point of a line.

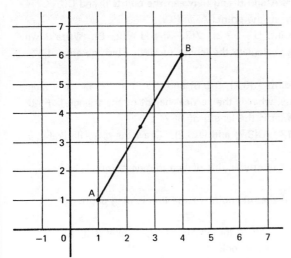

The x co-ordinate of the mid-point of line AB is half way between the x co-ordinates of A and B.

i.e. $1 + \frac{1}{2}(4 - 1) = 2\frac{1}{2}$

Similarly the y co-ordinates of the mid point of line AB is
$1 + \frac{1}{2}(6 - 1) = 3\frac{1}{2}$

EXERCISE 10.1

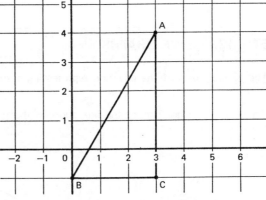

1.

a) Write down the co-ordinates of the points A, B and C.

b) What are the lengths of the lines AC and CB?

c) Calculate the length of the line AB.

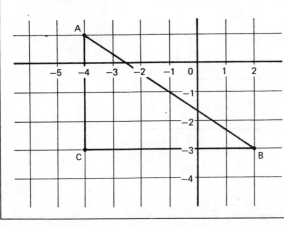

2.

a) Write down the co-ordinates of the points A, B and C.

b) What are the lengths of the lines AC and CB?

c) Calculate the length of the line AB.

3) On graph paper plot the points A(1,1), B(7,1) and C(7,6). Write down the distance between the points A and B and between the points B and C. Calculate the distance between the points A and C.

4) On graph paper plot the points U(−5,−3), V(2,−3) and W(2,−6). Write down the lengths UV and VW and calculate the length of UW. Find the area of triangle UVW.

5) On graph paper plot the points A(0,2), B(5,6) and C(7,2) and draw the triangle ABC. Taking AC as its base, what is the vertical height of the triangle? Find the area of the triangle. What is the length of BC?

6) Plot the points A(1,2), B(1,4), C(3,7) and D(3,2). Draw the quadrilateral ABCD and find its area.

7) What are the co-ordinates of the mid-point of line joining points A(1,2) and B(5,6)?

8) What are the co-ordinates of the mid-point of the line joining points C(−3,3) and D(2,−4)?

9) What is the length of the line joining the points A(−2,−3) and B(3,2). What are the co-ordinates of its mid point?

10) Find the area of the triangle bounded by the x axis, the y axis and the line joining the points (3,0) and (0,−5).

STRAIGHT LINE GRAPHS

The general form of the equation representing a straight line is

$$y = mx + c$$

Where m is the gradient of the line and c is the y intercept.

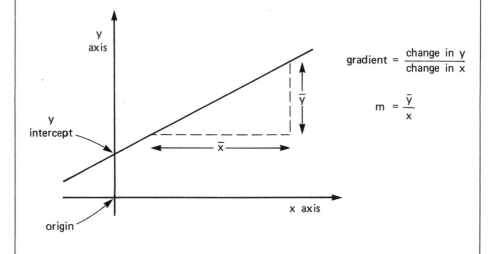

$$\text{gradient} = \frac{\text{change in } y}{\text{change in } x}$$

$$m = \frac{\bar{y}}{x}$$

Example 10.2

$3x - 2y + 4 = 0$ is the equation of a straight line. Re-arrange it into the form $y = mx + c$

$$3x - 2y + 4 = 0$$
$$3x + 4 = 2y$$
$$\frac{3}{2}x + 2 = y$$

i.e. $\quad y = \dfrac{3}{2}x + 2$

Example 10.3

Plot the graph of $y = 2x + 1$ between $x = 0$ and $x = 6$

For accuracy we need to plot 3 points
When $x = 0$ $\quad y = 2(0) + 1 = 1$
$\therefore$ plot point $(0,1)$
When $x = 2$ $\quad y = 2(2) + 1 = 4 + 1 = 5$
$\therefore$ plot point $(2,5)$
When $x = 4$ $\quad y = 2(4) + 1 = 8 + 1 = 9$
$\therefore$ plot point $(4,9)$

Plotting these three points gives this graph

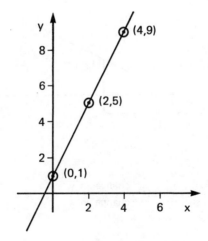

Example 10.4

Write down an equation in the form y = mx + c for the graph shown below.

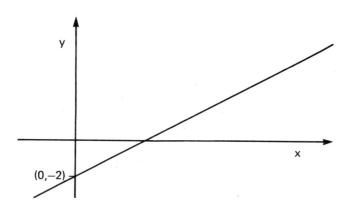

The y intercept is (0,−2) so c has the value −2.

For the gradient we must consider any two points on the line. Considering points (0,−2) and (12,4)

Between these two points the change in y = 6, change in x = 12

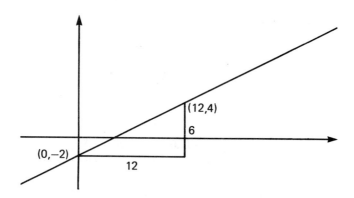

$$\therefore \text{gradient} = \frac{\text{change in y}}{\text{change in x}}$$

$$= \frac{6}{12} = \frac{1}{2}$$

$$\therefore \text{Equation of line is } y = \frac{1}{2}x - 2$$

Note that this can also be written as 2y = x − 4   or   2y − x + 4 = 0

Example 10.5
Graph with a negative gradient. Find the gradient of the graph shown below.

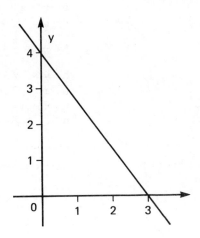

Consider the points (0,4) and (3,0)
As the x value increases from 0 to 3 the y value decreases from 4 to 0
∴ change of x is 3
change of y is −4
∴ gradient is $\dfrac{-4}{3}$ = $-\dfrac{4}{3}$ or $-1\dfrac{1}{3}$
∴ equation of this line is

$$y = -\frac{4}{3}x + 4$$

or multiplying throughout by 3   3y = −4x + 4
or 3y + 4x − 4 = 0

EXERCISE 10.2

---

1.   Re-arrange these equations into the form y = mx + c and write down
     (i)   the co-ordinates of the y intercept
     (ii) the gradient of their graphs

     a. y − 2x + 3 = 0   b. 2x − y − 3 = 0
     c. y + x + 3 = 0   d. 2y + 2x − 2 = 0
     e. 3x − 4 − 2y = 0   f. y − 2x + 4 = 0
     g. 2y − 3x + 4 = 0   h. 2y + 3 − 4x = 0
     i. 3y + 2x − 4 = 0   j. 4y + 3 − 2x = 0
     k. 2y − 3x + 2 = 0   l. 2x + 3y + 4 = 0

2. Using 1 cm to represent 1 unit on both the x axis and the y axis plot the following straight line graphs.

a. $y = x + 1$

b. $y = x + 3$

c. $y = x - 2$

d. $y = -x + 1$

e. $y = -2x - 1$

f. $-y = \dfrac{x}{2} + 1$

g. $y = 2x + 1$

h. $y = \frac{1}{2}x + 1$

i. $y = 2x - 3$

j. $2y - 2x + 1 = 0$

k. $x + 3 - y = 0$

l. $x - y - 2 = 0$

m. $4 + x - y = 0$

n. $2x + y - 2 = 0$

o. $y + 2x + 3 = 0$

3. Write down an equation of the form $y = mx + c$ for each of the following straight line graphs

(i)
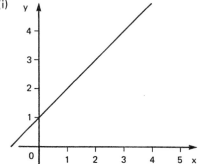

(ii)
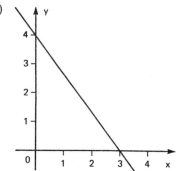

(iii)
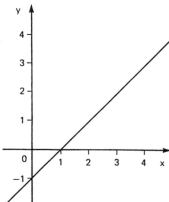

(iv)
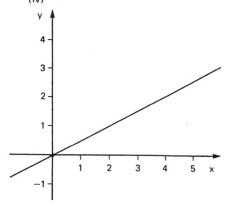

128

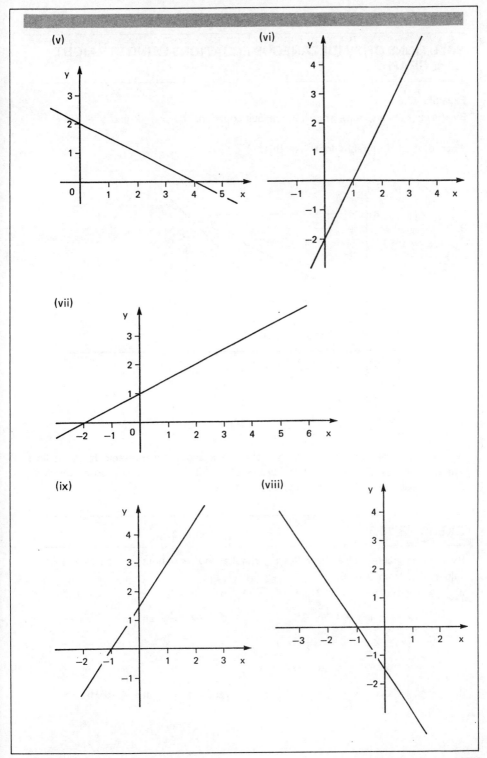

SOLUTIONS OF SIMULTANEOUS EQUATIONS USING STRAIGHT LINE GRAPHS

Example 10.6

By drawing graphs, solve the simultaneous equations $y = x - 2$ and $y = \frac{1}{2}x + 2$

When plotted the graphs look like this

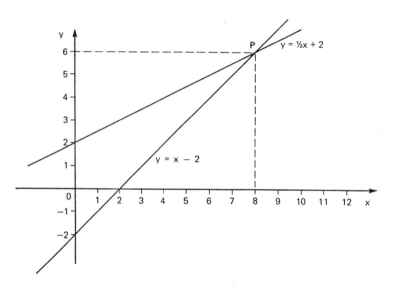

At their point of intersection (P) the values of x and y are the same for both lines. The co-ordinates of P represent the values of x and y which satisfy both equations. i.e.   the solution to the simultaneous equations is $y = 6$ $x = 8$

EXERCISE 10.3

By drawing graphs, solve the following simultaneous equations. In all cases plot values of x from 0 to 5.

a. $y = x$ and $y = \frac{1}{2}x + 2$

b. $y = \frac{1}{2}x$ and $y = x - 2$

c. $y = x - 1$ and $y = \frac{1}{2}x + 2$

d. $y = \frac{1}{3}x$ and $y = \frac{4}{3}x - 3$

e. $y = \frac{1}{4}x - 2$ and $y = -\frac{1}{2}x + 1$

f. $y - x = 0$ and $2y - x - 3 = 0$

g. $y + x = 2$ and $y + \frac{1}{2}x = 0$

h. $y = -\frac{3}{2}x$ and $y - \frac{x}{2} - 2 = 0$. In this case plot x from -4 to $+6$.

PLOTTING CURVES

In order to plot the curve of an equation or function it is necessary to first draw up a table of values.

Example 10.7

Plot the graph of $y = 2x^2 - 2x + 1$ for the values of x from -3 to $+4$ using a scale of 1 cm to 1 unit on the x axis and 1 cm to 5 units on the y axis.

First calculate each separate part of the equation for each value of x.
This is shown in the table below.

x =	-3	-2	-1	0	1	2	3	4
$x^2 =$	9	4	1	0	1	4	9	16
$2x^2 =$	18	8	2	0	2	8	18	32
$-2x =$	+6	+4	+2	0	-2	-4	-6	-8
$+1 =$	+1	+1	+1	+1	+1	+1	+1	+1
$y=2x^2-2x+1 =$	25	13	5	1	1	5	13	25

These values of x and y can now be plotted according to the scale asked for in the question.

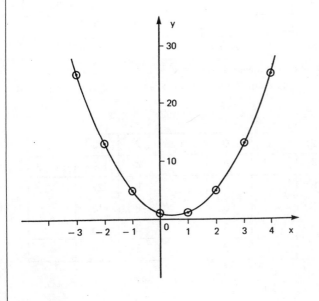

Take care in getting the curve correct — especially at a turning point

EXERCISE 10.4

1. Complete the table of values for the equation $y = 2x^2 - 2$ and plot its graph. Use a scale of 1 cm to 1 unit on the x axis and 2 cm to 5 units on the y axis.

x =	−3	−2	−1	0	1	2	3
x^2 =	9		1	0			9
$2x^2$	18		2	0			18
− 2	−2		−2	−2			−2
$y=2x^2-2$	16		0	−2			16

2. Complete the table of values for the equation $y = 5x + \dfrac{x^2}{2}$ and plot its graph using a scale of 1 cm to 1 unit on the x axis and 2 cm to 5 units on the y axis.

x =	0	1	2	3	4	5	6
x^2 =	0	1	4	9	16	25	36
$5x$	0		10		20	25	
$x^2/2$	0		2		8	12½	
$y=5x+x^2/2$	0		12		28	37½	

3. Complete the table of values for the equation $y = x^3 - 2x^2 - 3$ and plot its graph using a scale of 2 cm to represent 1 unit on the x axis and 2 cm to represent 5 units on the y axis.

x	−2	−1	0	1	2	3	4
x^2	4		0		4	9	
x^3	−8		0		8	27	
$-2x^2$	−8		0		−8	−18	
−3	−3		−3		−3	−3	
$y=x^3-2x^2-3$	−19		−3		−3	6	

4. Complete the table of values for the equation $y = 3x^2 - x^3$. Using a scale of 4 cm to represent 1 unit on the x axis and 4 cm to represent 1 unit on the y axis plot its graph.

x	0	0.5	1	1·5	2	2·5	3
x^2	0		1	2·25		6·25	9
$3x^2$	0		3	6·75		18·75	27
$-x^3$	0		−1	−3·375		−15·625	−27
$y=3x^2-x^3$	0		2	3·375		3·125	0

5. Complete the table of values for the equation $y = 6 - \dfrac{3}{x}$ and draw its graph, using a scale of 5 cm to represent 1 unit on the x axis and 4 cm to represent 10 units on the y axis.

x	0·1	0·2	0·5	1·0	2·0
6	6		6	6	
−3/x	−30		−6	−3	
y=6−3/x	−24		0	3	

SOLUTIONS TO EQUATIONS BY THE INTERSECTION OF TWO GRAPHS

Example 10.8

The diagram shows the graphs of $y = x^2 + 2x - 3$ and $y = x + 6$

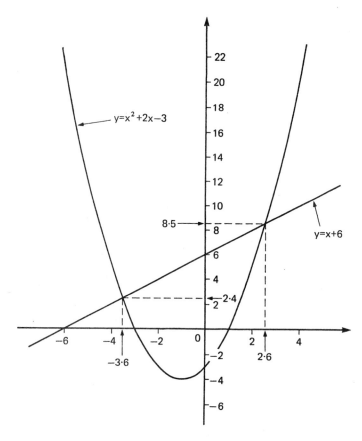

At the points of intersection of these graphs

$x^2 + 2x - 3 = x + 6$ ......(1)

By rearranging this it can also be expressed as

$x^2 + x - 9 = 0$ ....(2)

The approximate solutions to this equation, expressed as either (1) or (2) is $x = 2 \cdot 6$ or $x = -3 \cdot 6$ from the graph.

Also the points of intersection give the solutions to the simultaneous

equations　　　$y = x^2 + 2x - 3$

and　　　　　$y = x + 6$

which are　　$y = 8 \cdot 5$ when $x = 2 \cdot 6$

and　　　　　$y = 2 \cdot 4$ when $x = -3 \cdot 6$

Example 10.9

The diagram shows the graphs of $y = 2x^2 - 4x - 3$, $y = 0$ and $y = 4$

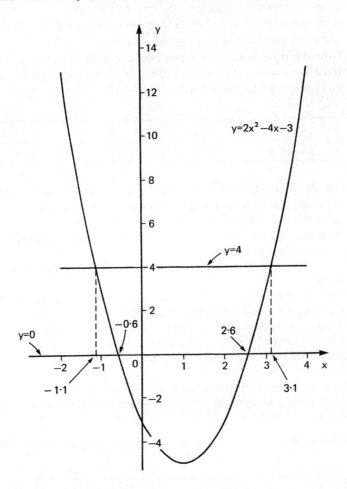

(a) The values of x at the intersections of the graphs $y = 2x^2 - 4x - 3$ and
$y = 0$ are approximate solutions to the quadratic equation
$$2x^2 - 4x - 3 = 0$$
i.e. $x = -0.6$ and 2.6

(b) The values of x at the intersections of the graphs $y = 2x^2 - 4x - 3$ and
$y = 4$ are approximate solutions to the equation
$$2x^2 - 4x - 3 = 4$$
or
$$2x^2 - 4x - 7 = 0$$
i.e. $x = -1.1$ and 3.1

EXERCISE 10.5

1. a) Draw the graph of $y = x^2 + 2x - 3$ for values of x from -4 to $+2$
    b) Using the same axes draw the graph of $y = x + 2$
    c) Write down the values of x where the two graphs intersect.
    d) Write down an equation which satisfies these two values of x.

2. a) Complete this table for the values of $y = x^3 - 2x + 2$

x	-2·5	-2	-1	0	1	2	2·5
y	-8·625		3			6	

   b) Plot the graph of $y = x^3 - 2x + 2$ using a scale of 2 cm to represent
       1 unit on the x axis and 2 cm to represent 2 units on the y axis.
   c) Using the same axes draw the graph of $y = 2x + 2$.
   d) Show that the equation $x^3 - 4x = 0$ has 3 solutions. Give approximate
       values of these solutions.

3. a) Draw up a table of values for $y = 4 + 3x - x^2$ for values of x from -4
        to $+4$.
    b) Draw the graph of $y = 4 + 3x - x^2$ using a scale of 2 cm to represent
        1 unit on the x axis and 2 cm to represent 4 units on the y axis.
    c) Using the same axes draw the line $y = 3$ and write down the approximate
        x co-ordinates of the point of intersection of the two graphs.
    d) Show that the x co-ordinate at this point is an approximate solution to
        the equation $3x - x^2 + 1 = 0$.
    e) What is the solution to the equation $4 + 3x - x^2 = 0$?
    f) By drawing a straight line find an approximate solution to the equation
        $8 + 3x - x^2 = 0$.

4. a) Draw up a table of values for $y = 2x + \dfrac{8}{x}$ for the following values of x

x =	0·5	1·0	1·5	2·0	2·5	3	4	6

   b) Using a scale of 2 cms to represent 1 unit on the x axis and 1 cm to
       represent 1 unit on the y axis plot the graph of $y = 2x + \dfrac{8}{x}$

   c) Using the same axes draw the lines representing $y = 14$ and $y = 12 - \dfrac{x}{2}$

   d) By considering points of intersection of two graphs write down the
       approximate solutions to the equation $2x + \dfrac{8}{x} - 14 = 0$.

e) Show that the intersection of graphs $y = 2x + \dfrac{8}{x}$ and $y = 12 - \dfrac{x}{2}$ gives a solution to the equation $5x^2 - 24x + 16 = 0$. What are the approximate solutions to this equation?

5. Using a scale of 2 cm to 1 unit on both the x and y axes draw the graph of $y = (x+3)(x-1)$ between $x = -4$ and $x = 2$.
   Using the same axes and scales draw the graph of $y = x - 1$. From your graph estimate the following
   a) the solution to the equation $(x+3)(x-1) = 1$
   b) the x co-ordinates of the points of intersection of the two graphs and write down the quadratic equation which these values of x satisfy.

6. Draw the graphs of $y = (3+x)(3-2x)$ and $y = \dfrac{3x + 5}{2}$ for values of x from -4 to $+2$ using a scale of 2 cm to 1 unit in the x direction and 1 cm to 1 unit in the y direction. From your graph estimate the solutions to the equations
   a) $13 - 9x - 4x^2 = 0$ and
   b) $3 - 3x - 2x^2 = 0$

SKETCHING GRAPHS

When a graph is sketched it does not have to be drawn accurately but it should show its main points.

$y = mx + c$
A straight line graph of gradient 'm' passing through the y axis at point (0,c)

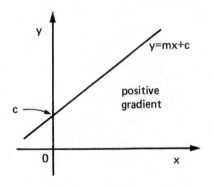

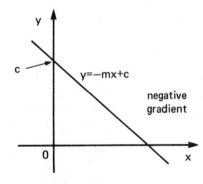

$y = mx$

When a straight line graph passes through the origin the value of c is zero.

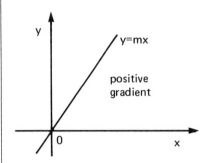

$y=a$

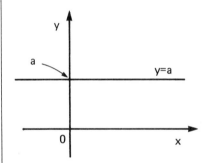

$x=b$

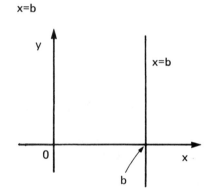

$y=x^2$

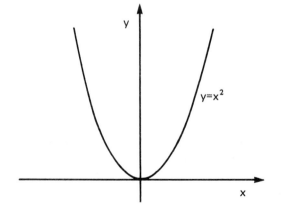

$y = 2x^2$ — for each value of x the value of y is double that for $y = x^2$

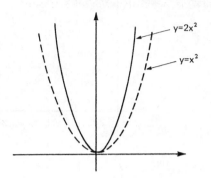

The graph of $2x^2$ is steeper than that of $y = x^2$

Notice that these two curves are symmetrical about the y axis

$y = \dfrac{1}{x}$

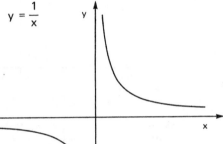

Notice that this graph has rotational symmetry of 180^0 about the origin.

$y = \dfrac{2}{x}$

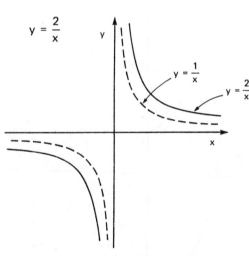

EXERCISE 10.6

1. By considering the sketches above, what equation best describes the sketches on the next page?

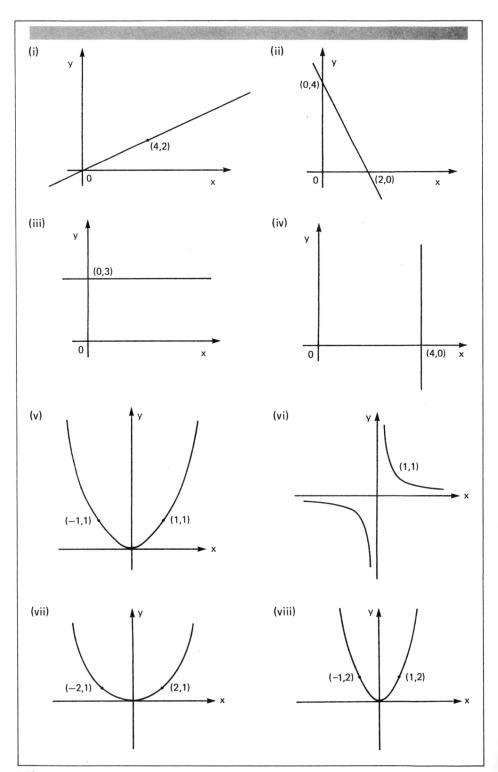

140

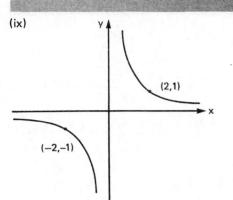

(ix)

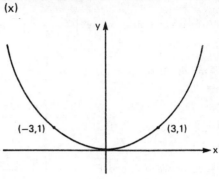

(x)

2. Sketch the following curves
   1) $y = 3x$
   2) $y = x + 1$
   3) $y = x - 2$
   4) $y = x$
   5) $x = 5$
   6) $y = -4x$
   7) $y = \frac{1}{2}x^2$
   8) $y = 3x^2$
   9) $y = \frac{2}{x}$
   10) $y = \frac{3}{x}$

AREA UNDER A GRAPH — TRAPEZOIDAL RULE

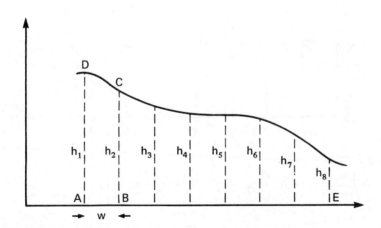

Each strip is treated as a trapezium because DC is approximately a straight line.
The narrower the strip, the more accurate the area becomes as DC becomes closer
to becoming a straight line

$\therefore$ Area of ABCD $= w\left[\dfrac{h_1 + h_2}{2}\right]$

Area of 2nd strip $= w \left[\dfrac{h_2 + h_3}{2} \right]$ and so on

Area of all seven strips is $= w \left[\dfrac{h_1 + h_2 + h_2 + h_3 + h_3 + h_4 \ldots \ldots h_8}{2} \right]$

$\qquad = w \left[\dfrac{h_1 + 2h_2 + 2h_3 + 2h_4 + 2h_5 + 2h_6 + 2h_7 + h_8}{2} \right]$

Area between A and E $= w \left[\dfrac{h_1 + h_8}{2} + h_2 + h_3 + h_4 + h_5 + h_6 + h_7 \right]$

i.e. the area underneath the graph is equal to the width of a strip multiplied by the sum of half the first and last ordinates and all the remaining ordinates.

Example 10.10

Find the area under the graph shown below. The height of each ordinate is given.

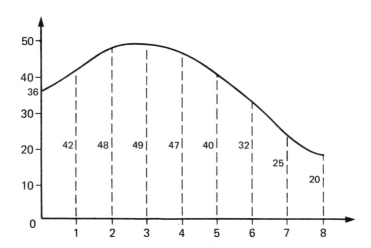

Here w = 1 unit

$\text{Area} = w \left[\dfrac{h_0 + h_8}{2} + h_1 + h_2 + h_3 + h_4 + h_5 + h_6 + h_7 \right]$

$\qquad = 1 \left[\dfrac{36 + 20}{2} + 42 + 48 + 49 + 47 + 40 + 32 + 25 \right] = 1\,(28 + 283)$

$\qquad\qquad\qquad\qquad\qquad\qquad\qquad\qquad\qquad\qquad\qquad\qquad = 311 \text{ units}$

EXERCISE 10.7

For questions 1 and 2 find the areas under the curves using the trapezoidal rule.

1. The curve $y = x^2$ between $x = 0\cdot20$ and $x = 1\cdot00$ given the following values.

x	0·20	0·40	0·60	0·80	1·00
y	0·04	0·16	0·36	0·64	1·00

2. The curve $y = x^2 + x$ between $x = 0\cdot2$ and $x = 1\cdot6$ given the following values.

x	0·2	0·4	0·6	0·8	1·0	1·2	1·4	1·6
y	0·24	0·56	0·96	1·44	2·0	2·64	3·36	4·16

3. The speed of a vehicle after time t seconds is given by the graph below. Use the trapezoidal rule to find the distance travelled in 20 seconds. Use strips of width 2 seconds and estimate from the graph the value of the ordinates.

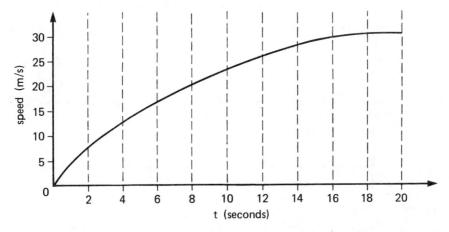

4. Estimate the area under the curve given by the following table, between $x = 10$ and $x = 35$ using a strip width of 5 units.

x	10	15	20	25	30	35
y	20	50	70	88	100	108

5. Find the approximate area underneath the curve below using the trapezoidal method taking a) strips of width 1 unit   b) strips of width 0·5 units.

Which of these answers is the most accurate? Explain why. How can you obtain a more accurate answer?

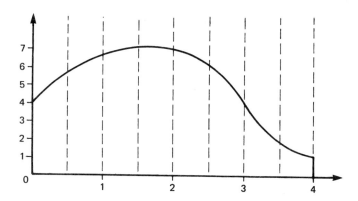

6. A vehicle moves in a straight line so that its velocity v at any time t is given as follows.

t (secs)	0	1	2	3	4	5
v (m/s)	1·5	2·3	3·6	5·4	7·5	10·1

Find the distance travelled in the first 5 seconds, using a strip width of 1 sec.

7. Find the area underneath the curve $y = \frac{1}{x}$ between $x = 1$ and $x = 3$, using 10 equal strips.

8. The diagram shows a speed/time graph for a train between two stations. Use the trapezoidal rule to find the distance between the stations taking strips of width 20 secs. where necessary.

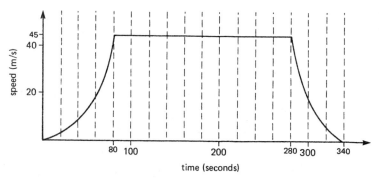

9. Find the values of $y = 4 + 3x + x^2$ for values of x from 1 to 3 at 0·2 intervals. Use them to find the approximate area beneath this curve between $x = 1$ and $x = 3$.

GRADIENTS OF CURVES

The gradient of a curve at a point is obtained by drawing a tangent to the curve at that point and calculating its gradient.

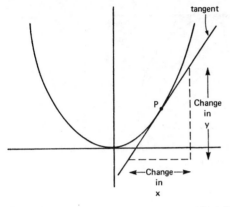

The gradient of this curve at point P is found by taking two points on the tangent and dividing the change in y by the change in x.

For accuracy it is best to use two well defined points on the tangent.

Example 10.11

Plot the curve of $y = \frac{1}{4}x^2$ between $x = -5$ and $x = 5$ and find the gradient when $x = -4$ and $x = 2$.

From the graph

At $x = -4$ gradient $= \dfrac{\text{change in y}}{\text{change in x}} = -\dfrac{8}{4} = -2$

At $x = 2$ gradient $= \dfrac{\text{change in y}}{\text{change in x}} = \dfrac{3}{3} = 1$

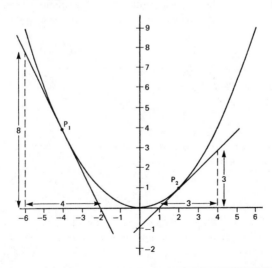

MAXIMUM AND MINIMUM POINTS

A **maximum** point on a curve is one where the curve changes from having a positive gradient to having a negative gradient. At this point the gradient is zero.

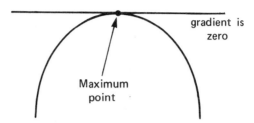

A **minimum** point on a curve is one where the gradient changes from being negative to being positive. At this point the gradient is zero.

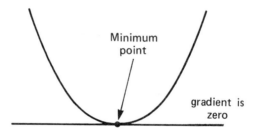

EXERCISE 10.8

Plot each of the following graphs and find (a) the gradients at the points indicated (b) the co-ordinates of the maximum or minimum points, stating whether the point is maximum or minimum.

1. $y = x^2$ at $x = -3$ and $x = 2$
2. $y = 2x^2 - 3$ at $x = -1$ and $x = 3$
3. $y = 3x^2$ at $x = -2$ and $x = 1$
4. $y = \frac{1}{2}x^2$ at $x = 1$ and $x = -2$
5. $y = 3 - x^2$ at $x = -2$ and $x = +2$
6. $y = x^2 - x$ at $x = -2$ and $x = 1$
7. $y = 2x(1 - x)$ at $x = -1\frac{1}{2}$ and $x = 4$
8. $y = 4 - \frac{1}{2}x^2$ at $x = -3$ and $x = +3$

GRAPHS 2

RATES OF CHANGE

The gradient of a curve at a point indicates the amount by which one variable (y) is changing compared with another variable (x) i.e. a gradient of 2 indicates that y is increasing by 2 units for every 1 unit y increases by.

Example 11.1

The table below shows the distance travelled (s) by a car in a time (t).

t (secs)	0	1	2	3	4
distance (metres)	0	20	40	60	80

Plotting time against distance travelled gives this straight line graph

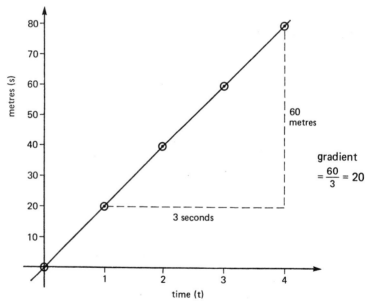

Taking any two points on this line gives a gradient of 20 i.e. the distance travelled is increasing by 20 metres every second or the speed is 20 metres per second.

Example 11.2

The curve shows the distance travelled (s) by a car in time (t). Find its speed when t = 40 secs. Explain what is happening to the car's speed between

(a)   t = 0 and t = 14 secs
(b)   t = 14 secs and t = 25 secs
(c)   t = 25 secs and t = 50 secs

148

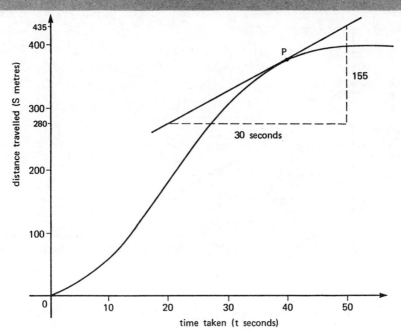

Speed of car when t = 40 secs is the gradient of the curve at this point

$$= \frac{155}{30} = 5 \cdot 17 \text{m per sec} \quad \text{(to 2 d.p.)}$$

a) when t = 0 the gradient of the curve is zero ∴ the speed of the car is zero. between t = 0 and t = 14 the gradient is increasing therefore the speed of the car is increasing

b) between t = 14 and t = 25 the gradient of the curve is constant (straight line) therefore the speed of the car is constant

c) between t = 25 and t = 50 the gradient of the curve is decreasing therefore the speed of the car is decreasing. At t = 50 the gradient is again zero so the car is stationary.

Example 11.3

The table below shows how the amount of water in a tank varies when the outlet tap is turned on and the water allowed to escape.

volume of water (m^3)	10	6	2½	1½
time t (secs)	0	300	600	900

Plot these values on a graph and draw a line through them. From the graph estimate

a) the rate in litres/sec at which the water is leaving the tank after 450 secs

b) at what time the tank will be empty

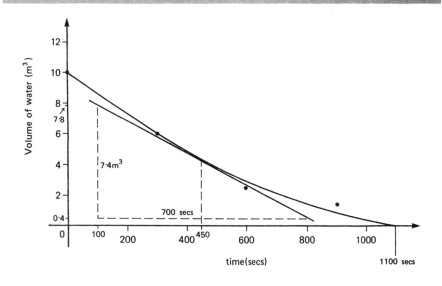

a) rate at which water leaves tank $= \dfrac{7\cdot 4}{700}$ m^3/sec $= \cdot 01057$ m^3/sec

but 1m^3 $=$ 1000 litres

$\therefore$ rate is $\cdot 01057 \times 1000$

$=$ 10·57 litres per second

b) from the graph, the tank will be empty approximately 1100 secs later or 18 mins 20 secs

---

EXERCISE 11.1

1. The table shows the distance covered d (metres) by a vehicle in time t

time t (secs)	15	30	45	60	75	90	105	120	135	150
distance d (metres)	10	40	100	200	310	430	540	650	710	750

Plot these points and draw a graph. Find the speed of the vehicle when
a) t = 135 secs and   b) the distance travelled is 400 metres.

2. The amount of water in a tank is shown in the table below, t seconds after it was allowed to drain out through a tap.

t seconds	0	10	20	30	40	50	60	70
litres	100	67	49	35	24	15	8	3½

Plot points to show this information using a scale of 2 cm to represent 10 seconds on the horizontal axis and 2 cm to represent 10 litres on the vertical axis. Join the points with a line. From the graph find
a) the rate of flow 40 seconds after the tap was turned on
b) the approximate time it takes for the tank to empty.

3. The profit obtained from sales of a particular item is given in the table below. Plot these points using a scale of 2 cm to represent 20 items sold on the horizontal axis and 2 cm to represent a profit of £100 on the vertical axis. Through these points draw a line and find from the graph
a) how the rate of increase in profit when 30 items are sold a week differs from that when 50 items are sold a week
b) How many items are sold per week when the rate of profit is the greatest?

no. of items sold per week	0	20	40	60	80	100	120	140
profit £	0	40	130	270	470	650	780	850

4. The number of newspapers sold by a newsagent between 6·00 am and 10·00 am is given in the table

time	6·00	6·30	7·00	7·30	8·00	8·30	9·00	9·30	10.00
sales	0	22	75	150	260	420	515	555	572

Plot these values on a graph using the scale of 4 cm to represent 1 hour on the horizontal axis and 2 cm to represent 100 newspapers on the vertical axis.
a) from your graph find the rate (newspapers per hour) at which the newspapers are being sold at (i) 7·00 am (ii) 8·00 am
b) at what time (approximately) are the most newspapers being sold?
c) If the newsagent employs an assistant for 1 hour in the morning, between what times would he be most usefully employed?

5. The cost of making engineering components is shown in the table below

no. of items	5	10	15	20	25	30	40	50	60	70
cost	220	320	390	450	490	520	570	610	650	690

Plot these values on a graph using the scale of 2 cm to represent 10 components on the horizontal axis and 2 cm to represent £100 on the vertical axis. From your graph find
a) the point at which the cost of components becomes constant
b) the cost of each component after this point
If the components are sold for £15 each, using the same axes, draw a straight line to represent this. From your diagram find how many components have to be sold to make a profit.

CONVERSION GRAPHS

A straight line is an example of direct proportion. If a straight line is plotted using some known information further information can be obtained by taking other points on the line.

Example 11.4
The table below shows the cost of electricity. Draw a straight line to show this and from the graph estimate
a) the cost of 450 units
b) the number of units used for £35

no. of units	0	300	600
cost	£7	£22	£37

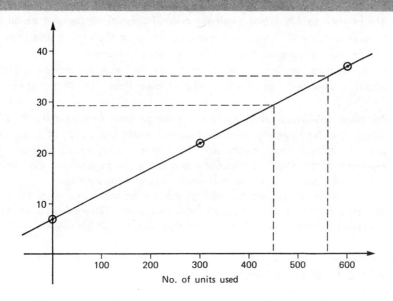

From the graph
a) the cost of 450 units is approximately £29·30
b) the number of units used for £35 is approximately 560

EXERCISE 11.2

---

1. The rate of exchange between the pound and French franc is £1 = 9·8 francs.
   Using a scale of 2 cm to represent £2 on the horizontal axis and 2 cm to
   represent 20 francs on the vertical axis draw a line to show this information.

   Use the graph to convert
   a) £4·37 into francs   b) £9·46 into francs   c) 49 francs into pounds
   d) 73 francs into pounds

2. There are two ways of paying for electricity. The first method is by paying a
   standard charge of £7·20 and each unit at 5·4p. The second method is by
   paying 7·3p for each unit. Using a scale of 2 cm to represent 100 units on
   the horizontal axis and 2 cm to represent £5 on the vertical axis, draw two
   lines to represent this information.
   From your graph find (a) the number of units used when the cost is the
   same for both schemes   (b) the difference between the cost of 500 units on
   both schemes.

3. Jennie has to make pastry but her scales measure in ounces and the recipe
   uses grams. She has a tin of beans which say on the label that 15½ ounces

is equivalent to 439 grams. Using a scale of 2 cm to represent 2 oz on the horizontal axis and 2 cm to represent 50 grams on the vertical axis draw a line to show the relationship between ounces and grams.

From the graph convert the following to the nearest half ounce, so that Jennie can use her scales.   (a)   285 g of plain flour   (b)   200 g of butter

4.   An old people's club wishes to hire a coach to take them on a trip of 70 miles. The first company contacted quoted a standing charge of £25 plus £1 per mile while a second quoted £1·30 per mile. Using a scale of 2 cm to represent 20 miles on the horizontal axis and 2 cm to represent £20 on the vertical axis plot two lines to represent these two price ranges.

(a)   From the graphs find the cost of the trip from both companies.

(b)   At a later date the old people find they have £125 in their funds to go on a mystery tour. How far can they go by each company?

DISTANCE / TIME GRAPHS

$$\text{Average speed} = \frac{\text{distance travelled}}{\text{time taken}}$$

Velocity is a measure of speed in a particular direction.

Units   distance — metres, kilometres, miles etc

time   — hours, minutes, seconds

speed and velocity — metres per second (m/s), miles per hour (m.p.h.) etc.

Example 11.5

If a car travels 80 miles in 2½ hours its average speed is

$$\frac{80}{2\frac{1}{2}} = \underline{32 \text{ m.p.h.}}$$

Example 11.6

Change a speed of 12 m/s into   a)   m/minute   b)   km/hour

a)   12 m/s =   12 × 60 m/min
= 720 m/min

b)   12 m/s =   12 × 60 × 60 m/hour
720 × 60
=   43200 metres/hour
= $\frac{43200}{1000}$ km/hr
= 43·2 km/hr

EXERCISE 11.3

1. Find the average speed of each of the following
   a) 72 km in 1½ hours   b) 120 miles in 3 hours   c) 65 metres in 10 seconds   d) 1500 metres in 20 mins   e) 200 miles in 2¾ hours.

2. Change each of the following
   a) 15 m/s into   (i) m/min   (ii) km/hr
   b) 20 km/hr into   (i) km/min   (ii) m/sec
   c) 30 m.p.h. into   (i) miles/min   (ii) miles/second
   d) 0·5 km/min into   (i) km/hr   (ii) m/s
   e) 0·5 mile/min into m.p.h.

Example 11.7
A journey is represented on the graph below.

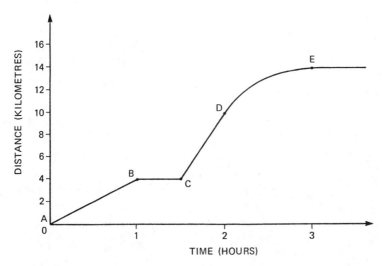

From the graph
A to B   represents a constant speed of 4 km in 1 hour i.e. 4 km/hr.
B to C   represents an increase in time but no change in distance i.e. no movement. The speed is zero.
C to D   represents a constant speed of 6 km in ½ hour or 12 km/hr.
D to E   represents a variable speed decreasing until E is reached.

Example 11.8
The graph shows a journey undertaken by a group of walkers.   (graph overleaf)

From the graph determine
a) their average speed between A and B.
b) their average speed between points B and C.

c) their speed at 2 p.m.

d) After arriving at C they rested for ½ hour and then returned to A at a constant speed. If they arrived home at 6.00 p.m. what was their speed?

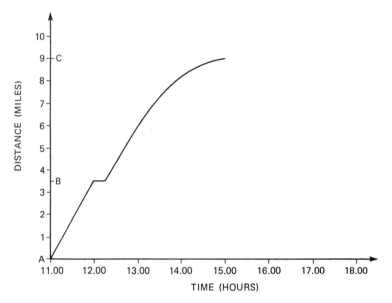

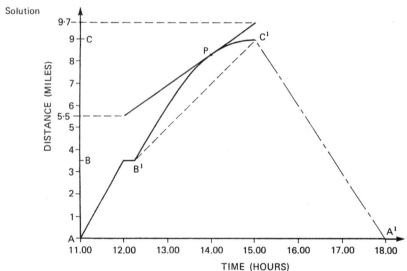

Solution

a) Average speed = $\dfrac{\text{distance}}{\text{time}}$ = $\dfrac{3 \cdot 5}{1}$ = 3·5 m.p.h.

b) The average speed between points B and C is the gradient of line B^1C^1

$= \dfrac{5 \frac{1}{2} \text{ miles}}{2 \frac{3}{4} \text{ hours}} = \dfrac{11}{2} \times \dfrac{4}{11} = 2$ mph

c) The speed at 2.00 p.m. is given by the gradient of the tangent at point P

$$= \frac{9 \cdot 7 - 5 \cdot 5}{15 - 12} = \frac{4 \cdot 2}{3} = 1 \cdot 4 \text{ mph}$$

d) Speed home is the gradient of line $C^1 A^1$

$$= \frac{9}{3} = 3 \text{ mph}$$

EXERCISE 11.4

1. The diagram below shows the journey of a lorry driver who leaves home at A and arrives at his destination D, 200 miles away.

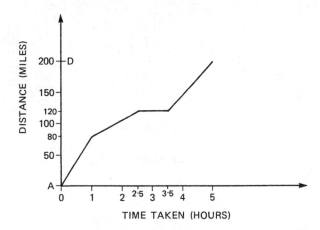

From the diagram find
a) His average speed when he is travelling fastest.
b) His average speed when he is travelling slowest.
c) The length of time he spent resting.

2. The diagram shows a speed/time graph for two buses, A and B travelling between towns F, G and H. Bus A travels from F to H and bus B from H to F.
Find
a) the average speed of bus A between F and G in m.p.h.
b) the length of time bus A stops at G.
c) the time at which bus B leaves H.
d) the average speed of bus B in m.p.h.
e) the time at which the buses pass each other.
f) the distance from G at which the buses pass.
g) the time at which bus B arrives at F.

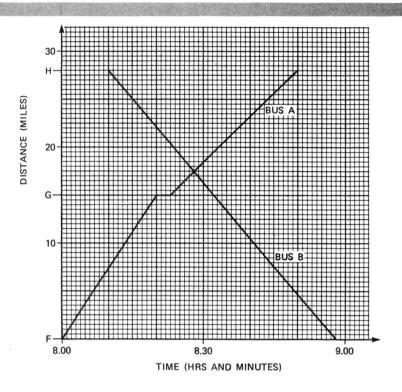

TIME (HRS AND MINUTES)

3. The diagram below shows the distance travelled by a car from rest in time t.

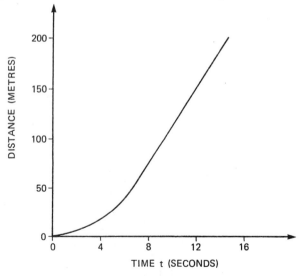

TIME t (SECONDS)

Find

a) the distance travelled in the 7th second (i.e. between t = 6 and t = 7 secs)

b) the distance travelled in the first 10 seconds.

c) the average speed of the car in km/hr after 7 secs.

4. An object moves so that its distance travelled d (metres) in time t (secs) is given in the table below. Using a scale of 2 cm to represent 1 second on the horizontal axis and 2 cm to represent 5 metres on the vertical axis draw a distance/time graph for values of t from 0 to 4 seconds.

t	0	0·5	1	1·5	2·0	2·5	3·0	4·0
d	0	0·5	1·5	4·0	8·0	13·5	19·0	30·5

From your graph find
a) the average velocity between t = 2 secs and t = 4 secs
b) the average velocity during the 2nd second.
c) the velocity when t = 1 second

5. An object is projected vertically upwards so that its height above the ground (h) in time (t) is given by the following table.

t (seconds)	0	0·5	1	1·5	2	2·5	3	3·5	4
h (metres)	0	7	12	15	16	15	12	7	0

Draw a graph to show this information using a scale of 2 cm to represent 1 second on the horizontal axis and 2 cm to represent 2 metres on the vertical axis.
From your graph find
a) the time, to the nearest 1/10th of a second it takes to reach 10 metres.
b) its average velocity.
c) at what time on the upward journey its velocity is equal to its average (mean) velocity.

6. An object is projected vertically upwards. Its height (h) above the ground after time (t) is given by the formula $h = 30t - 6t^2$ where h is measured in metres and t in seconds. Draw a graph to show this relationship for values of t from 0 to 5 seconds.
From your graph find
a) the height when t = 1·4 seconds
b) the approximate speed of the object when t = 2 seconds
c) the average speed of the object in the fourth second.
d) the distance travelled in the fourth second.
e) the maximum height gained by the object.

SPEED / TIME GRAPHS

When the speed (or velocity) of an object is plotted against time the gradient of the line gives the acceleration of the object.

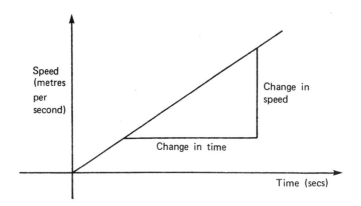

$$\text{Gradient} = \frac{\text{change in speed}}{\text{change in time}} = \text{Acceleration}$$

The area underneath the graph represents the distance travelled.

Units

Distance — metres, kilometres, feet, miles etc.

Time — seconds, minutes, hours etc.

Speed (or velocity) — metres per second (m/s), miles per hour (mph) etc.

Acceleration — metres per second^2 (m/s^2) etc.

Example 11.9

A train travelling at 15 m/s accelerates to 30 m/s in 1 minute. Find its acceleration.

$$\text{Acceleration} = \frac{\text{change of speed}}{\text{change of time}}$$

$$= \frac{30 - 15}{60} = \frac{15}{60} = \cdot25 \text{ m/s}^2$$

Example 11.10

A car's speed increases uniformly from 0 to 20 m/s in 1 minute and stays at that speed for a further 2 minutes. The car then decelerates uniformly until its speed is zero again, in another 30 seconds. Show this on a speed/time graph and find
a) its acceleration in m/s^2
b) its deceleration
c) the distance travelled

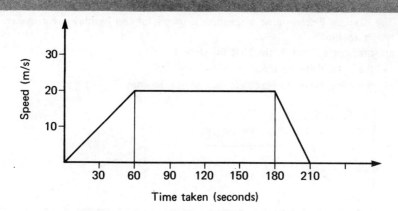

Acceleration $= \dfrac{\text{change in speed}}{\text{change in time}} = \dfrac{20}{60} = \dfrac{1}{3}$ m/s²

Deceleration $= \dfrac{20}{30} = \dfrac{2}{3}$ m/s²

Distance travelled = area under graph

= ½(60 × 20) + (120 × 20) + ½(30 × 20)

= 600 + 2400 + 300 = <u>3300 metres</u>

EXERCISE 11.5

1. A car accelerates uniformly from 15m/sec to 45m/sec in 1 minute. Find the acceleration.

2. A car travelling at 10m/s accelerates uniformly for 40 seconds at 0·6m/s². What is the new speed?

3. The diagram below shows a speed/time graph for the journey a car makes. Use it to find
   a) the total distance travelled in 120 secs
   b) the acceleration in the first 30 secs.

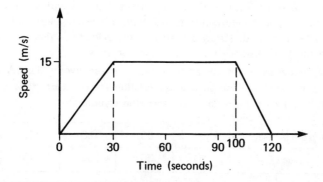

4. The diagram below shows a speed/time graph for the journey a car makes. Use it to find
   a) the acceleration in the first 50 seconds
   b) the total distance travelled
   c) the time taken to complete half of the journey

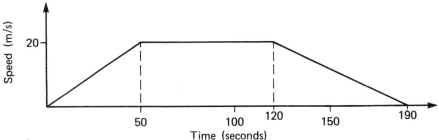

5.

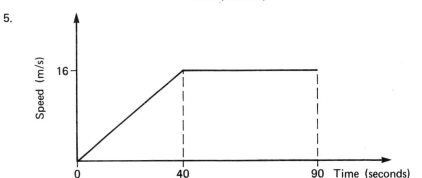

The diagram shows the first part of a journey a car makes. Calculate
a) its acceleration during the first 40 seconds
b) the distance travelled in the first 90 seconds
After 90 seconds the car decelerates uniformly, coming to rest after a further 60 seconds. Calculate
c) How far it will travel in coming to rest
d) the value of the deceleration

6. An electric vehicle starts from rest and moves with a constant acceleration for 15 seconds to reach a speed of 12 m/s. It then travels with a constant speed for 75 seconds and finally comes to rest with a constant deceleration 2 minutes after it started. Draw a sketch of the velocity — time graph and calculate the total distance travelled in the two minutes.

7. The table below shows the speed of a train between two stations A and B. Assuming that the acceleration and deceleration are constant, draw a speed/time graph and find the distance between the stations.

Time from A (secs)	30	60	90	120	150
Speed m/sec	15	30	30	20	10

8. The diagram shows a sketch of a speed/time graph for a train between stations A and B. Find the distance between the stations to the nearest 10 metres.

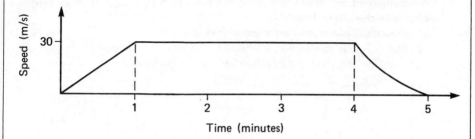

9. The diagram below shows the first part of a journey made by a car on a motorway. Find the distance travelled in the first five minutes, assuming that the speed is constant after the initial acceleration.

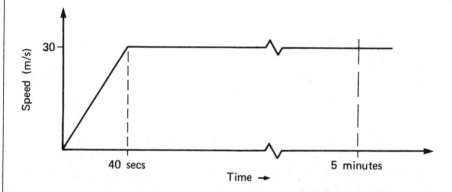

10. The diagram shows a speed/time graph for a train's journey between two stations. Find the approximate distance travelled.

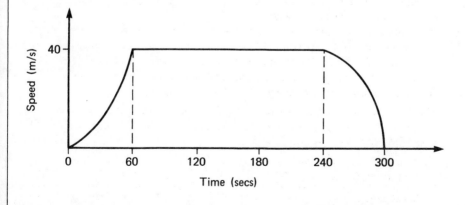

11. A particle is moving with an initial speed of 3 m/s. In the next 5 seconds its speed increases uniformly to 18 m/s. It then continues for 2 seconds at a constant speed and finally the speed decreases uniformly until it stops moving after a further 10 seconds.

a) show this information on a speed/time graph

b) find (i)   the acceleration in the last 10 seconds of motion
       (ii) the total distance travelled by the particle.

GEOMETRY 1
TRIANGLES

GEOMETRY

Angles

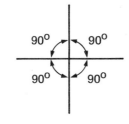

1 complete turn is divided into 360°

$\frac{1}{4}$ of a turn is 90°

$\frac{1}{2}$ of a turn is 180° and makes a straight line.

1° (degree) is made up of 60 smaller units called minutes (') i.e. 1° = 60'

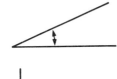

An **acute** angle is less than 90°

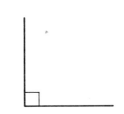

A 90° angle is called a **right** angle.

An angle bigger than 90° but less than 180° is called an **obtuse** angle.

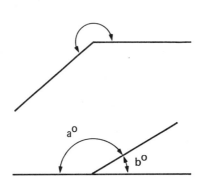

An angle greater than 180° and less than 360° is called a **reflex** angle.

Two angles which make a straight line are supplementary (i.e. they add to give 180°)

$a° + b° = 180°$

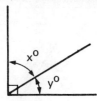

Two angles which make a right angle are said to be complementary (i.e. they add to give 90°)

$$x^\circ + y^\circ = 90^\circ$$

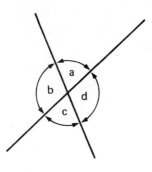

Two straight lines which cross form four angles of two different sizes

$\hat{a} = \hat{c}$ (vertically opposite angles)

$\hat{b} = \hat{d}$ (vertically opposite angles)

i.e. vertically opposite angles are equal

Parallel lines

> The arrows indicate the parallel lines

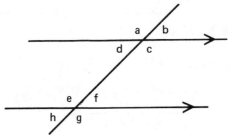

Two parallel lines and a transversal produce two similar crosses

$$\hat{a} = \hat{e} \qquad \hat{b} = \hat{f} \qquad \hat{c} = \hat{g} \qquad \hat{d} = \hat{h}$$

These angles are called **corresponding** angles i.e. **corresponding angles are equal**

These angles are called **alternate** angles (Look for the Z shape)

i.e. **Alternate angles are equal**

Example 12.1

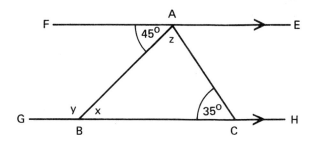

Find x, y and z.

(a) $F\hat{A}B = A\hat{B}C$ (alternate angles)

∴ $\hat{x} = 45^\circ$

(b) $\hat{y} + \hat{x} = 180^\circ$ (straight line)

∴ $\hat{y} = 180^\circ - 45^\circ = 135^\circ$

(c) $B\hat{C}A = C\hat{A}E$ (alternate angles)

∴ $C\hat{A}E = 35^\circ$

$F\hat{A}B + B\hat{A}C + C\hat{A}E = 180^\circ$ (straight line)

∴ $\hat{z} = 180^\circ - 80^\circ = 100^\circ$

EXERCISE 12.1

Find the sizes of the angles marked x, y, and z in the following questions.

(1)

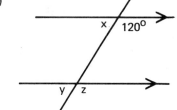

(2)

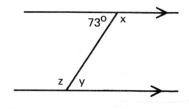

(3)

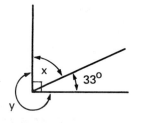

(4)

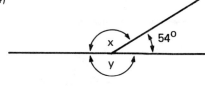

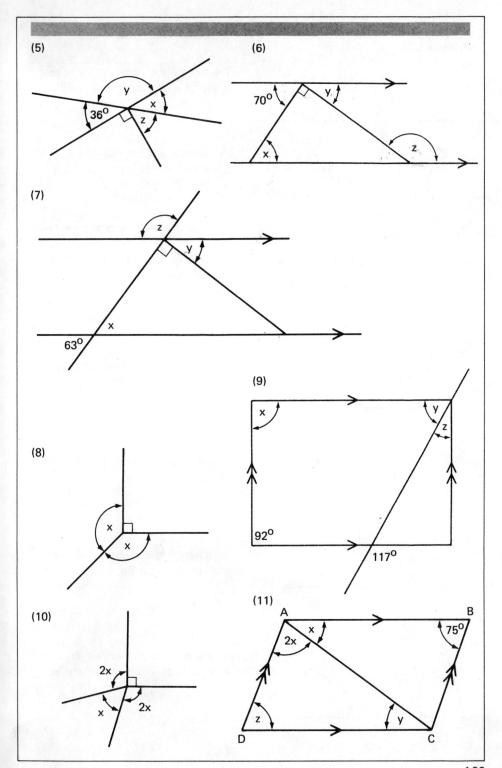

(5)

(6)

(7)

(8)

(9)

(10)

(11)

Triangles

1)

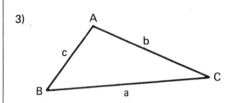

The sum of the three interior angles is $360°$ i.e. $a° + b° + c° = 360°$

2)

The exterior angle is equal to the sum of the two interior opposite angles i.e. $d° = a° + b°$

3)

The largest angle is opposite the largest side.

The smallest angle is opposite the smallest side

i.e. $\hat{A}$ is opposite side a (largest)

$\hat{C}$ is opposite side c (smallest)

4)

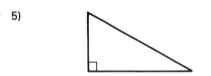

An **acute** angled triangle has each of its angles less than $90°$

5)

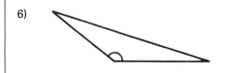

A **right angled** triangle has one angle of $90°$

6)

An **obtuse angled** triangle has one angle greater than $90°$

7)

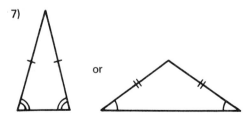

or

An **isoceles** triangle has two sides equal and the angles opposite these sides equal

170

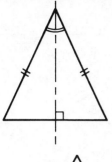

The bisector of the angle between the two equal sides bisects the third side at right angles.

8)

An **equilateral** triangle has all sides equal and internal angles of 60^0

9)   A triangle with three sides different in length is called **scalene**

Example 12.2

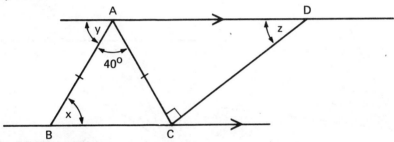

Find angles x, y and z

a)   In isoceles triangle ABC, $A\hat{B}C = A\hat{C}B$

$$\therefore \quad x = \frac{180^0 - 40^0}{2} = \underline{70^0}$$

b)   Since AD and BC are parallel
$\hat{x} = \hat{y}$ (alternate angles)
$\therefore \quad \underline{y = 70^0}$

c) $C\hat{A}D = A\hat{C}B$ (alternate angles)
and $A\hat{C}B = x = 70^0$

then $C\hat{A}D = 70^0$

In $\triangle A\hat{C}D$, ACD $= 90^0$ and $C\hat{A}D = 70^0$
$\therefore \quad \underline{A\hat{D}C = 20^0}$

171

EXERCISE 12.2

Find the sizes of the angles marked x, y and z in the following.

1)

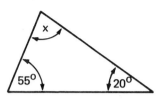

2)

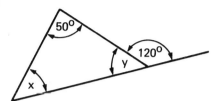

3)

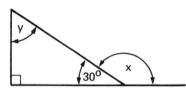

4)

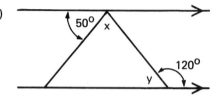

5)

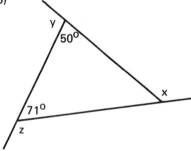

6)

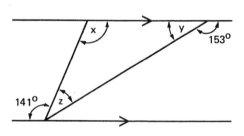

7)

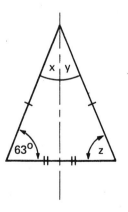

8)

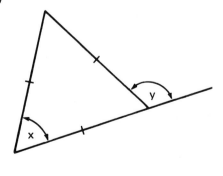

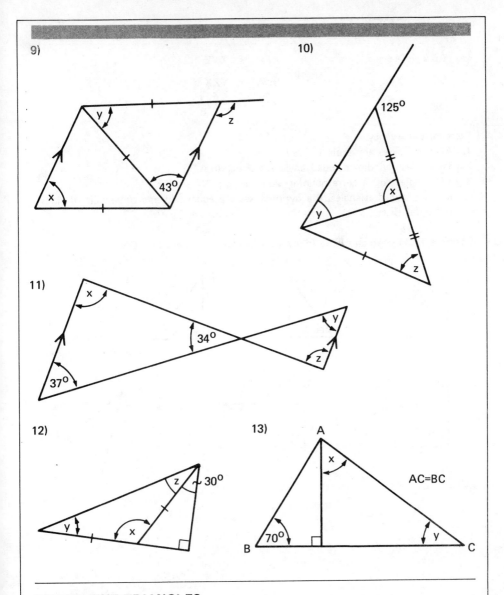

9)

10)

11)

12)

13)

CONGRUENT TRIANGLES

Congruent triangles are the same shape and the same size, i.e. they have the same size angles and the same size corresponding sides.

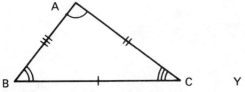

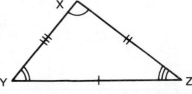

i.e. AB = XY   AB̂C = XŶZ

   BC = YZ   BĈA = YẐX

   AC = XZ   BÂC = YX̂Z

Tests for congruency
1. All three sides are equal (S.S.S.)
2. Two sides and the included angle are equal (S.A.S.)
3. Two angles and a corresponding side are equal (A.A.S.)
4. In right angled triangles, the hypotenuses are equal and one other pair of sides are equal (R.H.S.)

Example 12.3   Which of the following triangles are congruent? Give reasons.

1)

2)

3)

4)

5)

6)

7)

8)

1 and 4 are congruent   (R.H.S.)
2 and 7 are congruent   (S.A.S.)
3 and 6 are congruent   (A.A.S.)
5 and 8 are congruent   (S.S.S.)

Example 12.4 Prove that the line bisecting the angle between the equal sides in an isoceles triangle bisects the third side at right angles.

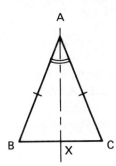

Proof Consider △ ABX and △ AXC

AB = AC (equal sides of an isoceles triangle)

$\hat{BAX} = \hat{XAC}$ ($\hat{BAC}$ is bisected)

AX is common to both triangles

∴ △ ABX and △ AXC are congruent

It follows therefore that BX = XC and $\hat{BXA} = \hat{CXA} = 90^\circ$

EXERCISE 12.3

In questions 1 to 5 say whether all, two or none of the triangles are congruent.

1)   a   b   c

2)   a   b   c

3)   a   b   c

4)   a   b   c

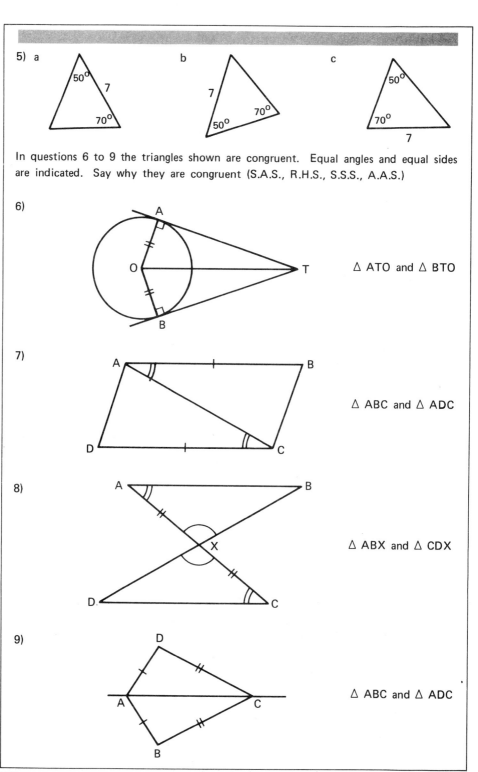

5) a

50°
7
70°

b

7
70°
50°

c

50°
70°
7

In questions 6 to 9 the triangles shown are congruent. Equal angles and equal sides are indicated. Say why they are congruent (S.A.S., R.H.S., S.S.S., A.A.S.)

6)

A

O — T

B

△ ATO and △ BTO

7)

A   B

D   C

△ ABC and △ ADC

8)

A   B

X

D   C

△ ABX and △ CDX

9)

D

A   C

B

△ ABC and △ ADC

176

10) a b c d

e 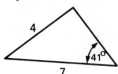 f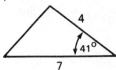

Which pairs of these triangles are congruent?

11) a b c

Which, if any of the following statements are true about the triangles above?

A. Triangles a and b are congruent
B. Triangles a and c are congruent
C. Triangles b and c are congruent

SIMILAR TRIANGLES

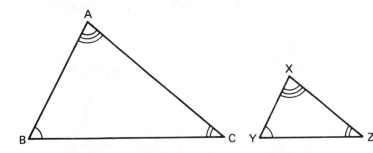

a) Two triangles are similar when they have the same angles.
AB corresponds to XY
AC corresponds to XZ
BC corresponds to YZ
The ratios of these corresponding sides are equal

i.e. $\dfrac{AB}{XY} = \dfrac{AC}{XZ} = \dfrac{BC}{YZ}$

b)   The areas of similar triangles are proportional to the squares of the corresponding sides

i.e. $\dfrac{\text{Area } \triangle ABC}{\text{Area } \triangle XYZ} = \dfrac{AB^2}{XY^2} = \dfrac{AC^2}{XZ^2} = \dfrac{BC^2}{YZ^2}$

c)   To prove that two triangles are similar it is sufficient to show that two angles in one triangle are the same as two in the other.

Example 12.5

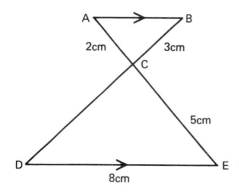

a)   Find the lengths of AB and DC
b)   Find the ratio of the area of △ ABC to △ DEC

Since AB and DE are parallel

$A\hat{B}C = C\hat{D}E$

$B\hat{A}C = C\hat{E}D$

$A\hat{C}B = D\hat{C}E$ (vertically opposite) $\therefore \triangle ABC$ and $\triangle CDE$ are similar

a) $\dfrac{AB}{DE} = \dfrac{AC}{CE} = \dfrac{BC}{CD}$

using the first two ratios

$\dfrac{AB}{8} = \dfrac{2}{5}$

$AB = \dfrac{2 \times 8}{5} = 3\tfrac{1}{5}$ cm.

using the last two ratios

$\dfrac{AC}{CE} = \dfrac{BC}{CD}$ or $\dfrac{CE}{AC} = \dfrac{CD}{BC}$ ⟵ this ratio can be used either way up

$\dfrac{5}{2} = \dfrac{CD}{3}$

$CD = \dfrac{3 \times 5}{2} = 7\tfrac{1}{2}$ cm

b)   Ratio $\triangle$ ABC : $\triangle$ DEC
      = AC^2 : CE^2
      = 2^2 : 5^2
      = 4 : 25

EXERCISE 12.4

1)

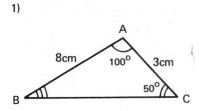
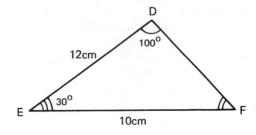

$\triangle$ ABC and $\triangle$ DEF are similar triangles. Find the sizes of BC and DF.

2)

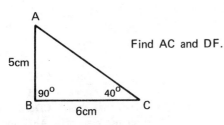

Find AC and DF.

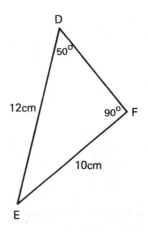

3)

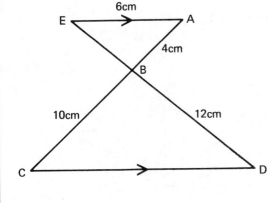

a) Complete $\dfrac{AB}{BC}$ = $\dfrac{EB}{\quad}$ = $\dfrac{\quad}{CD}$

b) Find EB and CD

c) Find the ratio of the area of triangle ABE to the area of triangle BCD.

179

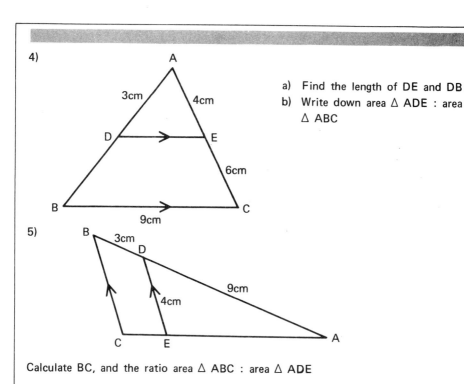

4)

a) Find the length of DE and DB
b) Write down area △ ADE : area △ ABC

5)

Calculate BC, and the ratio area △ ABC : area △ ADE

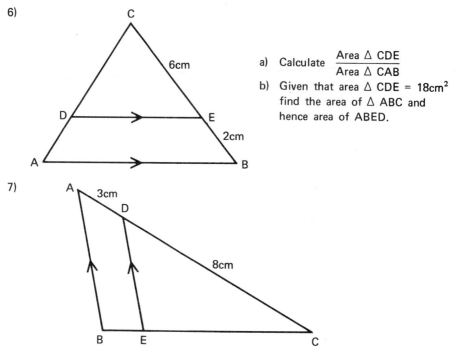

6)

a) Calculate $\dfrac{\text{Area } \triangle \text{ CDE}}{\text{Area } \triangle \text{ CAB}}$

b) Given that area △ CDE = 18cm² find the area of △ ABC and hence area of ABED.

7)

Given that the area of the trapezium ABED is 20cm² find the area of △ ABC.

180

8)

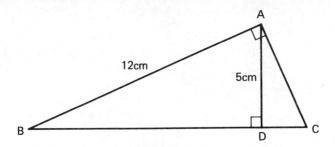

a) Show that triangles ABC, ABD and ADC are similar.
b) What is the ratio of area △ ABD : area △ ADC?

9)

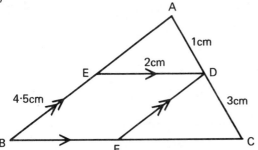

AD = 1 cm
DC = 3 cm
DE = 2 cm
BE = 4·5 cm

a) Name two triangles similar to AED.
b) Calculate the lengths of FC and AE.
c) Calculate the ratio of the areas of triangles AED and ABC.

10)

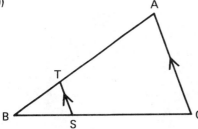

Point S is on BC such that SC = 2BS
If the area of △ ABC is 27cm^2 find
the area of the trapezium STAC.

GEOMETRY 2
PROPERTIES OF A CIRCLE

PROPERTIES OF A CIRCLE

AYB is the major arc
AXB is the minor arc
AB is a chord
Point 0 is the centre

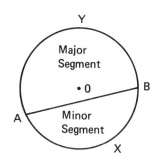

Angles in a circle

1. The angle subtended by a
   chord (BC) at the centre
   of a circle (0) is twice
   the angle at the
   circumference
   i.e. $B\hat{O}C = 2 \times B\hat{A}C$

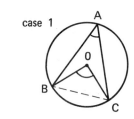

2. The angle in a semi-circle
   is a right angle
   i.e. $B\hat{A}C = 90°$

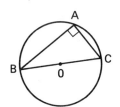

3. Angles subtended by a chord
   (BC) in the same segment
   are equal i.e. $B\hat{A}C = B\hat{D}C$

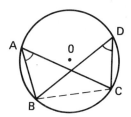

A quadrilateral whose vertices lie on the circumference of a circle is called a
cyclic quadrilateral

The opposite angles of a
cyclic quadrilateral are
supplementary

i.e. $\hat{a} + \hat{b} = 180^{\circ}$
    $\hat{c} + \hat{d} = 180^{\circ}$

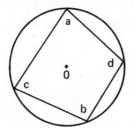

Example 13.1

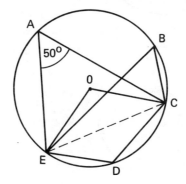

Find angles $C\hat{O}E$, $C\hat{B}E$, $C\hat{D}E$, $E\hat{C}O$

$C\hat{O}E = 100^{\circ}$ (angle at the centre is twice the angle at the circumference)

$C\hat{B}E = 50^{\circ}$ (angles in the same segment are equal)

$C\hat{D}E = 180^{\circ} - 50^{\circ} = 130^{\circ}$ (opposite angles of a cyclic quadrilateral are
                                                    supplementary)

for $E\hat{C}O$

Δ OEC is isoceles (OC = OE = radii)

$$\therefore E\hat{C}O = \frac{180^{\circ} - 100^{\circ}}{2} = 40^{\circ}$$

EXERCISE 13.1

Find the sizes of the angles marked by letters in the following diagrams.

1.

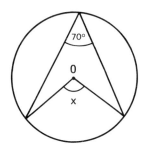

2.

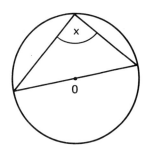

3.

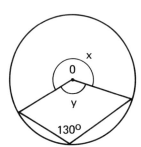

4.

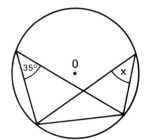

5.

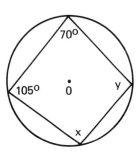

6.

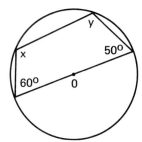

7.

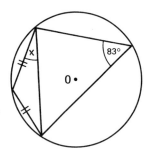

8.

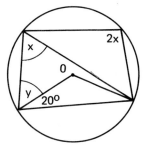

186

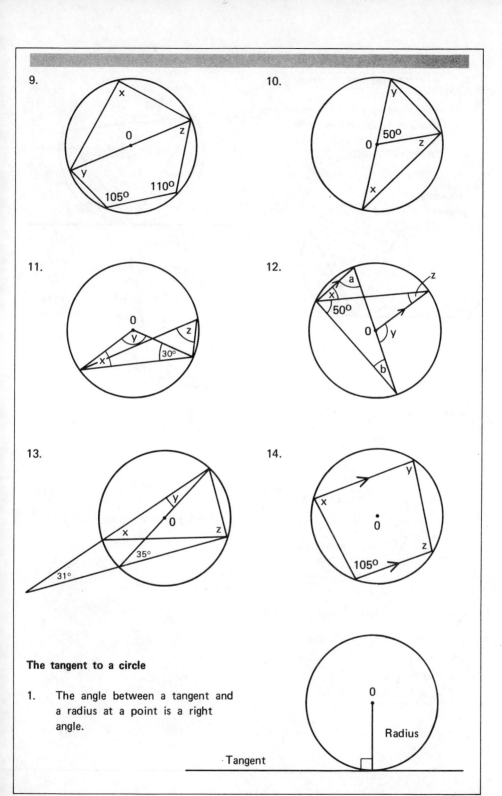

The tangent to a circle

1. The angle between a tangent and a radius at a point is a right angle.

Radius

Tangent

2. Alternate segment theorem

The angle between a tangent and a chord is equal to the angle subtended by the chord in the alternate segment.

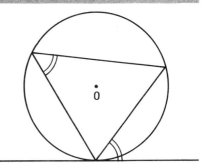

Alternate segment

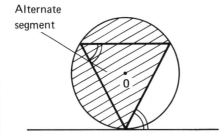

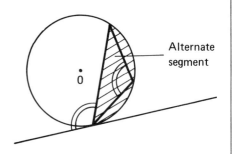

Alternate segment

Example 13.2

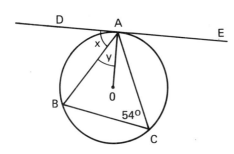

Find x and y

$\stackrel{\wedge}{DAB} = \stackrel{\wedge}{ACB}$ (Alternate segment theorem)

$\therefore x = 54^{o}$

$\stackrel{\wedge}{DAO} = 90^{o}$

$\therefore \hat{y} = 90^{o} - x$

$\hat{y} = 90^{o} - 54^{o} = 36^{o}$

EXERCISE 13.2

Find the size of the angles marked by the letters in the following diagrams.

1.

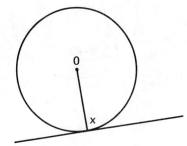

2.

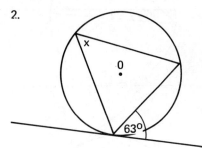

3.

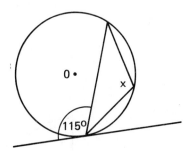

4.

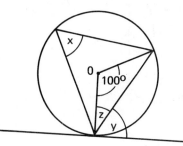

5.

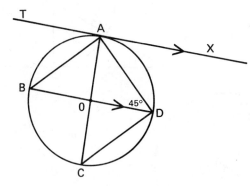

Find DÂX
TÂB
AĈD
AB̂D
CÂD
CÂB
AÔB

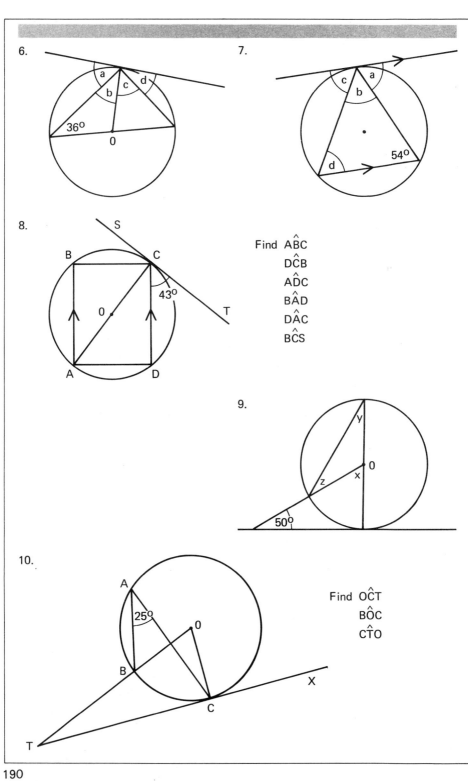

6.

7.

8.

Find AB̂C
DĈB
AD̂C
BÂD
DÂC
BĈS

9.

10.

Find OĈT
BÔC
CT̂O

CHORDS OF A CIRCLE

Intersecting chords

Rule

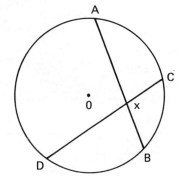

$$(AX) \times (XB) = (DX) \times (XC)$$

Example 13.3

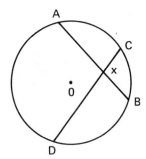

AB = 8 cm

AX = 6 cm

CX = 5 cm

Find the length of chord DC

$(AX) \times (XB) = (DX) \times (XC)$

$6 \times 2 = (DX) \times 5$

$12 = 5\,(DX)$

$DX = \dfrac{12}{5} = 2 \cdot 4$ cm

$\therefore DC = DX + CX = 2 \cdot 4 + 5 = 7 \cdot 5$ cm

Example 13.4

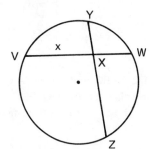

VW = 9 cm:

YX = 4 cm

XZ = 5 cm

Find x

$$(VX) \times (XW) = (YX) \times (XZ)$$
$$(x) \times (9-x) = 4 \times 5$$
$$9x - x^2 = 20$$
$$x^2 - 9x + 20 = 0$$
$$(x - 5)(x - 4) = 0$$
$$\therefore \underline{x = 5} \quad \text{or} \quad \underline{x = 4}$$

i.e. If VX = 5 cm   XW = 4cm

or if VX = 4cm   XW = 5cm

EXERCISE 13.3

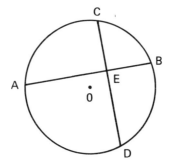

This diagram refers to questions 1, 2 and 3.

1) If AE = 4cm, EB = 3cm, CE = 2cm find ED
2) If AE = 8cm, ED = 5cm, EC = 4cm find EB
3) If AB = 10cm, EB = 3cm, CE = 4cm find ED

4)

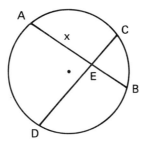

AB = 8cm
DE = 4cm
EC = 3cm
AE = x

a) Write down EB in terms of x.
b) Using the relationship AE $\times$ EB = DE $\times$ EC write down a quadratic equation in x and use it to find the values of AE and EB.
5) Two chords AB and CD cross at E. If ED = 3cm, CE = 4cm and AE = 5cm find BE.

6) A chord 8cm long is bisected by the diameter of a circle of radius 5cm. How far along the diameter does the chord cut it?

7)

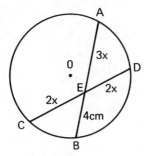

Two chords AB and CD cross at E. If AE = 3x cm, CE = ED = 2x cm and EB = 4 cm find the value of x and hence the length of CD

8)

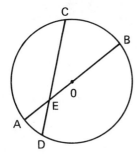

AB is the diameter of a circle of radius 5½cm. If DE = 3cm and EC = 8cm find the length of AE.

GEOMETRY 3
POLYGONS

POLYGONS

A polygon is a closed figure having straight sides.

Polygons have different names according to the number of sides they have.

A 3 sided polygon is a triangle
A 4 sided polygon is a quadrilateral
A 6 sided polygon is a hexagon
An 8 sided polygon is an octogon

Irregular polygons

Sum of the interior angles

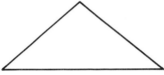

Triangle
Sum of interior angles is 180°

Quadrilateral (made from 2 triangles)
Sum of interior angles is
$2 \times 180° = 360°$

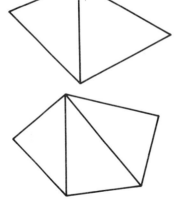

Pentagon (made from 3 triangles)
Sum of interior angles is
$3 \times 180° = 540°$

and so on.

This can be remembered in the form of the formula
Sum of interior angles = number of triangles $\times$ 180°

But number of triangles = number of sides — 2
$\therefore$ $\underline{S = (n - 2)180°}$ where S = sum of interior angles
n = number of sides

Example 14.1

The sum of the interior angles of a 12 sided figure =
$$(12 - 2) \times 180^0 = 10 \times 180^0 = \underline{1800^0}$$

Example 14.2

A pentagon (5 sides) has four interior angles of 120^0, 90^0, 110^0 and 80^0.
Find the fifth angle.

Sum of 5 interior angles = $(5 - 2) \times 180^0 = 540^0$

5th angle = $540^0 - (120^0 + 90^0 + 110^0 + 80^0)$
$$= 540^0 - 400^0 = \underline{140^0}$$

Example 14.3

In a pentagon (5 sides) ABCDE, AB is parallel to CD and $A\hat{B}C = 120^0$. If $B\hat{A}E = C\hat{D}E = 2x^0$ and $A\hat{E}D = x^0$, find x.

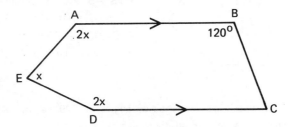

Sum of the interior angles is $(5 - 2) \times 180^0 = 540^0$

If $A\hat{B}C = 120^0$ then $B\hat{C}D = 60^0$ (supplementary angles)

∴ Sum of three unknown angles
$$= 540^0 - (180^0 + 60^0) = 360^0$$

∴ $2x + 2x + x = 360^0$

$5x = 360^0$

$\underline{x = 72^0}$

EXERCISE 14.1

---

1) A quadrilateral ABCD has $A\hat{B}C = 93^0$, $B\hat{C}D = 80^0$ and $C\hat{D}A = 104^0$.
   Find $D\hat{A}B$.

2) In a quadrilateral ABCD, AB is parallel to DC. If $A\hat{B}C = 110^0$ and $A\hat{D}C = 84^0$ find $B\hat{A}D$ and $B\hat{C}D$.

3)

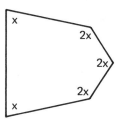

Find the sizes of the angles in this pentagon.

4) In a hexagon, three internal angles are each 120° and of the remaining three angles, two are each twice the size of the third. Find these angles.

5)

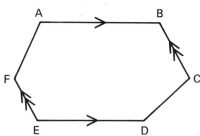

An irregular hexagon ABCDEF has sides AB and ED parallel and BC and FE parallel. If $A\hat{B}C = 130^O$, $B\hat{C}D = 115^O$, $C\hat{D}E = 102^O$ and $A\hat{F}E = 124^O$. Find angles $D\hat{E}F$ and $B\hat{A}F$.

6) An octogon (8 sides) has two interior angles of 129° each. All the other interior angles are equal. Find them.

7) Tiles are made so that four tiles of the same size (congruent) will fit together to form a cross. Find the interior angles of the tile.

8) A ten sided polygon has five interior angles which are twice the size of the other five angles. Find the sizes of these angles.

REGULAR POLYGONS

A regular polygon has all its sides equal in length and all its interior angles equal in size.

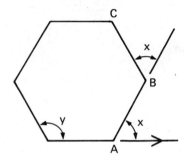

x is the exterior angle
y is the interior angle

Imagine a fly standing at corner A and looking in the direction of the arrow. To get to B it will have to turn through angle x first. Arriving at B it will have to turn through this angle again in order to get to C. If it does this at each corner it will eventually arrive at A again. It will now have turned through n exterior angles (n being the number of corners or sides) and 360° (because it is looking in the original direction)

$$\therefore \text{Exterior angles} = \frac{360^{\circ}}{n}$$

Since interior angles + exterior angle = 180°

$$\text{interior angle} = 180^{\circ} - \frac{360^{\circ}}{n}$$

Note that the interior angle of a regular polygon can also be found by dividing the sum of the interior angles by the number of sides

i.e. $\dfrac{(n-2)\ 180}{n}$

Example 14.4

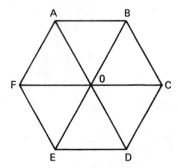

ABCDEF is a regular hexagon with centre 0. Find

a) $B\hat{C}D$ b) $B\hat{D}C$
c) $B\hat{E}D$ d) $E\hat{B}D$
e) $A\hat{O}B$

199

a) $B\hat{C}D$ is an interior angle

$= 180^0 - \dfrac{360^0}{6}$

$= 180^0 - 60^0 = \underline{120^0}$

b) Triangle BCD is isoceles since BC = CD $\therefore$ $B\hat{D}C = \dfrac{180^0 - 120^0}{2} = 30^0$

c) Line BE bisects the hexagon (line of symmetry)

$\therefore$ Interior angle $F\hat{E}D$ is bisected

$\therefore$ $B\hat{E}D = \dfrac{120^0}{2} = 60^0$

d) $E\hat{B}D = C\hat{B}E - C\hat{B}D$

$= 60^0 - 30^0 = \underline{30^0}$

e) $A\hat{O}B = \dfrac{360^0}{6} = 60^0$

EXERCISE 14.2

Find the interior and exterior angles of each of the regular polygons in questions 1 to 4.

1) A heptagon (7 sides)
2) A decagon (10 sides)
3) A 12 sided figure
4) A 20 sided figure

5)

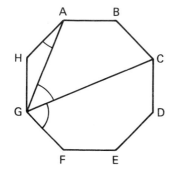

In the regular octogon shown find the sizes of the angles

a) $A\hat{B}C$ b) $H\hat{A}G$

c) $C\hat{G}F$ d) $A\hat{G}C$

6) ABCDEFG is a regular heptagon (7 sides) with 0 the centre. Find

a) $A\hat{O}B$ b) $O\hat{B}C$

7) A regular polygon has an interior angle of 160^0. Find how many sides it has.

8) A regular polygon has an interior angle of 168°. Find how many sides it has.

9) In a regular polygon the interior angle is five times bigger than the external angle. How many sides has it?

10) Four tiles, each in the shape of a regular octogon are placed together on a flat surface leaving a 'hole' in the middle. By calculating the interior angle of the regular octogon, show that the 'hole' **must** be a square.

11)

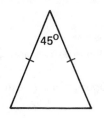

A number of the equilateral triangles shown will tessellate to form a regular polygon. How many sides will the polygon have?

12)

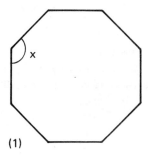

(1)

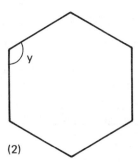

(2)

a) Find the size of the two interior angles marked on the regular polygons shown above.

b) Explain why a number of tiles of shape (1) will not fit together without leaving gaps when laid on a flat surface but those of shape (2) will.

QUADRILATERALS

A quadrilateral is a four sided figure.

Types of quadrilaterals

Parallelogram

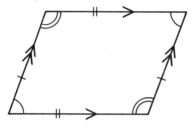

Properties
a) Opposite sides are equal and parallel
b) Opposite angles equal

Rectangle (or oblong)

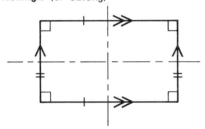

Properties
a and b — as a parallelogram
c) All interior angles are $90°$
d) Two lines of symmetry

Square

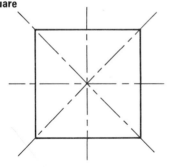

Properties
a, b and c — as a rectangle
d) Four lines of symmetry
e) All sides of same length
f) Diagonals cross at right angles

Rhombus

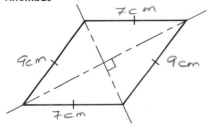

Properties
a and b as a rectangle
c) Two lines of symmetry
d) All sides of same length
e) Diagonals cross at right angles

Kite

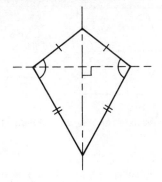

Properties
a) Two pairs of equal adjacent sides
b) Diagonals cross at right angles
c) 1 pair of opposite equal angles
d) 1 line of symmetry

Trapezium

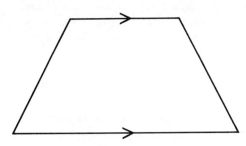

Properties
a) 1 pair of opposite sides parallel

EXERCISE 14.3

What shape is formed when the mid points of the sides of the shapes in question 1 to 5 are joined to the mid-points of adjacent sides?

1) Rectangle
2) Square
3) Parallelogram
4) Kite
5) Rhombus
6) Find all the internal angles in this trapezium

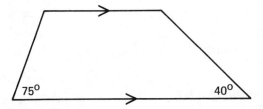

7)

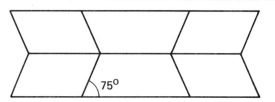

Parallelogram and trapezium tiles are to be tessellated in the way shown above. Find all the angles of the two tiles.

8)

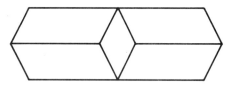

Four congruent parallelograms are put together as shown in the diagram. What is the shape of the 'hole' in the middle? If one of the angles of the 'hole' shape is 45° find the angles of the parallelogram.

9) Find the angles of a parallelogram where one angle is twice the size of the other angle.

10) ABC is an isoceles triangle where AB = AC. What quadrilateral is formed when ABC is reflected about line BC?

11) Two isoceles triangles ABC and BCD are joined by their common side BC. If BC is the unequal side in both triangles what quadrilateral is formed? If $A\hat{B}C = 70°$ and $B\hat{C}D = 40°$ find the four angles of the quadrilateral.

THE TANGENT KITE

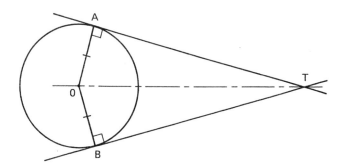

Considering triangles AOT and BOT

$O\hat{A}T = O\hat{B}T = 90°$

OA = OB = radii

OT is a common side

∴ △ AOT and △ BOT are congruent (R.H.S.)

It follows that

AT = BT

$\hat{AOT} = \hat{BOT}$

$\hat{ATO} = \hat{BTO}$

also $\hat{AOB} + \hat{ATB} = 180^\circ$ (since four angles of a quadrilateral add up to 360°)

Example 14.5

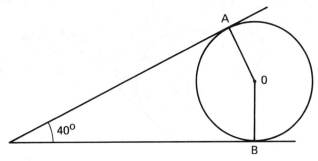

$\hat{AOB} = 180^\circ - 40^\circ = 140^\circ$

EXERCISE 14.4

In questions 1 to 6 find the sizes of the angles marked.

1)

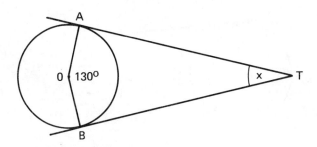

2)

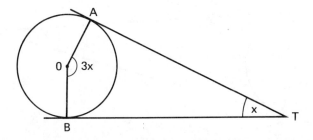

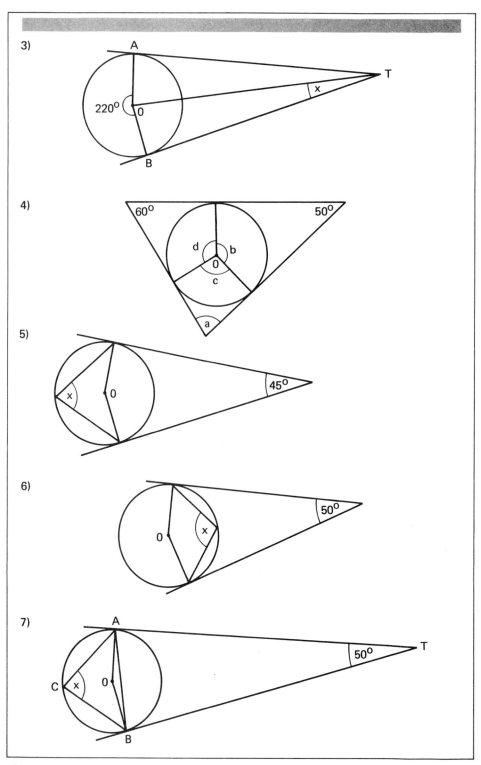

3)

4)

5)

6)

7)

206

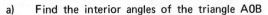

a) Find the interior angles of the triangle AOB

b) What type of triangle is △ ATB?

c) What is the relationship between TÂB and AĈB?

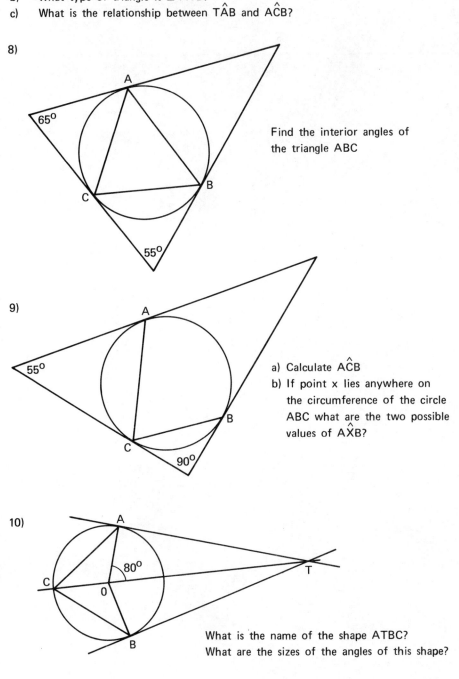

8)

65°

A

C

B

55°

Find the interior angles of
the triangle ABC

9)

55°

A

C

B

90°

a) Calculate AĈB

b) If point x lies anywhere on
the circumference of the circle
ABC what are the two possible
values of AX̂B?

10)

A

C

80°

0

T

B

What is the name of the shape ATBC?
What are the sizes of the angles of this shape?

GEOMETRICAL
DRAWING

GEOMETRICAL CONSTRUCTIONS

1. **Bisector of a line**

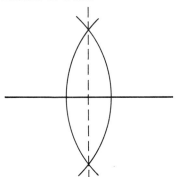

Draw two arcs of the same radius from the two ends of the line

2. **Bisector of an angle**

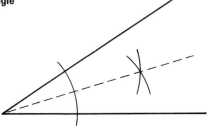

3. **A perpendicular from a point (P) on a line**

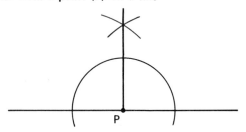

4. **A perpendicular from a point (P) to a line**

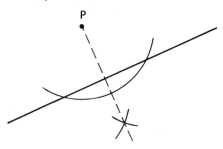

5. **A perpendicular from a point (P) at the end of a line**

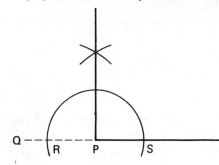

Extend the line to Q.
Draw an arc centre P to cut the line at R and S.
From R and S draw two arcs of equal radii.
Join the intersection of these arcs to point P.

6. **An angle of 60**

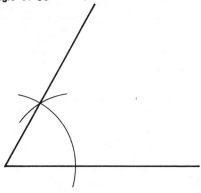

7. **A line through a point parallel to another line**

Mark any two points QR
From P draw an arc radius QR
From R draw an arc radius QP.
Join the intersection of these arcs to point P.

8. **A line parallel to another line at a known distance**

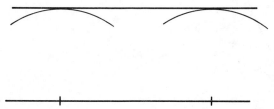

Draw two arcs of the given distance, from the line.
Draw the common tangent of these arcs.

211

EXERCISE 15.1

Construct each of the following
1) An angle of 45°
2) An angle of 30°
3) An angle of 120°
4) A square of sides 8cm.
5) A parallelogram with angles of 120° and 60° and sides of 5cm and 8cm.
6) An equilateral triangle with sides of 6cm.
7) An isoceles triangle ABC where AB = AC, BC = 4cm and a perpendicular height of 6cm.

LOCUS PROBLEMS

A locus is the path made by a moving point.

The locus of a point (P) which is equidistant from two straight lines is the bisector of the angle formed by the two lines.

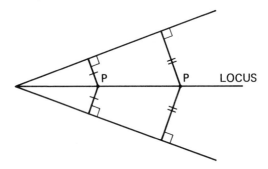

The locus of a point (P) which is equidistant from two points A and B is the perpendicular bisector of the line AB.

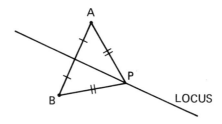

The locus of a point (P) which is equidistant from another point (0) is a circle, centre 0.

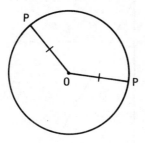

Example 15.1

ABCD is a rectangular lawn where AB = 10 metres and BC is 7 metres. Two paths cross the lawn. One is equidistant from the sides AB and BC and the other is equidistant from the corners A and D. Construct ABCD to a scale of 1cm representing 1 metre and clearly show the centre lines of the paths. A tree is to be planted at least 4 metres from the point of intersection of these paths and at least 2 metres from the centre lines of the paths. Show the area where it can be planted by shading.

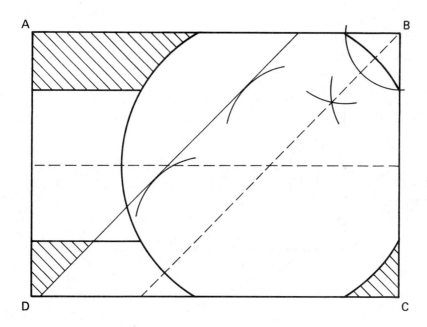

Example 15.2

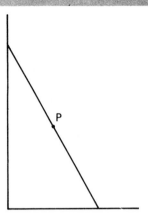

A ladder AB of length 6 metres rests against a wall. Beginning with it standing vertically against the wall, plot the locus of its mid point P by drawing the ladder in 7 different positions. Use a scale of 1cm to 1 metre.

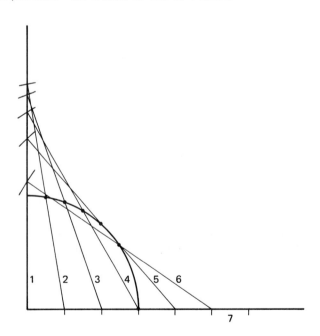

1.

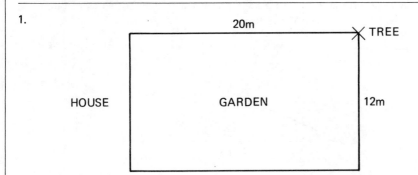

A garden is in the shape of a rectangle measuring 20 metres by 12 metres with a house at one end and a tree in one corner. A rose bed is to be made and must be at least 4m from the house and 6m from the tree. Using a scale of 1cm to represent 2m make a scale drawing of the garden and shade in the area in which the rose bed can be made.

2.

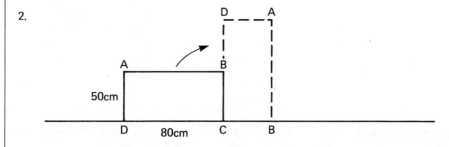

A rectangular box shown above is to be moved along a floor by pivoting it about corner C until side CB is on the floor, then pivoting it about corner B until AB is on the floor. This is continued until side AD is on the floor. Using a scale of 1cm to represent 20cm. Make a scale drawing of this and show the locus of point A.

3.

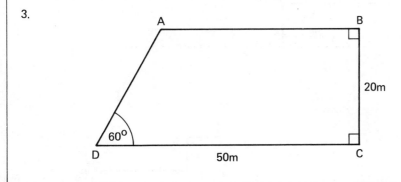

The diagram shows a small field in which a flagpole is to be placed. Its position is to be 5 metres from side AB and 35 metres from corner D. Using a ruler and compass only (no protractor) make a scale drawing with 1cm to represent 5m, indicating clearly the position of the flagpole.

4.

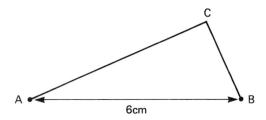

Two pins, A and B, are 6cm apart. A length of string measuring 10cm is tied to each of these pins and formed into a triangle ABC. By constructing a series of triangles, plot the locus of point C.

5.

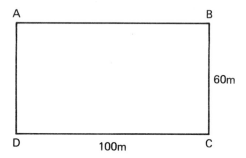

A town square is in the form of a rectangle ABCD, measuring 100m by 60m. Using a scale of 1cm representing 10m make an accurate drawing of it. It is known that water pipes run under the square. One runs parallel to AB so that it is equidistant from A and D and a second is equidistant from sides AB and BC. Find the position P where the pipes meet.

6.

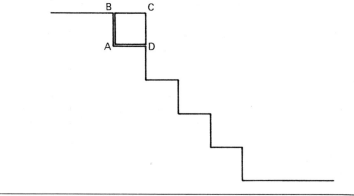

216

A square box ABCD whose sides are the same depth and height as a series of steps is to be rolled down the steps until point C reaches the bottom. Sketch the locus of the point C.

7.

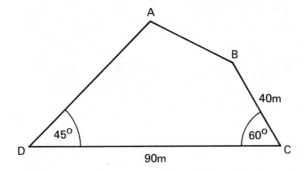

A field is in the shape of the quadrilateral ABCD shown above. Using a scale of 1cm to represent 10m construct, using a ruler and compass only, a scale drawing of it. It is proposed to plant a tree which is equidistant from points A and C and 50 metres from point D. Use a suitable method to find this point.

8.

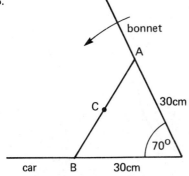
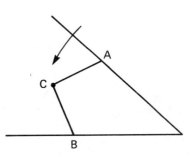

The bonnet of a car is held open by a prop AB. The prop is hinged to the bonnet at A, the car body at B and it is hinged in the middle. The drawing shows the bonnet fully open. When the bonnet closes point C moves forward. Show the locus of point A and C. Use a scale of 1cm to represent 5cm.

9.
Draw a line AB, 8cm long. Use this line to draw a triangle ABC such that $A\hat{C}B$ = 90°. Now using the same AB but a different C, draw other triangles with $A\hat{C}B$ = 90° and plot the locus of point C. What is the shape of the locus of C?

10.

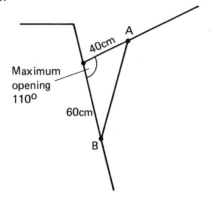

The tail boot of a car is kept in position by a stay AB. It is hinged on the door at A, but runs through a swivel guide at B. By drawing the boot door in various positions show the locus of the end (B) of the stay.

11.

A mechanism consists of a round card which rotates about its centre and a pencil which moves horizontally between points A and B. If the card rotates once while the pencil moves from A to B by considering 45° turns of the card plot the line made by the pencil.

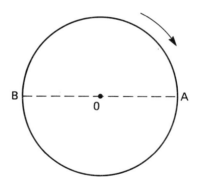

MEASUREMENTS

UNITS OF MEASUREMENT

Mass (referred to as **weight** in everyday speech but these are not scientifically the same)

$$1000 \text{ milligrams (mg)} = 1 \text{ gram (g)}$$
$$1000 \text{ g} = 1 \text{ kilogram (kg)}$$
$$1000 \text{ kg} = 1 \text{ tonne}$$

Length
$$10 \text{ millimetres (mm)} = 1 \text{ centimetre (cm)}$$
$$100 \text{ cm} = 1 \text{ metre (m)}$$
$$1000 \text{ m} = 1 \text{ kilometre (Km)}$$

Area The area within a square of sides 1cm is 1 square centimetre $1cm^2$

Other units are   square metre m^2

square millimetre mm^2

Volume The space within a cube of sides 1cm is 1 cubic metre $1cm^3$ or 1cc

Capacity The measure of liquid a vessel will hold

This can be expressed in terms of mm^3, cm^3, m^3 or **litre**

For most purposes 1 litre = 1000 cc

(the actual relationship is 1 litre = 1000·028cc)

The more precise relationship is 1 litre = 1000 millilitres (ml)

from which we assume 1 ml = 1cc

Example 16.1

1)
$$2560g = \frac{2560}{1000} \text{ kg} = 2 \cdot 56 \text{kg}$$

2) $6 \cdot 3 \text{ tonne} = 6 \cdot 3 \times 1000 \text{ kg} = 6300 \text{ kg}$

3) $\cdot 003 \text{ m} = \cdot 003 \times 1000 \text{ mm} = 3 \text{mm}$

4) $1cm^2 = (10mm)^2 = 100mm^2$

5)   Change 6500 cm^2 into m^2

$$1m^2 = (100cm)^2 = 10000cm^2$$
$$\therefore 6500cm^2 = \frac{6500m^2}{10000} = \cdot 65m^2$$

6) $1m^3 = (100cm)^3 = 1000000cm^3$

7)   Change $4cm^3$ into mm^3

$$1cm^3 = (10mm)^3 = 1000mm^3$$
$$\therefore 4cm^3 = 4 \times 1000 = 4000mm^3$$

8)   Change $1m^3$ into litres

$$1 \text{ litre} = 1000cm^3$$
$$1m^3 = (100cm)^3 = 1000000cm^3$$
$$1m^3 = \frac{1000000}{1000} = 1000 \text{ litre}$$

EXERCISE 16.1

1) Change into kg
a) 5g   b) 250g   c) 4531g   d) ·3 Tonne
e) 7·3 Tonnes   f) 2·300 mg   g) 500 mg   h) ·003 Tonnes

2) Change into grams
a) 7 mg   b) 7 kg   c) 93 mg   d) 564 mg
e) ·3 kg   f) 4560 mg   g) ·005 kg   h) 1·54 kg

3) Change into metres
a) 3000 cm   b) 246 cm   c) 56 cm   d) ·005 km
e) 3·4 km   f) ·17 km   g) $5·0 \times 10^4$ mm   h) 5426 mm

4) Change
a) $4 \ m^2$ into cm^2 b) $3·54 \ m^2$ into cm^2
c) $9 \ cm^2$ into mm^2 d) $1·2 \times 10^4 \ cm^2$ into m^2
e) $476 \ mm^2$ into cm^2 f) $26 \ mm^2$ into cm^2
g) $·003 \ m^2$ into cm^2 h) $40 \ cm^2$ into mm^2

5) Change
a) $2 \ cm^3$ into mm^3 b) $·003 \ cm^3$ into mm^3
c) $3·4 \ m^3$ into cm^3 d) $·015 \ m^3$ into cm^3
e) $5·0 \times 10^4 \ mm^3$ into cm^3 f) $1·2 \times 10^6 \ cm^3$ into m^3
g) $·5 \ m^3$ into litres   h) $5·3 \times 10^6$ ml into litres
i) 28 litres into ml   j) ·003 litres into ml

AREAS AND PERIMETERS

Rectangle

Area = length $\times$ breadth = ℓb
Perimeter = $2\ell + 2b = 2(\ell+b)$

Parallelogram

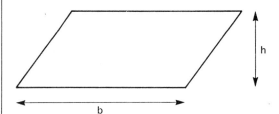

Area = ½ (base $\times$ perpendicular height)

= bh

Triangle

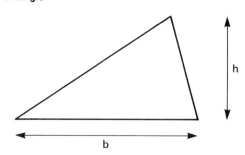

Area = ½ (base $\times$ perpendicular height)

= ½ bh

Trapezium

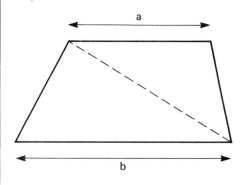

Area = ½ah + ½bh

= ½(a + b)h

Circle

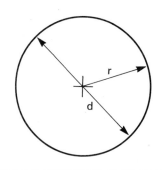

Area = πr^2

Circumference = $2\pi r$ or πd

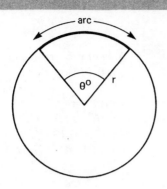

Sector of a circle

Area of sector $= \pi r^2 \times \dfrac{\theta}{360}$

Arc length $= 2\pi r \times \dfrac{\theta}{360}$

$\qquad$ or $\pi d \times \dfrac{\theta}{360}$

To find the areas of irregular shapes the figure is split up into standard shapes.

Example 16.2

1)

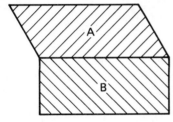

Total Area = Area of parallelogram A
$\qquad\qquad\qquad$ + Area of rectangle B

2)

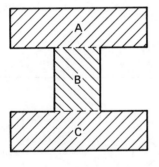

Total Area = Area of A + Area of B
$\qquad\qquad\qquad$ + Area of C

3)

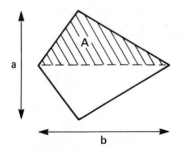

Area of kite
$= 2 \times$ area of triangle A
$= 2(\frac{1}{2}b \times \frac{1}{2}a)$
$= \frac{1}{2}ab$
i.e. $\frac{1}{2}$(product of diagonals)

223

4)

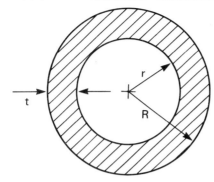

Area of ring or Annulus
= area of large circle − area of
small circle
$= \pi R^2 - \pi r^2$
$= \pi (R^2 - r^2)$
$= \pi (R + r) (R - r)$
$= \pi (R + r)t$

EXERCISE 16.2

Wherever necessary use $\pi = 3 \cdot 142$

1) Find the areas and perimeters of rectangles measuring
    a) 3 cm by 3 cm   b) 6 cm by 8 cm   c) 9 cm by 3·4 cm
    d) 8·4 cm by 9·3 cm

2) Find the areas of the following shapes

a)

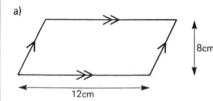

8cm

12cm

b)

4·8cm

13·3cm

c)

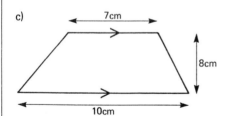

7cm

8cm

10cm

d)

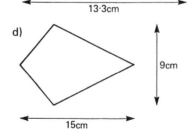

9cm

15cm

3) Find the area and circumference of circles with radii
    a) 9 cm   b) 3·4 cm   c) 8·9 cm
    d) 17 m

4) Find the area and arc length of the following sectors where r is the radius and θ is the angle subtended at the centre.
   a) r = 3 cm, θ = 40°   b) r = 9 cm, θ = 130°
   c) r = 10·5 cm, θ = 260°   d) r = 17·45, θ = 185°

5)

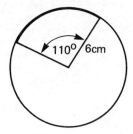

Find the area and perimeter of the sector shown

6) Find the areas of the shaded parts of these figures

a)

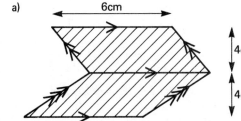

b)

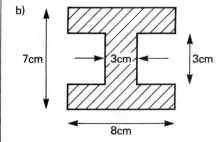

c)

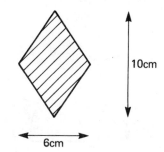

d)

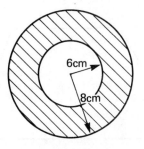

e)

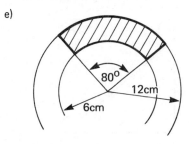

225

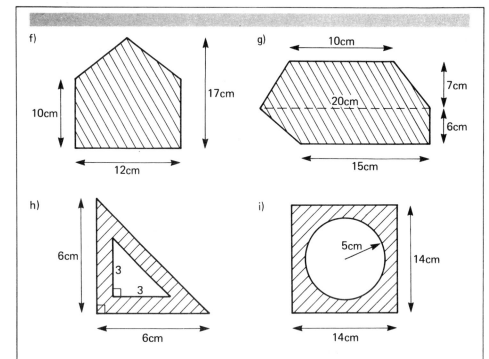

f) 17cm 10cm 12cm

g) 10cm 7cm 20cm 6cm 15cm

h) 6cm 3 3 6cm

i) 5cm 14cm 14cm

7) How many 30 cm square tiles are needed to cover the floor of a room measuring 3 metres by 4½ metres?

8) A bicycle wheel is of diameter 80 cm. How many revolutions must it turn through to cover 1 kilometre?

9) A lawn is in the form of a quadrant shown below. Find its area and perimeter.

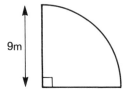

9m

10) By taking suitable measurements find the areas of the following shapes.

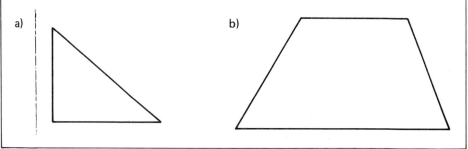

a)

b)

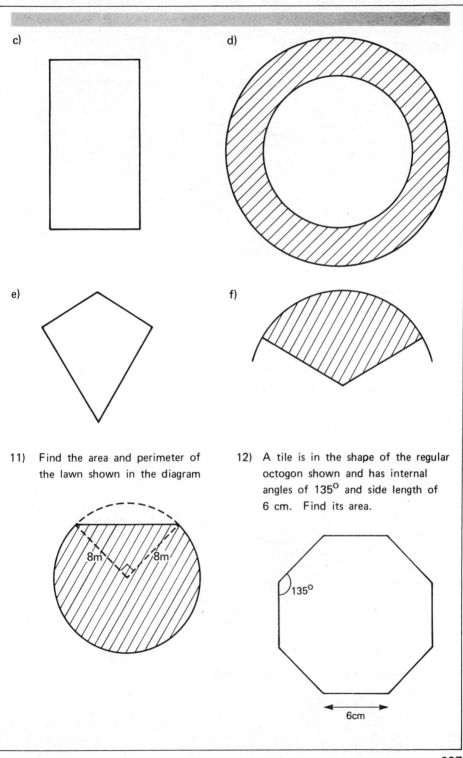

c)

d)

e)

f)

11) Find the area and perimeter of the lawn shown in the diagram

8m   8m

12) A tile is in the shape of the regular octogon shown and has internal angles of 135° and side length of 6 cm. Find its area.

135°

6cm

VOLUME

Prisms A prism is a three dimensional shape with a constant cross section.

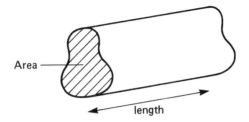

Volume = Area of end × length

Types of prisms

1) **Rectangular block** (cuboid)

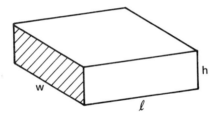

Volume = Area of end × length = whℓ

2) **Cylinder**

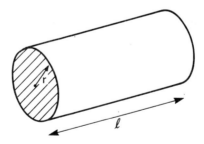

Volume = Area of end × length = $\pi r^2 \ell$

3) **Pipe**

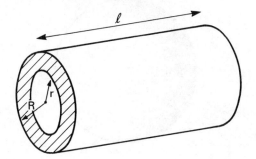

Volume = $\pi(R + r)\,t\,\ell$

4) **Triangular prism**

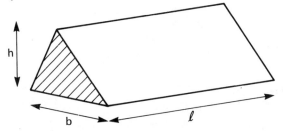

Volume = $\frac{1}{2}bh\ell$

Other shapes

Cone

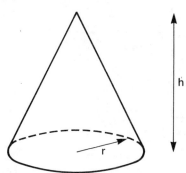

Volume = $\frac{1}{3}\pi r^2 h$

Pyramid

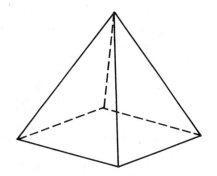

Volume = $\frac{1}{3}$(Area of base)h

Sphere

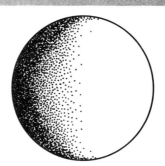

Volume = $\dfrac{4\pi r^3}{3}$

Example 16.3

A marble paperweight is in the shape of a hemisphere of radius 4 cm. Calculate its volume. A supplier packs them into boxes of 50. Find their weight if 1 cm³ of marble weighs 2·7 grams.

Volume of one paperweight = $\dfrac{1}{2} \times \dfrac{4}{3} \times 3{\cdot}142 \times 4^3$

= 134·06 cm³

Weight of one paperweight = 134·06 × 2·7 grams

= 361·96 grams

Weight of 50 paperweights = 361·96 × 50

= 18098 grams

= 18kg 98 grams

Example 16.4

A metal sphere of diameter 10 cm is lowered into a cylindrical jar of 16 cm height and 12 cm diameter which contains water to a depth of 10 cm. How far up the side of the jar will the water rise?

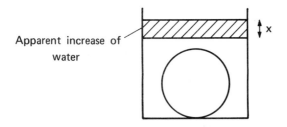

Apparent increase of water

x

Amount of water displaced = volume of sphere

= $\dfrac{4}{3} \times \pi \times 5^3$

= 523·67 cm³

Apparent increase in water = Area of jar base X x

= $\pi \times 6^2 \times x$

= 113·11 x cm³

But apparent increase in water = amount of water displaced

$$113 \cdot 11x = 523 \cdot 67$$

$$x = \frac{523 \cdot 67}{113 \cdot 11}$$

$$x = 4 \cdot 63 \text{ cm (to 2 d.p.)}$$

EXERCISE 16.3

1) The diagram shows the cross section (length) of a swimming pool of width 12m.

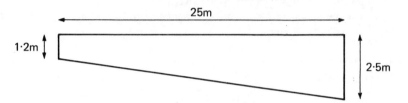

Calculate the amount of water it will hold to the nearest litre.

2) A trench ·7m wide by 1·2m deep and 20 metres long is dug on a building site. Calculate the amount of earth removed.

3) A box measuring 30 cm long by 10 cm wide by 15 cm high (outside dimensions) is made from wood 7mm thick. Calculate the volume of wood required and its weight (to the nearest gram) if 1 cm³ of wood weighs 0·47 g.

4) A circular pond of 4m diameter is to have a concrete path around it, 1 metre wide and 12 cm deep. Find the amount of concrete required.

5) A block of steel measuring 0·5m by 1m by 0·75m is rolled into a steel sheet 0·2 cm thick and 1·5m wide. Calculate the length of the sheet.

6) A metal tube has an outside diameter of 1·5 cm and a thickness of 4 mm. If its length is 5m calculate its volume to the nearest cm³.

7) A rolling pin is made from three pieces of wood as shown below. The

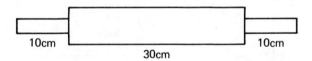

thicker piece is 5 cm diameter and the two end pieces are 2·3 cm diameter. If 1 cm of this wood weighs ·75g find its weight.

8) Find the volume of a 12 cm square based pyramid with a weight of 20 cm.

9) Find the height of a 4 cm square based pyramid whose volume is 40 cm³.

10) Find the volume of a pyramid whose base is a rectangle measuring 6 cm by 8 cm and whose height is 12 cm.

11) A wine glass is in the shape of an inverted cone. If the rim is 6 cm diameter and its depth 8 cm how much wine will it hold?

12) A wine glass in the shape of an inverted cone has a rim of 5 cm diameter and holds 92ml. What is its depth?

13) A piece of metal in the shape of a square based pyramid with height 10 cm and base side of 5 cm is melted down and re-cast into spheres with diameter of 3mm. How many spheres can be made?

14) Tennis balls of 6 cm diameter are packed into cubic boxes which hold 27. Find   a) the volume of a box   b) the percentage of the box filled by the tennis balls.

15) A measuring cylinder with a base diameter of 3·8 cm contains water. 500 spheres of diameter 5·3 mm are dropped in and completely covered. Calculate the height which the water level rises.

16) A hollow metal sphere has an outside diameter of 10 cm and is 1 cm thick. Find the volume of the metal.

NETS AND SURFACE AREA

Nets

A net is the opened out plan of all the surfaces of a three dimensional shape.

Example 16.5

a.   Cube

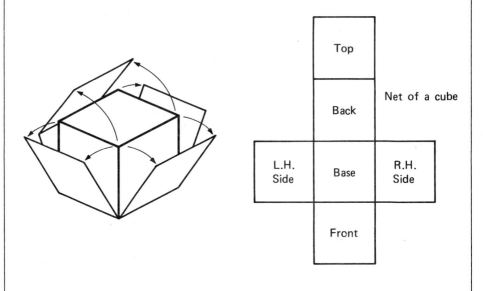

Net of a cube

	Top	
	Back	
L.H. Side	Base	R.H. Side
	Front	

b.   Square based pyramid

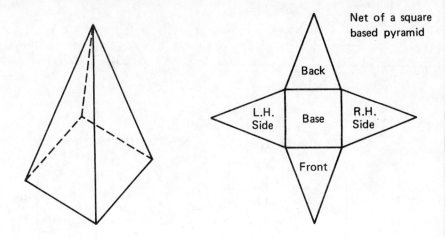

Net of a square based pyramid

c.   Tetrahedron (triangular based pyramid)

EXERCISE 16.4

Draw accurately the nets of the following shapes.

1.   Cuboid

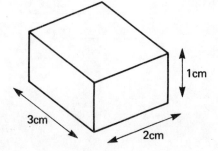

2.   Cube

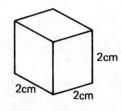

3. Regular tetrahedron with edges of 3cm

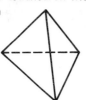

4. Triangular prism

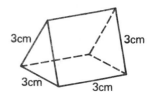

5.
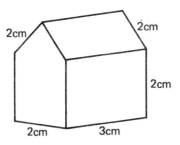

6.
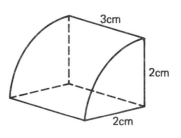

7. Sketch the net of a cube in eight different ways.
8. Sketch the net of a regular tetrahedron in two different ways.

SURFACE AREAS

---

1. **Rectangular block** (cuboid)

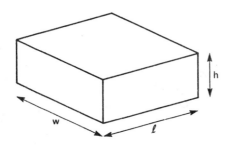

Net

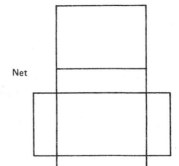

Surface area = 2 wh + 2ℓh + 2ℓw

        Two   Front Top and
        ends   and   bottom
               back

    = 2 (wh + ℓh + ℓw)

2. Cylinder

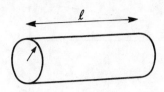

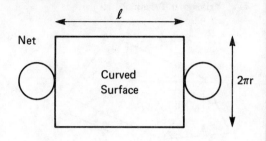

Net

Curved Surface

$2\pi r$

Surface area = area of curved surface + area of 2 ends
$$= 2\pi r \ell + 2\pi r^2$$
$$= 2\pi r \ (\ell + r)$$

3. Cone

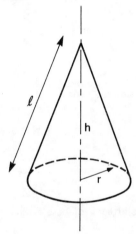

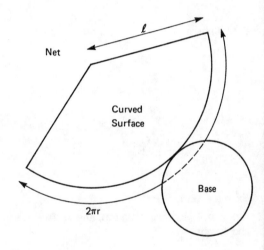

Net

Curved Surface

Base

$2\pi r$

Surface area = area of base + area of curved surface

$$= \pi r^2 + \pi \ell^2 \ \frac{2\pi r}{2\pi \ell} \ \begin{array}{l} \longleftarrow \text{arc length} \\ \longleftarrow \text{Circumference of circle} \end{array}$$

$$= \pi r^2 + \pi r \ell$$
$$= \pi r \ (r + \ell)$$

> curved surface is the area of the sector of the circle radius ℓ

235

4. Triangular Prism

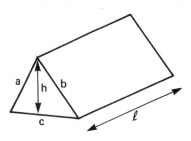
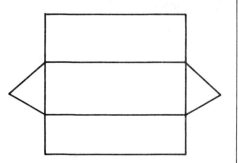

Surface area = area of two triangular ends + area of three rectangular faces
$$= \tfrac{1}{2}(bh) + a\ell + b\ell + c\ell$$
$$= \tfrac{1}{2}bh + \ell\,(a + b + c).$$

5. Sphere

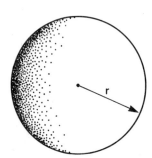

Surface area = $4\pi r^2$

Example 16.6

Find, to 4 significant figures, the surface area of a solid cone of base radius 4 cm and height 7 cm.

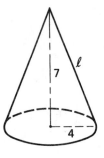

To find the slant height ℓ use Pythagoras theorem
$$\ell^2 = 7^2 + 4^2$$
$$\ell^2 = 49 + 16$$
$$\ell^2 = 65$$
$$\ell = 8.06 \text{ cm}$$

Surface area = $\pi r (r + \ell)$
$$= 3.142 \times 4(4 + 8.06)$$
$$= 3.142 \times 4 \times 12.06$$
$$= 151.6 \text{ cm (to 4 sig figs)}$$

Example 16.7

The ceiling of a church is in the form of a hemisphere. If its radius is 8 metres what is the cost of painting it if a 5 litre tin of paint costs £15·50 and covers 55m^2?

Curved surface area of a hemisphere
$$= \frac{1}{2} \times 4\pi r^2$$
$$= 2 \times 3·142 \times 64$$
$$= 402·176m^2$$

No. of tins required $= \dfrac{402·176}{55} = 7·3$ tins

∴ 8 tins have to be bought

Cost of paint $= 8 \times £15·50 = £124$

EXERCISE 16.5

Find the surface areas of the following shapes (give your answers in appropriate units correct to 4 significant figures)
1. A rectangular block (cuboid) measuring 6 cm wide by 5 cm high by 13 cm long.
2. A rectangular block (cuboid) measuring ·4 m by ·7 m by 1·1 m.
3. A solid cylinder of radius 12 mm and length 5 mm.
4. A solid cylinder of radius 70 mm and length 555 mm.
5. A cone of slant height 9 cm and base radius 4 cm.
6. A cone of height 40 cm and base radius 30 cm.
7. A prism of length 12 cm whose end is in the form of a right angled isosceles triangle having two sides of 4 cm.
8. A prism of length 22 cm whose end is in the form of a right angled triangle having an hypotenuse of 13 cm and a second side of 5 cm.
9.

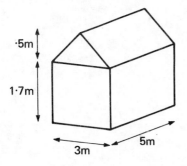

A greenhouse shown in the diagram is to be completely re-glazed. If glass costs £4·50 a square metre calculate the total cost of the glass.

10. A water tank is in the form of a cylinder of 4m diameter and 4m high, open at one end. It is to be made from sheet steel and painted with three coats of paint, both inside and outside. Calculate the amount of steel required and the number of tins of paint if 1 tin is sufficient to cover 28 m².

11. A conical lampshade is to be made from the piece of fabric shown. Calculate the radius of the base of the cone and its height.

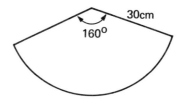

RATIOS OF AREAS AND VOLUMES OF SIMILAR SHAPES

Similar shapes look the same shape but are of a different size.

Ratio of length

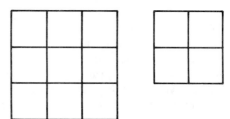

The ratio of these lines is 3:2

The ratio of these areas is 9:4

or $3^2 : 2^2$

i.e. Area ratio is the square of the length ratio

Ratio of volume

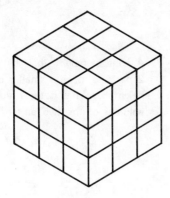 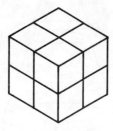

The ratio of these volumes is 27:8
$$\text{or } 3^3 : 2^3$$
i.e. the volume ratio is the cube of the length ratio

Example 16.8

Two hollow cylinders are similar in shape. One is 12 cm tall and the other is 18 cm tall. Find the ratio of (a) the areas of their ends (b) their volumes. If the smaller one has a volume of 1000 cm^2 what is the volume of the larger one?

Length ratio	Small : Large
=	12 : 18
=	2 : 3
Area ratio =	$2^2 : 3^2$
=	4 : 9
Volume ratio =	$2^3 : 3^3$
=	8 : 27

Since volume of smaller cylinder is 1000 cm^3

volume ratio = 1000 : x = 8 : 27

i.e. $\dfrac{x}{1000} = \dfrac{27}{8}$

$$x = \frac{27 \times 1000}{8} = 3375 \text{ cm}^3$$

Example 16.9

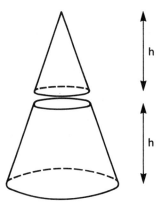

A cone of height 2h is cut into 2 parts to make a smaller cone of height h. What is the ratio of the volumes of the two parts?

The original cone of height 2h and the cone of height h are similar shapes

Ratio of their heights $\quad = \quad$ h : 2h

$\qquad\qquad\qquad = \quad$ 1 : 2

Ratio of their volumes $\quad = \quad 1^3 : 2^3$

$\qquad\qquad\qquad = \quad$ 1 : 8

$\therefore$ Ratio of the two cut parts are 1 : (8 $-$ 1)

$\qquad\qquad\qquad\qquad = \quad$ 1 : 7

Example 16.10

Two similar blocks of metal made from the same material have total surface areas of 25 and 64 cm. If the smaller one weighs 30 grams, what is the weight of the larger one?

Ratio of areas $\quad = \quad$ 25 : 64

Ratio of lengths $\quad = \quad \sqrt{25}$: $\sqrt{64}$

$\qquad\qquad\quad = \quad$ 5 : 8

Ratio of volumes $\quad = \quad 5^3 : 8^3$

$\qquad\qquad\quad = \quad$ 125 : 512

But since volume is directly proportional to weight (mass) then

$$\frac{512}{125} = \frac{x}{100} \quad \text{where x is the mass of the larger block}$$

$$x = \frac{512 \times 100}{125}$$

$$x = 409 \cdot 5 \text{ grams}$$

EXERCISE 16.6

1. Two similar blocks have corresponding sides of 3 cm and 6 cm. Find the ratio of their volumes.
2. Two similar triangular prisms have lengths of 12 cm and 15 cm. Find the ratio of their volumes.
3. Two similar cylinders have lengths of 50 cm and 75 cm. Find the ratios of
   a) the areas of their circular ends   b) their volumes
4. Two similar chocolate packages are in the shape of a triangular prism. One is 25 cm in length and the other 20 cm. Show that the larger package holds approximately twice as much chocolate as the smaller one.
5. A cylindrical can of height 30 cm holds one litre of orange juice. What height, to the nearest mm must a similar can be if it holds 500 ml?
6. A sauce bottle is 20 cm tall and holds 600 grams. How much to the nearest gram does a similar bottle 15 cm tall hold?
7. A model lorry is made to scale of 1 : 10. If the lorry can hold 24 m^3 what is the capacity of the model?
8. Two similar corn flakes packets have widths of 25 cm and 20 cm. Cornflakes are sold in packets of 750 g, 500 g and 350 g. If the 25 cm packet holds 750 g how much does the 20 cm packet hold?
9. Two similar boxes have lids with areas of 81 cm^2 and 225 cm^2. What is the ratio of their volumes?
10. A ball has a diameter of 8 cm and weighs 200 grams. Find the weight of a ball of 10 cm diameter made from the same material.

TRIGONOMETRY

TRIGONOMETRY

Calculating sides and angles of triangles

Trigonometric ratios
In a right angled triangle the side opposite a given angle is called the **opposite** side. The side opposite the right angle is called the **hypotenuse**. The side between these sides is called the **adjacent** side.

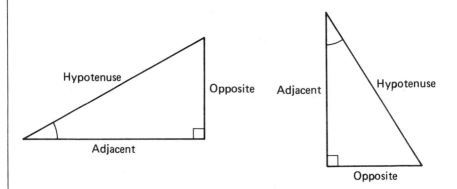

The sine of an angle
In a right angled triangle the ratio of the sides $\dfrac{\text{opposite}}{\text{hypotenuse}}$ is called the sine (sin) of the angle.

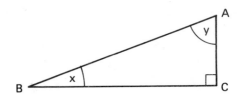

$$\text{Sin } x = \frac{AC}{AB} \qquad \text{Sin } y = \frac{BC}{AB}$$

To find the sine of an angle by using a calculator
a)   ensure it is in the 'degree' mode
b)   press in the angle
c)   press the SIN button
Example — to find the sine of $36\cdot4^{\circ}$ press the following buttons ⒊ ⒍ . ⒋ SIN this gives a display of $0\cdot5934188$ which can be rounded off to $0\cdot5934$ if necessary.

To find an angle given its sine by using a calculator

a)   ensure it is in the 'degree' mode

b)   press in the sine value

c)   press the $\boxed{\text{SIN}^{-1}}$ button (this may involve pressing the 2nd function button first)

Example — to find the angle whose sine is 0·4156 press the following buttons $\boxed{\cdot}\ \boxed{4}\ \boxed{1}\ \boxed{5}\ \boxed{6}\ \boxed{\text{SIN}^{-1}}$ this gives a display of 24·557107 which should be rounded off to 1 decimal place i.e. 24·6°.

Example 17.1

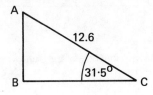

Find the length of side AB

$$\frac{AB}{12\cdot 6} = \sin 31\cdot5°$$

∴   AB = 12·6 × sin 31·5°

AB = 12·6 × 0·5225

AB = 6·58 cm   (to 2 d.p.)

Example 17.2

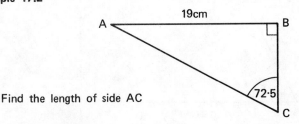

Find the length of side AC

$$\text{Sin } 72\cdot5° = \frac{19}{AC}$$

$$0\cdot9537 = \frac{19}{AC}$$

AC × 0·9537 = 19

∴ $AC = \dfrac{19}{0\cdot9537} = 19\cdot92$ cm   (to 2 d.p.)

Example 17.3

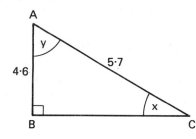

Find the sizes of angles x and y

$$\text{Sine } x = \frac{AB}{AC} = \frac{4 \cdot 6}{5 \cdot 7} = 0 \cdot 8070 \quad \text{(to 4 d.p.)}$$

$\therefore$ angle $x = 53 \cdot 8^\circ$ (to 1 d.p.)

      angle $y = 90 - 53 \cdot 8^\circ = 36 \cdot 2^\circ$

EXERCISE 17.1

1.   Find the length of the unknown side (x) in the following triangles

a)

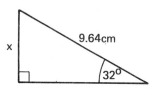

b)

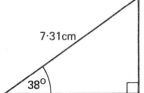

c)

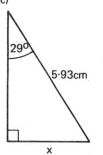

d)

e)

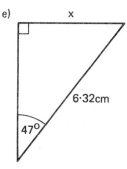

2.   Find the length of the unknown side (x) in the following triangles

a)

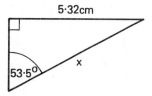

b)

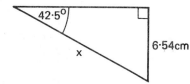

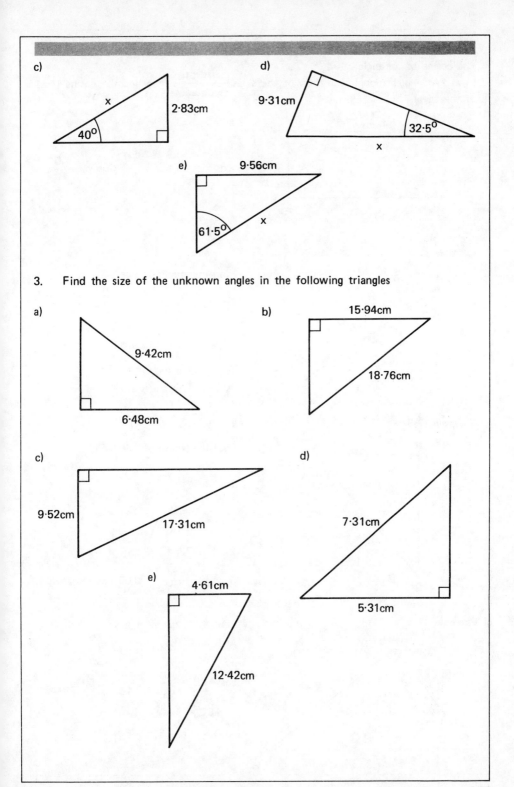

c)

x

2·83cm

40°

d)

9·31cm

32·5°

x

e)

9·56cm

61·5°

x

3. Find the size of the unknown angles in the following triangles

a)

9·42cm

6·48cm

b)

15·94cm

18·76cm

c)

9·52cm

17·31cm

d)

7·31cm

5·31cm

e)

4·61cm

12·42cm

The cosine of an angle

In a right angles triangle the ratio of the sides $\dfrac{\text{adjacent}}{\text{hypotenuse}}$ is called the cosine (cos) of the angle.

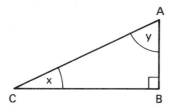

$$\text{Cos } x = \frac{BC}{AC} \qquad\qquad \text{Cos } y = \frac{AB}{AC}$$

Example 17.4

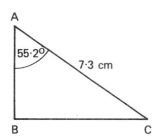

Find the length of side AB

$$\frac{AB}{AC} = \cos 55 \cdot 2^0$$

$$\frac{AB}{7 \cdot 3} = 0 \cdot 5707 \quad \text{(to 4 d.p.)}$$

$$AB = 7 \cdot 3 \times 0 \cdot 5707$$

$$AB = 4 \cdot 17 \text{ cm (to 2 d.p.)}.$$

Example 17.5

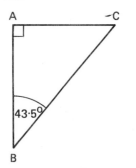

Find the length of side CB

$$\cos 43 \cdot 5^0 = \frac{AB}{BC}$$

$$0 \cdot 7254 = \frac{6 \cdot 58}{BC}$$

$$BC \times 0 \cdot 7254 = 6 \cdot 58$$

$$\therefore BC = \frac{6 \cdot 58}{0 \cdot 7254} = 9 \cdot 07 \text{ cm (to 2 d.p.)}$$

Example 17.6

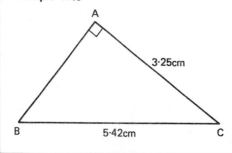

Find the sizes of angles
$A\hat{C}B$ and $A\hat{B}C$

$$\cos A\hat{C}B = \frac{AC}{BC} = \frac{3 \cdot 25}{5 \cdot 42} = 0 \cdot 5996$$

$$\therefore A\hat{C}B = 53 \cdot 2^0 \quad \text{(to 1 d.p.)}$$

$$ABC = 90 - 53 \cdot 2^0 = \underline{36 \cdot 8^0}$$

EXERCISE 17.2

1. Find the length of the unknown side (x) in the following triangles

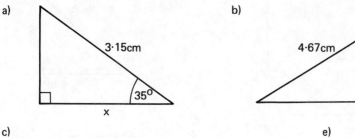

a)

3·15cm
35°
x

b)

4·67cm
62°
x

c)

2·41cm
51·5°
x

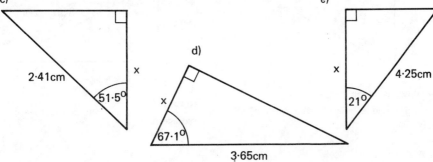

d)

x
67·1°
3·65cm

e)

x
21°
4·25cm

2. Find the length of the hypotenuse in each of the following

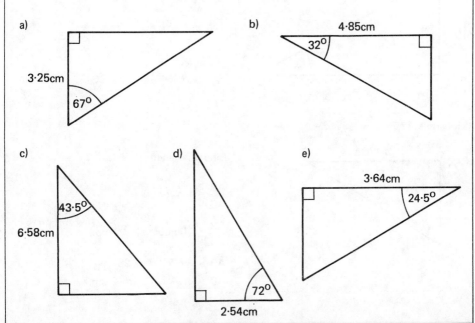

a)

3·25cm
67°

b)

4·85cm
32°

c)

43·5°
6·58cm

d)

72°
2·54cm

e)

3·64cm
24·5°

3. Find the sizes of the two unknown angles in each of the following triangles.

a)

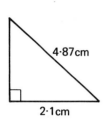

4·87cm

2·1cm

b)

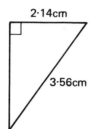

2·14cm

3·56cm

c)

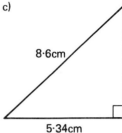

8·6cm

5·34cm

d)

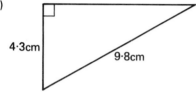

4·3cm

9·8cm

e)

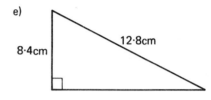

12·8cm

8·4cm

The tangent of an angle

In a right angled triangle the ratio of the sides $\dfrac{\text{opposite}}{\text{adjacent}}$ is called the tangent (tan) of the angle

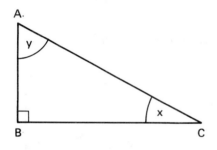

$$\text{Tan } x = \frac{AB}{BC} \qquad \text{Tan } y = \frac{BC}{AB}$$

Example 17.7

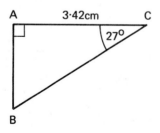

A   3·42cm   C

27°

B

Find the length of side AB

$$\frac{AB}{AC} = \tan 27°$$

$$\frac{AB}{3·42} = 0·5095 \quad \text{(to 4 d.p.)}$$

$$AB = 3·42 \times 0·5095$$

$$\underline{AB = 1·74 \text{ cm}} \quad \text{(to 2 d.p.)}$$

Example 17.8

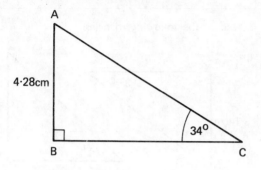

Find the length of side BC

$$\text{Tan } 34^o = \frac{AB}{BC}$$

$$0{\cdot}6745 = \frac{4{\cdot}28}{BC}$$

$$BC \times 0{\cdot}6745 = 4{\cdot}28$$

$$BC = \frac{4{\cdot}28}{0{\cdot}6745} = \underline{6{\cdot}35} \quad \text{(to 2 d.p.)}$$

Alternatively this can be done more easily by using the angle BAC

i.e. $\dfrac{BC}{AB} = \tan 56^o$

$$\frac{BC}{4{\cdot}28} = 1{\cdot}4826$$

$$BC = 1{\cdot}4826 \times 4{\cdot}28$$

$$BC = \underline{6{\cdot}35} \text{ cm} \quad \text{(to 2 d.p.)}$$

Example 17.9

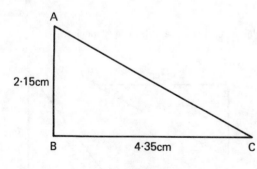

Find the angle BAC and ACB

$$\text{Tan } B\hat{A}C = \frac{4{\cdot}35}{2{\cdot}15} = 2{\cdot}0233$$

$$\therefore \ \underline{B\hat{A}C = 63{\cdot}7^o}$$

EXERCISE 17.3

1. Find the unknown side (x) in each of the following triangles.

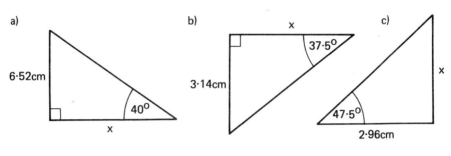

a)

6·52cm

40°

x

b)

x

37·5°

3·14cm

c)

x

47·5°

2·96cm

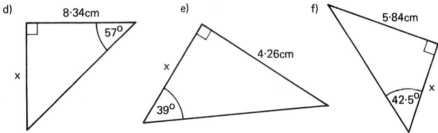

d)

8·34cm

57°

x

e)

4·26cm

x

39°

f)

5·84cm

42·5°

x

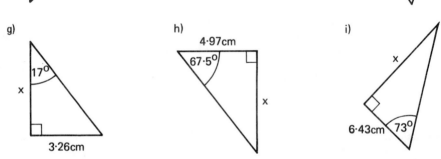

g)

17°

x

3·26cm

h)

4·97cm

67·5°

x

i)

x

6·43cm

73°

2. Find the two unknown angles in each of the following triangles.

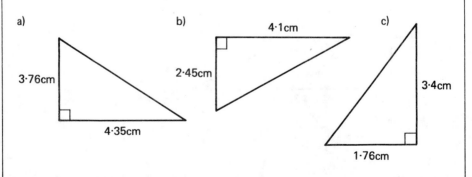

a)

3·76cm

4·35cm

b)

4·1cm

2·45cm

c)

3·4cm

1·76cm

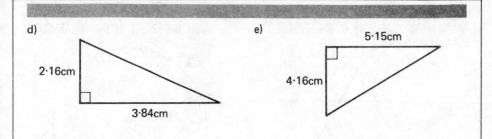

d) 2·16cm 3·84cm

e) 5·15cm 4·16cm

EXERCISE 17.4 (Mixed)

Solve each of the following by using the sine, cosine or tangent ratio.

1. Find the length of side x.

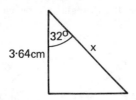

3·64cm 32° x

2. Find the length of side x.

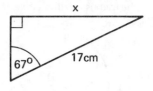

x 67° 17cm

3. Find the two unknown angles

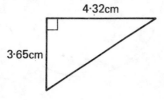

4·32cm 3·65cm

4. Find the length of side x.

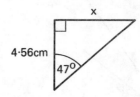

x 4·56cm 47°

5. Find the two unknown angles

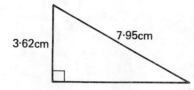

3·62cm 7·95cm

6. Find the two unknown angles

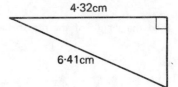

4·32cm 6·41cm

7. Find the height of this isosceles triangle

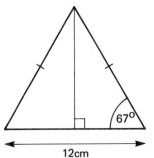

67°

12cm

8. Find the length of the chord AB

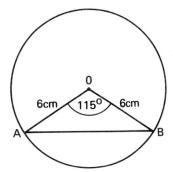

6cm 115° 6cm

A B

9. Find the radius of this circle if OB is 7 cm.

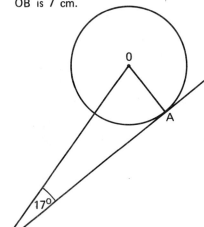

0

A

17°

B

10. Find the diameter of the circle.

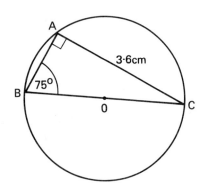

A

3·6cm

B 75°

0 C

11. Find the length of the major diagonal BD in this kite.

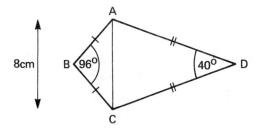

A

8cm B 96° 40° D

C

12. Given that the sides of this rhombus are 8cm, find the lengths of the two diagonals.

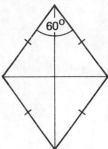

13. Calculate the angles of this isosceles triangle.

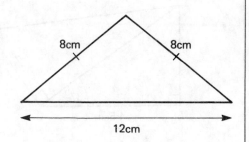

14. Find the length of chord AB and the radius of the circle.

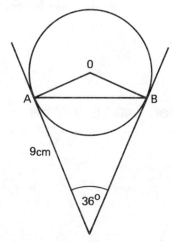

15. The rhombus has an exterior angle of 60° as shown. If the minor diagonal is 8 cm, find the length of each side.

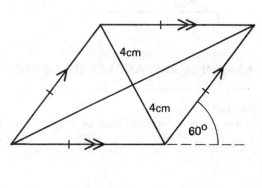

16. Find the length of the longer side of this parallelogram.

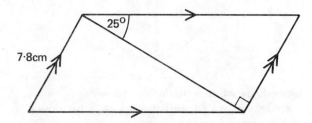

255

17. Find the length of the chord of a circle of radius 10 cm which subtends an angle of 110° at the centre.

18.

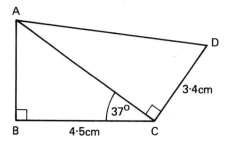

Find the length of side AD

19.

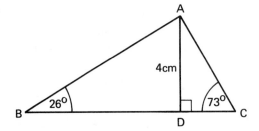

Find the length of side BC

BEARINGS AND ANGLES OF DEPRESSION AND ELEVATION

Bearings

A bearing is a direction given by the points of the compass

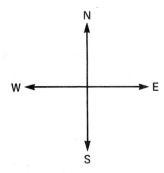

There are two methods by which a bearing can be written
a)   by using the points of the compass that are on either side of it
b)   by measuring clockwise from due north

Example 17.10

1) Between North and East

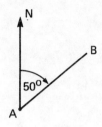

The bearing of B from A is
a)   N 50° E
b)   050°

2) Between East and South

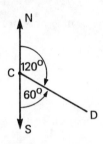

The bearing of D from C is
a)   S 60° E
b)   120°

3) Between South and West

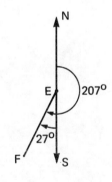

The bearing of F from E is
a)   S 27° W
b)   207°

4) Between West and North

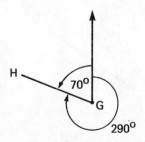

The bearing of H from G is
a)   N 70° W
b)   290°

5) If the bearing of A from B is 037° (N37°E) what is the bearing of B from A?

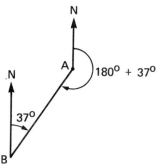

The bearing of B from A is 180° different from the bearing of A from B. i.e. the bearing of B from A is 217° or S 37° E.

EXERCISE 17.5

1. By measuring, write down the bearings of B from A in each of the following diagrams.

a)

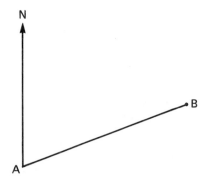

b)

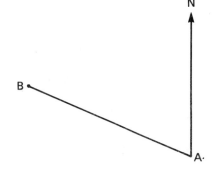

c)

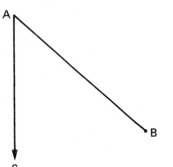

d)

258

e)
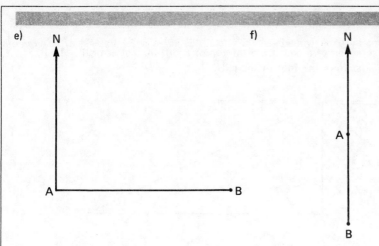

f)

2. In each of the diagrams in question 1 say what the bearing of A from B is.

Angle of Depression

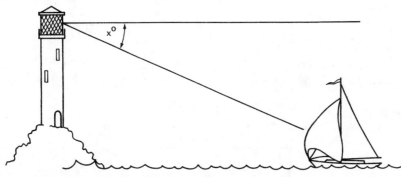

The **angle of depression** of the boat from the lighthouse is x°.

Angle of elevation

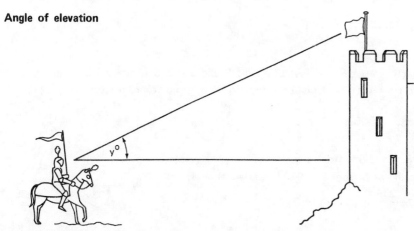

The **angle of elevation** of the flag from the knight is y°.

Example 17.11

The angle of depression of a boat from the top of a cliff 30 metres high is 17·1°. How far is the boat from the foot of the cliff?

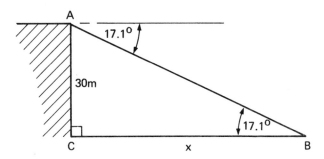

In triangle ABC, $A\hat{B}C$ is equal to the angle of depression

$$\therefore \ \text{Tan } 17\cdot1° = \frac{30}{x} \quad \text{or} \quad \text{Tan } (90 - 17\cdot1) = \frac{x}{30} = \tan 72\cdot9°$$

$$\frac{x}{30} = 3\cdot2506$$

$$x = 3\cdot2506 \times 30$$

$$x = 97\cdot52 \text{ metres} \ \text{(to 2 d.p.)}$$

Example 17.12

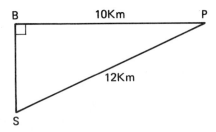

A boat B is 10 km due west of a port P and a ship S is due south of the boat and 12 km from port. Calculate the bearing of the ship from the port.

$$\text{Cos } B\hat{P}S = \frac{10}{12} = 0\cdot8333$$

$$\therefore \ B\hat{P}S = 33\cdot6° \ \text{(to 1 d.p.)}$$

$\therefore$ bearing of S from P is 270° (due west) − 33·6°

$$= 236\cdot4°$$

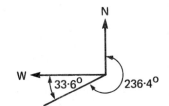

EXERCISE 17.6

1.

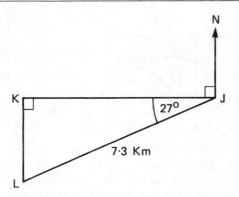

Point K is due west of J and L is due south of K. a) Write down the bearing of L from J. b) Calculate the distance KL correct to the nearest 10 metres.

2.

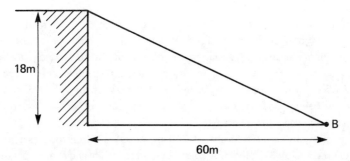

A boat is 60 m from the foot of a cliff 18 m high. Calculate the angle of elevation from the boat to the top of the cliff.

3. A radio mast AB is 25 m high. It is supported by a wire (BC) of length 29 metres. Calculate the angle of Elevation of the top of the mast from the bottom of the wire.

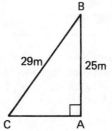

4. A boat, A, leaves port and steams due north for 9 km. At the same time a boat, B, travels 13 km due east. Find the bearing a) of A from B and b) B from A when at these positions.

5. A boat observes a lighthouse on the top of a cliff 55 m high. If the angle of elevation of the lighthouse from the boat is 16·2° how far is the boat from the foot of the cliff?

6.

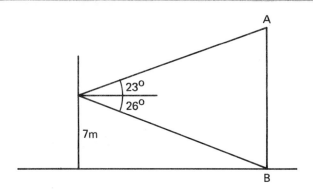

A building, AB, is observed across a street from the window of a house 7 m above the ground. If the angle of elevation of the top of the building is 23° and the angle of depression of the foot of the building is 26°, how high is the building?

7. A ship, S, travels 3 km due North from a port (P) and then travels 4½ km due east. Calculate a) its bearing from the port b) the bearing of the port from the ship.

8. A tower 30 m high stands on top of a 40 m high cliff. A man at the bottom of the tower observes a boat out at sea at an angle of depression of 21°. Find the angle of elevation of the top of the tower from the boat.

9. Two boats are sighted out at sea by an observer standing on the top of a cliff 35 m high. Boat A has an angle of depression of 25° and boat B, directly behind boat A, has an angle of depression of 17°. Find the distance between the two boats.

10. An aircraft, flying at a height of 200 m, observes a boat due east at an angle of depression of 37° and the coast, due west, at an angle of depression of 26°. How far is the boat from the coast?

PYTHAGORAS' THEOREM

This is used to calculate the length of one side of a right angled triangle given two other sides. Expressed formally "In any right angled triangle, the square on the hypotenuse is equal to the sum of the squares on the other two sides."

i.e.

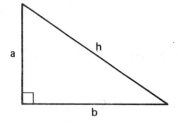

$h^2 = a^2 + b^2$
To find sides a or b this formula is rearranged thus
$a^2 = h^2 - b^2$ or $b^2 = h^2 - a^2$

Example 17.13

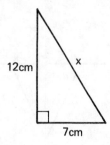

Find the length of the hypotenuse x.

$x^2 = 12^2 + 7^2$

$x^2 = 144 + 49$

$x^2 = 193$

$x = \sqrt{193} = 13.89$ cm   (to 2 decimal places)

It is important to remember triangles with sides of 3, 4 and 5

5, 12 and 13

7, 24 and 25 and multiples

of these. These are known as 'Pythagorean triples'. The use of Pythagoras' theorem appears in many problems and is therefore very useful.

Such problems may involve

a.

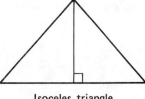

Isoceles triangle

b.

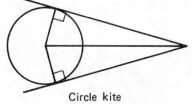

Circle kite

c.

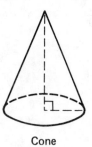

Cone

d.

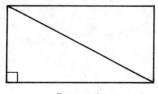

Rectangle

e.

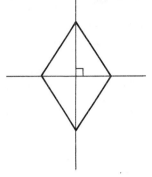

Rhombus

f.

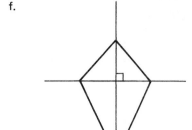

Kite

g.

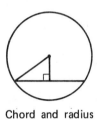

Chord and radius

h.

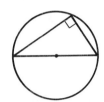

Angle in a semi-circle

Example 17.14

Find, correct to 3 significant figures, the height of a cone with base diameter of 40 cm and slant height of 50 cm.

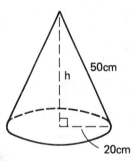

50cm

h

20cm

$$h^2 = 50^2 - 20^2$$
$$h^2 = 2500 - 400$$
$$h^2 = 2100$$
$$h = \sqrt{2100}$$
$$h = \underline{45{\cdot}8 \text{ cm}}$$

EXERCISE 17.7

1. Find the length of the hypotenuse in each of the following triangles.

a.

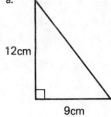

12cm

9cm

b.

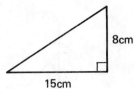

8cm

15cm

c.

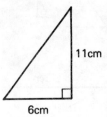

11cm

6cm

2. Find the length of the side marked x in each of the following triangles.

a.

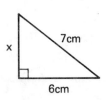

x   7cm

6cm

b.

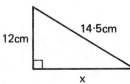

14·5cm

12cm

x

c.

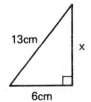

13cm

x

6cm

d.

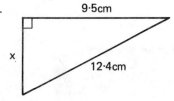

9·5cm

x

12·4cm

3. Use the Pythagorean triples 3, 4, 5; 5, 12, 13; or 7, 24, 25 to solve these triangles.

a.

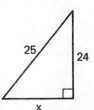

25   24

x

b.

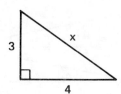

x

3

4

c.

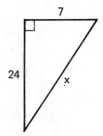

7

24

x

265

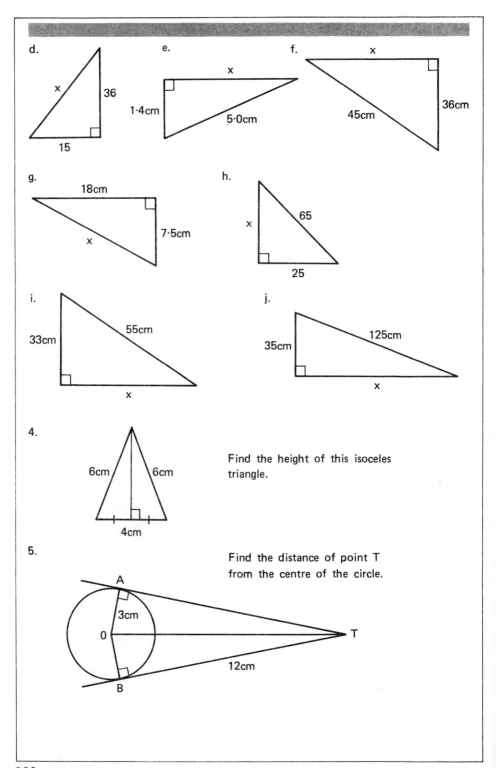

d.

x, 36, 15

e.

x, 1·4cm, 5·0cm

f.

x, 45cm, 36cm

g.

18cm, 7·5cm, x

h.

65, x, 25

i.

33cm, 55cm, x

j.

35cm, 125cm, x

4.

6cm, 6cm, 4cm

Find the height of this isoceles triangle.

5.

Find the distance of point T from the centre of the circle.

A, 3cm, 0, T, 12cm, B

6.

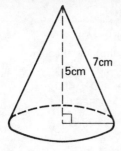

Find the base radius of a cone of height 5 cm and a slant height of 7 cm

7. Find the length of the diagonal of a rectangle measuring 9 cm by 12 cm.

8. A rhombus has diagonals of 7 cm and 4 cm. Find the length of its sides.

9. A square has a side of 7 cm. Find the length of its diagonals.

10. How far from the centre of a circle of radius 7 cm is a chord of length 7 cm.

11.

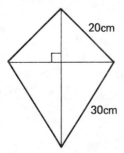

A kite has sides measuring 20 cm and 30 cm with the small diagonal measuring 28 cm. Find the length of the longer diagonal.

---

3 DIMENSIONAL PROBLEMS

Example 17.15

The diagram shows a square based right pyramid (a). If the base edges are 20 cm, find the length of the diagonal AB. (b) If the angle VBA is 55°, calculate the height VC.

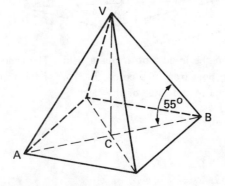

(a)

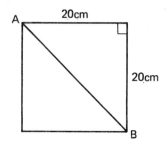

Length of AB
By pythagoras theorem
$AB^2 = 20^2 + 20^2$
$AB^2 = 400 + 400$
$AB = \sqrt{800}$
$AB = 28 \cdot 28$ cm

(b) Considering triangle VCB

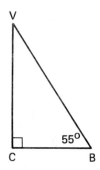

BC = ½ of AB = 14·14 cm
$\text{Tan } 55^\circ = \dfrac{VC}{14 \cdot 14}$

$1 \cdot 428 = \dfrac{VC}{14 \cdot 14}$

$\therefore VC = 1 \cdot 428 \times 14 \cdot 14$
$= 20 \cdot 19$ cm (to 2 d.p.)

EXERCISE 17.8

1. The height of a square based pyramid is 2 m and the sides of its base are 3 m. Calculate the length of each sloping edge.

2.

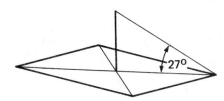

A flagpole stands in the middle of a square field. The angle of elevation of the top of the flag pole from one corner is 27°. If the flagpole is 12 metres high find the lengths of the sides of the field.

3.

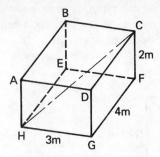

The diagram shows a box with vertices ABCDEFGH. Calculate the length of
(a) the diagonal of the base, HF and
(b) the diagonal of the box HC.

4. An air balloon is 200 m above the ground, immediately above one corner of a rectangular field. The angles of elevation of the balloon when viewed from A and B are 18° and 32°. Calculate the length AB of field.

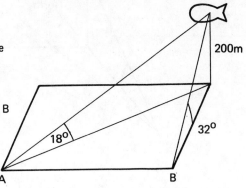

5.

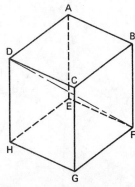

Find the length of the diagonal DF of the cube shown if its sides are each 1 metre square.

6. A radio mast is due east of an observer A and 150 metres away. Another observer, B, stands due north of A on level ground. If the angle of elevation of the top of the mast from B is 28° and the bearing of the mast is 132° from B, find the height of the mast.

7.

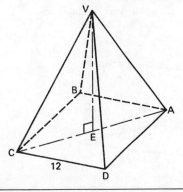

The diagram shows a pyramid with a rectangular base ABCD and vertex V. The diagonals of the base meet at E and EV is perpendicular to the base. If EV = 20 cm, BD = 15 cm and CD = 12 cm, calculate a) BC
b) VA   c) the angle CVA.

8. An aircraft, flying at a height of 3000 metres, is due north of an observer who measures the angle of elevation of the aircraft to be 24°. Later, when the aircraft has travelled due east, maintaining its height, the angle of elevation is 20°. Calculate the distance travelled by the aircraft and its bearing from the observer.

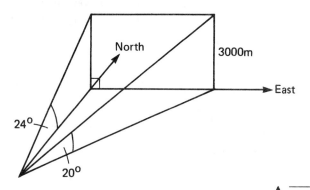

9. A block of wood is made by cutting the top off a pyramid as shown in the diagram parallel to the base. If the height of the block is 6 cm, find the angle between the edge CG and the base, and the length of the edge CG

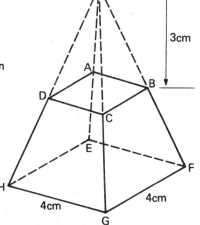

10. The roof of a building is in the shape of a triangular prism. Calculate
   a) the length of BC   b) the angle BFC

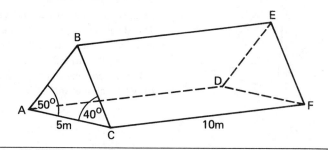

SOLUTIONS TO TRIANGLES WITHOUT RIGHT ANGLES

(a)   **Sine rule**

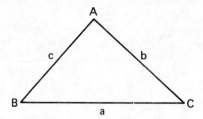

The angles A, B and C and the sides a, b and c are related by

$$\frac{a}{\text{Sin A}} = \frac{b}{\text{Sin B}} = \frac{c}{\text{Sin C}} \qquad \ldots\ldots\ldots\ldots (1)$$

$$\text{or} \quad \frac{\text{Sin A}}{a} = \frac{\text{Sin B}}{b} = \frac{\text{Sin C}}{c} \qquad \ldots\ldots\ldots\ldots (2)$$

This rule is used in the first form when a side is to be found and in the second form when an angle is to be found

Example 17.16

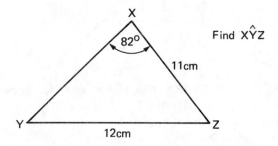

Find $X\hat{Y}Z$

$$\frac{\text{Sin } X\hat{Y}Z}{11} = \frac{\text{Sin } 82^\circ}{12}$$

$$\frac{\text{Sin } X\hat{Y}Z}{11} = \frac{\cdot 9903}{12}$$

$$\text{Sin } X\hat{Y}Z = \frac{\cdot 9903 \times 11}{12} = \cdot 9077$$

$$\therefore X\hat{Y}Z = 65 \cdot 20^\circ$$

Example 17.17 (Obtuse angle)

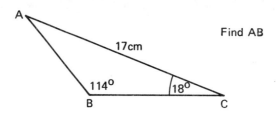

Find AB

$$\frac{AB}{\text{Sin } 18^O} = \frac{17}{\text{Sin } 114^O}$$

$$\frac{AB}{\cdot3030} = \frac{17}{\cdot8910}$$

$$AB = \frac{17 \times \cdot3030}{\cdot8910} = 5\cdot78 \text{ cm} \quad \text{(to two decimal places)}$$

(b) **Cosine rule**

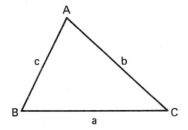

(I) **To find the third side of a triangle given two sides and their included angle.**

The general form is given by
$$a^2 = b^2 + c^2 - 2bc \text{ Cos A}$$
but this can be applied to the other sides as follows
$$b^2 = a^2 + c^2 - 2ac \text{ Cos B}$$
and $c^2 = a^2 + b^2 - 2ab \text{ Cos C}$

Example 17.18

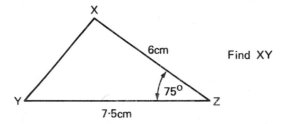

Find XY

$XY^2 = 7 \cdot 5^2 + 6^2 - 2 \times 7 \cdot 5 \times 6 \times Cos\ 75^o$

$XY^2 = 56 \cdot 25 + 36 - (90 \times \cdot 2588)$ ◄—— Note – do the subtraction last

$XY^2 = 92 \cdot 25 - 23 \cdot 294$

$XY^2 = 68 \cdot 956$

$XY = \sqrt{68 \cdot 956} = \underline{8 \cdot 30}$ (to 2 decimal places)

Example 17.19 (Obtuse angle)

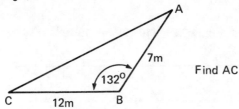

Find AC

$AC^2 = 12^2 + 7^2 - 2 \times 12 \times 7 \times Cos\ 132^o$

$AC^2 = 144 + 49 - (168 \times (-0 \cdot 6691))$

$AC^2 = 193 + 112 \cdot 409$ ◄—— Notice the sign change due to the obtuse angle

$AC^2 = 305 \cdot 41$

$AC = \sqrt{305 \cdot 41} = \underline{17 \cdot 48m}$ (to 2 decimal places)

(II) **To find an angle when three sides of a triangle are known.**

The general form $a^2 = b^2 + c^2 - 2bc\ Cos\ A$ can be re-arranged to form

$$Cos\ A = \frac{b^2 + c^2 - a^2}{2bc}$$

Example 17.20

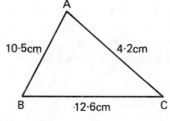

Find the three angles

(I) $\quad Cos\ A\hat{C}B = \dfrac{4 \cdot 2^2 + 12 \cdot 6^2 - 10 \cdot 5^2}{2 \times 4 \cdot 2 \times 12 \cdot 6}$

$\quad Cos\ A\hat{C}B = \dfrac{17 \cdot 64 + 158 \cdot 76 - 110 \cdot 25}{105 \cdot 84}$

$\quad Cos\ A\hat{C}B = \dfrac{66 \cdot 15}{105 \cdot 84} = \cdot 6250$

$\therefore \quad A\hat{C}B = 51 \cdot 32^o$

(II) $\text{Cos B}\hat{\text{A}}\text{C} = \dfrac{10\cdot5^2 + 4\cdot2^2 - 12\cdot6^2}{2 \times 10\cdot5 \times 4\cdot2}$

$\text{Cos B}\hat{\text{A}}\text{C} = \dfrac{110\cdot25 + 17\cdot64 - 158\cdot76}{88\cdot2}$

$\text{Cos B}\hat{\text{A}}\text{C} = \dfrac{30\cdot87}{88\cdot2} = -0\cdot35$

$\therefore \quad \text{B}\hat{\text{A}}\text{C} = 110\cdot49^\circ$

> Notice the negative Cosine gives an obtuse angle

(III) $\text{A}\hat{\text{B}}\text{C} = 180^\circ - (51\cdot32 + 110\cdot49) = 18\cdot19^\circ$

EXERCISE 17.9

Use the Sine rule to find the remaining sides and angles in the triangles in questions 1 to 6.

1. $\text{A}\hat{\text{B}}\text{C} = 61^\circ$, $\text{B}\hat{\text{A}}\text{C} = 46^\circ$ and AC = 4 cm
2. $\text{J}\hat{\text{K}}\text{L} = 49^\circ$, $\text{K}\hat{\text{J}}\text{L} = 57^\circ$ and JL = 6 cm
3. $\text{X}\hat{\text{Z}}\text{Y} = 43^\circ$, XY = 17 cm and XZ = 21 cm
4. $\text{S}\hat{\text{T}}\text{U} = 57^\circ$, SU = 12 cm and ST = 10 cm
5. $\text{P}\hat{\text{R}}\text{Q} = 110^\circ$, PQ = 13·5 cm and PR = 7·3 cm
6. $\text{D}\hat{\text{E}}\text{F} = 116^\circ$, DF = 12 cm and DE = 6cm

Use the Cosine rule to help find the remaining sides and angles in questions 7 to 12
7. $\text{A}\hat{\text{B}}\text{C} = 46^\circ$, AB = 3·5 cm and BC = 2·1 cm
8. $\text{D}\hat{\text{E}}\text{F} = 72^\circ$, DE = 17m and EF = 20m
9. $\text{X}\hat{\text{Y}}\text{Z} = 106^\circ$, YZ = 7·3m and XY = 6·2m
10. $\text{J}\hat{\text{K}}\text{L} = 120^\circ$, JK = 9cm and KL = 6cm
11. PQ = 6·3m, QR = 4·5m and RP = 7·4m
12. AB = 2·9 cm, BC = 5·6 cm and AC = 3·6 cm

13.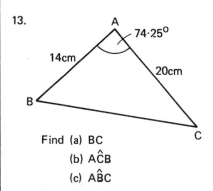

Find (a) BC
    (b) A$\hat{\text{C}}$B
    (c) A$\hat{\text{B}}$C

14.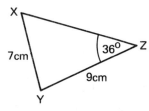

Find (a) Y$\hat{\text{X}}$Z
    (b) X$\hat{\text{Y}}$Z
    (c) XZ

15.

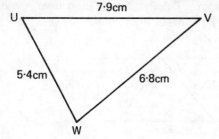

Find the sizes of three angles of this triangle

16.

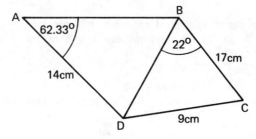

Use the Sine rule to find all angles and lengths in the above figure.

17.

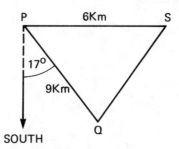

The diagram shows the position of a port P and a ship 6km due east of it. Another ship Q is 9km from P on a bearing of South 17° East. Find the distance between the two ships, to the nearest ten metres.

18.

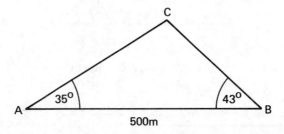

A straight length of motorway AB is 500 metres long. A church, C, is observed from A at an angle of 35° to the motorway and from B an angle of

43° (as shown on the diagram). Calculate its distances from A and B. Also calculate the shortest distance between it and the motorway.

19.

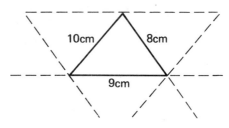

The diagram shows a series of congruent triangles used in the making of a patchwork design. If the sides measure 8cm, 9cm, and 10cm calculate its angles.

20. A rosebed is made in the corner of a garden where two walls meet at 117°, as shown in the diagram. Calculate the length of path AB.

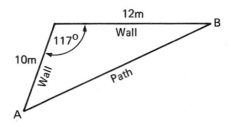

(c) **Area of a triangle**

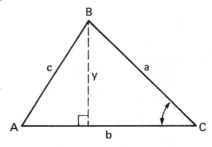

Area of triangle = ½ base × perpendicular height
                  = ½by
but y = a Sin C
∴ Area of triangle = ½ ab Sin C ⟵ Note: two sides and included angle

Example 17.21

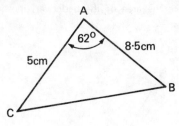

Area = ½ ab Sin C
  = ½ × 5 × 8·5 × Sin 62°
  = 21·25 × ·8829
  = 18·76 cm

EXERCISE 17.10

Find the areas of the triangles in questions 1 to 5

1. $A\hat{B}C = 57°$, AB = 5cm and BC = 7cm
2. $X\hat{Y}Z = 73°$, XY = 8·2cm and YZ = 12·3cm
3. $C\hat{D}E = 108°$, CD = 5·4cm and DE = 8·3cm
4. $P\hat{Q}R = 120°$, PQ = 7·3cm and QR = 8·5cm
5. $R\hat{S}T = 53·33°$, RS = 19·5cm and ST = 15cm

6.

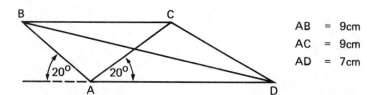

AB = 9cm
AC = 9cm
AD = 7cm

By using the sine rule show that the area of triangle ACD is equal to the area of triangle ABD

7.

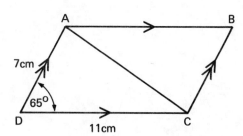

By finding the area of triangle ADC find the area of the parallelogram ABCD

8.   A patchwork bedcover is to be made from 300 pieces of fabric cut into the
      shape of the triangle shown. Calculate the area of the bedcover, in square
      metres correct to three decimal places.

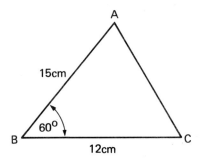

MATRICES

MATRICES

A matrix is a rectangular array of numbers. It is used to store information which can be used to solve a mathematical problem.

Order of matrix — this is the number of rows (r) and the number of columns (c) the matrix has.

$$\begin{pmatrix} 1 & 4 & 3 \\ 1 & 2 & 5 \end{pmatrix}$$ this is a 2 by 3 matrix   (2 × 3)

$$\begin{pmatrix} 1 \\ 3 \end{pmatrix}$$ this is a column matrix. Its order is 2 by 1   (2 × 1)

$$\begin{pmatrix} 5 & 1 & 2 & 3 \end{pmatrix}$$ this is a row matrix. Its order is 1 by 4   (1 × 4)

$$\begin{pmatrix} 3 & 5 \\ 4 & 2 \end{pmatrix}$$ this is a square matrix of order 2 by 2   (2 × 2)

$$\begin{pmatrix} 0 & 0 \\ 0 & 0 \end{pmatrix}$$ this is a null matrix as all its numbers are zero

Addition of matrices

Matrices of the same order can be added together by adding corresponding elements.

e.g. $\begin{pmatrix} 5 & 4 \\ 3 & 1 \end{pmatrix} + \begin{pmatrix} 3 & 2 \\ 4 & 1 \end{pmatrix} = \begin{pmatrix} 5+3 & 4+2 \\ 3+4 & 1+1 \end{pmatrix} = \begin{pmatrix} 8 & 6 \\ 7 & 2 \end{pmatrix}$

$\begin{pmatrix} 4 & 3 \\ -1 & 3 \end{pmatrix} - \begin{pmatrix} 2 & -3 \\ 4 & 1 \end{pmatrix} = \begin{pmatrix} 4-2 & 3-(-3) \\ -1-4 & 3-1 \end{pmatrix} = \begin{pmatrix} 2 & 6 \\ -5 & 2 \end{pmatrix}$

Multiplication of matrices

Multiplication by a scalar

$3\begin{pmatrix} 2 & 4 \\ 1 & 3 \end{pmatrix} = \begin{pmatrix} 3×2 & 3×4 \\ 3×1 & 3×3 \end{pmatrix} = \begin{pmatrix} 6 & 12 \\ 3 & 9 \end{pmatrix}$

Multiplication of one Matrix by another

This is done by multiplying rows in the 1st matrix by columns in the second matrix, as shown on the following page.

Example 18.1

1st multiplication

$$\text{1st row} \longrightarrow \begin{pmatrix} \boxed{1 \quad 2} \\ 3 \quad 4 \end{pmatrix} \quad \begin{pmatrix} \boxed{5} \quad 6 \\ \boxed{7} \quad 8 \end{pmatrix} = \begin{pmatrix} 1 \times 5 + 2 \times 7 \\ \uparrow \end{pmatrix} \leftarrow \text{1st row}$$

$$\qquad\qquad\qquad\qquad \underset{\text{column}}{\text{1st}} \qquad\qquad \underset{\text{column}}{\text{1st}}$$

2nd multiplication

$$\text{1st row} \longrightarrow \begin{pmatrix} \boxed{1 \quad 2} \\ 3 \quad 4 \end{pmatrix} \quad \begin{pmatrix} 5 \quad \boxed{6} \\ 7 \quad \boxed{8} \end{pmatrix} = \begin{pmatrix} 19 & 1 \times 6 + 2 \times 8 \\ & \uparrow \end{pmatrix} \leftarrow \text{1st row}$$

$$\qquad\qquad\qquad\qquad\qquad \underset{\text{column}}{\text{2nd}} \qquad\qquad \underset{\text{column}}{\text{2nd}}$$

3rd multiplication

$$\text{2nd row} \longrightarrow \begin{pmatrix} 1 \quad 2 \\ \boxed{3 \quad 4} \end{pmatrix} \quad \begin{pmatrix} \boxed{5} \quad 6 \\ \boxed{7} \quad 8 \end{pmatrix} = \begin{pmatrix} 19 & 22 \\ 3 \times 5 + 4 \times 7 & \\ \uparrow & \end{pmatrix} \leftarrow \text{2nd row}$$

$$\qquad\qquad\qquad\qquad \underset{\text{column}}{\text{1st}} \qquad\qquad \underset{\text{column}}{\text{1st}}$$

4th multiplication

$$\text{2nd row} \longrightarrow \begin{pmatrix} 1 \quad 2 \\ \boxed{3 \quad 4} \end{pmatrix} \quad \begin{pmatrix} 5 \quad \boxed{6} \\ 7 \quad \boxed{8} \end{pmatrix} = \begin{pmatrix} 19 & 22 \\ 43 & 3 \times 6 + 4 \times 8 \\ & \uparrow \end{pmatrix} \leftarrow \text{2nd row}$$

$$\qquad\qquad\qquad\qquad\qquad \underset{\text{column}}{\text{2nd}} \qquad\qquad \underset{\text{column}}{\text{2nd}}$$

$$\therefore \begin{pmatrix} 1 & 2 \\ 3 & 4 \end{pmatrix} \begin{pmatrix} 5 & 6 \\ 7 & 8 \end{pmatrix} = \begin{pmatrix} 19 & 22 \\ 43 & 50 \end{pmatrix}$$

In order to multiply two matrices together the number of columns in the last matrix must equal the number of rows in the 2nd matrix.

Example 18.2

$$\begin{pmatrix} 3 & -2 \\ 1 & 5 \end{pmatrix} \begin{pmatrix} -4 \\ 1 \end{pmatrix} = \begin{pmatrix} 3 \times -4 + -2 \times 1 \\ 1 \times -4 + 5 \times 1 \end{pmatrix} = \begin{pmatrix} -14 \\ 1 \end{pmatrix}$$

Example 18.3

If A $\begin{pmatrix} 1 & 3 \\ -2 & 1 \end{pmatrix}$ and B $= \begin{pmatrix} 2 & 1 \\ -4 & 3 \end{pmatrix}$

find   a) $A - B$ b) $2B$ c) AB d) B^2

a) $A - B = \begin{pmatrix} 1 & 3 \\ -2 & 1 \end{pmatrix} - \begin{pmatrix} 2 & 1 \\ -4 & 3 \end{pmatrix} = \begin{pmatrix} 1-2 & 3-1 \\ -2-(-4) & 1-3 \end{pmatrix}$

$$= \begin{pmatrix} -1 & 2 \\ 2 & -2 \end{pmatrix}$$

b) $2B = 2 \begin{pmatrix} 2 & 1 \\ -4 & 3 \end{pmatrix} = \begin{pmatrix} 4 & 2 \\ -8 & 6 \end{pmatrix}$

c) $AB = \begin{pmatrix} 1 & 3 \\ -2 & 1 \end{pmatrix} \begin{pmatrix} 2 & 1 \\ -4 & 3 \end{pmatrix} = \begin{pmatrix} 2-12 & 1+9 \\ -4-4 & -2+3 \end{pmatrix} = \begin{pmatrix} -10 & 10 \\ -8 & 1 \end{pmatrix}$

d) $B^2 = \begin{pmatrix} 2 & 1 \\ -4 & 3 \end{pmatrix} \begin{pmatrix} 2 & 1 \\ -4 & 3 \end{pmatrix} = \begin{pmatrix} 4-4 & 2+3 \\ -8-12 & -4+9 \end{pmatrix} = \begin{pmatrix} 0 & 5 \\ -20 & 5 \end{pmatrix}$

EXERCISE 18.1

1. If $A = \begin{pmatrix} 1 & 3 \\ 5 & 2 \end{pmatrix}$ and $B = \begin{pmatrix} -2 \\ 1 \end{pmatrix}$

   find a) AB   b) A^2

   Explain why $A + B$, BA and B^2 cannot be formed.

2. If $A = \begin{pmatrix} 4 & 1 \\ 3 & 2 \end{pmatrix}$ and $B = \begin{pmatrix} 2 & 1 \\ 5 & -3 \end{pmatrix}$ find

   a) $A + B$ b) $A - B$ c) AB   d) BA
   e) A^2 f) B^2
   What do you notice about the results to c and d?

IDENTITY MATRICES

The identity element of a set is the element which when combined with any other element of the set leaves it unchanged.

Example 18.4

The identity element for ordinary multiplication is 1 since

$$1 \times 3 = 3 \times 1 = 3$$
$$1 \times (-2) = (-2) \times 1 = -2 \qquad \text{etc}$$

The identity element for ordinary addition is 0 since

$$3 + 0 = 0 + 3 = 3$$
$$-2 + 0 = 0 + (-2) = -2 \qquad \text{etc}$$

The identity matrix for a 2×2 matrix under multiplication is $\begin{pmatrix} 1 & 0 \\ 0 & 1 \end{pmatrix}$

since $\begin{pmatrix} 1 & 0 \\ 0 & 1 \end{pmatrix} \begin{pmatrix} 1 & 2 \\ 3 & 4 \end{pmatrix} = \begin{pmatrix} 1+0 & 2+0 \\ 0+3 & 0+4 \end{pmatrix} = \begin{pmatrix} 1 & 2 \\ 3 & 4 \end{pmatrix}$

also $\begin{pmatrix} 1 & 2 \\ 3 & 4 \end{pmatrix} \begin{pmatrix} 1 & 0 \\ 0 & 1 \end{pmatrix} = \begin{pmatrix} 1+0 & 0+2 \\ 3+0 & 0+4 \end{pmatrix} = \begin{pmatrix} 1 & 2 \\ 3 & 4 \end{pmatrix}$

$I = \begin{pmatrix} 1 & 0 \\ 0 & 1 \end{pmatrix}$

Inverse of a matrix

The inverse of an element is an element which when combined with the first element gives the identity element.

Example 18.5   Under ordinary multiplication

$3 \times \frac{1}{3} = 1$ $\therefore$ $\frac{1}{3}$ is the inverse of 3

also 3 is the inverse of $\frac{1}{3}$

$-2 \times -\frac{1}{2} = 1$ $\therefore$ $-\frac{1}{2}$ is the inverse of -2

also -2 is the inverse of $-\frac{1}{2}$

under ordinary addition

$3 + (-3) = 0$ $\therefore$ -3 is the inverse of 3

also 3 is the inverse of -3 etc

Matrices

If $AB = I$ then B is the inverse of A and A is the inverse of B
The inverse of A is referred to as A^{-1} $\therefore$ $I = AA^{-1}$

If $A = \begin{pmatrix} a & b \\ c & d \end{pmatrix}$ then $A^{-1} = \dfrac{1}{ad - bc} \begin{pmatrix} d & -b \\ -c & a \end{pmatrix}$

Example 18.6

If $B = \begin{pmatrix} 1 & 3 \\ 2 & 4 \end{pmatrix}$ find B^{-1}

$B^{-1} = \dfrac{1}{(1 \times 4)-(3 \times 2)} \begin{pmatrix} 4 & -3 \\ -2 & 1 \end{pmatrix}$

$= \dfrac{1}{4-6} \begin{pmatrix} 4 & -3 \\ -2 & 1 \end{pmatrix} = -\frac{1}{2} \begin{pmatrix} 4 & -3 \\ -2 & 1 \end{pmatrix}$

$= \begin{pmatrix} -2 & \frac{3}{2} \\ 1 & -\frac{1}{2} \end{pmatrix}$

check $\begin{pmatrix} 1 & 3 \\ 2 & 4 \end{pmatrix} \begin{pmatrix} -2 & \frac{3}{2} \\ 1 & -\frac{1}{2} \end{pmatrix} = \begin{pmatrix} -2+3 & \frac{3}{2}-\frac{3}{2} \\ -4+4 & 3-2 \end{pmatrix}$

$$= \begin{pmatrix} 1 & 0 \\ 0 & 1 \end{pmatrix}$$

Example 18.7

If $M = \begin{pmatrix} 1 & -2 \\ 2 & 1 \end{pmatrix}$ find the matrix $\begin{pmatrix} a \\ b \end{pmatrix}$ such that $M \begin{pmatrix} a \\ b \end{pmatrix} = \begin{pmatrix} 0 \\ 5 \end{pmatrix}$

Since $M \begin{pmatrix} a \\ b \end{pmatrix} = \begin{pmatrix} 0 \\ 5 \end{pmatrix}$ then $\begin{pmatrix} a \\ b \end{pmatrix} = M^{-1} \begin{pmatrix} 0 \\ 5 \end{pmatrix}$

$M^{-1} = \dfrac{1}{1+4} \begin{pmatrix} 1 & 2 \\ -2 & 1 \end{pmatrix} = \dfrac{1}{5} \begin{pmatrix} 1 & 2 \\ -2 & 1 \end{pmatrix}$

$\therefore \begin{pmatrix} a \\ b \end{pmatrix} = \dfrac{1}{5} \begin{pmatrix} 1 & 2 \\ -2 & 1 \end{pmatrix} \begin{pmatrix} 0 \\ 5 \end{pmatrix} = \dfrac{1}{5} \begin{pmatrix} 10 \\ 5 \end{pmatrix} = \begin{pmatrix} 2 \\ 1 \end{pmatrix}$

EXERCISE 18.2

Find the inverses of the following matrices

1. $\begin{pmatrix} 2 & 3 \\ 5 & 5 \end{pmatrix}$ 2. $\begin{pmatrix} 3 & 2 \\ 4 & 3 \end{pmatrix}$ 3. $\begin{pmatrix} 7 & 2 \\ 3 & 1 \end{pmatrix}$ 4. $\begin{pmatrix} 6 & 10 \\ 4 & 7 \end{pmatrix}$

5. $\begin{pmatrix} -5 & 3 \\ -3 & 2 \end{pmatrix}$ 6. $\begin{pmatrix} 6 & 2 \\ 11 & 4 \end{pmatrix}$ 7. $\begin{pmatrix} 3 & 3 \\ 5 & 4 \end{pmatrix}$ 8. $\begin{pmatrix} -4 & 3 \\ 5 & -4 \end{pmatrix}$

9. $\begin{pmatrix} 6 & 4 \\ 5 & 3 \end{pmatrix}$ 10. $\begin{pmatrix} 4 & -3 \\ 6 & -5 \end{pmatrix}$

11. If $M = \begin{pmatrix} 3 & 1 \\ 2 & 1 \end{pmatrix}$ find the matrix $\begin{pmatrix} a \\ b \end{pmatrix}$ such that $M \begin{pmatrix} a \\ b \end{pmatrix} = \begin{pmatrix} 7 \\ 5 \end{pmatrix}$

12. If $M = \begin{pmatrix} 1 & 2 \\ 2 & 1 \end{pmatrix}$ find the matrix $\begin{pmatrix} a \\ b \end{pmatrix}$ such that $M \begin{pmatrix} a \\ b \end{pmatrix} = \begin{pmatrix} 7 \\ 8 \end{pmatrix}$

ROUTE MATRICES

A route matrix tells us how many routes (arcs) there are between two points (nodes)

Example 18.8

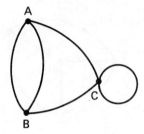

The routes are

A	to	B	2 routes
B	to	A	2 routes
A	to	C	1 route
C	to	A	1 route
B	to	C	1 route
C	to	B	1 route
C	to	C	2 routes

> Note the two routes from C to C – one going one way and the other in the opposite direction.

and can be expressed in the form of a matrix like this

$$\text{from}\quad\begin{matrix} & & \text{to} & \\ & A & B & C \\ A & \\ B & \\ C & \end{matrix}\begin{pmatrix} 0 & 2 & 1 \\ 2 & 0 & 1 \\ 1 & 1 & 2 \end{pmatrix}$$

EXERCISE 18.3

1. Write down route matrices for the following network diagrams

a)

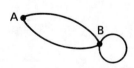

b)

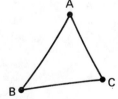

285

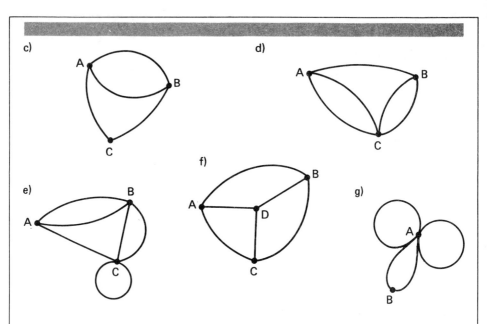

c)

d)

e)

f)

g)

2. Draw network diagrams from the following route matrices

a)
$$\begin{array}{c} \text{from} \end{array} \begin{array}{c} A \\ B \end{array} \begin{pmatrix} \overset{\displaystyle A}{2} & \overset{\displaystyle B}{1} \\ 1 & 2 \end{pmatrix}$$
to

b)
$$\begin{array}{c} \text{from} \end{array} \begin{array}{c} A \\ B \end{array} \begin{pmatrix} \overset{\displaystyle A}{2} & \overset{\displaystyle B}{2} \\ 2 & 2 \end{pmatrix}$$
to

c)
$$\begin{array}{c} \text{from} \end{array} \begin{array}{c} A \\ B \\ C \end{array} \begin{pmatrix} \overset{\displaystyle A}{0} & \overset{\displaystyle B}{1} & \overset{\displaystyle C}{2} \\ 1 & 0 & 2 \\ 2 & 2 & 0 \end{pmatrix}$$
to

d)
$$\begin{array}{c} \text{from} \end{array} \begin{array}{c} A \\ B \\ C \end{array} \begin{pmatrix} \overset{\displaystyle A}{2} & \overset{\displaystyle B}{2} & \overset{\displaystyle C}{1} \\ 2 & 0 & 1 \\ 1 & 1 & 2 \end{pmatrix}$$
to

e)
$$\begin{array}{c} \text{from} \end{array} \begin{array}{c} A \\ B \\ C \end{array} \begin{pmatrix} \overset{\displaystyle A}{2} & \overset{\displaystyle B}{1} & \overset{\displaystyle C}{1} \\ 1 & 2 & 1 \\ 1 & 1 & 0 \end{pmatrix}$$
to

f)
$$\begin{array}{c} \text{from} \end{array} \begin{array}{c} A \\ B \\ C \end{array} \begin{pmatrix} \overset{\displaystyle A}{2} & \overset{\displaystyle B}{2} & \overset{\displaystyle C}{2} \\ 2 & 0 & 1 \\ 2 & 1 & 0 \end{pmatrix}$$
to

g)
$$\begin{array}{c} \text{from} \end{array} \begin{array}{c} A \\ B \\ C \end{array} \begin{pmatrix} \overset{\displaystyle A}{0} & \overset{\displaystyle B}{2} & \overset{\displaystyle C}{1} \\ 2 & 0 & 2 \\ 1 & 2 & 0 \end{pmatrix}$$
to

Directed route matrices

Example 18.9

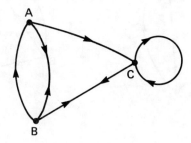

Here we take into account the direction
The routes are

A ——→ B	1 route	
A ——→ C	1 route	
B ——→ A	2 routes	
B ——→ C	1 route	
C ——→ B	1 route	
C ——→ C	1 route	

These can be expressed in the form of a matrix like this

$$\begin{array}{c} \\ \text{from} \\ \\ \end{array} \begin{array}{c} \\ A \\ B \\ C \end{array} \overset{\begin{array}{ccc} & \text{to} & \\ A & B & C \end{array}}{\begin{pmatrix} 0 & 1 & 1 \\ 2 & 0 & 1 \\ 0 & 1 & 1 \end{pmatrix}}$$

EXERCISE 18.4

1. Write down directed route matrices for each of the following network diagrams

a)

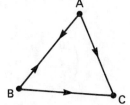

b)

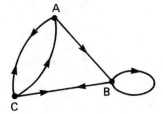

c)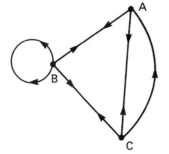

d)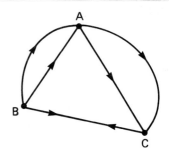

e)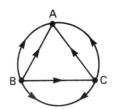

f)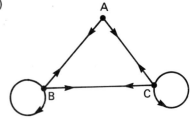

g)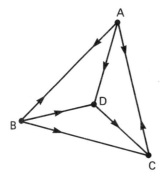

h)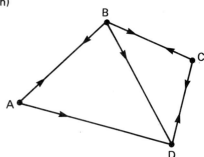

2. Draw network diagrams from the following directed route matrices.

a)

		A	B	C
	A	0	2	1
from	B	1	2	1
	C	0	0	1

b)

		A	B	C
	A	1	2	3
from	B	2	1	1
	C	2	3	1

c)

	A	B	C
A	1	2	1
B	1	1	2
C	2	1	0

d)

	A	B	C
A	0	1	2
B	2	0	3
C	2	1	0

e)

	A	B	C
A	1	2	3
B	3	0	1
C	2	2	0

f)

	A	B	C
A	0	2	1
B	2	0	1
C	2	2	0

g)

	A	B	C
A	0	2	3
B	3	1	2
C	2	1	1

	A	B	C
A	0	2	1
B	2	0	1
C	2	3	2

2 stage route matrices

These show the number of 2 stage routes

Example 18.10

This has the following one stage routes

A	to	A	1 route
A	to	B	2 routes
B	to	A	1 route

and its route matrix is

$$M = \begin{matrix} & \begin{matrix} A & B \end{matrix} \\ \begin{matrix} A \\ B \end{matrix} & \begin{pmatrix} 1 & 2 \\ 1 & 0 \end{pmatrix} \end{matrix}$$

It also has the following 2 stage routes

From A to A	$A \rightarrow A \rightarrow A$	1 route
3 routes	$A \rightarrow B \rightarrow A$	2 routes

From A to B	$A \rightarrow A \rightarrow B$	2 routes
2 routes		

From B to A	$B \rightarrow A \rightarrow A$	1 route
1 route		

From B to B	$B \rightarrow A \rightarrow B$	2 routes

and its route matrix is

$$N = \begin{matrix} & \begin{matrix} A & B \end{matrix} \\ \begin{matrix} A \\ B \end{matrix} & \begin{pmatrix} 3 & 2 \\ 1 & 2 \end{pmatrix} \end{matrix}$$

Matrix N can be obtained by squaring matrix M

i.e. $M = \begin{pmatrix} 1 & 2 \\ 1 & 0 \end{pmatrix} \begin{pmatrix} 1 & 2 \\ 1 & 0 \end{pmatrix} = \begin{pmatrix} 3 & 2 \\ 1 & 2 \end{pmatrix}$

EXERCISE 18.5

For each of the following network diagrams write down a directed route matrix and verify that its square represents the matrix of all the two stage routes.

1)

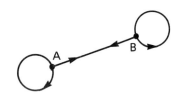

2)

3)

4)

5)

6)

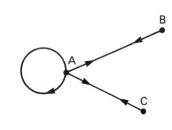

7)

8)

9)

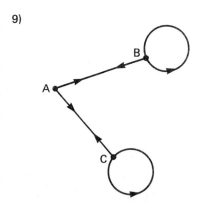

10)

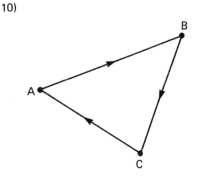

TRANSFORMATION AND SYMMETRY

GEOMETRICAL TRANSFORMATION

1. **Translations**

   A translation is a movement from one position to another along a straight line. The translation is represented by the matrix $\begin{pmatrix} a \\ b \end{pmatrix}$ where 'a' indicates the distance moved parallel to the x axis and 'b' the distance moved parallel to the y axis.

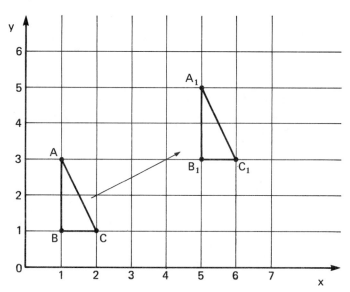

The translation of ABC to $A_1 B_1 C_1$ is indicated by the matrix $\begin{pmatrix} 4 \\ 2 \end{pmatrix}$

EXERCISE 19.1

If $\triangle$ ABC is translated to $\triangle A_1 B_1 C_1$ by matrix M find the co-ordinates of $A_1 B_1 C_1$ when

1) A(1,1) B(2,1) C(1,3) is translated by $\begin{pmatrix} 1 \\ 4 \end{pmatrix}$

2) A(2,1) B(2,3) C(1,3) is translated by $\begin{pmatrix} 2 \\ 1 \end{pmatrix}$

3) A(−2,3) B(−1,3) C(−1,1) is translated by $\begin{pmatrix} 4 \\ -2 \end{pmatrix}$

4) A(−1,−2) B(−3,−2) C(−2,−4) is translated by $\begin{pmatrix} -1 \\ 2 \end{pmatrix}$

2. Enlargements

An enlargement changes a shape into a similar shape.

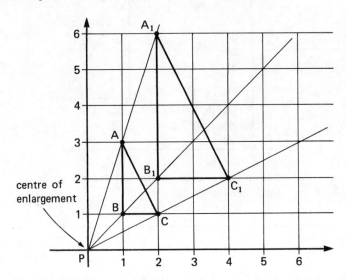

$\triangle$ ABC is enlarged onto $\triangle$ $A_1 B_1 C_1$

Point A and its image A_1 lie on a straight line. Similarly points B and B_1 and C and C_1. All of these lines meet at point P. Point P is called the **centre of enlargement**

PA_1 is twice as long as PA

also $PB_1 = 2PB$

$PC_1 = 2PC$

This enlargement has a **scale factor of 2.**

An enlargement with a positive scale factor such as this has its centre of enlargement behind the object, relative to the image.

Enlargements with a negative scale factor

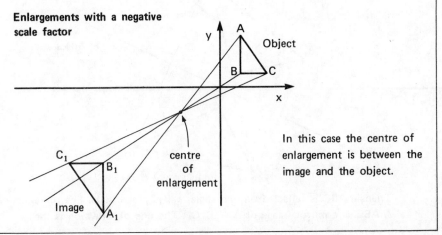

In this case the centre of enlargement is between the image and the object.

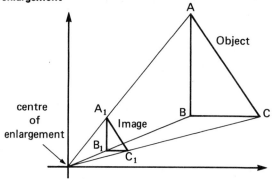

Fractional enlargement

In this case the image appears between the object and the centre of enlargement. Its size is diminished.

EXERCISE 19.2

Plot the following triangles and in each case enlarge them through the point P with the given scale factors. Write down the co-ordinates of the image points A, B and C.

1. A(1,1)   B(2,1)   C(1,3)   through   P(0,0)   scale factor 3.
2. A(−1,0)   B(−3,0)   C(−2,3)   through   P(−4,2)   scale factor 3.
3. A(2,2)   B(4,2)   C(3,4)   through   P(0,0)   scale factor −1.
4. A(2,0)   B(4,0)   C(3,−2)   through   P(0,1)   scale factor −2.
5. A(6,6)   B(6,4)   C(3,4)   through   P(0,0)   scale factor ½.
6. A(0,6)   B(0,3)   C(4,3)   through   P(4,−3)   scale factor ⅓.

3. **Reflections in a line**

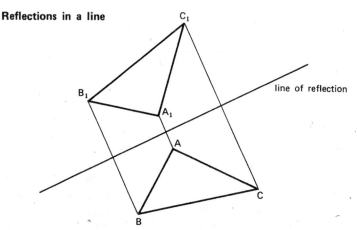

Triangle ABC is reflected onto triangle $A_1B_1C_1$ across the line of reflection.
$\triangle$ ABC is a mirror image of $\triangle A_1B_1C_1$. The line of reflection is the

294

perpendicular bisector of lines AA_1, BB_1 and CC_1. The image is congruent to the object.

Example 19.1

a)   Reflections in the x and y axis.

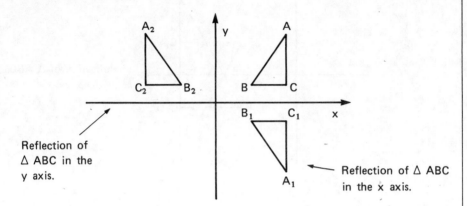

Reflection of
△ ABC in the
y axis.

Reflection of △ ABC
in the x axis.

b)   Reflection in the lines y = x and y = −x.

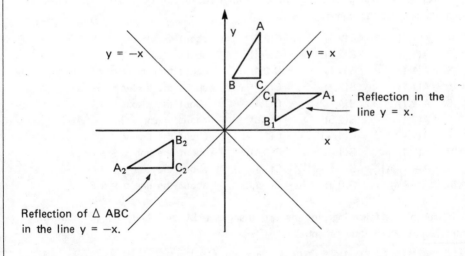

Reflection in the
line y = x.

Reflection of △ ABC
in the line y = −x.

c)   Reflection when the line of reflection goes through the object.

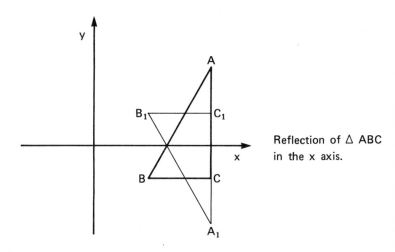

Reflection of △ ABC
in the x axis.

EXERCISE 19.3

Reflect the following triangles about the lines stated. In each case write down the co-ordinates of the images.

1. A(1,1)   B(2,1)   C(2,4)   about y axis.
2. A(1,1)   B(2,1)   ⌐   C(2,4)   about x axis.
3. A(1,1)   B(2,1)   C(2,4)   about the line y = x
4. A(1,1)   B(2,1)   C(2,4)   about the line y = −1
5. A(4,1)   B(4,−2)   C(1,1)   about the x axis.
6. A(2,1)   B(2,5)   C(4,5)   about line x = 2
7. A(1,−1)   B(4,−1)   C(1,−4)   about the line y = −x
8. A(1,1)   B(1,4)   C(3,4)   about the line y = −x
9. A(−4,−1)   B(−1,−1)   C(−1,−4)   about the line y = 1
10. A(−4,4)   B(0,4)   C(−4,0)   about the line y = x

In each of the following plot the two triangles (ABC and $A_1B_1C_1$) and state the line about which they reflect.

11. A(1,1)   B(3,1)   C(3,4)   and A_1(1,−1) B_1(3,−1) C_1(3,−4)
12. A(−1,1)   B(2,1)   C(2,3)   and A_1(1,1) B_1(−2,1) C_1(−2,3)
13. A(2,0)   B(4,0)   C(2,2)   and A_1(0,−2) B_1(0,−4) C_1(−2,−2)
14. A(0,−2)   B(0,−4)   C(2,−2)   and A_1(−2,0) B_1(−4,0) C_1(−2,2)

4. Rotations

A rotation turns a shape through an angle about a point. All points on the object turn through the same angle.

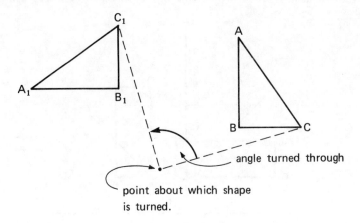

point about which shape is turned.

angle turned through

Constructing the centre of rotation

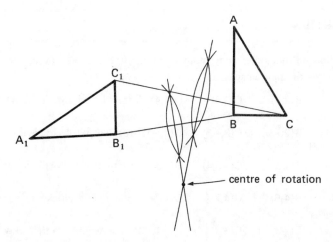

centre of rotation

The centre of rotation can be found by joining together two pairs of corresponding points on each triangle and bisecting these lines. The centre of rotation is the point at which these bisections cross.

Example 19.2

Plot the rectangle A(2,2)   B(4,2)   C(4,7)   D(2,7). Find the image of ABCD when it is rotated 90° anticlockwise about the point (1,1)

Draw line PA

Measure 90° anticlockwise at P

Measure PA_1 = PA. This gives the new position for A.

The other points can be found in the same way or obtained by inspection.

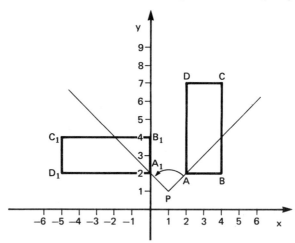

EXERCISE 19.4

Plot the following rectangles and rotate them about the points given. Write down the co-ordinates of their images.

1. A(1,1)   B(3,1)   C(3,4)   D(1,4) rotated 90° anticlockwise about origin (0,0)

2. A(2,−1) B(2,−5) C(3,−5) D(3,−1) rotated 180° clockwise about the origin.

3. A(−3,1) B(−5,1) C(−5,4) D(−3,4) rotated 90° clockwise about the origin.

4. A(1,5)   B(4,5)   C(4,7)   D(1,7) rotated 90° clockwise about point (1,1)

5. A(−1,1) B(−3,−1) C(−3,−4) D(−1,−4) rotated 90° anticlockwise about (−1,−1)

6. A(1,1)   B(1,4)   C(5,4)   D(5,1) rotated 90° clockwise about (3,1)

Find, by constructing or otherwise the centre of rotation and the angle rotated through in each of the following where $\triangle A_1 B_1 C_1$ is the image of $\triangle$ ABC.

7. A(1,1)   B(3,1)   C(1,4) mapped to A_1(−1,1) B_1(−3,3) C_1(−4,1)
8. A(1,−2) B(1,−4) C(3,−4) mapped to A_1(−1,2) B_1(−1,4) C_1(−3,4)
9. A(1,1)   B(1,4)   C(3,1) mapped to A_1(1,1) B_1(1,−2) C_1(−1,1)
10. A(1,3)   B(1,6)   C(3,3) mapped to A_1(3,1) B_1(6,1) C_1(3,−1)
11. A(−2,2) B(−4,2) C(−2,4) mapped to A_1(0,4) B_1(2,4) C_1(0,2)

298

SYMMETRY

Line Symmetry (Axial symmetry)
A line (or axis) of symmetry divides a shape into matching left hand and right hand halves.

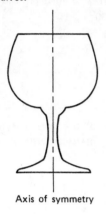

Axis of symmetry

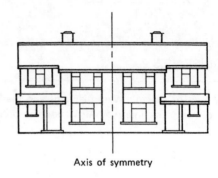

Axis of symmetry

Some shapes have more than one axis of symmetry

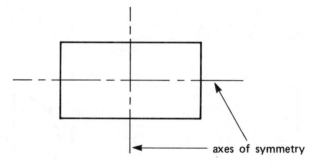

axes of symmetry

Rotational symmetry (point symmetry)
A figure which has rotational symmetry will be superimposed onto its own shape when rotated about a point through less than 360°.
e.g.
A rectangle has rotational symmetry of order 2. When rotated about the point where its diagonals intersect it becomes superimposed onto itself when rotated through 180° and 360°.

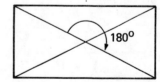

180°

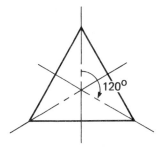

An equilateral triangle has rotational symmetry of order **3**. When rotated about its centroid it becomes superimposed onto itself when rotated through 120°, 240° and 360°.

EXERCISE 19.5

Sketch each of the following diagrams and mark on them   a) the lines of symmetry   b) the centre of symmetry.   Also state the order of rotational symmetry.

1)
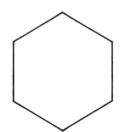

2)

3)

4)

5)
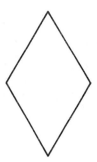

6)
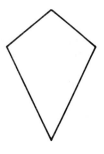

7)

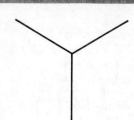

8)

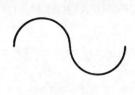

9. Copy these diagrams and put in the lines of symmetry, then complete the following table.

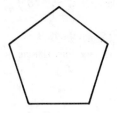

	No of axes of symmetry	Order of rotational symmetry	Angle between adjacent axes of symmetry
Equilateral triangle			
Square			
Pentagon			
Hexagon			
Heptagon			
Octogon			
Nonogon			
Decagon			
n sided			

10. List the letters in the word U N I V E R S A L which have neither line nor point symmetry.
11. Add one line to this shape to give it rotational symmetry but not line symmetry.

TRANSFORMATION MATRICES

A point (x,y) can be transformed by a 2 by 2 matrix $\begin{pmatrix} a & b \\ c & d \end{pmatrix}$ by multiplying

the matrix by the point written as a column matrix of the form $\begin{pmatrix} x \\ y \end{pmatrix}$

i.e. $\begin{pmatrix} x \\ y \end{pmatrix}$ maps to $\begin{pmatrix} a & b \\ c & d \end{pmatrix}\begin{pmatrix} x \\ y \end{pmatrix}$

where $\begin{pmatrix} a & b \\ c & d \end{pmatrix}$ represents a transformation

Example 19.3

Draw the triangle A(1,1)   B(3,1)   C(3,4) and transform it using the matrix
$M = \begin{pmatrix} 0 & -1 \\ 1 & 0 \end{pmatrix}$ Plot the image formed and describe the transformation.

Multiplying each point by the matrix M

$\begin{pmatrix} 0 & -1 \\ 1 & 0 \end{pmatrix}\begin{pmatrix} 1 \\ 1 \end{pmatrix} = \begin{pmatrix} -1 \\ 1 \end{pmatrix}$ $\therefore$ (1,1)   maps to $\longrightarrow$ (−1,1)

$\begin{pmatrix} 0 & -1 \\ 1 & 0 \end{pmatrix}\begin{pmatrix} 3 \\ 1 \end{pmatrix} = \begin{pmatrix} -1 \\ 3 \end{pmatrix}$ $\therefore$ (3,1) $\longrightarrow$ (−1,3)

$\begin{pmatrix} 0 & -1 \\ 1 & 0 \end{pmatrix}\begin{pmatrix} 3 \\ 4 \end{pmatrix} = \begin{pmatrix} -4 \\ 3 \end{pmatrix}$ $\therefore$ (3,4) $\longrightarrow$ (−4,3)

Showing this on a diagram

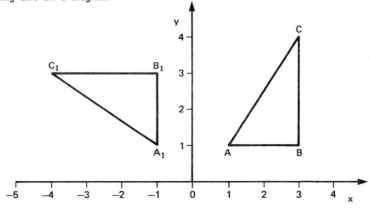

By inspection matrix M represents a rotation of 90° anticlockwise about the origin (0,0)

EXERCISE 19.6

By first drawing the triangle A(1,1)   B(3,1)   C(3,4)   use each of the following matrices to transform it. State what transformation each matrix represents.

1. $\begin{pmatrix} -1 & 0 \\ 0 & -1 \end{pmatrix}$ 2. $\begin{pmatrix} 0 & 1 \\ -1 & 0 \end{pmatrix}$ 3. $\begin{pmatrix} 1 & 0 \\ 0 & -1 \end{pmatrix}$ 4. $\begin{pmatrix} -1 & 0 \\ 0 & 1 \end{pmatrix}$

5. $\begin{pmatrix} 0 & 1 \\ 1 & 0 \end{pmatrix}$ 6. $\begin{pmatrix} 0 & -1 \\ -1 & 0 \end{pmatrix}$ 7. $\begin{pmatrix} 2 & 0 \\ 0 & 2 \end{pmatrix}$ 8. $\begin{pmatrix} \frac{1}{2} & 0 \\ 0 & \frac{1}{2} \end{pmatrix}$

9. $\begin{pmatrix} -2 & 0 \\ 0 & -2 \end{pmatrix}$

10. Write down, in general terms, the matrix used for enlargements through the origin indicating its scale factor.

Combining transformation

Two transformations following each other can be represented by a single transformation by multiplying their two matrices together.

e.g.   transformation A followed by transformation B can be represented by matrix C where   C = BA

i.e.   the product of two matrices gives the same result as using one matrix after the other.

Example 19.4

Triangle A(1,1),   B(2,2)   C(1,4)   is transformed onto triangle $A_1 B_1 C_1$ by the matrix M where M $= \begin{pmatrix} 1 & 0 \\ 0 & -1 \end{pmatrix}$ and triangle $A_1 B_1 C_1$ is transformed by the matrix N where N $= \begin{pmatrix} 0 & -1 \\ -1 & 0 \end{pmatrix}$ onto triangle $A_1 B_1 C_2$

a)   Find the co-ordinates of $A_1 B_1 C_1$ and C_2 and draw the three triangles.
b)   What single transformation will transform $\triangle$ ABC onto $\triangle A_1 B_1 C_2$?
c)   By calculating the matrix W = N M show that this matrix represents the transformation found in part b.
d)   Find W^{-1} and use it to find the co-ordinates of the point whose image is $\begin{pmatrix} 3 \\ -5 \end{pmatrix}$

a) For point A_1 $\begin{pmatrix} 1 & 0 \\ 0 & -1 \end{pmatrix} \begin{pmatrix} 1 \\ 1 \end{pmatrix} = \begin{pmatrix} 1 \\ -1 \end{pmatrix}$ $\therefore$ co-ordinates of A_1 are $(1,-1)$

For point B_1 $\begin{pmatrix} 1 & 0 \\ 0 & -1 \end{pmatrix} \begin{pmatrix} 2 \\ 2 \end{pmatrix} = \begin{pmatrix} 2 \\ -2 \end{pmatrix}$ $\therefore$ co-ordinates of B_1 are $(2,-2)$

For point C_1 $\begin{pmatrix} 1 & 0 \\ 0 & -1 \end{pmatrix} \begin{pmatrix} 1 \\ 4 \end{pmatrix} = \begin{pmatrix} 1 \\ -4 \end{pmatrix}$ $\therefore$ co-ordinates of C_1 are $(1,-4)$

For point C_2, C_1 is mapped onto C_2 by N

$\begin{pmatrix} 0 & -1 \\ -1 & 0 \end{pmatrix} \begin{pmatrix} 1 \\ -4 \end{pmatrix} = \begin{pmatrix} 4 \\ -1 \end{pmatrix}$ $\therefore$ co-ordinates of C_2 are $(4,-1)$

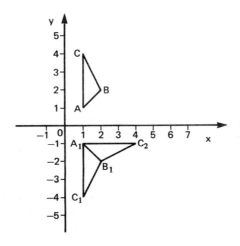

b) By inspection $\triangle$ ABC is mapped to $\triangle A_1B_1C_1$ by a clockwise rotation of 90° about the origin.

c) $W = NM = \begin{pmatrix} 0 & 1 \\ -1 & 0 \end{pmatrix} \begin{pmatrix} 1 & 0 \\ 0 & -1 \end{pmatrix} = \begin{pmatrix} 0 & 1 \\ -1 & 0 \end{pmatrix}$

For point A_1 $\begin{pmatrix} 0 & 1 \\ -1 & 0 \end{pmatrix} \begin{pmatrix} 1 \\ 1 \end{pmatrix} = \begin{pmatrix} 1 \\ -1 \end{pmatrix}$ A maps to A_1

For point B_1 $\begin{pmatrix} 0 & 1 \\ -1 & 0 \end{pmatrix} \begin{pmatrix} 2 \\ 2 \end{pmatrix} = \begin{pmatrix} 2 \\ -2 \end{pmatrix}$ B maps to B_1

For point C_2 $\begin{pmatrix} 0 & 1 \\ -1 & 0 \end{pmatrix} \begin{pmatrix} 1 \\ -4 \end{pmatrix} = \begin{pmatrix} -4 \\ -1 \end{pmatrix}$ C maps to C_2

$\therefore$ Matrix W represents the transformation found in part b

d) $W^{-1} = \dfrac{1}{0-(-1)} \begin{pmatrix} 0 & -1 \\ 1 & 0 \end{pmatrix} = \begin{pmatrix} 0 & -1 \\ 1 & 0 \end{pmatrix}$

If the co-ordinates of the point are (a,b) then

$\text{(W)} \begin{pmatrix} a \\ b \end{pmatrix} = \begin{pmatrix} 3 \\ -5 \end{pmatrix}$

$\therefore \begin{pmatrix} a \\ b \end{pmatrix} = \left(W^{-1} \right) \begin{pmatrix} 3 \\ -5 \end{pmatrix}$

$\begin{pmatrix} a \\ b \end{pmatrix} = \begin{pmatrix} 0 & -1 \\ 1 & 0 \end{pmatrix} \begin{pmatrix} 3 \\ -5 \end{pmatrix} = \begin{pmatrix} 5 \\ 3 \end{pmatrix}$

point (5,3) is mapped onto (3,−5)

EXERCISE 19.7

1. A transformation is given by the matrix $M = \begin{pmatrix} -1 & 1 \\ 1 & 1 \end{pmatrix}$. Find M^{-1} and use it to find the co-ordinates of the point whose image is (1,3).

2. As question 1 but $M = \begin{pmatrix} 1 & 1 \\ 1 & -1 \end{pmatrix}$ and point is (4,0)

3. M is the image of triangle A after it has been reflected about the y axis and N the image of triangle A after it has been rotated 180° about the origin. If triangle A has co-ordinates (1,1), (2,1) and (1,3) draw triangle A and its images M and N. What single transformation would map M to N?

4. Triangle A has co-ordinates (1,1), (3,2) and (1,2). Triangle M is the image of △ A when rotated through 180° about point (1,1). Draw triangles A and M. △ M is now translated using the matrix $\begin{pmatrix} -2 \\ -2 \end{pmatrix}$ to form △ N. Draw △ N. Which single transformation maps △ A onto △ N?

5. Triangle W has co-ordinates A(−3,1), B(−1,−1) and C(−1,2)
   a) draw △ W and △ V formed when △ W is rotated through 90° clockwise about point (−3,0).
   b) △ V is reflected about the Y axis to form △ U. △ U is reflected about the x axis to form △ T. Draw triangles U and T.
   c) What single transformation maps   (i) W onto T   (ii) V onto T

6. △ ABC has co-ordinates A(1,1), B(3,1) and C(1,4). △ ABC is reflected about line y = −x onto △ $A_1B_1C_1$ and △ ABC is reflected about the line y = 0 onto △ $A_2B_2C_2$. Draw these three triangles. What single transformation maps △ $A_1B_1C_1$ onto △ $A_2B_2C_2$?

7. △ ABC is transformed using the matrix M where $M = \begin{pmatrix} -0.6 & 0.8 \\ 0.8 & 0.6 \end{pmatrix}$ onto △ $A_1B_1C_1$. If A(0,5), B(−1,8) and C(2,4) represents △ ABC, draw triangles ABC and $A_1B_1C_1$ and describe the transformation.

8. $\triangle$ ABC is transformed using the matrix M where M = $\begin{pmatrix} 0.8 & 0.6 \\ -0.6 & 0.8 \end{pmatrix}$ onto

$\triangle$ A$_1$B$_1$C$_1$. Draw the points A(0,0), B(2,4) and C(−1,3) and their images.

If matrix N = $\begin{pmatrix} 1.6 & 1.2 \\ -1.2 & 1.6 \end{pmatrix}$ draw $\triangle$A$_2$B$_2$C$_2$ the image of $\triangle$ ABC under

this matrix. Describe the transformation determined by matrix N in geometric terms.

9. $\triangle$ ABC has co-ordinates A(1,2), B(3,3) and C(1,3). Transformation V is

given by $\begin{pmatrix} 0 & -1 \\ -1 & 0 \end{pmatrix}$ and transformation W by the matrix $\begin{pmatrix} 4 \\ 4 \end{pmatrix}$

a) Draw $\triangle$ ABC and $\triangle$ A$_1$B$_1$C$_1$, the image of $\triangle$ ABC under the transformation V

b) Draw $\triangle$ A$_2$B$_2$C$_2$, the image of $\triangle$ A$_1$B$_1$C$_1$, under the transformation W.

c) What single transformation maps $\triangle$ ABC onto $\triangle$ A$_2$B$_2$C$_2$?

10. $\triangle$ ABC has co-ordinates of A(2,5), B(2,2) and C(4,2). Draw the images of

this triangle under the transformation given by the matrices i) $\begin{pmatrix} -\frac{1}{2} & 0 \\ 0 & -\frac{1}{2} \end{pmatrix}$

ii) $\begin{pmatrix} \frac{1}{2} & 0 \\ 0 & \frac{1}{2} \end{pmatrix}$. Label these triangles J and K. What is the single transform-

ation that maps $\triangle$ J onto $\triangle$ K?

If the area of $\triangle$ K is x square units what is the area of $\triangle$ ABC?

11. Transformation J is represented by the matrix J = $\begin{pmatrix} 1 & 0 \\ 0 & -1 \end{pmatrix}$ and

transformation K by the matrix K = $\begin{pmatrix} 0 & 1 \\ 1 & 0 \end{pmatrix}$. $\triangle$ ABC has co-ordinates

A(1,0), B(1,2) and C(4,2).

a) Draw the image of $\triangle$ ABC when transformed by J. Call this $\triangle$ A$_1$B$_1$C$_1$.

b) Draw the image of $\triangle$ A$_1$B$_1$C$_1$ when transformed by K. Call this

$\triangle$ A$_2$B$_2$C$_2$

c) What single transformation will transform $\triangle$ ABC onto $\triangle$ A$_2$B$_2$C$_2$?

Show that this transformation can be expressed in terms of the matrix product KJ.

12. As question 11 but let J = $\begin{pmatrix} 1 & 0 \\ 0 & -1 \end{pmatrix}$ and K = $\begin{pmatrix} -1 & 0 \\ 0 & -1 \end{pmatrix}$

13. $\triangle$ ABC is represented by the points A(0,0), B(0,3) and C(2,3). Draw this

triangle and its image when transformed by the matrix $\begin{pmatrix} 1 & 1 \\ -1 & 1 \end{pmatrix}$. From

your diagram describe two separate transformations which are equivalent to this transformation.

VECTORS

VECTORS

A vector is a quantity which has both magnitude and direction. It is a movement in a straight line (as in a **translation**). Any quantity which relies on direction as well as size to describe it is a vector. For example, speed is described in terms of size only (20 km/hr) but velocity is a vector quantity (20 km/hr in a southerly direction).

Vectors can be expressed as a column matrix $\begin{pmatrix} x \\ y \end{pmatrix}$ where x describes the horizontal movement and y the vertical movement, eg.

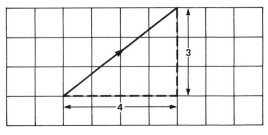

This vector is $\begin{pmatrix} 4 \\ 3 \end{pmatrix}$

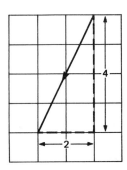

This vector is $\begin{pmatrix} -2 \\ -4 \end{pmatrix}$

Notice that the direction of the vector is given by the arrow.

Adding vectors

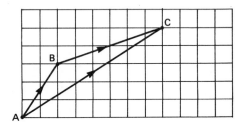

Vector $\overrightarrow{AB}$ followed by vector $\overrightarrow{BC}$ represents a movement from A to C

i.e. $\overrightarrow{AB} + \overrightarrow{BC} = \overrightarrow{AC}$

or $\begin{pmatrix} 2 \\ 3 \end{pmatrix} + \begin{pmatrix} 6 \\ 2 \end{pmatrix} = \begin{pmatrix} 8 \\ 5 \end{pmatrix}$

Notice that vectors are added like column matrices

Magnitude of a vector

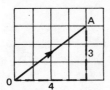

By Pythagoras' theorem the length of OA $= \sqrt{4^2 + 3^2} = \sqrt{25} = 5$

i.e. the magnitude of vector $\begin{pmatrix} x \\ y \end{pmatrix}$ is $\sqrt{x^2 + y^2}$

Vectors can be written in the form of a lower case letter

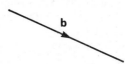

Equivalent vectors
These must have the same magnitude (length) and the same direction (parallel to each other)

a = b

Multiplying a vector by a scalar

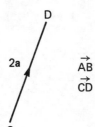

$\overrightarrow{AB} = a$
$\overrightarrow{CD} = 2a$

$\overrightarrow{AB}$ is parallel to $\overrightarrow{CD}$

$\overrightarrow{CD}$ is twice as long as $\overrightarrow{AB}$

if $\overrightarrow{AB} = \begin{pmatrix} 2 \\ 3 \end{pmatrix}$ then $\overrightarrow{CD} = 2 \begin{pmatrix} 2 \\ 3 \end{pmatrix} = \begin{pmatrix} 4 \\ 6 \end{pmatrix}$

Vectors ka and la are parallel

Negative vectors

$$\overrightarrow{AB} = \mathbf{a}$$ $$\overrightarrow{BA} = -\mathbf{a}$$

Notice that $\overrightarrow{BA}$ is the negative of $\overrightarrow{AB}$

If $\overrightarrow{AB} = \begin{pmatrix} 2 \\ 3 \end{pmatrix}$ then $\overrightarrow{BA} = \begin{pmatrix} -2 \\ -3 \end{pmatrix}$

Example 20.1

In the quadrilateral ABCD, A has co-ordinates $(1, -1)$, C has co-ordinates $(3,1)$,

$\overrightarrow{DC} = \begin{pmatrix} 1 \\ 3 \end{pmatrix}$ and $\overrightarrow{AB} = 2\overrightarrow{DC}$

Find

(a) $\overrightarrow{AB}$ (b)   the co-ordinates of B
(c)   the geometrical relations between AB and DC

(a) $\overrightarrow{AB} = 2\overrightarrow{DC}$

$= 2 \begin{pmatrix} 1 \\ 3 \end{pmatrix}$

$\overrightarrow{AB} = \begin{pmatrix} 2 \\ 6 \end{pmatrix}$

(b)   Co-ordinates of B are

$(1 + 2, -1 + 6) = (3,5)$ ◀───── By combining the co-ordinates of A with the vector $\overrightarrow{AB}$

(c) $\overrightarrow{AB} = 2\overrightarrow{DC}$
∴ AB and DC are parallel and DC is twice the length of AB

Example 20.2

0 is the origin and OAB is a triangle with point P on AB such that PB = 3AP.

Given that $\overrightarrow{OA} = 8\mathbf{a}$ and $\overrightarrow{OB} + 12\mathbf{b}$ find in terms of $\mathbf{a}$ and $\mathbf{b}$ the following

(a) $\overrightarrow{AB}$ (b) $\overrightarrow{AP}$ (c) $\overrightarrow{OP}$

Draw a sketch first

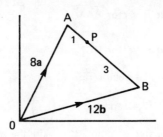

(a) From the diagram $\vec{AB} = \vec{AO} + \vec{OB}$

$= -8a + 12b$

$\vec{AB} = 12b - 8a$

or $4(3b - 2a)$

(b) $\vec{AP} = 1/4 (\vec{AB})$

$= 1/4 \times 4 (3b - 2a)$

$= 3b - 2a$

(c) $\vec{OP} = \vec{OA} + \vec{AP}$

$= 8a + 3b - 2a$

$= 6a + 3b$

or $3 (2a + b)$

EXERCISE 20.1

1. $\vec{AB} = \begin{pmatrix} 2 \\ 3 \end{pmatrix}$ and $\vec{BC} = \begin{pmatrix} 3 \\ 5 \end{pmatrix}$ calculate $\vec{AC}$

2. $\vec{OP} = \begin{pmatrix} 1 \\ -1 \end{pmatrix}$ and $\vec{PQ} = \begin{pmatrix} -3 \\ 1 \end{pmatrix}$ calculate $\vec{OQ}$

3. Express $\vec{AB} + \vec{BC} + \vec{CD}$ in its simplest form.

4. Find the magnitude of the following vectors

(a) $\begin{pmatrix} 3 \\ 4 \end{pmatrix}$ (b) $\begin{pmatrix} 5 \\ 12 \end{pmatrix}$ (c) $\begin{pmatrix} -3 \\ 4 \end{pmatrix}$ (d) $\begin{pmatrix} 4 \\ -3 \end{pmatrix}$ (e) $\begin{pmatrix} -12 \\ 5 \end{pmatrix}$

5. (a) If $\vec{AB} = 3a$ and $\vec{CD} = 6a$ write down the geometrical relationship between $\vec{AB}$ and $\vec{CD}$.

(b) What is the geometrical relationship between vectors $4a + 2b$ and $6a + 3b$?

(c) What is the geometrical relationship between vectors $\vec{AB} = \begin{pmatrix} 4 \\ 1 \end{pmatrix}$ and $\vec{CD} \begin{pmatrix} 2 \\ \frac{1}{2} \end{pmatrix}$?

6. (a) If $\vec{AB} = \begin{pmatrix} 6 \\ 3 \end{pmatrix}$ what is vector $\vec{BA}$?

(b) If $\vec{CD} = \begin{pmatrix} -3 \\ 2 \end{pmatrix}$ what is vector $\vec{DC}$?

(c) If $\vec{EF} = 6\mathbf{a} + 2\mathbf{b}$ what is vector $\vec{FE}$?

7. Point A has co-ordinates (2,4) and $\vec{AB} = \begin{pmatrix} 4 \\ 3 \end{pmatrix}$

Calculate (i) the co-ordinates of point B   (ii) the magnitude of $\vec{AB}$.

8. OPQR is a quadrilateral such that $\vec{OP} = \mathbf{a} + 2\mathbf{b}, \vec{PQ} = 5\mathbf{a}$ and $\vec{RQ} = 3\mathbf{a} = 6\mathbf{b}$.
Find (i) $\vec{OQ}$ (ii) the geometrical relationship between $\vec{OP}$ and $\vec{RQ}$

(iii) $\vec{RP}$

9. In triangle ABC, A has co-ordinates (1, −2) B has co-ordinates (2,3) and

$AC = \begin{pmatrix} 4 \\ -1 \end{pmatrix}$

Calculate (i)   the co-ordinates of C

(ii)   the vector $\vec{AB}$ in the form $\begin{pmatrix} x \\ y \end{pmatrix}$

10. OABC is a parallelogram with O the origin. $\vec{OA} = 12\mathbf{m}$ and $\vec{OB} = 12\mathbf{n}$.
Y is the mid point of AC and X is a point on the line AB such that
$AX = \frac{1}{2}XB$. Find in terms of $\mathbf{m}$ and $\mathbf{n}$.

(a) $\vec{OX}$ (b) $\vec{AC}$ (c) $\vec{AY}$ (d) $\vec{OY}$
What is the geometrical relationship between points O, X and Y?

11.

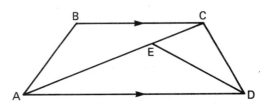

If $\vec{AD} = 12\mathbf{b}$, $\vec{DC} = 6\mathbf{a}$, AD is parallel to BC and AE = 5EC find
(a) $\vec{AC}$ (b) $\vec{DE}$ (c) $\vec{AB}$ in terms of $\mathbf{a,b}$ and k given that $\vec{BC} = k\mathbf{b}$.

12. If $\vec{AC} = \begin{pmatrix} 3 \\ 4 \end{pmatrix}$ and $\vec{AB} = \begin{pmatrix} 4 \\ 1 \end{pmatrix}$ write down $\vec{BC}$ as a column vector.

13. In triangle OAB $\vec{OA} = 6\mathbf{a}$ and $\vec{OB} = 9\mathbf{b}$. Point P is on AB such that
AP = $\frac{1}{2}$PB. Find in terms of $\mathbf{a}$ and $\mathbf{b}$

(a) $\vec{AB}$ (b) $\vec{AP}$ (c) $\vec{OP}$.

14. OABC is a parallelogram. If $\vec{OA}$ = **4a** and $\vec{OC}$ = **4c** find

(a) $\vec{AC}$ (b) $\vec{AP}$ where P is the mid point of AC   (c) $\vec{OP}$.

If X is the mid point of CB find   (d) $\vec{PX}$. What is the geometrical relationship between OX and OC?

15. ABCDEF is a regular hexagon with centre O. $\vec{OA}$ = **a** and $\vec{OB}$ = **b**

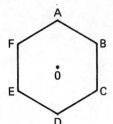

Express in terms of **a** and **b** the vectors

(a) $\vec{OD}$ (b) $\vec{OE}$ (c) $\vec{DA}$

(d) $\vec{BC}$ (e) $\vec{OC}$ (f) $\vec{CF}$

16. O, A, B and C are points such that $\vec{OA}$ = $\begin{pmatrix} 2 \\ 4 \end{pmatrix}$, $\vec{AB}$ = $\begin{pmatrix} 4 \\ 2 \end{pmatrix}$ and $\vec{CB}$ = $\begin{pmatrix} 5 \\ 5 \end{pmatrix}$

(a) Express $\vec{OC}$ in the form of a column vector

(b) Express $\vec{CB}$ in the form k $\vec{OC}$ where k is a scalar.

D is a point such that $\vec{OD}$ is $\begin{pmatrix} -1 \\ 2 \end{pmatrix}$

(c) Find $\vec{DB}$

(d) What is the geometrical relationship between points D, A and B?

STATISTICS AND
PROBABILITY

STATISTICS

Presentation of data

a) **Horizontal bar chart**

> Note — the length of each bar is proportional to the number of pupils it represents.

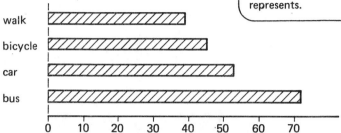

Bar chart showing how pupils get to school

b) **Vertical bar chart**

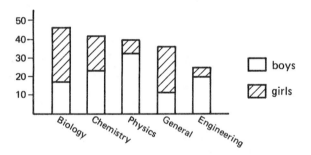

Bar chart showing the number of 4th year pupils opting for science subjects

c) **Pie charts**

Each quantity or number is represented by a sector of a circle. The angle at the centre of the circle for each sector is found using the formula

$$\text{Angle} = \frac{\text{Number in sector}}{\text{Total number}} \times 360°$$

Example 21.1

A class of 36 pupils were asked how they normally came to school. 15 said they came by bus, 10 walked, 8 came by car and 3 by bicycle. Show this on a pie chart.

Bus   Angle at centre = $\frac{15}{36} \times 360° = 150°$

Walk   Angle at centre = $\frac{10}{36} \times 360° = 100°$

Car   Angle at centre = $\frac{8}{36} \times 360° = 80°$

Bicycle   Angle at centre = $\frac{3}{36} \times 360° = 30°$

Total $\underline{360°}$

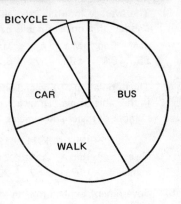

c)   **Pictogram**

    Using the example of the pie chart this can be shown as follows

        Bus   ☥ ☥ ☥ ☥ ☥ ☥ ☥ ☥ ♀

        Walk   ☥ ☥ ☥ ☥ ☥   Scale ☥

                                         represents 2 pupils

        Car   ☥ ☥ ☥ ☥

        Bicycle   ☥ ♀

Pictogram showing how pupils go to school.

EXERCISE 21.1

---

1)

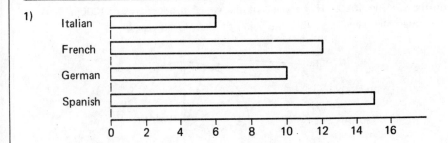

    The bar chart shows the number of people who take Languages in the 5th form.
    How many take each language?

2)   The United Kingdom is made up of the following approximate areas.
    England 12·8m hectares, Wales 2m hectares, Scotland 7·8m hectares and
    Northern Ireland 1·4m hectares. Display this information on a pie chart.

3) The average monthly rainfall for England is given in the table below. Display this on a suitable bar chart. (All dimensions are in m.m.)

Jan	Feb	Mar	Apr	May	Jun	Jul	Aug	Sep	Oct	Nov	Dec
85	84	58	57	68	60	72	89	83	82	96	91

4) The population of England and Wales (to the nearest hundred thousand) is shown in the table below. Draw a bar chart of this data, distinguishing between the number of males and females.

	1901	1911	1921	1931	1941	1951	1961	1971	1981
Males	18·5	20·4	21·0	22·0	N/A	24·1	25·5	27·0	27·1
Females	19·7	21·7	23·0	24·0	N/A	26·1	27·2	28·6	28·7

5) Government expenditure in the Housing and Social Security sector in 1983 were, approximately, Housing £6000m, Education £16000m, National Health Service £14500m, Social Services £3000m and Social Security £32500m. Represent this information on a pie chart.

6) The pie chart shows the amount of Engineering Production carried out in the United Kingdom in 1983. If the total expenditure was £54000m calculate the expenditure in (a) Mechanical Engineering (b) Motor Vehicle Production. What percentage of the total does Electrical and Electronic Engineering represent?

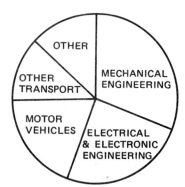

7) The diagram shows the approximate value of the output of Agricultural crops in the U.K. in 1983. If the value of the wheat produced was £1200m, find
   (a) the total value   (b) the value of the oilseed rape.

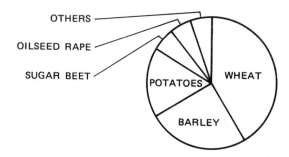

318

8) The pie chart shows the approximate amount of net income spent by an average family. Calculate (a) the percentage of their income spent on food (b) the amount spent on housing per week if their weekly wage is £170.

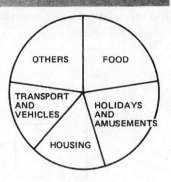

9) Christian   🧍🧍🧍🧍🧍🧍🧍🧍🧍🧍

Islamic   🧍🧍🧍🧍🧍

Hindi   🧍🧍🧍🧍 ○

Confucianism   🧍🧍🧍🧍

Buddhists   🧍 🧍   🧍 = 100 million people

The pictogram shows the approximate number of followers of the main religions of the world. Estimate the number of followers of each.

10) The main languages of the world are shown below. Draw a pictogram to show these allowing one symbol (🧍) to represent 50 million people.

Chinese	550 million	English	300 million
Spanish	190 million	Hindi	175 million
Russian	130 million	Arabic	115 million

Collection and Classification of data

Data is collected together by means of a tally chart. Each classification is counted by means of a tally (/) to obtain the frequency.

Example 21.2

A class of 30 pupils were asked what their shoe sizes were. The results are given below.

4,3,5,5,4,5,6,4,5,7,5,7,4,5,6,6,8,4,3,5,8,7,3,6,5,6,6,4,5,6.

Shoe size	Tally	Frequency
3	///	3
4	##// /	6
5	##// ////	9
6	##// //	7
7	///	3
8	//	2
	Total	30

This tally chart shows a **frequency distribution** which can be represented in the form of a **histogram**.

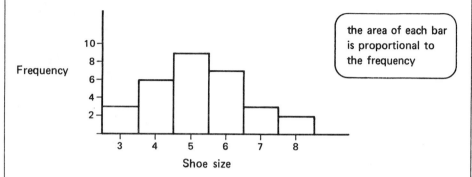

the area of each bar is proportional to the frequency

A **frequency diagram** (or polygon) can also be used to illustrate a frequency distribution. The mid-points of the tops of the rectangles of the histogram are plotted.

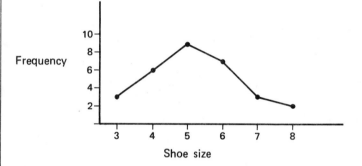

Class intervals are used when the range of values are large.

Example 21.3

Draw up a frequency table for the following set of raw data putting it into class intervals of 0–9, 10–19, etc

24, 44, 43, 41, 62, 81, 36, 35, 33, 62, 63, 59, 87, 51 70, 45 57, 60, 59, 55, 2, 43, 44, 73, 55, 19, 54, 83, 71, 12, 23, 67, 55, 62, 27, 51, 91, 38, 46, 75, 59, 65, 51, 61, 91, 8, 15, 56.

Classification	Tally	Frequency
0–9	//	2
10–19	///	3
20–29	///	3
30–39	////	4
40–49	//// //	7
50–59	//// //// //	12
60–69	//// ///	8
70–79	////	4
80–89	///	3
90–99	//	2

This can now be represented by a histogram thus

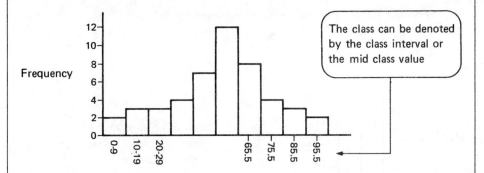

The class can be denoted by the class interval or the mid class value

For the frequency diagram (polygon) the mid class mark should be used.

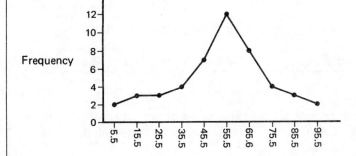

EXERCISE 21.2

1) Complete this tally chart

height		frequency
120cm	//	2
121cm	//// /	6
122cm	//// //// ////	
123cm	////	
124cm	///	
	total	

2) Construct a tally chart for the raw data given below

   3, 4, 5, 2, 5, 4, 3 1, 3, 3, 4, 6, 5, 2, 3, 2, 3, 2, 5, 3, 1, 2, 4, 6, 5, 4, 3, 1, 4, 1.

3)

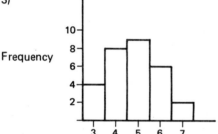

From this histogram construct a frequency chart (or tally chart) of the distribution.

4) Construct a frequency diagram from the following frequency distribution.

Height of tomato plants	89cm	90cm	91cm	92cm	93cm
Distribution	2	4	5	6	3

5) Draw up a frequency table for the following set of marks (out of 30) obtained by a class of 36 pupils in a test. Use the class intervals 0—4, 5—9, 10—14, 15—19, 20—24, and 25—30.
   9, 15, 28, 24, 3, 29, 22, 15, 18, 12, 19, 24, 23, 17, 24, 16, 17, 1, 6, 13, 12, 13, 11, 21, 27, 22, 16, 13, 8, 2, 5, 14, 17, 19, 8, 16.

6) Draw a histogram from the data in question 5.
7) Draw a frequency polygon using the data in question 5. Use mid class marks of 2, 7 etc.

AVERAGES

Mean

This is the average most often used. It makes use of all the data and is therefore representative of the whole distribution.

$$\text{Mean} = \frac{\text{Sum of all the values}}{\text{Number of values}}$$

Example 21.4

Find the mean of the numbers 6, 4, 3, 8, 5, 6, 4, 7, 2, 5.

$$\text{Mean} = \frac{6+4+3+8+5+6+4+7+2+5}{10} = \frac{50}{10} = 5$$

Median

This is the middle value. Its most important use is when extreme values are unknown.

Example 21.5

Find the median of the following numbers

Numbers	under 10	10	11	12	13	14	over 14
Frequency	2	3	4	2	2	1	2

Putting these numbers down in order
−, −, 10, 10, 10, 11, 11, 11, 11, 12, 12, 13, 13, 14, −, −
Since there are 16 numbers there are two middle numbers the 8th and 9th.
These are both 11   ∴ Median is 11

Note (1)   If the 8th and 9th values had been different we would take the average (mean) of the two as the median.

Note (2)   The position of the middle number can be found by adding 1 to the number of values and dividing by 2. In this case

Mid number is $\dfrac{16 + 1}{2} = 8\frac{1}{2}$ i.e. 8th and 9th

Mode

This is the most commonly occurring value. It is used when an exact value is needed, e.g. the average family car is designed for the most popular family size of 2 rather than the impractical size of 2.5 (the mean size)

Example 21.6

The table below shows the shoe sizes for 30 people

Shoe size	3	4	5	6	7	8
Frequency	3	6	9	7	3	2

From the table 9 people have size 5

∴ Mode is 5

EXERCISE 21.3

Find the mean of each of the sets of numbers in questions 1 to 6

1) 13, 16, 20, 24, 27, 29, 33.
2) 221, 352, 234, 421, 301, 383.
3) 2·6, 1·9, 2·7, 2·1, 3·2, 3·0.
4) 43½, 47½, 39½, 34½.
5) 179, 111, 152, 233, 244, 221.
6) 141, 126, 117, 64, 72, 65, 85, 120, 141, 132.

Find the median number in each of the sets of numbers in questions 7 to 10.

7) 41, 85, 72, 17, 41, 16, 54, 55, 10.
8) 71, 44, 72, 33, 100, 58.
9) 87, 31, 10, 94, 78, 85, 88, 94, 20, 41.
10) 28, 22, 78, 78, 96, 70, 34, 30, 58, 23, 24, 89, 80.

Find the modal class (or mode) of the sets of numbers in questions 11 to 15.

11)

Class	1	2	3	4	5	6	7	8	9	10
Frequency	5	8	17	20	23	19	14	12	8	6

12)

Class	2	4	6	8	10
Frequency	4	7	8	12	8

13)

Class	10	20	30	40	50
Frequency	62	73	53	27	19

14)

Class Interval	0 — 9	10 — 19	20 — 29	30 — 39
Frequency	18	36	30	16

15)

Class Interval	0 — 99	100 — 199	200 — 299	300 — 399
Frequency	8	18	40	26

CUMULATIVE FREQUENCY

The table below shows the heights of 60 tomato plants to the nearest centimetre.

height (cm)	40	41	42	43	44	45
frequency	4	10	14	17	10	5

The cumulative frequency table gives the number of plants which are less than 40½ cm in height etc.

height (cm) (class limit)	40½	41½	42½	43½	44½	45½
cumulative frequency	4	14	28	45	55	60

(Note that a recorded height of 40 cm can lie between 39·5 and 40·5 cm. This means that its class limit is 40·5)

The diagram below shows the cumulative frequency plotted against the height and is called the **cumulative frequency curve** or Ogive.

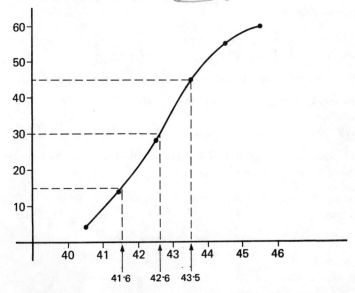

Since half of the plants (30) have a height of under 42·6 cm this height is the **median**.

Since a quarter of the plants (15) have a height of under **41·6** this is the **lower quartile**.

Since three quarters (45) have heights of under **43·5** this is the **upper quartile**.

The difference between the upper quartile and the lower quartile is known as the **interquartile range**. In this case the interquartile range is **43·5 − 41·6 = 1·9 cm.**

EXERCISE 21.4

1) The frequency table below shows the lengths (to the nearest centimetre) of 36 leaves taken from a tree. Use it to write down a cumulative frequency table with class limits of 1·5, 2·5 cm etc.

Length	1	2	3	4	5	6	7	8	9	10
Frequency	1	1	4	6	9	7	4	2	1	1

2) The table below shows the frequency distribution of the wages (measure to the nearest £) for weekly paid employees in a factory. Using class limits of £59.50, £79.50 etc write down a cumulative frequency table. Use this table to construct a cumulative frequency polygon and from it estimate
   (a) the median   (b) the lower quartile   (c) the upper quartile
   (d) the interquartile range.

weekly wages (£)	Under 60	60 − 79	80 − 99	100 − 119	120 − 139
no. of employees	8	15	31	20	7

3) The table below shows measurements of a manufactured item correct to the nearest millimetre.

length (mm)	42	43	44	45	46
frequency	4	20	33	27	6

Copy and complete the following cumulative frequency table

length (mm)	42½	43½	44½	45½	46½
cumulative frequency	4	24			

4) Thirty pupils were asked how many children there were in their family. The table below shows the replies.

No. in family	1	2	3	4	5	6	7
Frequency	7	13	5	2	1	1	1

Copy and complete the cumulative frequency table

No. in family	1	2	3	−	−	−	−
Cumulative frequency	7	20					

Construct a cumulative frequency polygon and from it estimate the median number of children per family.

5) The diagram below shows a cumulative frequency curve for the length of 100 engineering components

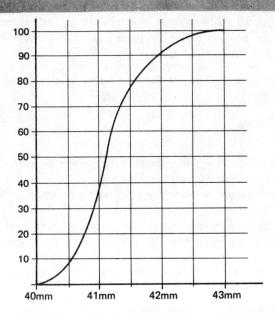

From the curve estimate   a) the median length   b) the upper quartile
                          c) the lower quartile   d) the interquartile range

6) The table below shows the runs scored by batsmen in a game of cricket.

Runs scored	1–10	11–20	21–30	31–40	41–50
Frequency	5	11	13	7	1

Construct a cumulative frequency table and write down the number of
innings where   a) less than 31 runs were scored
                b) more than 20 runs were scored

7) From the histogram below produce a cumulative frequency table and write
down the number of plants that are   a) less than 63·5 cm high
                                          b) greater than 61·5 cm in height
                                          Also find the mean of the
                                          distribution

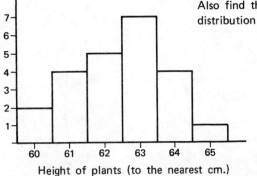

Height of plants (to the nearest cm.)

8) Batteries are tested by using them in an electric toy and recording the length of time the toy operates before the battery fails. The results of 40 batteries are as follows (to the nearest hour)

10	12	10	12	11	12	13	11	13	12
11	12	12	13	10	12	14	12	11	13
10	13	11	13	14	14	11	12	12	14
11	13	12	13	12	13	13	11	12	14

a) Construct a frequency table from this data with class sizes of 10, 11, 12, 13, and 14 hours.
b) Construct a cumulative frequency table with class limits of 10.5 hrs, 11.5 hrs etc.
c) Draw a cumulative frequency curve and from it estimate (1) the median (2) the upper and lower quartiles (3) the interquartile range.

9) The number of absentees from a class during a period of a 60 day term are given in the table below

No. of absentees	0	1	2	3	4	5	6	7
Frequency (days)	9	12	15	11	6	4	2	1

a) Write down a cumulative frequency table
b) Draw the cumulative frequency curve
c) From the curve estimate the median number of days

10) The speed of vehicles (to the nearest 1 mile per hour) passing a point on a motorway were as follows

speed (m.p.h.)	20–29	30–39	40–49	50–59	60–69	70–79	80–89
frequency	3	26	41	48	37	26	5

a) Write down the class limits
b) Construct a cumulative frequency table
c) Draw a cumulative frequency curve
d) From the curve estimate the median, upper and lower quartiles and the interquartile range.

PROBABILITY

Probability is the measure of the chance of an event happening.

Tossing a coin can have two different outcomes, a head or a tail. The probability of any one of these happening is ½ (1 chance in 2)

Throwing a dice can have six different outcomes. The probability of any one of these happening is 1/6 (1 chance in 6). Also the probability of throwing an even number is 3/6 = ½ (3 chances in 6)

The impossibility of an event happening is indicated by 0 (zero). The certainty of an event happening is indicated by 1. All other events have probabilities lying between 0 and 1.

Mutually exclusive events are events which cannot happen at the same time.
e.g.   getting a 5 or 6 with one throw of a dice
getting a King or Ace when drawing one card from a pack
getting a head or tail when tossing a coin once

To find the probabilities of either one or the other of these happening we add their respective probabilities
P (A or B) = P (A) + P (B)
Also for three events
P (A or B or C) = P(A) + P(B) + P(C) etc.
e.g.   the probability of throwing a 5 or 6 with a dice is
1/6 + 1/6 = 2/6 = 1/3

The probability of drawing a king or ace from a pack is

$$\frac{4}{52} + \frac{4}{52} = \frac{8}{52} = \frac{2}{13}$$

Independent events are events which do not affect each other, e.g. tossing a coin and throwing a dice.
To find the probability that two independent events will happen we multiply their respective probabilities
P (A and B) = P (A) X P (B)
Also for three events
P (A and B and C). P (A) X P (B) X P (C) etc.
e.g.   the probability of getting a head and a 3 when a coin and dice are thrown together is   1/2 X 1/6 = 1/12

If the probability of an event happening is P then the probability of it not happening is 1 − P
e.g.   the probability of not getting a 3 when throwing a dice is 1 − 1/6 = 5/6
(i.e. probability of getting a 1, 2, 4, 5, or 6)

Example 21.7

A bag contains 10 sweets, 2 red, 3 green and 5 orange. What is the probability of taking out

(a)   a red sweet
(b)   a sweet which is not red
(c)   a green sweet
(d)   a green or red sweet
(e)   a red sweet followed by a green sweet after replacing the red one
(f)   a red sweet and then a green sweet without replacing the red one.

(a) $\dfrac{2}{10} = \dfrac{1}{5}$ (b) $1 - \dfrac{1}{5} = \dfrac{4}{5}$ (c) $\dfrac{3}{10}$

(d)   For mutually exclusive events P (green) + P (red) = $1 + \dfrac{3}{10} = \dfrac{5}{10} = \dfrac{1}{2}$

(e)   For independent events P (red) $\times$ P (green) = $\dfrac{1}{5} \times \dfrac{3}{10} = \dfrac{3}{50}$

(f)   This time there are only 9 sweets left after the first has gone

$\therefore$ P (red) $\times$ P (green) = $\dfrac{1}{5} \times \dfrac{3}{9} = \dfrac{1}{5} \times \dfrac{1}{3} = \dfrac{1}{15}$

3 green and 9 sweets left

Using a tree diagram

Example 21.8

A coin is tossed three times. Draw a tree diagram to show all the probabilities. From the diagram determine the probability of obtaining two tails and one head.

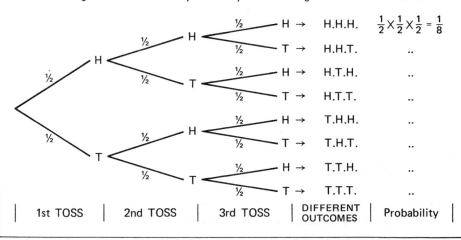

| 1st TOSS | 2nd TOSS | 3rd TOSS | DIFFERENT OUTCOMES | Probability |

There are 8 different outcomes
There are 3 outcomes of 2 tails and 1 head
∴ Probability of two tails and 1 head is 3/8
(or since the probability of each outcome is 1/8, the probability of 3 outcomes
is 3/8).

Example 21.9
Two dice are thrown and their values added. Draw up a table to show their sums
and find the probability that the sum is 8.

Table

2nd dice

1st dice		1	2	3	4	5	6
	1	2	3	4	5	6	7
	2	3	4	5	6	7	8
	3	4	5	6	7	8	9
	4	5	6	7	8	9	10
	5	6	7	8	9	10	11
	6	7	8	9	10	11	12

There are 36 possible outcomes
There are 5 outcomes giving a sum of 8
∴ Probability of giving 8 is 5/36

EXERCISE 21.5

Find the probability of the events in questions 1 to 6 happening
1) Throwing the number 2 on a dice
2) Drawing a king from a pack of cards
3) Selecting a girl from a class containing 20 boys and 15 girls
4) Winning first prize in a raffle if you hold 10 tickets and 200 have been sold
5) Picking an even number from the numbers 1 to 20 inclusive
6) Throwing an odd number on a dice
7) Find the probability of an event not happening if the probability of it
   happening is (a) 1/2   (b) 1/4   (c) 1/3   (d) 4/5   (e) 3/4
8) Find the probability of drawing a picture card or an ace from a pack of
   playing cards
9) Find the probability of throwing a 5 or a 3 with a dice
10) Find the probability of choosing either a red or a black ball from a bag
    containing 3 red, 4 black and 5 green balls
11) If P(A) is 1/3 and P(B) is 1/2 what is the probability of A or B happening
    when A and B are mutually exclusive events.

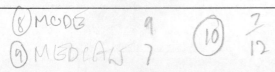

12) What is the probability of drawing an ace from one pack of cards and a king from a second pack

13) What is the probability of drawing an ace followed by a king from a pack of cards without replacement

14) What is the probability of obtaining a head and a 6 when a coin and a dice are thrown together

15) If the probability of two independent events A and B happening is 1/4 and 1/2 find the probability of
    (a) both happening
    (b) both failing
    (c) A happening and B failing
    (d) A failing and B happening

16) What is the probability of drawing two red balls from a bag containing 6 red and 8 blue balls if the first ball drawn is not replaced

17) Two dice bearing the numbers 1, 1, 2, 2, 3, 3 are thrown together and the numbers shown are added. The table below shows the results that can be obtained. Find the probability of obtaining
    (a) 2   (b) 3   (c) 4   (d) 5   (e) 6

1st dice

		1	1	2	2	3	3
	1	2	2	3	3	4	4
	1	2	2	3	3	4	4
2nd dice	2	3	3	4	4	5	5
	2	3	3	4	4	5	5
	3	4	4	5	5	6	6
	3	4	4	5	5	6	6

18) Construct a table to show the sums which can be obtained by taking one number from each of the sets $\{1, 2, 3, 4, 5, 6\}$ and $\{2, 3, 4\}$. Find the probabilities of obtaining a sum of   (a) 6   (b) 4 or 6   (c) a number other than 6

19) A bag contains 3 red sweets and 3 green sweets. A sweet is drawn out and not replaced. A second sweet is then drawn out. By drawing a probability tree diagram calculate the probability of obtaining
    (a) 2 red sweets   (b) a red sweet followed by a green sweet

20) The order of play in a badminton competition is decided by drawing names from a hat. Six names, James, David, Stephen, Abigail, Hannah and Jennie are put into the hat and drawn out at random. Find the probabilities of drawing
    (a) Abigail's name first
    (b) A boy's name first
    (c) A girl's name followed by a boy's name

21) A game of chance has the probability of 2/5 of winning and 3/5 of losing. Copy the following tree diagram showing the outcomes for 3 games and fill in the missing probabilities.

Find the probability of winning

(a) twice in a row

(b) three times in a row

(c) winning the first two times and losing on the third try.

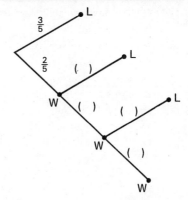

22) A bag contains 3 red counters and 3 blue counters. The tree diagram below shows the probabilities of drawing two counters without replacement. Copy and complete the diagram and find

(a) the probability of drawing a red followed by a blue counter

(b) the probability of drawing two red counters.

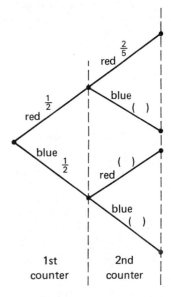

1st counter   2nd counter

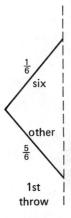

1st throw

23) What is the probability of throwing a 6 on a dice?

What is the probability of throwing a number other than 6 on a dice?

Complete the tree diagram for three throws of a dice, the first has been done for you.

From the diagram find the probability of gaining

(a) three sixes

(b) exactly two sixes (in any order)

(c) exactly one six (in any order)

INVESTIGATIONS

INVESTIGATIONS

1.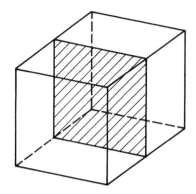

   When a cube is sliced through parallel to one side the shape formed is a square. Investigate what other shapes can be formed by slicing in different ways.

2. a) A 4 X 4 square is cut up into smaller squares (with lengths of whole numbers). How many different ways can this be done? How many squares are produced each time?

   b) Investigate this for other squares. What is the minimum number of squares each can be cut into? (Not 1). Is there any pattern in these numbers?

3. Find sets of fractions, with numerators of unity, which sum to the following fractions   (i) 5/6   (ii) 19/28   (iii) 2/3   (iv) 11/12   (v) 47/60   (vi) 9/11

   example 5/6 = 1/2 + 1/3   Explain how this can be done.

4. A cube measuring n centimetres (n being a whole number) is cut into unit cubes. How many cuts are needed (in terms of n) to do this?

   Investigate also a cuboid measuring ℓ by m by n centimetres (ℓ, m and n being whole numbers).

5. 1 + 2 = 3   4 + 5 + 6 = 7 + 8.   Investigate and find other sets of numbers which behave like this. Can you find a rule to discover these sets?

6. Find a number with 13 factors. Describe how such a number can be found.

7. A 4 squared polyomino is a shape made up of 4 squares, like this. How many 4 squared polyominoes are there?

   How many different 5 squared polyominoes (petominoes) are there?

   How many different 7 squared polyominoes do you expect there to be?

8.

This circle has 2 dots on its circumference and a chord joining them. It produces 2 regions.

This circle has 3 dots, 3 chords and 4 regions. Continue this process and determine whether there is any relationship between the number of dots and the number of chords.

9.

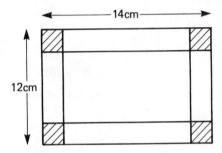

An open box is to be made from a sheet of card measuring 14 cm by 12 cm. Equal size squares are to be cut from the corners, and the sides folded up. What size squares (to the nearest 1/4 cm) need to be cut in order that the volume of the box is a maximum?

10. This is one way of cutting a 4 X 4 board into two identical pieces. How many ways are there altogether, by just using horizontal and vertical cuts?

What is special about a square whose sides are an odd number of units long? Explain why this is so.

Draw all the ways of cutting a 6 X 6 board into identical halves.

11.

1	2	3
4	5	6
7	8	9

Without going onto the same square twice and moving horizontally and vertically only, find how many different ways there are of getting from square 1 to square 9. What is the maximum number of moves? What is the minimum number of moves?

Investigate a 4 X 4 square.

Is there a route requiring an odd number of moves?

12.
What is the maximum number of sides that a polygon drawn on a 4X4 dot grid can have? Investigate for other square grids.

13. Exactly half the prime numbers are the sum of two squares.
i.e. $13 = 9 + 4 = 3^2 + 2^2$. Make a list of primes formed in this way and a list of those which are not.
Find a rule which tests whether or not a prime can be made in this way.

14.
a)

Can you draw this shape (a) without going over the same line twice and without taking your pen off the paper?

b)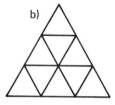

Now try this shape (b).
Can you extend these ideas to larger shapes and write down a general method?

15.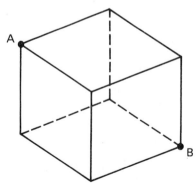
a) Investigate the number of different routes there are from A to B travelling along the edges of the cube.
(i) without any restrictions
(ii) without going over the same edge twice. What is the length of the longest route?

(iii) without going over the same edge twice and moving down and across only, what is the length of the shortest route?
b) Investigate for other prisms, where corners A and B are opposite corners, using the restrictions given in (iii) above and determine a relationship between the number of faces (F) the number of edges (E) and the number of different routes (R).

16. 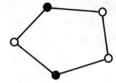 How many different necklaces can be made with 2 black and 3 white beads?
Investigate for other combinations of beads.

17. How many ways are there of cutting a square of 16 dots up into two equal parts using only cuts which join the dots?

18. The diagram is made from 10 straight lines making 15 squares.
a) Find the smallest number of lines needed to make 100 squares.
b) Are there any shapes where the number of lines equals the number of squares?

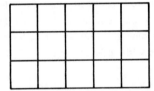

19. Is it possible to have a fraction with a numerator of unity, equal to the sum of two other fractions both with a numerator of unity?
Give examples.
Can you write down a general rule for finding them?

20. By investigating different polyhedra (cube, tetrahedron etc), find a relationship between the number of faces (F), the number of vertices (V) and the number of edges (E).

21. Frogs
Three red counters and three green counters are arranged as shown below with a space in the middle.

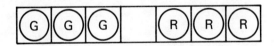

The object is for the three red counters to move to the positions occupied by the three green counters and for the three green counters to move to the positions occupied by the three red counters. This has to be done according to the rules.
(i) The red counters can only move to the left and the green counters can only move to the right.

(ii) The counters can move to an adjacent free space.

(iii) The counters can jump over another counter of the other colour into a free space.

a) How many moves can this be done in?

Write down the series of moves needed.

b) Extend this to other numbers of counters and write down a general rule.

22.

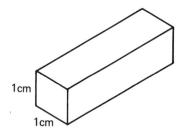

Wooden rods like the one shown are 1, 2, 3, 4 and 5 centimetres long. You have a large supply of all sizes.

a) How many different ways can you make up a length of 5 centimetres?

b) Consider making up other lengths up to 5 centimetres and write down a general rule for determining the number of different ways of making up a length of x centimetres with rods of length 1, 2, 3 . . . x centimetres.

23. **Picks Theorem**

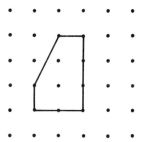

Draw a series of closed figures on dotty-paper (like the one shown). The figures must all have straight edges with their vertices being the dots. Each figure can be described in terms of the number of dots its sides go through (p) and the number of dots within it (i).

In the above figure p = 8 and i = 2. Find the relationship between p, i and A where A is the area of the figure.

ANSWERS

EXERCISE 1.1

1.	$14^{\circ}c$	2.	$1^{\circ}c$	3.	$-6^{\circ}c$
4.	$-2^{\circ}c$	5.	$3^{\circ}c$	6.	$5^{\circ}c$
7.	$-4^{\circ}c$	8.	$-2^{\circ}c$	9.	$9^{\circ}c$
10.	$-11^{\circ}c$	11.	$-14^{\circ}c$	12.	$14^{\circ}c$
13.	$-6^{\circ}c$	14.	$0^{\circ}c$	15.	$0^{\circ}c$
16.	$-23^{\circ}c$	17.	$-17^{\circ}c$	18.	$9^{\circ}c$
19.	$-26^{\circ}c$	20.	$58^{\circ}c$	21.	$4^{\circ}c$
22.	$15^{\circ}c$	23.	$9^{\circ}c$	24.	$9^{\circ}c$
25.	$3^{\circ}c$	26.	$7^{\circ}c$	27.	$3^{\circ}c$
28.	$9^{\circ}c$	29.	$8^{\circ}c$	30.	$5^{\circ}c$
31.	$4^{\circ}c$	32.	$12^{\circ}c$	33.	$5^{\circ}c$
34.	$24^{\circ}c$	35.	$6^{\circ}c$		

EXERCISE 1.2

1. 1,3,5,15
2. 1,2,4,5,10,20
3. 1,2,3,4,6,8,12,24
4. 1,2,3,5,6,10,15,30
5. 1,2,4,8,16,32
6. 1,2,4,5,8,10,20,40
7. 1,3,5,9,15,45
8. 1,2,3,4,5,6,10,12,15,20,30,60
9. 1,71
10. 1,2,3,4,6,7,12,14,21,28,42,84
11. 1,2,3,5,6,9,10,15,18,30,45,90
12. 1,2,4,5,10,20,25,50,100
13. $2 \times 3 \times 5^2$
14. $2^5 \times 5$
15. $2^3 \times 5^2$
16. $2 \times 3 \times 5 \times 7$
17. $2^2 \times 5 \times 13$
18. $3^3 \times 5^2$
19. $3^3 \times 5 \times 7$
20. 5×7^3
21. $3 \times 5 \times 7 \times 11$
22. $3^2 \times 5 \times 23$
23. $2^2 \times 3$ multiply by 3
24. 2×3^2 multiply by 2
25. $2^2 \times 3^2 \times 5$ multiply by 5
26. $2^4 \times 5$ multiply by 5
27. 2×3^4 multiply by 2
28. $2^2 \times 3^2 \times 7$ multiply by 7
29. $5^2 \times 11$ multiply by 11
30. $2^2 \times 3^2 \times 13$ multiply by 13
31. $2^5 \times 19$ multiply by 38
32. $2^2 \times 5 \times 7^2$ multiply by 5
33. $2^3 \times 3 \times 5^2$ multiply by 6
34. $2^3 \times 3^2 \times 5$ multiply by 10
35. $2^2 \times 3^3 \times 5$ multiply by 15
36. $2^2 \times 3 \times 11^2$ multiply by 3
37. 27
38. 45
39. 25
40. 271
41. 147
42. 63
43. 147
44. 45
45. 195

EXERCISE 1.3

1.	3/4	2.	5/8	3.	1	4.	1 1/8
5.	1 3/8	6.	5/8	7.	1 2/5	8.	1 3/8
9.	2 3/4	10.	5/8	11.	3 5/8	12.	1 3/4
13.	5 1/4	14.	3½	15.	3/4	16.	2 1/8
17.	1 1/20	18.	6 1/5	19.	1 13/24	20.	8 1/6
21.	1/6	22.	3/8	23.	7/32	24.	2/5
25.	1 1/8	26.	7/12	27.	2	28.	3 1/8
29.	6 9/16	30.	3/4	31.	2½	32.	1 1/6
33.	1 3/5	34.	1 5/7	35.	2	36.	1 2/5
37.	1 21/44	38.	3 4/7	39.	2 2/3	40.	17/25

EXERCISE 1.4

1.	0·375	2.	0·625	3.	0·15	4.	0·35
5.	0·65	6.	0·0625	7.	0·3125	8.	0·4375
9.	0·8125	10.	0·12	11.	0·52	12.	0·84
13.	0·325	14.	0·425	15.	0·825		

16. $\dfrac{106}{409}$, 0·25920, $\dfrac{239}{922}$, $\dfrac{7}{27}$.

17. $\dfrac{7}{43}$, 0·16280, $\dfrac{387}{2376}$, $\dfrac{170}{1043}$.

18. a) $\quad$ 1/9 = ·1111111 $\qquad$ b) $\quad$ 1/11 = 0·0909090
$\qquad\quad$ 2/9 = ·222222 $\qquad\qquad\qquad$ 2/11 = 0·1818181
$\qquad\quad$ 3/9 = ·333333 $\qquad\qquad\qquad$ 3/11 = 0·2727272
$\qquad\quad$ etc. $\qquad\qquad\qquad\qquad\quad$ 4/11 = 0·3636363
$\qquad\qquad\qquad\qquad\qquad\qquad\qquad\quad$ etc.

EXERCISE 1.5

1.	a)	36	b)	3600	c)	0·36	
	d)	0·0025	e)	250 000	f)	1	
	g)	0·000001	h)	10 000	i)	400	
	j)	900	k)	0·0004	l)	0·09	
2.	a)	27	b)	0·027	c)	−27 000	
	d)	−125	e)	·125	f)	−125 000	
	g)	1	h)	−0·000001	i)	−343	
	j)	0·000343	k)	−343 000	l)	343 000	

3.	a)	0·25	b)	0·5	c)	1	
	d)	−2·5	e)	5	f)	−0·1	
	g)	0·01	h)	0·025	i)	−0·05	
	j)	−0·02	k)	2	l)	−100	
4.	a)	±8	b)	±10	c)	±20	
	d)	±25	e)	±0·2	f)	±0·1	
	g)	±0·4	h)	±0·7	i)	±0·5	
	j)	±30	k)	±40	l)	±0·8	
5.	a)	3	b)	−5	c)	1	
	d)	−4	e)	0·4	f)	−10	
	g)	0·1	h)	2	i)	0·2	
	j)	−0·3	k)	6	l)	−20	
6.	a)	9	b)	36	c)	81	
	d)	100	e)	400	f)	900	
	g)	0·01	h)	0·64	i)	0·016	
	j)	0·0064	k)	160000	l)	360000	
7.	a)	8	b)	64	c)	1	
	d)	−125	e)	−0·027	f)	343	
	g)	−1000	h)	−0·008	i)	−0·000064	
	j)	−0·001	k)	8000	l)	−80000	
8.	a)	0·2	b)	0·5	c)	0·1	
	d)	−5	e)	2	f)	−0·1	
	g)	0·01	h)	0·025	i)	−0·05	
	j)	− 0·025	k)	2	l)	−40	
9.	a)	±3	b)	±6	c)	±8	
	d)	±10	e)	±1	f)	±0·3	
	g)	±0·8	h)	±0·6	i)	±20	
	j)	±30	k)	±40	l)	±50	
10.	a)	1	b)	−3	c)	5	
	d)	−2	e)	0·2	f)	−0·1	
	g)	−4	h)	0·4	i)	−20	
	j)	−10	k)	6	l)	−0·3	
11.	a)	18·49	b)	32·49	c)	88·36	
	d)	204·49	e)	·0961	f)	·000961	
	g)	0·0000022	h)	·005776	i)	64009	
	j)	3317·76	k)	8892·49	l)	16384	
12.	a)	2·2997	b)	−107·85	c)	−131·097	
	d)	781·23	e)	0·0000021	f)	−·068921	
	g)	−·000389	h)	0·157464	i)	398688·26	
	j)	111215·25	k)	2593941·6	l)	16777216	
13.	a)	0·2932551	b)	0·1779359	c)	−0·1190476	
	d)	0·138$\dot{3}$	e)	2·4390244	f)	32·258065	
	g)	−17·857143	h)	−322·58065	i)	0·0135869	
	j)	−0·027$\dot{7}$	k)	−0·0119047	l)	0·0061349	

14. a) ±2·5455844   b) ±2·8896367   c) ±4·4045431
     d) ±6·6037868   e) ±0·7348469   f) ±0·1897366
     g) ±0·1378404   h) ±0·0380788   i) ±11·269428
     j) ±16   k) ±24·310492   l) ±37·709415
15. a) 1·38208   b) 2·13633   c) 2·6357
     d) 2·89488   e) 0·745904   f) 0·878503
     g) 0·24385   h) 0·284387   i) 3·86665
     j) 5·01899   k) 9·22636   l) 20·9203

EXERCISE 1.6

1. $3·6 \times 10$
2. $4·26 \times 10^2$
3. $8·3 \times 10^3$
4. $9·4 \times 10^4$
5. $5·62 \times 10^5$
6. $1·5 \times 10^{-1}$
7. $3·14 \times 10^{-2}$
8. $5·4 \times 10^{-3}$
9. $2·3 \times 10^{-4}$
10. $1·5 \times 10^{-5}$
11. $1·43 \times 10^{-3}$
12. $1·573 \times 10^2$
13. $2·741 \times 10$
14. $4·31 \times 10^{-2}$
15. $3·574 \times 10^2$
16. 13
17. 3400
18. 1485000
19. ·21
20. ·000341
21. 4320000
22. ·00218
23. 936000
24. ·0421
25. 59700
26. 32600
27. ·00485
28. ·0763
29. 621500
30. 0·0000000432

EXERCISE 1.7

1. 11
2. 4
3. 3
4. 9
5. 6
6. 12·8
7. 6·5
8. 3·1
9. 5·25
10. 2 3/4
11. 1 2/3
12. 2 9/10
13. 6 3/4
14. 3/16
15. 3
16. 42½
17. 1
18. 13/20
19. 10
20. 5½

EXERCISE 2.1

1. 200
2. 200
3. 700
4. 3300
5. 2100
6. 3600
7. 35700
8. 68300
9. 31500
10. 24200
11. 70
12. 150
13. 80
14. 90
15. 100
16. 180
17. 170
18. 260
19. 3420
20. 5760

EXERCISE 2.2

1.	a)	7·416	b)	7·42	c)	7·4	d)	7
2.	a)	5·035	b)	5·04	c)	5·0	d)	5
3.	a)	530	b)	500				
4.	a)	3450	b)	3500	c)	3000		
5.	a)	0·0055	b)	0·005				
6.		1·7321						
7.		3·16						
8.		7·52						
9.	a)	5·154	b)	5·15	c)	5·2		
10.	a)	5·014	b)	5·01	c)	5·0		
11.	a)	154·30	b)	154·3				
12.	a)	256·101	b)	256·10	c)	256·1		
13.		15·40						
14.		2·45						

EXERCISE 2.3

1.	18	2.	600	3.	1200	4.	0·72
5.	·06	6.	·00004	7.	4	8.	4
9.	3	10.	22	11.	3	12.	3
13.	10	14.	4	15.	4	16.	2
17.	·2	18.	6	19.	·7	20.	·5
21.	20	22.	60	23.	12	24.	8
25.	100000						

EXERCISE 2.4

1.	235	245	2.	725	775	3.	1250	1350
4.	2495	2505	5.	1345	1355	6.	55·5	56·5
7.	36·5	37·5	8.	4·995	5·005	9.	£25·50	£26·50
10.	5·65	5·75	11.	16·335	16·345	12.	7·85	7·95
13.	16·95	17·05	14.	450·5	451·5	15.	5475	5485

16. a) 9·5 10·5 b) 3·5 4·5 c) 47·25 m^2
    d) 33·25 m^2

17. a) Max 6999
    b) Min 5001

EXERCISE 3.1

1. a) 25%   b) 75%   c) 20%   d) 12½%
    e) 8 1/3%   f) 37½%   g) 56%   h) 33 1/3%
    i) 62½%   j) 14%
2. a) 40%   b) 80%   c) 45%   d) 31%
    e) 58%   f) 71·5%   g) 84·3%   h) 54·3%
    i) 59·4%   j) 65·4%
3. a) 2/5   b) 3/10   c) 13/20   d) 17/20
    e) 11/50   f) 19/50   g) 83/100   h) 9/25
    i) 63/100   j) 97/100
4. a) ·15   b) ·6   c) ·75   d) ·95
    e) ·36   f) ·24   g) ·27   h) ·61
    i) ·73   j) ·17
5. a) 18p   b) 75p   c) £1·19   d) £1·60
    e) £3·96   f) £6·72   g) £5·76   h) £9·12
    i) £3·87   j) £11·00   k) 85p   l) 8·84 m
    m) 445·2 m n) 125 m   o) 1·3 kg   p) 825 g
6. a) 40%   b) 26·7%   c) 65%   d) 26%
    e) 70%   f) 56·7%   g) 40%   h) 52·5%
    i) 29·3%   j) 42·5%   k) 47%   l) 27·1%
7. 62·7%
8. £4620
9. 52 or 53
10. 48%

EXERCISE 3.2

1. 1·06   2. 1·15   3. 1·75
4. 2·00   5. 3·50   6. ·93
7. ·73   8. ·25   9. £5·30
10. £9·10   11. £8·04   12. £10
13. £9·25   14. £9·15   15. 5·85 m
16. 9·1875 m   17. 7·875 m   18. 18·275
19. £7·92   20. £12·32 or £12·33   21. £5·25
22. £41·58   23. £6·27   24. 6·09 m
25. £14·06   26. 8·235 m   27. a) £90
                                                      b) £162
                                                      c) £56·70

28. a) £1·79   b) £1·61
29. a) £517·50   b) £43·13
30. £1·24

EXERCISE 3.3

1. £80	2. £43500	3. £110
4. £65·45	5. £6500	6. £220
7. £48	8. £3	9. £15
10. £370	11. 42300	12. 5m 51cm
13. £9000	14. £55	

EXERCISE 3.4

1. £4·50	2. £36	3. £60
4. £27	5. £48·40	6. £21
7. £38·16	8. £82·75	9. £40·62
10. £140·82	11. £2251·69	12. 31 years
13. £413·28	14. 4375·80, 32·68%	15. 5·92%, 23520
16. 65·3%	17. £613525	

EXERCISE 3.5

1. £5·18	2. £2·99	3. £4·49
4. £11·96	5. £10·06	6. £21·51
7. £29·27	8. £80·96	9. £129·95
10. £180·55	11. £878·60	12. £1177·60
13. £23·66	14. £86·25	15. £475
16. 1st is the cheapest by £45		

EXERCISE 4.1

1. £87·55	2. £56·83	3. £1787·85
4. £2889·85	5. £43·42	6. £1735·65
7. £677·68	8. £160·17	9. £949·87
10. £669·42		

EXERCISE 4.2

1. Fr 526·4	2. DM416·1	3. DR14269·5
4. Es 26059	5. Ptas 476·16	6. $ 42·50
7. £17·75	8. £24·04	9. £4·13
10. £3·62	11. £7·70	12. £34·04
13. Fr 10·75	14. 37p=Fr 3·94 ∴ cheaper in Britain	

EXERCISE 4.3

1.	£506·25	2.	£5536	3.	96p	4.	£1·23
5.	£273	6.	£370	7.	£1·23, £25·90	8.	14p

EXERCISE 4.4

1. £18·66   2. £52·70   3. £36·
4. a) 940 units   b) £53·11   c) 60·51
5. a) 209·44   b) £77·49   c) £86·69
6. £37·99   7. £68.95   8. £17·74

EXERCISE 5.1

1.	3:2	2.	3:2	3.	15:13	4.	2:3
5.	16:7	6.	4:1	7.	9:4	8.	30:13
9.	1:5	10.	9:7	11.	23:50	12.	5:1
13.	20:7	14.	3:1	15.	£2·50	16.	75 cm
17.	£1·40, £1·60	18.	10:11	19.	£9000, £15000.		
20.	£14·25, £19, £23·75			21.	£3750, £2500, £1250.		
22.	50 g						
23.	£10000, £6250, £3750.						

EXERCISE 5.2

1. 7 km   2. 850 m   3. 3·2 km
4. 5 cm   5. 3·4 cm   6. 3·75 km^2
7. 10 sq cm   8.a) 4 1/4 m b) 35 cm c) 1·5 m^2 d) 20 cm^2
9. a) 42·0 cm b) 2·1 cm
10. a) 1050 metres b) 78·75 hectares c) 16·67 cm

EXERCISE 5.3

1. 50·625 mph   2. 122·5 miles   3. 5 hrs 50 mins
4. 60 mph   5. 38·4 miles   6. 15·53
7. 22·31 litres (to 2 d.p.)   8. a) 200 km b) 18·2 litres c) £6·80

9. 11·04 mph   10. 45 mph

11. 5 hrs 32½ mins

EXERCISE 6.1

1. a) $\{1,2,3,4,5\}$ b) $\{$Monday, Tuesday, Wednesday, Thursday, Friday$\}$
    c) $\{$January, February, March, April, September, October, November, December.$\}$
    d) $\{2,3,5,7\}$ e) $\{2,3,5,7,11\ldots\}$
2. a) T   b) F   c) T   d) T   e) T   f) F
    g) F   h) F
3. a) $\{1,2,3\}$ b) $\{3,4,5\}$ c) $\{3\}$ d) $\{1,2,3,4,5\}$
    e) $A' = \{4,5,6,7\}$ f) $B' = \{1,2,6,7\}$ g) $\{1,2,4,5,6,7\}$
    h) $\{6,7\}$
4. $P \cap Q = \{10,12,20\}$ $Q' = \{11,13,14,16,17,18,19\}$

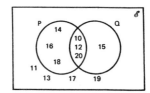

5. $P = \{1,3,5,7,9,11,13,15\}$
    $Q = \{2,3,5,7,11,13\}$
    $P \cap Q = \{3,5,7,11\}$ $P \cup Q = \{1,2,3,5,7,9,11,13,15\}$
6. a) 6
    b) $(A \cap B)' = \{30,31,32,33,34,35,37,38,39\}$
7. $A = \{1,2,3,4,5\}$ $B = \{1,2\}$ $A \cup B = \{1,2,3,4,5\}$
    $A \cap B = \{1,2\}$ $B' = \{3,4,5,6,7,8\}$
8. a) A   b) B   c) $A \cap B$ d) $\mathscr{E}$ e) $A \cup B$
    f) $(A \cap B)'$ g) A' h) B' i) $(A \cup B)'$ j) $A \cap B'$
    k) $A' \cap B$ l) $A \cup B'$ m) $A' \cup B$

EXERCISE 6.2

1. a) 3   b) 4   c) 6   d) 1   e) 7   f) 5
    g) 2
2. a) 24   b) 13   c) 4   d) 35   e) 6   f) 1
    g) 47

3. a) A∩B∩C   b) B∩C   c) B   d) A∪C
   e) C'   f) (A∪B∪C)'

4. a) B = {2,3,5,7,11,13,17,19}   C = {1,2,4,5,10,20}
   b) (i) T   (ii) T   (iii) F   (iv) T
   c) {2,5}
   d)

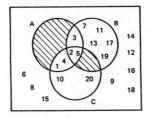

5. a) {3}   b) {1,2,3,5,7,9}   c) {4,6,8,10}
   d) {1,2,3,5,7,9}   e) {2}

6. x = 3
   a) 43   b) 50

7. a) (B∪C)'∩A   b) (B∩C)∩A'   c) B'∩C
   d) B'∩(A∪C)   e) B∩(A∪C)   f) B∪(A∩C)
   g) B∩C   h) C∩A∩B'   i) C∩A'

8.
a)   b)   c)

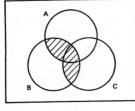 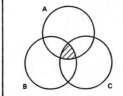 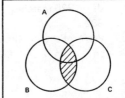

d)   e)   f)

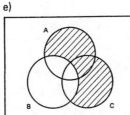 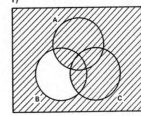

9. a) B∩(A∪C)   b) A∩B∩C   c) B∩C
   d) A∪B

EXERCISE 7.1

1. 11y
2. 3y
3. −2y
4. −9y
5. −23a
6. 15b + 5a
7. 7b + 7a
8. 4a + 7b
9. 8a + 2b
10. 6x − y
11. − 2x − 3y
12. − 4xy + 3y²
13. − 13ab + 2b
14. − 5ab + 5bc
15. 14xy − 9x²
16. $\frac{5x}{6}$
17. $\frac{3y}{4}$
18. $\frac{11x}{12}$
19. $\frac{3a}{4}$
20. $\frac{7a}{12}$
21. 2x + y
22. x + 3y
23. 8x − y

EXERCISE 7.2

1. a) 9 b) 11 c) 2n−1 d) 79
2. a) 20 b) 30 c) n(n+1) or n² + n d) 420
3. a) 15 b) 21 c) $\frac{n^2 + n}{2}$ d) 465
4. a) 15 b) 20 c) 5(n − 1)
5. a) 40 matches b) 60 matches c) 2n(n + 1)
   d) 220 matches
6. 982
7.

Pen	Posts	Crossbars
n	2n+2	6n+2

8. 773
9. a) £5·40
   b) 20 ℓ + 20w + ℓ w + 100
   c) £9·00

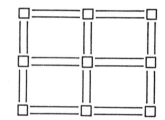

EXERCISE 7.3

1. 11
2. 5
3. 9
4. −1
5. −3
6. −3
7. 4
8. 3
9. 6
10. −8
11. −11
12. −15
13. 3
14. 0
15. 1
16. −6
17. −1
18. −1
19. −4
20. 0
21. −62
22. −15
23. −15
24. −4
25. 3
26. −16
27. −19
28. −11
29. 13
30. −15

EXERCISE 7.4

1. 24	2. −36	3. −18
4. 12	5. 10	6. −6
7. −4	8. 3	9. −3
10. 3	11. 12	12. −6
13. 2	14. $-\dfrac{3}{2}$	15. −1
16. 1	17. −27	18. 81
19. 8	20. −4	

EXERCISE 7.5

1. $3x + 3y$	2. $18x + 24$	3. $-2x + 3$
4. $-3x - 2$	5. $-8x - 20$	6. $-21x + 28$
7. $-12x - 12$	8. $10x - 15$	9. $9x + 6$
10. $13x + 20y$	11. $4x - 5y$	12. $20y - 4x$
13. $2x - 5y$	14. $8x + 5y$	15. $5x + y$
16. $15x + 13y$	17. $38x - 19y$	18. $3x - 26y$
19. $5x - 15y$	20. $6x^2 + 17x$	21. $-3x^2 - 22x$
22. $27x^2 - 5x$	23. $7x^2 + 3x$	24. $15x^2 - 6x$
25. $16x^2 + 27x$		

EXERCISE 7.6

1. $x^2 + 5x + 6$	2. $2x^2 + 5x + 2$	3. $3x^2 + 14x + 8$
4. $30x^2 + 47x + 14$	5. $6x^2 - x - 12$	6. $12x^2 - 5x - 25$
7. $24x^2 - 24x - 18$	8. $15x^2 + x - 6$	9. $8x^2 - 2x - 3$
10. $3x^2 + 2x - 8$	11. $24x^2 - 2x - 15$	12. $6x^2 - 38x + 56$
13. $42x^2 - 58x + 20$	14. $12x^2 - 33x + 18$	15. $72x^2 - 70x + 12$
16. $9x^2 + 12x + 4$	17. $25x^2 + 30x + 9$	18. $36x^2 - 24x + 4$
19. $16x^2 - 40x + 25$	20. $16x^2 - 72x + 81$	

EXERCISE 7.7

1. $2x$	2. ab	3. $2ab$
4. x	5. $3xy$	6. $3(a + 2)$
7. $2(2x + 3)$	8. $3b(a - 2)$	9. $5(ab - 2c)$
10. $5x(2y - x)$	11. $3a(2a - 3b)$	12. $2ab(2 + 3ab)$
13. $1/8a(4b + 1)$	14. $a(1 + b - a)$	15. $a(6b - c + bc)$

16. $a^2 b(7b - 4a)$ 17. $2xy(3 - 2x)$ 18. $\frac{a}{4}(2a - 1)$

19. $2x(xy + 3y - 6x^2)$ 20. $x(5x^2 - x + 1)$ 21. $2(3a^3 - 2ab + 5b)$

22. $xy(5 + 6x - 4y + 3x^2)$ 23. $4ab(ab + 2b - 3a)$ 24. $\frac{ab}{4}(ab - 2)$

25. $\frac{2n}{3}(2 + n)$

EXERCISE 7.8

1. $(m + n)(m - n)$ 2. $(a + 2)(a - 2)$
3. $(xy + z)(xy - z)$ 4. $(ab + 3)(ab - 3)$
5. $(ab + 3c)(ab - 3c)$ 6. $(5a + 3b)(5a - 3b)$
7. $(b + 1)(b - 1)$ 8. $2(2a + 5)(2a - 5)$
9. $3(2x + 3y)(2x - 3y)$ 10. $(x^2 + y)(x^2 - y)$
11. $(x^2 + y^2)(x + y)(x - y)$ 12. $(2a^2 + b)(2a^2 - b)$
13. $(3x^2 + y^2)(3x + y)(3x - y)$ 14. $2x(y + 2x)(y - 2x)$

EXERCISE 7.9

1. $(x + 5)(x + 4)$ 2. $(x - 2)(x - 1)$
3. $(x + 2)(x - 1)$ 4. $(x + 2)(x - 4)$
5. $(x + 6)(x + 5)$ 6. $(x - 6)(x - 4)$
7. $(x + 7)(x - 3)$ 8. $(x + 7)(x - 2)$
9. $(x + 7)(x + 6)$ 10. $(x - 7)(x + 6)$
11. $(x - 10)(x + 2)$ 12. $(x - 12)(x - 3)$
13. $(x - 11)(x + 4)$ 14. $(x + 10)(x - 6)$

EXERCISE 7.10

1. $(2x + 1)(x + 1)$ 2. $(2x + 1)(x + 4)$
3. $(2x + 1)(x + 3)$ 4. $(2x + 2)(x + 3)$
5. $(2x + 3)(x - 2)$ 6. $(3x + 2)(x - 3)$
7. $(2x - 1)(x - 4)$ 8. $(3x - 1)(x - 3)$
9. $(3x - 2)(x - 4)$ 10. $(3x + 7)(x - 2)$
11. $(3x + 4)(x + 5)$ 12. $(3x - 6)(x - 2)$
13. $(2x + 3)(2x + 2)$ 14. $(2x - 3)(2x - 2)$
15. $(x + 3)(4x + 1)$ 16. $(x - 5)(4x - 1)$
17. $(5x - 2)(x + 3)$ 18. $(4x + 1)(x + 5)$
19. $(3x + 1)(2x + 1)$ 20. $(3x + 2)(3x + 2)$
21. $(8x + 3)(x + 1)$ 22. $(4x - 3)(x - 5)$
23. $(5x + 2)(x - 3)$ 24. $(4x - 3)(3x - 1)$

EXERCISE 7.11

1. 1/6

2. 1/6

3. 3/4

4. $\dfrac{xv}{yw}$

5. $\dfrac{2a}{3b}$

6. $\dfrac{v}{y}$

7. $\dfrac{2x^2}{y}$

8. $\dfrac{a^2}{2}$

9. 1 3/4

10. $\dfrac{3}{8}$

11. $\dfrac{6b}{35}$

12. $\dfrac{6a}{5b}$

13. $\dfrac{3}{2(x-1)}$

14. $\dfrac{4}{2x+1}$

15. $\dfrac{5(x+3)}{4(x-1)}$

16. $\dfrac{x+2}{x-1}$

17. $\dfrac{x+3}{3(x-1)}$

18. $\dfrac{5(3x+1)}{4(x+2)}$

19. $\dfrac{3(x-1)^2}{20}$

20. 1 1/7

EXERCISE 7.12

1. 1/6

2. 7/12

3. 1/24

4. $\dfrac{y+x}{xy}$

5. $\dfrac{3y-2x}{xy}$

6. 3/a

7. $\dfrac{5x}{6}$

8. $\dfrac{a}{10}$

9. $\dfrac{a}{2}$

10. $\dfrac{3x-2y}{6}$

11. $\dfrac{8a+3b}{12}$

12. $\dfrac{9a-b}{6}$

13. $\dfrac{8a+6b-3c}{24}$

14. $\dfrac{12a+3b+4c}{18}$

15. $\dfrac{3a+11}{4(a+1)}$

16. $\dfrac{4x-11}{5(x+1)}$

17. $\dfrac{3x+7}{5(x-1)}$

18. $\dfrac{10x-3}{12}$

19. $\dfrac{-x-3}{4}$

20. $\dfrac{53x+6}{18}$

21. $\dfrac{6-x}{4}$

22. $\dfrac{7x-6}{5}$

23. $\dfrac{7x+5}{3}$

24. $\dfrac{-x-14}{12}$

25. $\dfrac{27-3x}{8}$

EXERCISE 7.13

1. a) x^5 b) x^{11} c) a^{12} d) y^{13}
2. a) a^2 b) a^3 c) x^2 d) 64
3. a) a^{24} b) x^{18} c) y^8 d) b^{18}
4. a) $x^4 y^2$ b) $a^5 b^3$ c) $x^4 y^6$ d) $a^3 b^6$
5. a) $9x^2$ b) $8x^3$ c) $27x^3$ d) $25a^2$
6. a) 3 b) $3x^3$ c) $5b^3$ d) $5x^5$
7. a) $12x^5$ b) $108a^7$ c) $30y^9$
8. a) x^6 b) $3/32\, x^3$ c) x^3 d) $\dfrac{x^{13}}{12}$

EXERCISE 7.14

1. a) $\dfrac{2}{a}$ b) $\dfrac{12}{x}$ c) $\dfrac{3}{2x}$ d) $12ab$

2. a) 2 b) 5 c) 3 d) $\dfrac{1}{4}$
      e) $\dfrac{1}{3}$ f) $\dfrac{1}{5a}$ g) $\dfrac{a}{5}$ h) $\dfrac{1}{2}$
      i) 3

3. a) 8 b) 4 c) 27 d) 27
      e) 16 f) 8 g) 125 h) $\dfrac{1}{125}$
      i) $\dfrac{1}{32}$

4. a) $\dfrac{5}{2}$ b) $\dfrac{3}{2}$ c) $\dfrac{3}{4}$ d) $\dfrac{25}{4}$
      e) $\dfrac{9}{4}$

EXERCISE 8.1

1. 10   2. 4   3. 21   4. 3
5. 8   6. −2   7. 5   8. 4 2/3
9. −6   10. 3   11. 9   12. 12
13. 6   14. 4   15. 120   16. 150
17. 12   18. ½   19. 1   20. 2
21. 7/10   22. 1   23. 2   24. 8
25. 3   26. 5   27. 5   28. 7
29. 8   30. 2   31. 7   32. 24
33. 20   34. 63   35. 29 3/5   36. 11
37. 8   38. 1 1/9   39. 6   40. −11

EXERCISE 8.2

1. 8½ cm and 11½ cm
2. 6 1/4, 12½ and 9 1/4 cm
3. 26, 27 and 28
4. 3·2 km
5. 30, 32 and 34
6. 36 and 12
7. 8, 11 and 14 years
8. £300
9. 30 10p coins and 10 50p coins
10. 11 5p articles and 9 3p articles
11. 6,8.
12. £1800
13. a) $10n + 6m = 200$
    b) $n = 8$
14. 20 hours

EXERCISE 8.3

1. 5,6,7 . . .
2. . . . −2,−10,1
3. 4,5,6 . . .
4. . . . 5,6,7
5. 3,4,5 . . .
6. . . . 2,3
7. 7,8,9 . . .
8. . . . −2,−1,0,1
9. . . . 3,4,5
10. . . . 0,1,2
11. . . . 16,17,18
12. 9,10,11 . . .
13. 3,4,5 . . .
14. . . . 2,3,4
15. 2,3,4 . . .
16. . . . 4,5,6
17. 5,6,7 . . .
18. . . . −2,−1,0,+1
19. 3,4,5 . . .
20. −3,−2,−1,0 . . .
21. 4,5,6 . . .
22. 4,5,6 . . .
23. . . . −4,−3,−2
24. 0,1,2 . . .
25. 3,4,5 . . .
26. . . . 5,6,7
27. . . . 2,3,4
28. . . . −2,−1,0,1
29. −5,−4,−3 . . .
30. . . . −6,−5,−4 . . .

EXERCISE 8.4

1. $\dfrac{c}{\pi}$
2. $\dfrac{c}{2\pi}$
3. $\dfrac{F}{a}$
4. $\dfrac{2A}{b}$
5. $\dfrac{V}{\ell b}$
6. $\dfrac{3V}{\pi r^2}$
7. $y - mx$
8. $\dfrac{y - c}{x}$
9. $\dfrac{V}{\pi r^2}$
10. $\sqrt{\dfrac{V}{\pi h}}$
11. $\dfrac{9c}{5} + 32$
12. $\dfrac{100I}{PT}$
13. $\dfrac{V^2}{2g}$
14. $\dfrac{V^2 - u^2}{2a}$
15. $\dfrac{2(S - ut)}{t^2}$

16. $\dfrac{2S}{t} - u$

17. $\dfrac{T^2 g}{4\pi^2}$

18. $\dfrac{y}{y-1}$

19. $\dfrac{3A-y}{2}$

20. $\dfrac{6P+5y}{5}$

21. $\sqrt{\dfrac{2y}{R}}$

22. $\dfrac{DX^2}{CZ}$

23. $\dfrac{bx}{x-b}$

24. $\dfrac{a(1-x^2)}{x^2}$

25. $\dfrac{bx^2}{1-x^2}$

26. $\sqrt{\dfrac{A+\pi r^2}{\pi}}$

27. $\sqrt{\dfrac{\pi R^2 - A}{\pi}}$

28. $\left(\dfrac{c-d}{t}\right)^2$

29. $\dfrac{a^2 b + Cc}{C}$

EXERCISE 8.5

1. 25	2. 11	3. -6
4. -3	5. 4	6. 7
7. -3	8. -13	9. 20
10. -4	11. 6	12. -3
13. 3·5	14. 20·27 (2 d.p.)	15. 20·423
16. 13	17. 23·56 (2 d.p.)	18. 28°c
19. £71·25	20. 19·58 to 2 d.p.	21. 15·34 to 2 d.p.
22. 96·875	23. 10 1/3	24. (a) 36·75 (b) $-1·2$
25. 29·25	26. (a) 43 (b) 8	27. (a) 66 (b) 6
28. (a) -6 (b) 0	29. (a) 152 (b) 22	30. 7½

EXERCISE 9.1

1. ±5	2. ±9	3. ±6
4. ±3	5. -2 or 3	6. 6 or -5
7. $-4/3$ or 1/2	8. 1½ or 3/4	9. 0 or 2/3
10. 0 or $-3/4$	11. 0 or 4	12. 0 or 3
13. 0 or 3/4	14. 0 or 2/3	15. 0 or 3/5
16. 0 or 1/4	17. 3 or -2	18. -2 or 1
19. 3/2 or -1	20. $\frac{1}{3}$ or -1	21. 5 or -2
22. 3 or 4	23. 2 or -4	24. 2/3 or -4
25. -3 or ½	26. 5/2 or $-5/2$	27. $\frac{3}{2}$ or $-\frac{5}{4}$
28. 0 or 3/4		

EXERCISE 9.2

1. 5·16 or 1·16	2. 5·24 or ·76	3. 4·65 or −0·65
4. −6·61 or ·60	5. −1·62 or 0·62	6. 1·59 or 0·16
7. −0·73 or 0·23	8. −0·94 or 0·74	9. −2·33 or 1·08
10. 4·79 or 0·21	11. 7·54 or 0·46	12. 2·58 or −0·58
13. 0·28 or 1·78	14. 1·55 or −0·23	15. 0·77 or 0·43

EXERCISE 9.3

1. $x = 4 \ y = 1$	2. $x = 5 \ y = 3$	3. $x = 1 \ y = -1$
4. $x = 3 \ y = 1$	5. $x = 3 \ y = -2$	6. $x = 3 \ y = 5$
7. $x = 4 \ y = 1$	8. $x = 3 \ y = 3$	9. $x = 5 \ y = -3$
10. $x = -4 \ y = 2$	11. $x = -2 \ y = -3$	12. $x = -2 \ y = 5$
13. $x = 5 \ y = 6$	14. $x = 9 \ y = -1$	15. $x = 2\frac{1}{2} \ y = 1$
16. $x = 4 \ y = -2$	17. $x = 2 \ y = 1$	18. $x = -2 \ y = -3$
19. $x = -1 \ y = 6$	20. $x = -3 \ y = 4$	

EXERCISE 9.4

1. £1·10, £2·40	2. 24, 15	3. 12·9 cm, 8·1 cm
4. 120g, 90g	5. 86p, 51p	6. 18p, 13p
7. 17 £10 notes and 6 £5 notes	8. 5 points, 3 points	
9. £11, £6	10. 7 litres, 11 litres	

EXERCISE 9.5

1. $x = -1 \ y = 0$
   $x = -\frac{3}{2} \quad y = -\frac{1}{2}$
2. $x = -\frac{3}{7} \ y = \frac{2}{7}$
   $x = -\frac{1}{2} \ y = \frac{1}{2}$
3. $x = 2 \ y = 1\frac{1}{2}$
   $x = -3 \ y = -1$
4. $x = 1 \ y = -1$
   $x = 2 \ y = -4$
5. $x = -\frac{1}{2} \ y = 5$
   $x = 3 \ y = -2$
6. $x = -\frac{2}{3} \ y = 3\frac{1}{3}$
   $x = -3 \ y = 1$
7. $x = \frac{3}{2} \ y = 0$
   $x = 1 \ y = 1$
8. $x = -2 \ y = -1$
   $x = -1 \ y = 1$
9. $x = -1 \ y = 4$
   $x = 5 \ y = 10$
10. $x = -1 \ y = -2$
    $x = 3 \ y = 10$

EXERCISE 9.6

1. $3\cdot73$ to 2 d.p.   2. $5\cdot30$ to 2 d.p.   3. $3\cdot79$ to 2 d.p.
4. $1\cdot72$ to 2 d.p.   5. $3\cdot89$ to 2 d.p.   6. $9\cdot22$ to 2 d.p.
7. a) $3\cdot162$ b) $5\cdot477$ c) $6\cdot325$

EXERCISE 9.7

1. a) 3   b) 4   c) 22   d) $n+2$
2. $\{4,6,8,10,12\}$
3. a) -3 b) 9   c) 102
4. a) 13   b) $1\frac{1}{3}$ c) 1
5. a) $2\frac{2}{9}$ b) $1\frac{31}{47}$ c) -4
6. a) 3   b) -8 c) -37 d) -17 e) $8\frac{3}{4}$
   f) $11-12x$ g) $11-12x$
7. a) 24   b) 3   c) 0   d) 1 or 3   e) 3 or 2
8. a) -8 b) 24   c) $-4\cdot46$ or $2\cdot46$
9. a) 104   b) 10 or 5   c) 12 or 3   d) $2(x-4)(2x-3)$
   e) 4 or $\frac{3}{2}$
10. a) -9 b) 4   c) $16x+15$
11. $m=3$, $c=2$

EXERCISE 9.8

1. $4/3$ 2. 256   3. $3/4$ 4. $\dfrac{3}{2}$

5.

x	1/8	1	8	64
y	3/8	3/4	1·5	3

6. a) 3   7. ½   8. $5/3$ 9. 62
   b) 1/8

10. $y = \dfrac{3}{2x^2}$ 11. $4/25$ 12. $\dfrac{8}{x}+3x$

1. a) A (3,4)   B (0,−1)   C (3,−1)
    b) AC = 5   CB = 3   c) AB = 5·83 to 2 d.p.
2. a) A (−4,1)   B (2,−3)   C (−4,−3)
    b) AC = 4   CB = 6   c) 7·21 to 2 d.p.
3. AB = 6   BC = 5   AC = 7·81
4. UV = 7   VW = 3   UW = 7·62
5. Vertical height = 4 units   Area = 14   BC = 4·47
6. AREA = 7 sq. units
7. (3,4)
8. (−½, −½)
9. 7·07 to 2 d.p.
10. AREA = 7½ sq. units

EXERCISE 10.2

1. a) $y = 2x-3$ y intercept $(0,-3)$ gradient 2
    b) $y = 2x-3$ .. $(0,-3)$ ..   2
    c) $y = -x-3$ .. $(0,-3)$ .. -1
    d) $y = -x+1$ .. $(0,1)$ .. -1
    e) $y = \frac{3}{2}x-2$ .. $(0,-2)$ .. $\frac{3}{2}$
    f) $y = 2x-4$ .. $(0,-4)$ ..   2
    g) $y = \frac{3}{2}x -2$ .. $(0,-2)$ .. $\frac{3}{2}$
    h) $y = 2x-\frac{3}{2}$ .. $(0,-\frac{3}{2})$ ..   2
    i) $y = \frac{2}{3}x+\frac{4}{3}$ .. $(0,\frac{4}{3})$ .. $-\frac{2}{3}$
    j) $y = \frac{1}{2}x-\frac{3}{4}$ .. $(0,-\frac{3}{4})$ .. $\frac{1}{2}$
    k) $y = \frac{3}{2}x-1$ .. $(0,-1)$ .. $\frac{3}{2}$
    l) $y = -\frac{2}{3}x-2$ .. $(0,-2)$ .. $\frac{2}{3}$

2.

a)

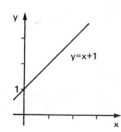

b)

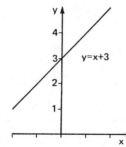

c)

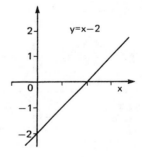

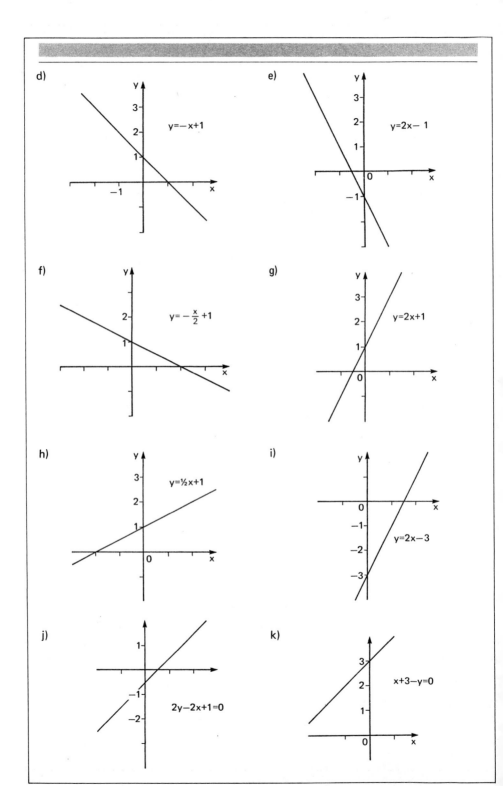

d) $y=-x+1$

e) $y=2x-1$

f) $y=-\frac{x}{2}+1$

g) $y=2x+1$

h) $y=\frac{1}{2}x+1$

i) $y=2x-3$

j) $2y-2x+1=0$

k) $x+3-y=0$

l)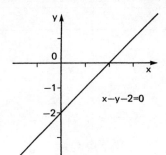

x−y−2=0

m)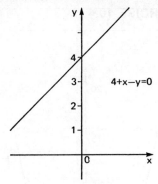

4+x−y=0

n)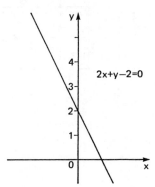

2x+y−2=0

o)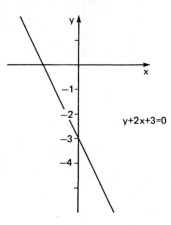

y+2x+3=0

3. i) $y = x+1$ ii) $y = -\frac{4}{3}x+4$
    iii) $y = x-1$ iv) $y = \frac{1}{2}x$
    v) $y = -\frac{1}{2}x+2$ vi) $y = 2x-2$
    vii) $y = \frac{1}{2}x+1$ viii) $y = -\frac{3}{2}x-\frac{3}{2}$
    ix) $y = \frac{3}{2}x+\frac{3}{2}$

EXERCISE 10.3

---

a) $x = 4,\ y = 4$ b) $x = 4,\ y = 2$ c) $x = 6,\ y = 5$
d) $x = 3,\ y = 1$ e) $x = 4,\ y = -1$ f) $x = 3,\ y = 3$
g) $x = 4,\ y = -2$ h) $x = -1,\ y = 1\frac{1}{2}$

EXERCISE 10.4

1.

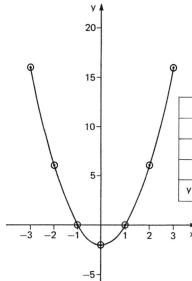

x	−3	−2	−1	0	1	2	3
x^2	9	4	1	0	1	4	9
$2x^2$	18	8	2	0	2	8	18
−2	−2	−2	−2	−2	−2	−2	−2
$y = 2x^2 - 2$	16	6	0	−2	0	6	16

2.

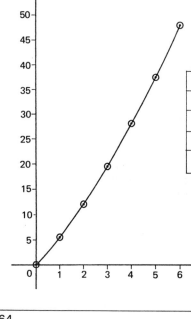

x	0	1	2	3	4	5	6
x^2	0	1	4	9	16	25	36
$5x$	0	5	10	15	20	25	30
$x^2/2$	0	½	2	4½	8	12½	18
$y = 5x + x^2/2$	0	5½	12	19½	28	37½	48

3.

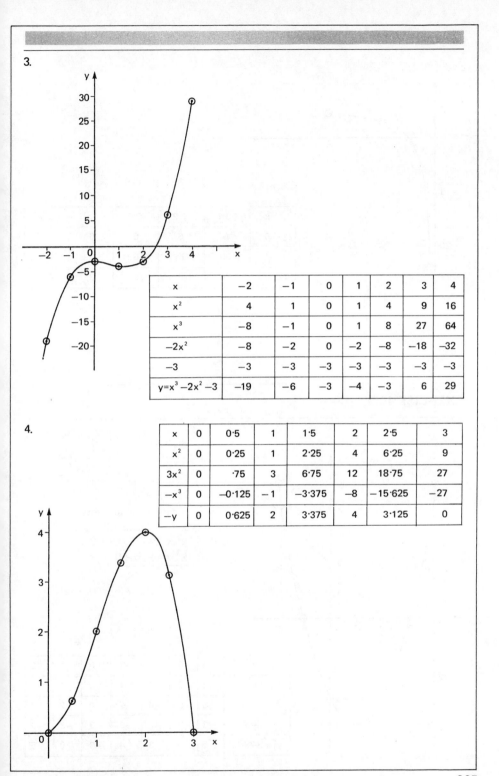

x	−2	−1	0	1	2	3	4
x^2	4	1	0	1	4	9	16
x^3	−8	−1	0	1	8	27	64
$-2x^2$	−8	−2	0	−2	−8	−18	−32
−3	−3	−3	−3	−3	−3	−3	−3
$y=x^3-2x^2-3$	−19	−6	−3	−4	−3	6	29

4.

x	0	0·5	1	1·5	2	2·5	3
x^2	0	0·25	1	2·25	4	6·25	9
$3x^2$	0	·75	3	6·75	12	18·75	27
$-x^3$	0	−0·125	−1	−3·375	−8	−15·625	−27
−y	0	0·625	2	3·375	4	3·125	0

365

5.

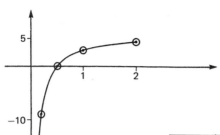

x	0·1	0·2	0·5	1·0	2·0
6	6	6	6	6	6
$-\dfrac{3}{x}$	−30	−15	−6	−3	−1·5
$y=6-\dfrac{3}{x}$	−24	−9	0	3	4·5

EXERCISE 10.5

1.

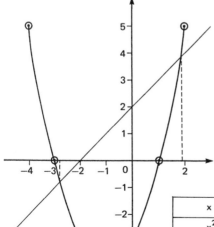

c) where the graphs intersect
$x = -2.8$ and 1.9

d) $x^2 + 2x - 3 = x + 2$
$\underline{x^2 + x - 5 = 0}$

x	−4	−3	−2	−1	0	1	2
x^2	16	9	4	1	0	1	4
+2x	−8	−6	−4	−2	0	+ 2	+ 4
−3	−3	−3	−3	−3	−3	−3	−3
$y=x^2+2x-3$	5	0	−3	−4	−3	0	5

2.

x	−2·5	−2	−1	0	1	2	2·5
x³	−15·625	−8	−1	0	1	8	15·625
−2x	+ 5	+4	+2	0	−2	−4	−5
+2	+ 2	+2	+2	+2	+2	+2	+2
y	−8·625	−2	+3	+2	0	+6	12·625

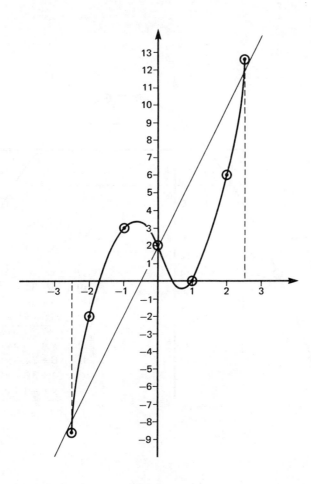

d) approximate solutions
are x = −2·5, 0 and 2·5

3.

x	−4	−3	−2	−1	0	1	2	3	4
4	4	4	4	4	4	4	4	4	4
+3x	−12	−9	−6	−3	0	+3	+6	+9	+12
$-x^2$	−16	−9	−4	−1	0	−1	−4	−9	−16
y	−24	−14	−6	0	4	6	6	4	0

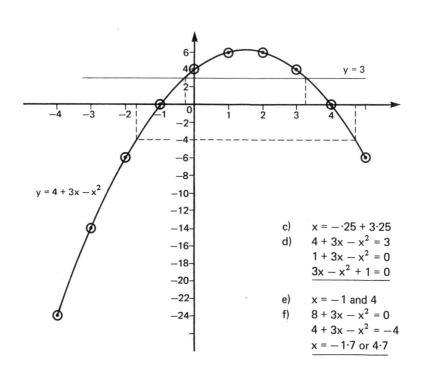

c) $x = -\cdot25 + 3\cdot25$

d) $4 + 3x - x^2 = 3$
    $1 + 3x - x^2 = 0$
    $3x - x^2 + 1 = 0$

e) $x = -1$ and 4

f) $8 + 3x - x^2 = 0$
    $4 + 3x - x^2 = -4$
    $x = -1\cdot7$ or $4\cdot7$

4.

x	0·5	1·0	1·5	2·0	2·5	3	4	6
2x	1·0	2·0	3·0	4·0	5·0	6·0	8·0	12·0
$+\frac{8}{x}$	+16·0	+8·0	+5·$\dot{3}$	+4·0	+3·2	+2·$\dot{6}$	2·0	1·$\dot{6}$
y	17·0	10·0	8·$\dot{3}$	8·0	8·2	8·$\dot{6}$	10·0	13·$\dot{6}$

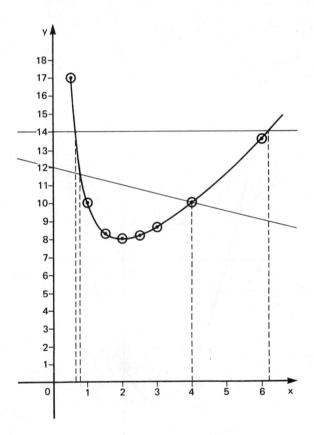

d)   0·65 & 6·2

e) $2x + \frac{8}{x} = 12 - \frac{x}{2}$
$2x^2 + 8 = 12x - \frac{x^2}{2}$
$2\frac{1}{2}x^2 - 12x - 8 = 0$
$5x^2 - 24x + 16 = 0$

Approximate solutions are
0·8 and 4·0

5.

x	−4	−3	−2	−1	0	1	2
x + 3	−1	0	1	2	3	4	5
x−1	−5	−4	−3	−2	−1	0	1
y=(x+3)(x−1)	5	0	−3	−4	−3	0	5

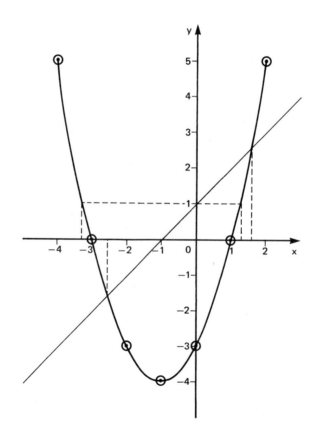

a)   x = −3·3 & 1·3
b)   x = −2·55 & 1·6
      (x + 3) (x − 1) = (x − 1)
      (x + 2) (x − 1) = 0

6.

x	−4	−3	−2	−1	0	1	2
(3 + x)	−1	0	1	2	3	4	5
(3 − 2x)	11	9	7	5	3	1	−1
y	−11	0	7	10	9	4	−5

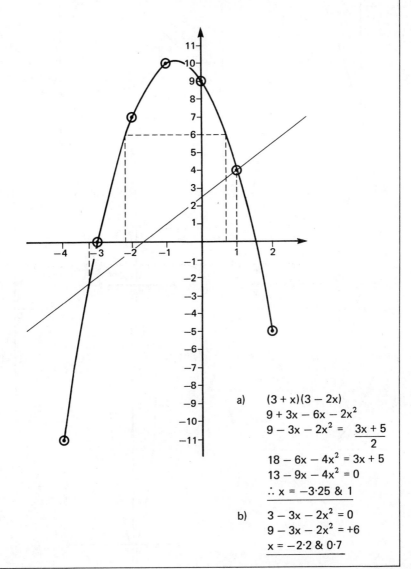

a) $(3 + x)(3 − 2x)$
$9 + 3x − 6x − 2x^2$
$9 − 3x − 2x^2 = \dfrac{3x + 5}{2}$
$18 − 6x − 4x^2 = 3x + 5$
$13 − 9x − 4x^2 = 0$
$\therefore x = −3\cdot25 \ \& \ 1$

b) $3 − 3x − 2x^2 = 0$
$9 − 3x − 2x^2 = +6$
$x = −2\cdot2 \ \& \ 0\cdot7$

371

1.   (i) $y = \frac{1}{2}x$ (ii) $y = -2x + 4$ (iii) $y = 3$

       (iv) $x = 4$ (v) $y = x^2$ (vi) $y = \frac{1}{x}$

       (vii) $y = \frac{1}{4}x^2$ (viii) $y = 2x^2$

                                                           (ix) $y = \frac{2}{x}$

       (x) $y = \frac{1}{9}x^2$

2.

(i)

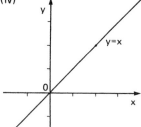

(ii)

(iii)

(iv)

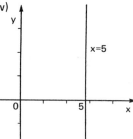

(v)

(vi)

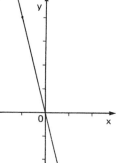

(vii)

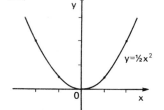

(viii)

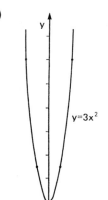

(ix)

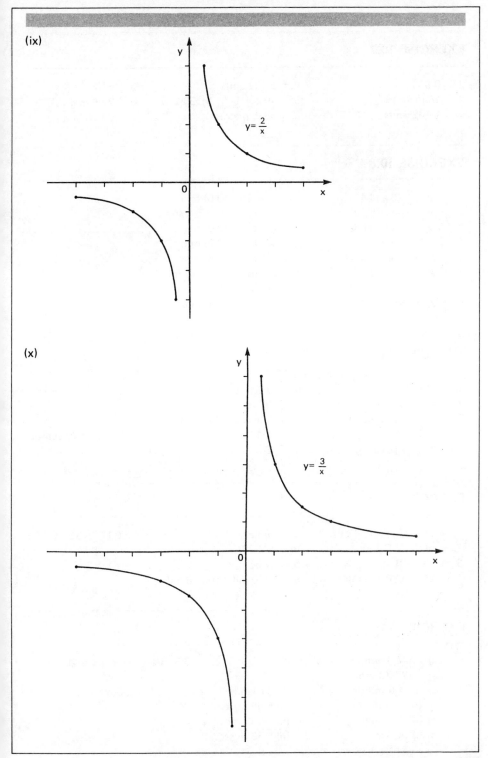

(x)

EXERCISE 10.7

1. 0·336	2. 2·632 units	3. 418m
4. 1860 units	5. a) 20·15 b) 20·275	6. 24·6 metres
7. 1·102 units	8. 6315 metres	9. 33·08 units

EXERCISE 10.8

1.	a)	−6 and 4	b) (0,0) min
2.	a)	−4 and 12	b) (0,−3) min
3.	a)	−12 and 3	b) (0,0) min
4.	a)	1 and −2	b) (0,0) min
5.	a)	4 and −4	b) (0,3) max
6.	a)	−5 and 1	b) (½, − ¼) min
7.	a)	8 and −14	b) (½, ½) max
8.	a)	3 and −3	b) (0,4) max

EXERCISE 11.1

1.	a)	3 m/s	b)	7·6 m/s		
2.	a)	0·96 litres/sec	b)	85 secs.		
3.	a)	£2·75 per item	b)	Approximately 70		
4.	a) (i) 130 (ii) 270		b)	8·10 am	c)	7·30 to 8·30 approx
5.	a)	Approx. 40 items	b)	£4	c)	37

EXERCISE 11.2

1.	a)	Approx. 43 Fr.	b)	93 Fr.	c) £5.00	d)	7·50
2.	a)	375 units	b)	£2·30			
3.	a)	10 oz.	b)	7 oz.			
4.	a)	£90 and £94	b)	100 miles and 96 miles.			

EXERCISE 11.3

1. a) 48 km/hr b) 40 mph c) 6·5 m/s d) 1·25 m/s
   e) 72·73 mph
2. a) (i) 900 m/min (ii) 54 km/hr e) 30 mph
   b) (i) ⅓ km/min (ii) 5·56 m/sec
   c) (i) ½ m/min (ii) ·0083 miles/sec
   d) (i) 30 km/hr (ii) 8·33 m/sec

EXERCISE 11.4

1.	a)	80 mph	b)	26·67 mph	c)	1 hour
2.	a)	45 mph	b)	3 mins	c)	8·10
	d)	35 mph	e)	8·28	f)	2½ miles
	g)	8·58				
3.	a)	15 metres	b)	115 secs	c)	68·4 Km/hr
4.	a)	11·25 m/s	b)	6·5 m/s	c)	3 m/s
5.	a)	0·8 sec	b)	8 m/s	c)	Approx 1 second
6.	a)	31 metres	b)	4½ m/s	c)	10 m/s
	d)	10 metres	e)	37½ metres		

EXERCISE 11.5

1. ½ m/sec^2
2. 34 m/s
3. a) 1425 metres   b) 0·5 m/s^2
4. a) ·4 m/s^2 b) 2600 m   c) 90 secs
5. a) 0·25 m/s^2 b) 1120 m   c) 480 metres
   d) 0·267 m/s^2
6. 1170 metres
7. 3150 metres
8. 10·6 Km
9. 8400 metres
10. 9600 metres
11. b) (i) −1·8 m/s^2 (ii) 178·5 m

EXERCISE 12.1

1. $x = 60^o$ $y = 60^o$ $z = 120^o$ 2. $x = 107^o$ $y = 73^o$ $z = 107^o$
3. $x = 57^o$ $y = 270^o$ 4. $x = 126^o$ $y = 180^o$
5. $x = 36^o$ $y = 144^o$ $z = 54^o$ 6. $x = 70^o$ $y = 20^o$ $z = 160^o$
7. $x = 63^o$ $y = 27^o$ $z = 117^o$ 8. $x = 135^o$
9. $x = 88^o$ $y = 63^o$ $z = 29^o$ 10. $x = 54^o$ $2x = 108^o$
11. $x = 35^o$ $2x = 70^o$ $y = 35^o$ $z = 75^o$

EXERCISE 12.2

1. $x = 105^o$ 2. $x = 70^o$ $y = 60^o$
3. $x = 150^o$ $y = 60^o$ 4. $x = 70^o$ $y = 60^o$
5. $x = 121^o$ $y = 130^o$ $z = 109^o$ 6. $x = 141^o$ $z = 120^o$

7. $x = 27^o$ $y = 27^o$ $z = 63^o$ 8. $x = 60^o$ $y = 120^o$
9. $x = 43^o$ $y = 94^o$ $z = 137^o$ 10. $x = 90^o$ $y = 35^o$ $z = 55^o$
11. $x = 109^o$ $y = 37^o$ $z = 109^o$ 12. $x = 120^o$ $y = 30^o$ $z = 30^o$
13. $x = 50^o$ $y = 40^o$

EXERCISE 12.3

1. All   2. a and c   3. a and c
4. b and c   5. None   6. R.H.S.
7. S.A.S.   8. A.A.S.   9. S.S.S.
10. c and d(AAS)   b and g(SAS)
11. A is true, B and C are not.

EXERCISE 12.4

1. $DF = 4\frac{1}{2}$, $BC = 6\frac{2}{3}$ 2. $AC = 7 \cdot 2$cm, $DF = 8$ cm
3. a) $\dfrac{AB}{BC} = \dfrac{EB}{BD} = \dfrac{EA}{CD}$ b) $EB = 4 \cdot 8$ cm   c)   4:25
                                                                        $CD = 15$ cm
4. a) $DB = 4\frac{1}{2}$cm $DE = 3 \cdot 6$ cm   b)   4:25
5. $BC = 5\frac{1}{3}$ cm 16:9
6. a)   9:16   b)   14 cm^2
7. Area $ABC = 42\dfrac{26}{57}$ cm^2
8. a) $\triangle$ ABD has angles of x, y and 90° b)   144:25
          $\triangle$ ADC has angles of x, y and 90°
          $\triangle$ ABC has angles of x, y and 90°
9. a) $\triangle$ ABC and $\triangle$ DFC
   b) $AE = 1 \cdot 5$ cm $FC = 6$ cm   c)   1:16
10. Area STAC = 24 cm^2

EXERCISE 13.1

1. 140° 2. 90° 3. $x = 260^o$ $y = 100^o$
4. 35° 5. $x = 110^o$ $y = 75^o$ 6. $x = 130^o$ $y = 120^o$
7. $41\frac{1}{2}^o$ 8. $x = 70^o$ $y = 20^o$
9. $x = 90^o$ $y = 70^o$ $z = 75^o$
10. $x = 25^o$ $y = 65^o$ $z = 25^o$
11. $= 30^o$ $y = 120^o$ $z = 60^o$
12. $x = 40^o$ $y = 100^o$ $z = 40^o$ $a = 80^o$ $b = 10^o$
13. $x = 35^o$ $y = 4^o$ $z = 86^o$
14. $x = 5^o$ $y = 75^o$ $z = 105^o$

EXERCISE 13.2

1. 90°
2. 63°
3. 115°
4. $x = 50^{\circ}$ $y = 50^{\circ}$ $z = 40^{\circ}$
5. $D\hat{A}X = T\hat{A}B = A\hat{C}D = A\hat{B}D = C\hat{A}D = C\hat{A}B = 45^{\circ}$
   $A\hat{O}B = 90^{\circ}$
6. $a = 54^{\circ}$ $b = 36^{\circ}$ $c = 54^{\circ}$ $d = 36^{\circ}$
7. $a = 54^{\circ}$ $b = 72^{\circ}$ $c = 54^{\circ}$ $d = 54^{\circ}$
8. $ABC = 90^{\circ}$ $DCB = 90^{\circ}$ $ADC = 90^{\circ}$ $BAD = 90^{\circ}$ $DAC = 43^{\circ}$ $BCS = 47^{\circ}$
9. $x = 40^{\circ}$ $y = 20^{\circ}$ $z = 20^{\circ}$
10. $OCT = 90^{\circ}$ $BOC = 50^{\circ}$ $CTO = 40^{\circ}$

EXERCISE 13.3

1. 6 cm
2. 2½ cm
3. 5¼ cm
4. 6 cm and 2 cm
5. 2·4 cm
6. Chord cuts diameter 2 cm from one end
7. CD = 12 cm
8. AE = 3 cm

EXERCISE 14.1

1. 83°
2. $BAD = 96^{\circ}$ $BCD = 70^{\circ}$
3. $67\tfrac{1}{2}^{\circ}, 67\tfrac{1}{2}^{\circ}, 135^{\circ}, 135^{\circ}, 135^{\circ}$
4. $144^{\circ}, 144^{\circ}$ and 72°
5. $DEF = 130^{\circ}$ $BAF = 119^{\circ}$
6. 137°
7. $90^{\circ}, 90^{\circ}, 90^{\circ}, 135^{\circ}$ and 135°
8. 96° and 192°

EXERCISE 14.2

1. $51·43^{\circ}$ and $128·57^{\circ}$
2. 36° and 144°
3. 30° and 150°
4. 18° and 162°
5. a) 135° b) $22\tfrac{1}{2}^{\circ}$ c) $67\tfrac{1}{2}^{\circ}$ d) 45°
6. a) $51·43^{\circ}$ b) $64·29^{\circ}$
7. 18
8. 30
9. 12
11. 8
12. a) 135° and 120°
    b) Interior angle of (i) is not a factor of 360° whereas the interior angle of (ii) is a factor.

EXERCISE 14.3

1. Rhombus   2. Square   3. Parallelogram
4. Rectangle   5. Rectangle   6. 105° and 140°
7. 75° and 105° 8. Rhombus. $67\frac{1}{2}^\circ$ and $112\frac{1}{2}^\circ$
9. 60° and 120° 10. Rhombus
11. Kite 40° 110° 110° 100°

EXERCISE 14.4

1. 50° 2. 45° and 135° 3. 20°
4. $a = 70^\circ$, $b = 130^\circ$, $c = 110^\circ$ and $d = 120^\circ$ 5. $67\frac{1}{2}^\circ$
6. 115° 7. a) 130°, 25°, 25°
           b) Isosceles   c) equal
8. $62\frac{1}{2}^\circ$, $57\frac{1}{2}^\circ$, 60° 9. a) $72\frac{1}{2}^\circ$ b) $107\frac{1}{2}^\circ$, $72\frac{1}{2}^\circ$
10. Kite; 80°, 20°, 130° and 130°

EXERCISE 15.1

1.

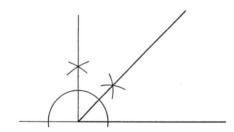

2.

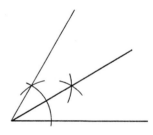

3.

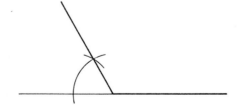

4.

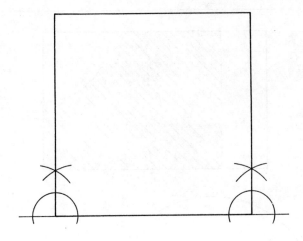

5.

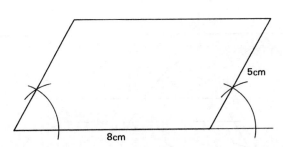

6.

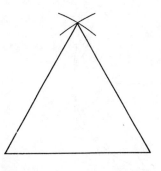

7.

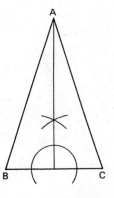

EXERCISE 15.2

1.

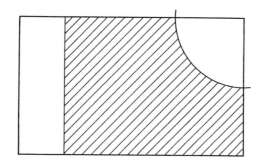

2.

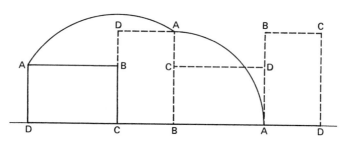

3.

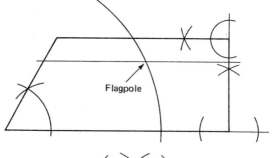

4.

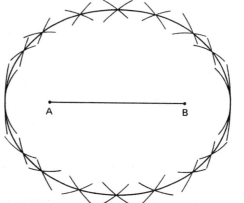

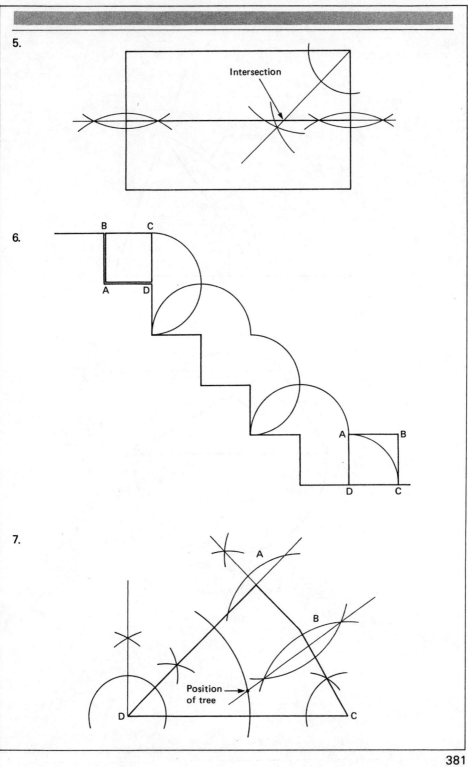

5.

Intersection

6.

B   C

A   D

A   B

D   C

7.

A

B

Position
of tree

D   C

8.

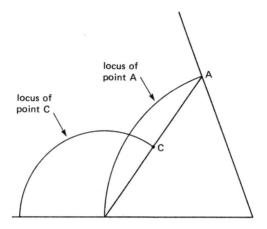

9.

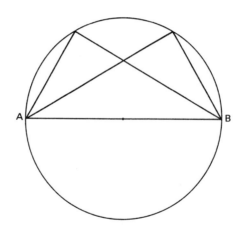

A circle of diameter AB.

10.

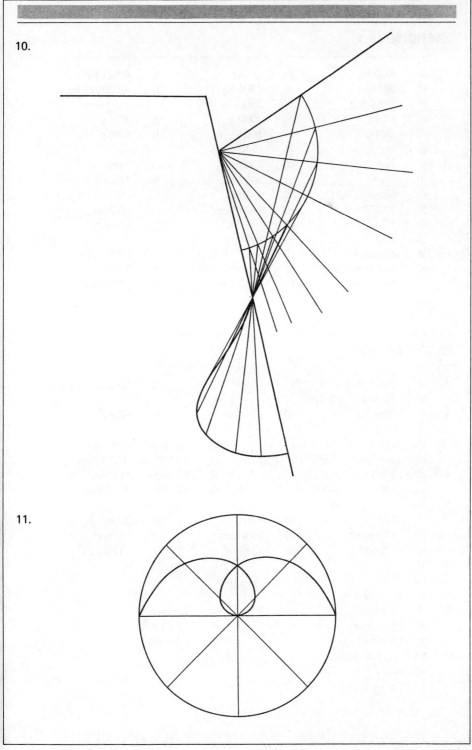

11.

EXERCISE 16.1

1. a) ·005 kg   b) ·25 kg   c) 4·531 kg
   d) 300 kg   e) 7300 kg   f) ·0000023 kg
   g) ·0005 kg   h) 3 kg
2. a) ·007 g   b) 7000 g   c) ·093 g
   d) ·564 g   e) 300 g   f) 4·56 g
   g) 5 g   h) 1540 g
3. a) 30m   b) 2·46m   c) ·56m
   d) 5m   e) 3400m   f) 170m
   g) 50m   h) 5·426m
4. a) 40 000cm^2 b) 35 400cm^2 c) 900mm^2
   d) 1·2m^2 e) 4·76cm^2 f) ·26cm^2
   g) 30cm^2 h) 4000
5. a) 2000mm^3 b) 3mm^3 c) 3 400 000
   d) 15000cm^3 e) 50cm^3 f) 1·2m^3
   g) 500 litres   h) 5300 litres   i) 28000 ml
   j) 3 ml

EXERCISE 16.2

1. a) 9cm^2, 12cm   b) 48cm^2, 28cm   c) 30·6cm^2, 24·8cm^2
   d) 78·12cm^2, 35·4cm
2. a) 96cm^2 b) 31·92cm^2 c) 68cm^2
   d) 67·5cm^2
3. a) 254·50cm^2, 56·56cm   b) 36·32cm^2, 21·37cm
   c) 248·88cm^2, 55·93cm   d) 908·04cm^2, 106·83cm
4. a) 3·142cm^2, 2·09cm   b) 91·90cm^2, 20·42cm
   c) 250·18cm^2, 47·65cm   d) 491·66cm^2, 56·35cm
5. 34·56cm^2, 23·52cm
6. a) 48cm^2 b) 41cm^2 c) 30cm^2
   d) 87·98cm^2 e) 75·41cm^2 f) 162cm^2
   g) 210cm^2 h) 13·5cm^2 i) 117·45cm^2
7. 150
8. 398
9. 63·63m^2, 32·14m
10. a) 3·75cm^2 b) 13·35cm^2
    c) 11·25cm^2 d) 17·28cm^2
    e) 5·25cm^2 f) 6·54cm^2
11. 49·02m, 182·82m^2
12. 191·82cm^2

EXERCISE 16.3

1.	555000 litres	2.	16·8m³	3.	542·82 g
4.	1·89m³	5.	125m	6.	6912cm³
7	504·1 g	8.	960cm³	9.	7·5cm
10.	192cm³	11.	75·4 ml	12.	140·5 mm
13.	5894	14.	a) 5832cm³ b) 52·37%		
15.	34·4 mm	16.	225·5cm³		

EXERCISE 16.4

1.

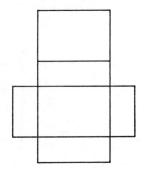

2.

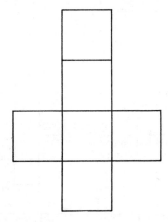

3.

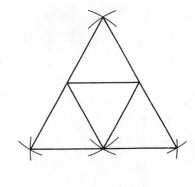

4.

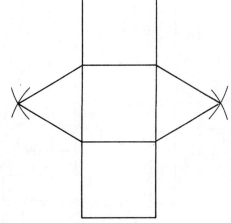

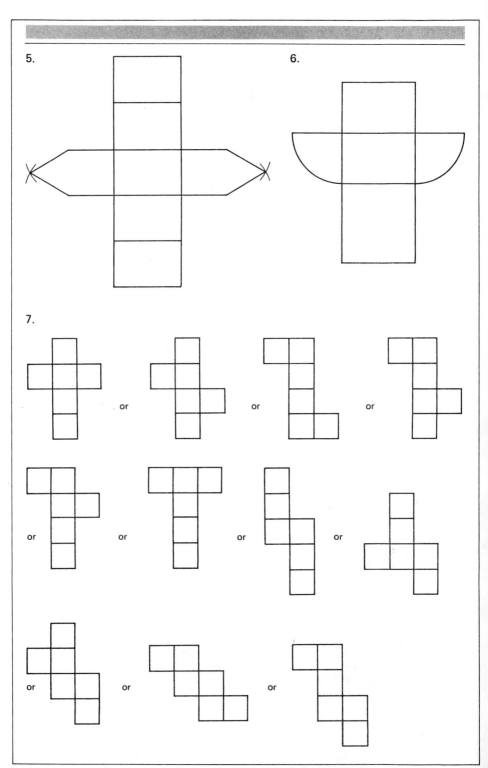

5.

6.

7.

or

or

or

or

or

or

or

or

or

or

8

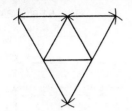

EXERCISE 16.5

1. 346cm^2 2. 2·98m^2 3. 5052mm^2
4. 2749cm^2 5. 163·4cm^2 6. 7541cm^2
7. 179·9cm^2 8. 720cm^2
9. £208·40   10. 62·84m^2, 14 tins
11. 13·33cm, 26·87cm

EXERCISE 16.6

1. 1:8   2. 64:125
3. a) 4:9   b) 8:27
4. Ratio of vol 125:64 ∴ approx twice
5. 23cm 8mm   6. 253 grams   7. ·024m^3
8. 350 g size   9. 729:5625   10. 390·6 g

EXERCISE 17.1

1. a) 5·11   b) 4·50   c) 2·87
   d) 3·54   e) 4·62
2. a) 6·62   b) 9·68   c) 4·40
   d) 17·33   e) 10·88
3. a) 43·5°, 46·5° b) 58·2°, 31·8° c) 33·4°, 56·6°
   d) 21·8°, 68·2° e) 46·5°, 43·4°

EXERCISE 17.2

1. a) 2·58   b) 2·19   c) 1·50
   d) 1·43   e) 3·97
2. a) 8·32   b) 5·72   c) 9·07
   d) 8·22   e) 4·00

3. a) 64·5°, 25·5°   b) 53·1°, 36·9°   c) 51·6°, 38·4°
    d) 64°, 26°   e) 49°, 41°

EXERCISE 17.3

1. a) 7·7   b) 4·09   c) 3·23
    d) 12·84   e) 5·5   f) 6·37
    g) 10·66   h) 12·00   i) 21·03
2. a) 40·8° and 49·2° b) 30·9° and 59·1° c) 62·6° and 27·4°
    d) 29·4° and 60·6° e) 51·1° and 38·9°

EXERCISE 17.4

1. 4·29   2. 15·65   3. 40·19° and 49·81°
4. 4·89   5. 27·09° and 62·91°   6. 42·37° and 47·63°
7. 14·14   8. 10·12   9. 2·05 cm
10. 3·73   11. 14·59 cm   12. 13·86cm and 8cm
13. 41·41°, 41·41° and 97·18°
14. 2·92cm and 5·56cm   15. 8 cm   16. 18·46cm
17. 16·38 cm   18. 6·58 cm   19. 9·42 cm

EXERCISE 17.5

1. a) 070 (N70°E)   b) 292° (N68°W)   c) 131° (S49°E)
    d) 236° (S56°W)   e) 090 (due east)   f) 180° (due south)
2. a) 250° (S70°W)   b) 112° (S68°E)   c) 311° (N49°W)
    d) 056° (N56°E)   e) 270° (due west)   f) 000° (due north)

EXERCISE 17.6

1. a) 243° (S63°W)   b) 3 km 310 m
2. 16·70°
3. 59·55°
4. a) A from B 304·7° (N55·3°W)
    b) B from A is 124·7° (S55·3°E)
5. 189·31 metres
6. 13·092 m
7. a) 056·31° (N56·31°E)   b) 236·31° (S56·31°W)
8. 32·50°
9. 39·42 m   10. 675·47 metres

EXERCISE 17.7

1. a) 15 cm   b) 17 cm   c) 12·53 cm
2. a) 3·606   b) 8·14 cm   c) 11·53 cm
   d) 7·97
3. a) 7   b) 5   c) 25
   d) 39   e) 4·8   f) 27
   g) 19½   h) 60   i) 44
   j) 120
4. 5·66 cm   5. 12·37 cm   6. 4·90 cm
7. 15 cm   8. 2·87 cm   9. 9·90 cm
10. 6·06 cm   11. 40·82 cm

EXERCISE 17.8

1. 2·92 m   2. 33·31 m   3. a) 5m b) 5·39m
4. 525·78 m   5. 1·732   6. 107·32 m
7. a) 9 cm   b) 21·36 cm   c) 41·11° 8. 4747 m
9. 64·8°, 3·32   10. i) 3·83   ii) 16·8°

EXERCISE 17.9

1. AB = 4·37   BC = 3·29
2. JK = 7·64   KL = 6·67
3. 24·52 cm, 57·4°, 79·6°
4. 14·03 cm, 44·3°, 78·7°
5. 9·13 cm, 30·5°, 39·5°
6. 8·09 cm, 26·7°, 37·3°
7. 97·5°, 36·5°, 2·54
8. 47·6°, 60·4°, 21·88
9. 33·5°, 40·5°, 10·80
10. 36·6°, 23·4°, 13·08
11. 58°, 37·3°, 84·8°
12. 27·05°, 34·37°, 27·05°
13. a) 21·07 cm   b) 39·75° c) B = 66°
14. a) 49·09° b) 94·91° c) 11·87 cm
15. 57·91°, 42·28°, 79·81°
16. B$\hat{D}$C = 45·04°, B$\hat{C}$D = 112·96°, BD = 22·12cm, A$\hat{B}$D = 34·09°, A$\hat{D}$B = 83·58°

    AB = 24·82cm
17. 9 Km 240m
18. 348·62m, 293·20m, 199·96m
19. 58·75°, 71·79°, 49·46° 20. 18·79m

1. 14·68 cm²
2. 48·23 cm²
3. 21·31 cm²
4. 26·87 cm²
5. 117·31 cm²
6. 10·77 cm²
7. 69·79 cm²

EXERCISE 18.1

1. a) $\begin{pmatrix} 1 \\ -8 \end{pmatrix}$
    b) $\begin{pmatrix} 16 & 9 \\ 15 & 19 \end{pmatrix}$

    A + B cannot be formed because the matrices are not of the same order.
    BA cannot be formed because the number of columns in the first matrix must
    equal the number of rows in the second matrix.
    B^2 as BA

2. a) $\begin{pmatrix} 6 & 2 \\ 8 & -1 \end{pmatrix}$
    b) $\begin{pmatrix} 2 & 0 \\ -2 & 5 \end{pmatrix}$
    c) $\begin{pmatrix} 13 & 1 \\ 16 & -3 \end{pmatrix}$

    d) $\begin{pmatrix} 11 & 4 \\ 11 & -1 \end{pmatrix}$
    e) $\begin{pmatrix} 19 & 6 \\ 18 & 7 \end{pmatrix}$
    f) $\begin{pmatrix} 9 & -1 \\ -5 & -4 \end{pmatrix}$

EXERCISE 18.2

1. $\begin{pmatrix} -1 & 3/5 \\ 1 & -2/5 \end{pmatrix}$
2. $\begin{pmatrix} 3 & -2 \\ -4 & 3 \end{pmatrix}$
3. $\begin{pmatrix} 1 & -2 \\ -3 & 7 \end{pmatrix}$

4. $\begin{pmatrix} 7/2 & -5 \\ -2 & 3 \end{pmatrix}$
5. $\begin{pmatrix} -2 & 3 \\ -3 & 5 \end{pmatrix}$
6. $\begin{pmatrix} 2 & -1 \\ -\frac{1}{2} & 3 \end{pmatrix}$

7. $\frac{1}{3}\begin{pmatrix} -4 & 3 \\ 5 & -3 \end{pmatrix}$
8. $\begin{pmatrix} -4 & -3 \\ -5 & -4 \end{pmatrix}$
9. $\frac{1}{2}\begin{pmatrix} -3 & 4 \\ 5 & -6 \end{pmatrix}$

10. $\frac{1}{2}\begin{pmatrix} 5 & -3 \\ 6 & -4 \end{pmatrix}$
11. $\begin{pmatrix} 2 \\ 1 \end{pmatrix}$
12. $\begin{pmatrix} 3 \\ 2 \end{pmatrix}$

1. a) $\begin{pmatrix} 0 & 2 \\ 2 & 2 \end{pmatrix}$

    b) $\begin{pmatrix} 0 & 1 & 1 \\ 1 & 0 & 1 \\ 1 & 1 & 0 \end{pmatrix}$

    c) $\begin{pmatrix} 0 & 2 & 1 \\ 2 & 0 & 1 \\ 1 & 1 & 0 \end{pmatrix}$

    d) $\begin{pmatrix} 0 & 1 & 2 \\ 1 & 0 & 2 \\ 2 & 2 & 0 \end{pmatrix}$

    e) $\begin{pmatrix} 0 & 2 & 1 \\ 2 & 0 & 2 \\ 1 & 2 & 2 \end{pmatrix}$

    f) $\begin{pmatrix} 0 & 1 & 1 & 1 \\ 1 & 0 & 1 & 1 \\ 1 & 1 & 0 & 1 \\ 1 & 1 & 1 & 0 \end{pmatrix}$

    g) $\begin{pmatrix} 4 & 2 \\ 2 & 0 \end{pmatrix}$

2. a)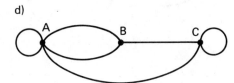

    b)

    c)

    d)

    e)

    f)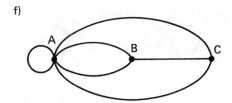

    g)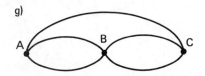

1. a) $\begin{pmatrix} 0 & 1 & 1 \\ 1 & 0 & 1 \\ 0 & 0 & 0 \end{pmatrix}$
    b) $\begin{pmatrix} 0 & 1 & 1 \\ 0 & 1 & 1 \\ 2 & 1 & 0 \end{pmatrix}$

    c) $\begin{pmatrix} 0 & 1 & 1 \\ 1 & 2 & 1 \\ 2 & 1 & 0 \end{pmatrix}$
    d) $\begin{pmatrix} 0 & 0 & 2 \\ 2 & 0 & 1 \\ 0 & 1 & 0 \end{pmatrix}$

    e) $\begin{pmatrix} 0 & 0 & 0 \\ 2 & 0 & 2 \\ 2 & 1 & 0 \end{pmatrix}$
    f) $\begin{pmatrix} 0 & 1 & 1 \\ 1 & 1 & 1 \\ 1 & 1 & 1 \end{pmatrix}$

    g) $\begin{pmatrix} 0 & 1 & 1 & 1 \\ 1 & 0 & 1 & 1 \\ 1 & 0 & 0 & 0 \\ 0 & 0 & 1 & 0 \end{pmatrix}$
    h) $\begin{pmatrix} 0 & 1 & 0 & 1 \\ 1 & 0 & 1 & 1 \\ 0 & 1 & 0 & 1 \\ 0 & 0 & 1 & 0 \end{pmatrix}$

2. a)

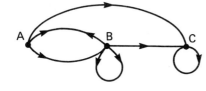

    b)

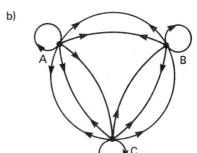

    c)

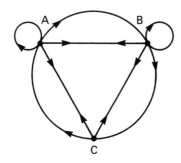

    d)

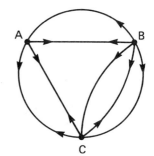

e)

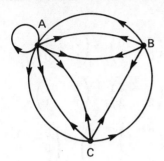

f)

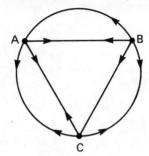

g)

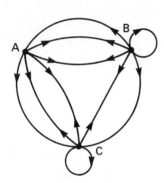

h)

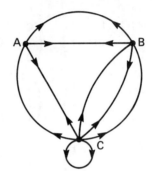

EXERCISE 18.5

2 stage matrices are:

1. $\begin{pmatrix} 1 & 1 \\ 1 & 2 \end{pmatrix}$

2. $\begin{pmatrix} 2 & 0 \\ 0 & 2 \end{pmatrix}$

3. $\begin{pmatrix} 4 & 0 \\ 0 & 4 \end{pmatrix}$

4. $\begin{pmatrix} 2 & 2 \\ 2 & 2 \end{pmatrix}$

5. $\begin{pmatrix} 5 & 4 \\ 4 & 5 \end{pmatrix}$

6. $\begin{pmatrix} 0 & 1 & 1 \\ 0 & 1 & 0 \\ 0 & 0 & 1 \end{pmatrix}$

7. $\begin{pmatrix} 1 & 1 & 1 \\ 0 & 1 & 1 \\ 1 & 1 & 1 \end{pmatrix}$

8. $\begin{pmatrix} 3 & 1 & 1 \\ 1 & 1 & 1 \\ 1 & 1 & 1 \end{pmatrix}$

9. $\begin{pmatrix} 2 & 1 & 1 \\ 1 & 2 & 1 \\ 1 & 1 & 2 \end{pmatrix}$

10. $\begin{pmatrix} 0 & 0 & 1 \\ 1 & 0 & 0 \\ 0 & 1 & 0 \end{pmatrix}$

1 stage matrices are:

1. $\begin{pmatrix} 1 & 1 \\ 1 & 2 \end{pmatrix}$ $\begin{pmatrix} 0 & 1 \\ 1 & 1 \end{pmatrix}$ 2. $\begin{pmatrix} 2 & 0 \\ 0 & 2 \end{pmatrix}$ $\begin{pmatrix} 0 & 2 \\ 1 & 0 \end{pmatrix}$

3. $\begin{pmatrix} 4 & 0 \\ 0 & 4 \end{pmatrix}$ $\begin{pmatrix} 0 & 2 \\ 2 & 0 \end{pmatrix}$ 4. $\begin{pmatrix} 2 & 2 \\ 2 & 2 \end{pmatrix}$ $\begin{pmatrix} 1 & 1 \\ 1 & 1 \end{pmatrix}$

5. $\begin{pmatrix} 5 & 4 \\ 4 & 5 \end{pmatrix}$ $\begin{pmatrix} 1 & 2 \\ 2 & 1 \end{pmatrix}$ 6. $\begin{pmatrix} 0 & 1 & 1 \\ 0 & 1 & 0 \\ 0 & 0 & 1 \end{pmatrix}$ $\begin{pmatrix} 0 & 1 & 1 \\ 0 & 0 & 1 \\ 0 & 1 & 0 \end{pmatrix}$

7. $\begin{pmatrix} 1 & 1 & 1 \\ 0 & 1 & 1 \\ 1 & 1 & 1 \end{pmatrix}$ $\begin{pmatrix} 0 & 1 & 1 \\ 1 & 0 & 0 \\ 0 & 1 & 1 \end{pmatrix}$

8. $\begin{pmatrix} 3 & 1 & 1 \\ 1 & 1 & 1 \\ 1 & 1 & 1 \end{pmatrix}$ $\begin{pmatrix} 1 & 1 & 1 \\ 1 & 0 & 0 \\ 1 & 0 & 0 \end{pmatrix}$

9. $\begin{pmatrix} 2 & 1 & 1 \\ 1 & 2 & 1 \\ 1 & 1 & 2 \end{pmatrix}$ $\begin{pmatrix} 0 & 1 & 1 \\ 1 & 1 & 0 \\ 1 & 0 & 1 \end{pmatrix}$

10. $\begin{pmatrix} 0 & 0 & 1 \\ 1 & 0 & 0 \\ 0 & 1 & 0 \end{pmatrix}$ $\begin{pmatrix} 0 & 1 & 0 \\ 0 & 0 & 1 \\ 1 & 0 & 0 \end{pmatrix}$

EXERCISE 19.1

1. A, (2,5) B, (3,5) C, (2,7)
2. A, (4,2) B, (4,4) C, (3,4)
3. A, (2,1) B, (3,1) C, (3,−1)
4. A, (−2,0) B, (−4, 0) C, (−3,−2)

EXERCISE 19.2

1. (3,3), (6,3), (3,9) 2. (5,−4), (−1,−4), (2,5)
3. (−2,−2), (−4,−2), (−3,−4) 4. (−1,0), (−5,0), (−3,4)
5. (3,3), (3,2), (1½,2) 6. (2⅔,0), (2⅔,−1), (4,−1)

EXERCISE 19.3

1. $(-1,1), (-2,1), (-2,4)$
2. $(1,-1), (2,-1), (2,-4)$
3. $(1,1), (1,2), (4,2)$
4. $(1,-3), (2,-3), (2,-6)$
5. $(4,-1), (4,2), (1,-1)$
6. $(2,1), (2,5), (0,5)$
7. $(1,-1), (1,-4), (4,-1)$
8. $(-1,-1), (-4,-1), (-4,-3)$
9. $(-4,3), (-1,3), (-1,6)$
10. $(4,-4), (4,0), (0,-4)$
11. $y=0$ (x axis)
12. $x=0$ (y axis)
13. $y=-1$
14. $y=x$

EXERCISE 19.4

1. $(-1,1), (-1,3), (-4,3), (-4,1)$
2. $(-2,1), (-2,5), (-3,5), (-3,1)$
3. $(1,3), (1,5), (4,5), (4,3)$
4. $(5,1), (5,-2), (7,-2), (7,1)$
5. $(-1,-1), (-1,-3), (2,-3), (2,-1)$
6. $(3,3), (6,3), (6,-1), (3,-1)$
7. 90° anticlockwise about $(0,0)$
8. 180° about $(0,0)$
9. 180° about $(1,1)$
10. 90° clockwise about $(1,1)$
11. 180° about $(-1,3)$

EXERCISE 19.5

1.

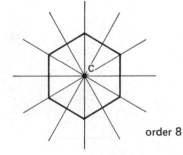

order 8

2.

order 2

3.

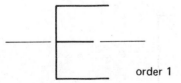

order 1

4.

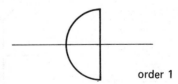

order 1

5.

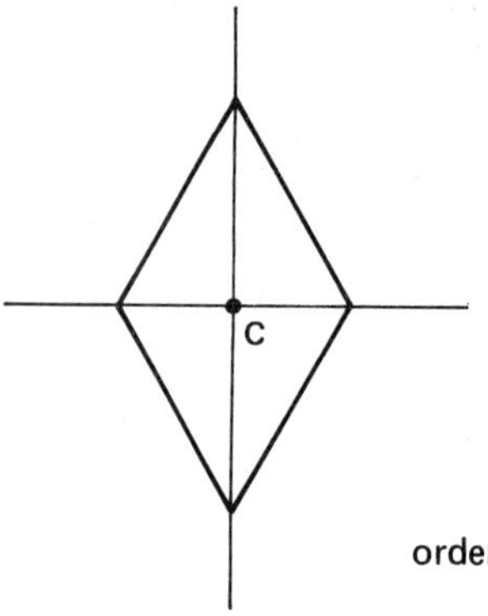

order 2

6.

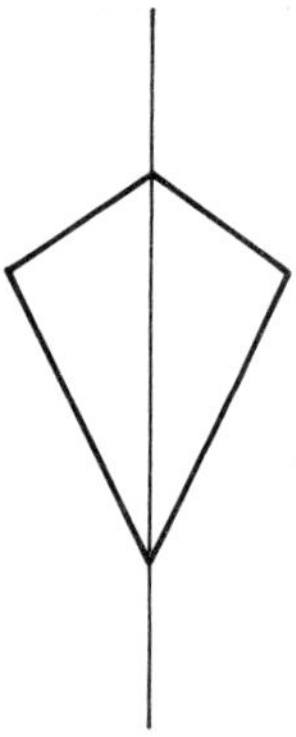

order 1

7.

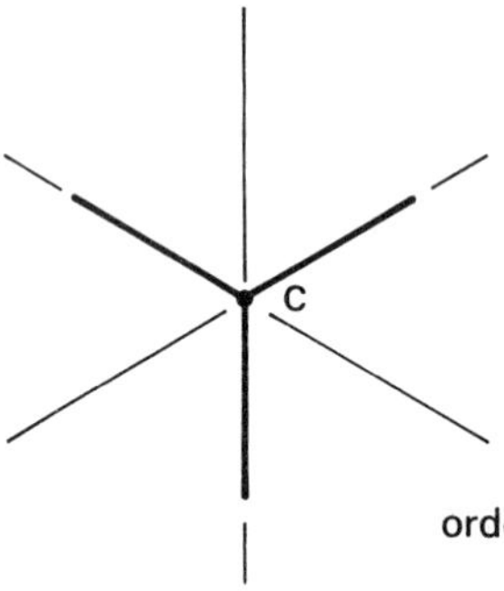

order 3

8.

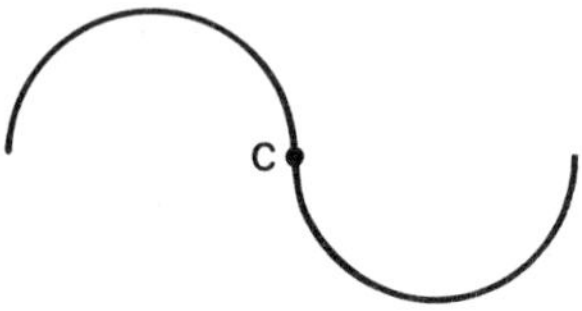

order 2

9.

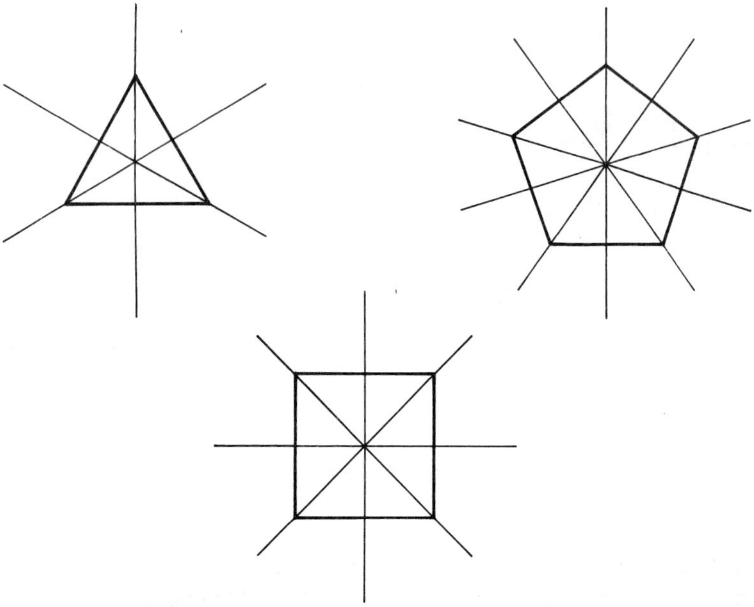

Regular Polygon	No. of axes of symmetry	Order of rotational symmetry	Angle between adjacent axes of symmetry
Equi. triangle	3	3	120°
Square	4	4	90°
Pentagon	5	5	72°
Hexagon	6	6	60°
Heptagon	7	7	$51\ 3/7^{\circ}$
Octogon	8	8	45°
Nonogon	9	9	40°
Decagon	10	10	36°
n sides	n	n	$360^{\circ} \div n$

10. R and L
11.

EXERCISE 19.6

1. Rotation of 180° about (0,0)
2. Rotation of 90° clockwise about (0,0)
3. Reflection in the x axis.
4. Reflection in the y axis.
5. Reflection in line y = x.
6. Reflection in line y = $-$x.
7. Enlargement, centre (0,0) $\times$ 2.
8. Enlargement, centre (0,0) ($\times \frac{1}{2}$).
9. Enlargement, centre (0,0) $\times\ -2$.
10.
$$\begin{pmatrix} n & 0 \\ 0 & n \end{pmatrix}$$ where n is the scale factor.

EXERCISE 19.7

1. $\begin{pmatrix} 1 \\ 2 \end{pmatrix}$

2. $\begin{pmatrix} 2 \\ 2 \end{pmatrix}$

3. Single transformation is reflection in the x axis.
4. Single transformation as a rotation of 180° about the origin.

5. c(i.) Rotation of 90° clockwise about (0,3) ii) Rotation of 180° about (0,0).
6. Rotation of 90° about (0,0).
7. Reflection in the line y = 2x.
8. N is a rotation of $36\cdot87^\circ$ clockwise together with an enlargement of 2.
9. Reflection in the line y = −x+4.
10. J maps to K by rotation of 180° about the origin.
   4x sq units
11. Rotation of 90° anticlockwise about origin.
12. Single transformation is a reflection in y axis.
13. Rotation about origin and enlargement.

EXERCISE 20.1

1. $\overrightarrow{AC}$ = $\begin{pmatrix} 5 \\ 8 \end{pmatrix}$

2. $\overrightarrow{OQ}$ = $\begin{pmatrix} -2 \\ 0 \end{pmatrix}$

3. $\overrightarrow{AD}$
4. a) 5   b) 13   c) 5   d) 5   e) 13
5. a) CD is parallel to AB and twice as long.
   b) 6a + 3b is parallel to 4a + 2b and 1½ times as long.
   c) AB = 2CD

6. a) $\overrightarrow{BA}$ = $\begin{pmatrix} -6 \\ -3 \end{pmatrix}$ or $-\overrightarrow{AB}$ b) $\overrightarrow{DC}$ = $\begin{pmatrix} 3 \\ -2 \end{pmatrix}$ or $-\overrightarrow{CD}$
   c) $\overrightarrow{FE}$ = −6a−2b

7. i) B (6,7)   ii) 5

8. (i) $\overrightarrow{OQ}$ = 6a + 2b   (ii) $\overrightarrow{RQ}$ = 2$\overrightarrow{OP}$ (iii) $\overrightarrow{RP}$ = 6b − 2a
9. (i) (5,−3)   (ii) $\begin{pmatrix} 1 \\ 5 \end{pmatrix}$
10. (a) 8m + 4n   (b) 12n   (c) 6n   (d) 12m + 6n
   O, X and Y form a straight line.
11. a) 12b + 6a   b) 5a − 2b   c) 6a + (12−k)b
12. $\begin{pmatrix} -1 \\ 3 \end{pmatrix}$
13. a) 9b − 6a   b) 3b − 2a   c) 4a + 3b
14. a) 4c − 4a   b) 2c − 2a   c) 2a + 2c
   d) 2c   e) 2PX = OC

15. a) −a   b) −b   c) 2a
    d) −a   e) b − a   f) 2(a − b)

16. a) $\begin{pmatrix} 1 \\ 1 \end{pmatrix}$ b) $5\overrightarrow{OC}$ c) $\begin{pmatrix} 8 \\ 4 \end{pmatrix}$

d) D, A and B lie on a straight line.

EXERCISE 21.1

1. Italian 6, French 12, German 10, Spanish 15.

2.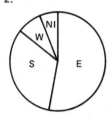

3.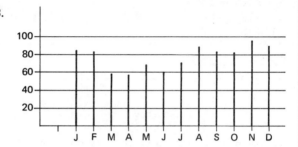

4.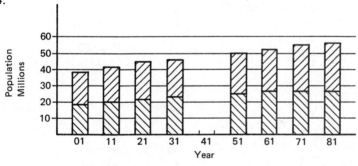

5.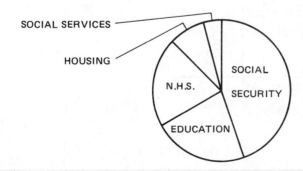

399

6. a)   16500 m   b)   10500 m   c)   25%
7. a)   £2880 m   b)   £160 m
8. a)   22.8%   b)   £28.33
9. Christian 950 million   Islamic 450 million   Hindi 430 million
    Confucianism 350 million   Buddhists 150 million
10. Chinese ♀♀♀♀♀♀♀♀♀♀♀
    English ♀♀♀♀♀♀
    Spanish ♀♀♀♀
    Hindi   ♀♀♀♀
    Russian ♀♀♀
    Arabic   ♀♀ o

EXERCISE 21.2

1. 14, 5, 3, 30.

2. | no. | | frequency |
    | --- | --- | --- |
    | 1 | //// | 4 |
    | 2 | ///// | 5 |
    | 3 | ///// /// | 8 |
    | 4 | ///// / | 6 |
    | 5 | ///// | 5 |
    | 6 | // | 2 |
    | | total | 30 |

3. | no. | frequency |
    | --- | --- |
    | 3 | 4 |
    | 4 | 8 |
    | 5 | 9 |
    | 6 | 6 |
    | 7 | 2 |
    | total | 29 |

4.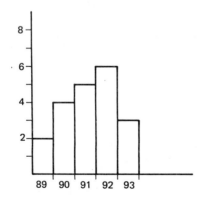

5. | Classification | | Frequency |
    | --- | --- | --- |
    | 0 – 4 | /// | 3 |
    | 5 – 9 | ///// | 5 |
    | 10 – 14 | ///// // | 7 |
    | 15 – 19 | ///// ///// / | 11 |
    | 20 – 24 | ///// // | 7 |
    | 25 – 30 | /// | 3 |
    | | total | 36 |

6.

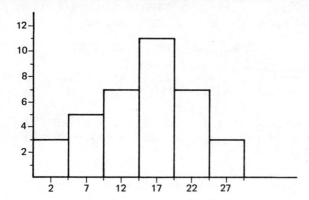

7.

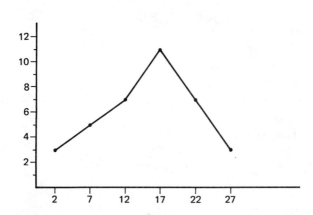

EXERCISE 21.3

1.	23·14 (2 d.p.)	2.	318·7	3.	2·58 (2 d.p.)
4.	41¼	5.	190	6.	106·3
7.	41	8.	64½	9.	81½
10.	58	11.	5	12.	8
13.	20	14.	10 − 19	15.	200 − 299

EXERCISE 21.4

1.

Length (class limit)	1·5	2·5	3·5	4·5	5·5	6·5	7·5	8·5	9·5	10·5
Cumulative frequency	1	2	6	12	21	28	32	34	35	36

2. | Wage | 59·50 | 79·50 | 99·50 | 119·50 | 139·50 |
   |---|---|---|---|---|---|
   | Cumulative frequency | 8 | 23 | 54 | 74 | 81 |

   a) £91   b) £76   c) £105   d) £29

3. | Length (mm) | 42½ | 43½ | 44½ | 45½ | 46½ |
   |---|---|---|---|---|---|
   | Cumulative frequency | 4 | 24 | 57 | 84 | 90 |

4. | No. in family | 1 | 2 | 3 | 4 | 5 | 6 | 7 |
   |---|---|---|---|---|---|---|---|
   | Cumulative frequency | 7 | 20 | 25 | 27 | 28 | 29 | 30 |

   Median 1·5

5. a) 41·1mm   b) 40·9mm   c) 41·4mm   d) ·5mm

6. | Runs | 10·5 | 20·5 | 30·5 | 40·5 | 50·5 |
   |---|---|---|---|---|---|
   | Cumulative frequency | 5 | 16 | 29 | 36 | 37 |

   a) 29   b) 21

7. | Height of plant | 60·5 | 61·5 | 62·5 | 63·5 | 64·5 | 65·5 |
   |---|---|---|---|---|---|---|
   | Cumulative frequency | 2 | 6 | 11 | 18 | 22 | 23 |

   a) 18   b) 17
   Mean 62·43 (to 2 d.p.)

8. a)
Time (hours)	Frequency
10	4
11	8
12	13
13	10
14	5
total	40

   b) | Time | 10·5 | 11·5 | 12·5 | 13·5 | 14·5 |
   |---|---|---|---|---|---|
   | Cumulative frequency | 4 | 12 | 25 | 35 | 40 |

   c) (i) 12·1 hours   (ii) 13 hours and 11·3 hours
   (iii) 1·7 hours

9. a)
No. of absentees	0	1	2	3	4	5	6	7
Cumulative frequency	9	21	36	47	53	57	59	60

   c) Median 1·6 days

10. a)
$$
\begin{array}{rcl}
19\cdot5 & - & 29\cdot5 \\
29\cdot5 & - & 39\cdot5 \\
39\cdot5 & - & 49\cdot5 \\
49\cdot5 & - & 59\cdot5 \\
59\cdot5 & - & 69\cdot5 \\
69\cdot5 & - & 79\cdot5 \\
79\cdot5 & - & 89\cdot5 \\
\end{array}
$$

b)

19·5 −29·5	29·5 −30·5	39·5 −49·5	49·5 −59·5	59·5 −69·5	69·5 −79·5	79·5 −89·5
3	29	70	118	155	181	186

d) Median 54·5 m.p.h.   Upper quartile 65 m.p.h.
Lower quartile 44 m.p.h.   Interquartile range 21 m.p.h.

EXERCISE 21.5

1. 1/6   2. 1/13   3. 3/7   4. 1/20
5. ½   6. ½
7. a) ½   b) 3/4   c) 2/3   d) 1/5   e) 1/4
8. 4/13   9. ⅓   10. 7/12   11. 5/6
12. 1/169   13. 4/663   14. 1/12
15. a) 1/8   b) 3/8   c) 1/8   d) 3/8   16. $\dfrac{15}{161}$
17. a) 1/9   b) 2/9   c) 4/9   d) 2/9   e) 1/9

18.

	1	2	3	4	5	6	
2	3	4	5	6	7	8	a) 1/6
3	4	5	6	7	8	9	b) 5/18
4	5	6	7	8	9	10	c) 5/6

19. a) 1/5   b) 3/10
20. a) 1/6   b) ½   c) 3/10

21.

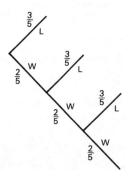

a) 4/25
b) 8/125
c) 12/125

22.

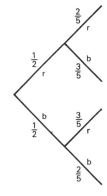

a)   3/10
b)   1/5

23.

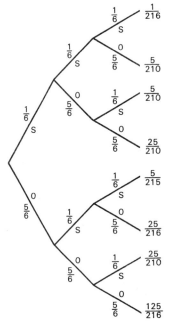

$\frac{1}{6}$, $\frac{5}{6}$

a)   1/216
b)   5/72
c)   25/72

INVESTIGATIONS

These answers and suggestions are not the only solutions. It is quite likely that yours will be different in some way.

1.   Equilateral triangle, isosceles triangle, scalene triangle (NO right angle triangle), square, rectangle, Hexagon, Pentagon.

2. a) 16, 13, 10, 7 and 4 squares (i.e. 5 different ways)

    b) 4 X 4 square − minimum 4

        5 X 5   8

        6 X 6   4

        7 X 7   10

        8 X 8   4

        9 X 9   12

                    etc.

3. (i)   1/2 + 1/3   (ii)   1/2 + 1/7 + 1/28   (iii)   1/2 + 1/6

    (iv) 1/4 + 1/2 + 1/6   (v)   1/2 + 1/6 + 1/12 + 1/30

4. $3(n - 1)$, $\ell + m + n - 3$

5. Use the values of n where $a^2 \leqslant n < (a + 1)^2$

    Where n and a are whole numbers

6. 2^{12} − method   2 has 2 factors

                           4 has 3 factors

                           8 has 4 factors

                           etc.

7. 4, 8, 32.

8. $\dfrac{n\,(n - 1)}{2}$

9. 2·5 cm.

10. 5   A square whose sides are an odd number of units long cannot be halved
     because it has an odd number of squares in it.

11. Maximum 8, minimum 4.

12. 14

13. 5, 13, 17, 29, 37 . . .

14.

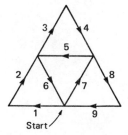

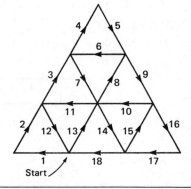

15. a) (i) There has to be restrictions otherwise there is an infinity of routes.
    (ii) Longest route is 6 edges.
    (iii) 16 different routes, shortest route is 3 edges
    b) F + E = R − 2

16. 2

17. 50 (including reflections and rotations)

18. a) 22   b) A 2 × 4 rectangle giving 8 squares is the only one.
    This can be proved by equating axb = a + 1 + b + 1

giving $a = \dfrac{b + 2}{b - 1}$

19. $\dfrac{1}{a} = \dfrac{1}{b} + \dfrac{1}{c}$ where a x b = c and b − a = 1

20. F + V − E = 2

21.
Move 1	G	G	G	←R	R	R	
Move 2	G	G	G	R		R	R
Move 3	G	G→		R	G	R	R
Move 4	G		G	R	G	R	R
Move 5	G	R	G		G	R	R
Move 6	G	R	G	R	G	←R	
Move 7	G	R	G	R	G	R	
Move 8	G	R	G	R		R	G
Move 9	G	R		R	G	R	G
Move 10	←R	G	R	G	R	G	
Move 11	R		G	R	G	R	G
Move 12	R	R	G		G	R	G
Move 13	R	R	G	R	G→		G
Move 14	R	R	G	R		G	G
Move 15	R	R	←R	G	G	G	

R	R	R		G	G	G

22. a) 16   b) 2^{x-1}

23. $A = i + \frac{1}{2}p − 1$

INDEX

GW00482277

Liberty Phi

PISCES

INTRODUCTION

Astrology is all about the planets in our skies and what energy and characteristics influence us. From ancient times, people have wanted to understand the rhythms of life and looked to the skies and their celestial bodies for inspiration, and the ancient constellations are there in the 12 zodiac signs we recognise from astrology. The Ancient Greeks devised narratives related to myths and legends about their celestial ancestors, to which they referred to make decisions and choices. Roman mythology did the same and over the years these ancient wisdoms became refined into today's modern astrology.

The configuration of the planets in the sky at the time and place of our birth is unique to each and every one of us, and what this means and how it plays out throughout our lives is both fascinating and informative. Just knowing which planet rules your sun sign is the beginning of an exploratory journey that can provide you with a useful tool for life.

Understanding the meaning, energetic nature and power of each planet, where this sits in your birth chart and what this might mean is all important information and linked to your date, place and time of birth, relevant *only* to you. Completely individual, the way in which you can work with the power of the planets comes from understanding their qualities and how this might influence the position in which they sit in your chart.

What knowledge of astrology can give you is the tools for working out how a planetary pattern might influence you, because of its relationship to your particular planetary configuration and circumstances. Each sun sign has a set of characteristics linked to its ruling planet – for example, Pisces is ruled by Neptune – and, in turn, to each of the 12 Houses (see page 81) that form the structure of every individual's birth chart (see page 78). Once you know the meanings of these and how these relate to different areas of your life, you can begin to work out what might be relevant to you when, for example, you read in a magazine horoscope that there's a Full Moon in Capricorn or that Jupiter is transiting Mars.

Each of the 12 astrological or zodiac sun signs is ruled by a planet (see page 52) and looking at a planet's characteristics will give you an indication of the influences brought to bear on each sign. It's useful to have a general understanding of these influences, because your birth chart includes many of them, in different house or planetary configurations, which gives you information about how uniquely *you* you are. Also included in this book are the minor planets (see page 102), also relevant to the information your chart provides.

PISCES

Our sun sign is determined by the date of our birth wherever we are born, and if you are a Pisces you were born between February 19th and March 20th. Bear in mind, however, that if you were born on one or other of those actual dates it's worth checking your *time* of birth, if you know it, against the year you were born and where. That's because no one is born 'on the cusp' (see page 78) and because there will be a moment on those days when Aquarius shifts to Pisces, and Pisces shifts to Aries. It's well worth a check, especially if you've never felt quite convinced that the characteristics of your designated sun sign match your own.

The constellation of Pisces (Latin for fishes) is a large configuration of stars formed of two geometric shapes joined by a V. Greek mythology tells the story of Aphrodite, goddess of love, and her son Eros, and how they transformed into fish to escape the wrath of Gaia, their tails tied together so they wouldn't lose each other in the waters of the Euphrates.

Pisces is ruled by the planet Neptune, god of the seas, and embodies their emotional, ever-fluctuating tides. The constantly changing oceans can be mysterious, the shimmering of reflected light creating n illusionary effect and hiding their depth.

A water sign (like Cancer and Scorpio), Pisces experiences the world very much through their feelings and is often extremely intuitive and in-tune with other people. Pisces is also a mutable sign (like Gemini, Virgo and Sagittarius) and well able to adapt to almost any situation they find themselves in, moving fluidly through the different social groups in which they might find themselves. This fluidity may make setting boundaries necessary, otherwise Pisces can sometimes find themselves overwhelmed by trying to be all things to all people, and the word No is a very useful one for Pisces to learn as they mature. Imagination (which can also lead to great empathy) is another of their creative gifts and their ability to weave magic through writing, art, music or dramatic performance is a very Pisces trait.

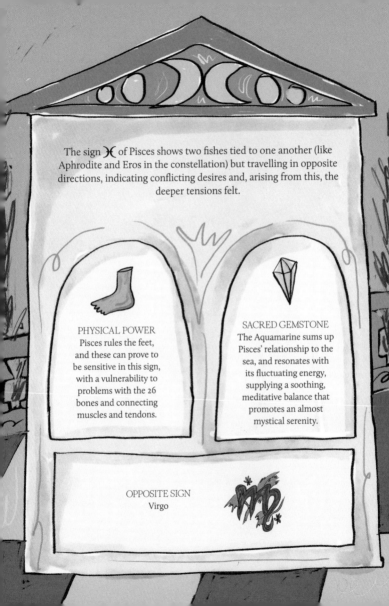

The sign ♓ of Pisces shows two fishes tied to one another (like Aphrodite and Eros in the constellation) but travelling in opposite directions, indicating conflicting desires and, arising from this, the deeper tensions felt.

PHYSICAL POWER
Pisces rules the feet, and these can prove to be sensitive in this sign, with a vulnerability to problems with the 26 bones and connecting muscles and tendons.

SACRED GEMSTONE
The Aquamarine sums up Pisces' relationship to the sea, and resonates with its fluctuating energy, supplying a soothing, meditative balance that promotes an almost mystical serenity.

OPPOSITE SIGN
Virgo

Pisces is depicted by the fish, with two of them linked together, swimming through the seas of life and forever navigating the shallow and deeper reaches of water, which represents their imaginative and emotional life.

Pisces' strength lies in their ability to respond and adapt fluidly to situations and people, thanks to their emotional intelligence and imagination. Being able to imagine other people's realities lies at the heart of empathy, another Pisces trait. A sensitivity to others needs boundaries, however, in order not to be overwhelmed, and finding this balance is very important for Pisces. This tension between being too responsive and having reservations is seen symbolically in the depiction of the two fish swimming in opposite directions. As Pisces grows and matures, this tension becomes easier to reconcile and they learn to say No when necessary for their own wellbeing, without causing offence.

Ruled by Neptune, the Roman god of the sea, there's a lot of deep water in which it's also possible for Pisces to hide. Neptune can also alter perception, creating a sense of illusion and Pisces sometimes deals with the more mundane aspects of life by hiding from reality. Subterfuge can also become something of a default for Pisces, especially to avoid being overwhelmed by an emotional response.

Pisces is also the most spiritual sign of the zodiac and it rules the 12th House of subconscious desires and secrets (see page 85), connecting to what's mystical and unseen, and how this can be used to evolve personally. For many Pisces this is about a spiritual journey, in whatever form this spirituality might manifest itself, and for some this might mean a conventional religious belief, for others an escapism through alcohol or drugs, or through dedication to a life of service to others. Again, there's an element of hiding the true self in this way, so it's important for Pisces to be true to their own self-realisation and find a way to do this that's authentic to them.

There's a very creative energy around Pisces and this is often expressed through artistic outlets and ventures. Visual art, the theatre, writing and cinema are all areas that attract a lot of Pisces who may make this their profession in some way – or, if not, through amateur or recreational activity. Certainly a lot of Pisces love to perform in front of an audience, finding expression through making music or theatre or just storytelling to enraptured children. And when it comes to friendships, Pisces is the sign of kindness and thoughtfulness. Gentle natured, they can also be real charmers, paying close attention to those they love and care for, often willing to go the extra mile for them.

THE MOON IN YOUR CHART

While your zodiac sign is your sun sign, making you a sun sign Pisces, the Moon also plays a role in your birth chart and if you know the time and place of your birth, along with your birth date, you can get your birth chart done (see page 78). From this you can discover in which zodiac sign your Moon is positioned in your chart.

The Moon reflects the characteristics of who you are at the time of your birth, your innate personality, how you express yourself and how you are seen by others. This is in contrast to our sun sign which indicates the more dominant characteristics we reveal as we travel through life. The Moon also represents the feminine in our natal chart (the Sun the masculine) and the sign in which our Moon falls can indicate how we express the feminine side of our personality. Looking at the two signs together in our charts immediately creates a balance.

MOON IN PISCES

The Moon spends roughly 2.5 days in each zodiac sign as it moves through all 12 signs during its monthly cycle. This means that the Moon is regularly in Pisces, and it can be useful to know when this occurs and in particular when we have a New Moon or a Full Moon in Pisces because these are especially good times for you to focus your energy and intentions.

A New Moon is always the start of a new cycle, an opportunity to set new intentions for the coming month, and when this is in your own sign, Pisces, you can benefit from this additional energy and support. The Full Moon is an opportunity to reflect on the culmination of your earlier intentions.

NEW MOON
IN PISCES AFFIRMATION

'I look to my dreams for inspiration but will be mindful of what work might be necessary to bring these to fruition.'

FULL MOON
IN PISCES AFFIRMATION

'I trust in the culmination of the Full Moon's energy to illuminate the depths of what I must consider in the realisation of my dreams.'

PISCES HEALTH

Pisces rules the feet, which is curious for a sign depicted by fish, although its glyph is sometimes said to represent a pair of feet. While they may have beautifully shaped feet as children, Pisces can be susceptible to bunions, chilblains, sprains and metatarsal fractures, so it's best to be aware of this and look after them. And because of this, Pisces is one of the signs most likely to have their podiatrist on speed dial.

Because of their affinity to water, many Pisces love water sports and to swim and this puts their feet at less risk. They often like the freedom of movement that being in water provides, and Pisces are as happy to dive and play as much as to swim lengths for exercise. Windsurfing, water-skiing and surfing or body-boarding also have their allure, although for many Pisces this is an occasional recreational event rather than regular exercise. The confined nature of a local swimming pool is often less attractive and it takes the more committed of Pisces to regularly show up for exercise there. For others, a complete contrast to swimming appeals and many Pisces enjoy long-distance running, finding it helps them ground their watery energy. For this, Pisces needs to have good supportive running shoes to protect their feet.

POWER UP
YOUR PISCES
ENERGY

There are often moments or periods when we feel uninspired, demotivated and low in energy. At these times it's worth working with your innate sun sign energy to power up again, and paying attention to what Pisces relishes and needs can help support both physical and mental health.

While watery environments resonate and can help restore and calm Pisces, sometimes it's also important to ground, and fire up, energy that might have become a little stagnant. It's important for Pisces to connect with the environment, walk the earth and turn their face towards the healing Sun. Natural surroundings and full-spectrum light are really helpful in lifting mood, and gentle Pisces can be all too susceptible to SAD (seasonal affective disorder) in the winter months when days are short. Ultraviolet light on the skin will ensure vitamin D production, which can also become depleted over the winter months.

Imaginative, creative Pisces will also thrive on cultural input – whether from visiting art galleries, music concerts or through their own reading and writing – and this too can help lift their soul. And socialising with like-minded friends can help stimulate their mood, preventing that constant internalising and rumination that can sap energy and cause depression. Exercise too will help Pisces, for their bodies and through the increase in feel-good endorphins in the brain that occurs with physical activity. Otherwise, restorative yoga or more dynamic Pilates can help them shift to a higher gear too.

As ever, a nutritious diet is an important aspect of Pisces' self-care, and while they often extol the virtues of fruit and vegetables, Pisces doesn't always follow the advice of five to seven portions a day. So a first step in powering up Pisces energy is to take a good look at what they are eating, jettisoning empty calories and going for a better mix of low-glycaemic carbohydrates, quality protein intake and lots of fruit and vegetables to help reinvigorate both body and mind. Iron-rich foods like spinach, watercress, beets, sweet potatoes, edamame, kidney beans, asparagus and dried apricots help provide this reinvigoration. Hydration too is important, particularly for a water sign, but low-caffeine and less alcohol will probably serve Pisces better. Herbs and spices with a bit of bite can help revive the appetite and Pisces should try dill, paprika, ginger tea and freshly ground black pepper while using sea salt rather than rock salt.

Utilise a New Moon in Pisces with a ritual to set your intentions and power up: light a candle, use essential oil of sandalwood to help ground your mood and concentration (this oil blends well with soothing lavender and uplifting ylang ylang), focus your thoughts on the change you wish to see and allow time to meditate on this. Place your gemstone (see page 13) in the moonlight. Write down your intentions and keep in a safe place. Meditate on the New Moon in Pisces affirmation (see page 21).

At a Full Moon in Pisces you will have the benefit of the Sun's reflected light to help illuminate what is working for you and what you can let go, because the Full Moon brings clarity. Reflect on the Full Moon in Pisces affirmation (see page 21) and make a note of your thoughts and feelings, strengthened by the moon in your sign.

PISCES'
SPIRITUAL
HOME

K nowing where to go to replenish your soul and recharge your batteries both physically and spiritually is important and worth serious consideration. For some Pisces, their spiritual home will always be something of a fantasy world in their own heads, something they take with them wherever they go. For others, it is the home they've created to showcase their dreams, whatever the geographic location.

Wherever they hail from, there are also a number of countries where Pisces will feel comfortable, whether they choose to go there to live, work or just take a holiday. Locations that resonate with Pisces' spirituality include Samoa, Chile, Portugal and North African countries Morocco, Egypt and Tunisia, along with Mauritius.

Cities with a spiritual feel like Jerusalem, Kyiv and Rio de Janeiro are places where Pisces is likely to feel at home, along with Warsaw, Seville and Dublin. There's a unique combination of history and drama in these places that appeals to Pisces' imagination and where they might feel most creative and inspired.

P I S

W O M A N

C E S

Pisces women can be a captivating mix of sensuality and blunt talking. This is because she is usually gifted with such acute insight that she sees no point beating about the bush when it comes to expressing an opinion, while also creating the disarming illusion of being a romantic and a dreamer. This can make her something of a challenge, because which Pisces woman is going to show up? Either is great as long as it's working in her favour, but Pisces can sometimes find the balance tricky. And while she definitely enjoys being a bit of a mystery, others can find her charms a little too other-worldly.

This is also a woman who likes to dress with an eye on what expresses her version of spirituality, which can sometimes mean deep purples or turquoise colours worn in a block or more subtly in accessories, jewellery or underwear. But there's a fluidity to her garments, often with floating silk scarves or a trailing fishtail detail to her coat. The way Pisces moves too is often graceful and fluid, with beautiful arm movements, as if serenely moving through gentle waters. Creativity is at the heart of many decisions Pisces

women make, from the way they dress to the decor in their home, and there's often something charmingly artistic about Pisces women that captivates.

Another notable trait in Pisces woman, along with her mysterious charming ways, is her kindness. This is a woman who will often go out of her way to comfort someone. Friend or stranger alike, Pisces finds it difficult to ignore another's discomfort or distress and her instinct is always to offer a supportive gesture, from a hug to a financial loan, should she judge their need to be greater than her own. Pisces is the woman who will often prioritise someone else's needs above her own and will selflessly give of her time, listening to someone's woes. It's a great gift to be so empathetic, but it can sap and drain Pisces' energy too. From childhood to grave, Pisces woman is likely to be a giver, and as she matures she needs to learn that she can give more if she takes better care of herself. Putting herself first isn't selfish, but enables Pisces woman to prioritise better how to be the friend and lover she wants to be without losing sight of herself.

PISCES MAN

Pisces man is one of the most interesting in the zodiac because it's not always clear, thanks to planet Neptune, that what you see is what you get. Very often gregarious and outgoing, Pisces man often keeps his deeper, more sensitive side under wraps. What you do see, however, is a man with an ease of movement, as Pisces is very seldom sluggish but fluid in the way they move, often making them great dancers. Pisces men can be very creative in their dress and are often beautifully dressed too, in lovely fabrics from linen to cashmere, which can be vintage, high street or designer-label.

He is also likely to have kept some heirloom family linen, china or silver, because Pisces values the spirituality of much-loved items, and his home often reflects this. Another trait is that Pisces often has, despite their dreamy ways, a strong practical streak. He's a man who likes to get things done now, rather than in a week's time, so the recycling (he cares about the Earth's future) is always done, the sink is unblocked or that flatpack furniture built, without delay.

This is also a man who makes a lovely friend as well as a lover, because Pisces men express their interest and concern through kindness. You may only need to mention once that something needs fixing, and Pisces man could surprise you by turning up the next day with a bag of tools because there's often a practical element to their care.

The downside of a Pisces man can be their regular need to escape, into fantasy or sometimes through literally disappearing off on some expedition, as they like to explore new waters to reinvigorate their lives. Sometimes that escape can be via mind-altering substances, or some religious sect, with which they like to escape or explore their own minds. Again, as for all Pisces, there's often a need for boundaries to avoid their fantasy lives drifting too completely into their real lives.

But mostly Pisces men are charming and kind, and the best friend in an hour of need. As a lover or partner, they show great commitment to those they love while still being capable of offering a stranger a shoulder to cry on.

PISCES IN
LOVE

Pisces can have a very romantic view of being in love, to the point of sometimes being unrealistic. Certainly, once they fall in love Pisces tends to move heaven and earth to have it reciprocated, to find their soulmate fish to which they can be joined. Once smitten, Pisces will often adapt, responding as intuitively as they can to meet their lover's needs and can be as committed to this quest as they are to their actual lover.

What's important for Pisces in love to remember is that they deserve to be loved just as much. There can be a tendency to give everything, and expect little in return, and there can be a tendency for Pisces to try and rescue another in return for love. But for an intimate relationship to thrive, Pisces mustn't delude themselves for the sake of romance; it must be rooted in equally real commitment to love on both sides.

PISCES AS
A LOVER

For all their charming and seductive ways, Pisces can be a surprisingly serious lover because this is a sign that takes love, in all its forms, seriously. Even at their most playful, Pisces is a thoughtful and engaged lover, focused on what makes it pleasurable for both. Again, the joining of two entities is often at the heart of Pisces' approach to making love, and this means their erotic pleasure is linked to a real appreciation of their partner's.

Pisces' strong imagination means that fantasy is often a part of how they operate as a lover, whether playing out their own fantasies in their head, or incorporating this in some sort of role play. What's also a typical Pisces trait is that this should be consensual, their dreams and desires matched to another's and not just foisted unwillingly upon them. This is very much part of Pisces' playful side too, where an element of performance becomes part of the game and they can easily adapt to whatever shared experience might enhance this.

There's often a spiritual side that comes into the bedroom with Pisces, and they may look towards spiritual practices like tantric sex to deepen their experience. For Pisces, an emotional connection is a first step towards sexual connection and only occasionally will physical attraction be the only precursor. It can happen, but there's often an underlying emotional connection that Pisces has already intuited.

All this seeking for an emotional connection can make some Pisces feel a tad vulnerable in their bodies, making them cautious and more tentative in their approach. However, as they mature this pays off because they learn to trust their intuitive side and their physical response which makes Pisces feel more secure.

WHAT'S IN PISCES'
BEDSIDE CABINET?

Rhythmic, sexy sea
music on a loop

Water-based
lubricant, for
enhancing sensual
pleasure

The Heart of Tantric Sex by Diana Richardson

WHICH SIGN SUITS PISCES?

In relationships with Pisces, the sun sign of the other person and the ruling planet of that sign can bring out the best, or sometimes the worst, in a lover. Knowing what might spark, smoulder or suffocate love is worth closer investigation, but always remember that sun sign astrology is only a starting point for any relationship.

PISCES AND ARIES

Deep, thoughtful Neptune finds Aries' dynamism inspiring if occasionally exhausting, but Mars does much to fire up Pisces' dreamier side, so together they can create wonderful ideas and realise great dreams.

PISCES AND TAURUS

Both Neptune and Venus share great charm, often making this an easy partnership, with Taurus' earthiness bringing much needed groundedness to some of Pisces' more fantastical moods. As long as this doesn't cause friction, it can work.

PISCES AND GEMINI

Mercury can sometimes find that Pisces puts a damper on events, while Neptune can find Gemini a little too frivolous, but when the air/water balance is right this can be a memorable partnership, bringing light to one and greater depth to the other.

PISCES AND CANCER

Two water signs that understand each other, and the Moon's influence on the sea resonates with its gentle influence on Neptune, but Cancer understands Pisces' need for a secure home in which to thrive, and is happy to supply this.

PISCES AND LEO

The Sun's strength does much to warm Pisces' watery depths, but Leo often needs much more obvious appreciation than is possible from such a spiritual soul, who, in return, can find that too much heat can become an irritant to them.

PISCES AND VIRGO

Again Mercury's airiness can ruffle Neptune's waters, but earth sign Virgo can offer a very welcome and stabilising effect on this relationship, while also benefiting from and appreciating Pisces' gentleness, often making this a very secure partnership.

PISCES AND LIBRA

In Libra, Venus has all the diplomatic skills to rein in Neptune's more dreamy aspects, helping Pisces realise some of their creative endeavours more productively, although at heart there may be too much air for this water sign to cope.

PISCES AND SCORPIO

Neptune and Pluto together may be just too deep to survive in partnership, as the way they express their feelings can aggravate each other, and unless Scorpio can reduce the sting in their tail, many Pisces may be too thin-skinned to survive.

PISCES AND SAGITTARIUS

Both love to explore, but Neptune and Jupiter may find it difficult to align their preferences for where. But the outgoing nature of Sagittarius is often just what Pisces needs, as long as they can travel together in the same direction.

PISCES AND CAPRICORN

Unless Saturn finds their gentler side, Capricorn can sometimes be too much of a taskmaster for Pisces, but if they can find a balance, then complementing this potent energy with Neptune can literally move mountains.

PISCES AND AQUARIUS

Neptune and Uranus can be so explosive together that this can either unite or separate the two, so this combined energy needs to be well managed. But if this is possible then Pisces can accommodate Aquarius' occasional unpredictability.

PISCES AND PISCES

With so much Neptune between them, it just depends whether this enables a partnership that swims happily through life in a compatible way, with the boundaries necessary to avoid literally drowning each other in emotion.

PISCES AT WORK

With their kind, sympathetic natures, Pisces are a welcome member of any team but they do need to make sure they don't get taken advantage of. Because they tend to want the best for everybody, Pisces can sometimes forget the necessity for boundaries and of not taking on extra work that should be done by someone else, or compensating for a team member who refuses to pull their weight. And delegation is another skill that Pisces often needs to learn.

When it comes to professions, however, Pisces often find themselves in work situations that require a performative element, as they are very good at adapting to and emulating a role in order to deliver. This can be in the acting profession itself, and many Pisces find this an attractive outlet for their creativity, but it can also be seen in careers like teaching, the law, and even medicine, all of which include a concern and interest in others. Whether teaching children or lecturing to adults, defending a client in a court of law, or carrying out surgery, these all combine a degree of performance in their delivery.

Creativity is such a strong element in Pisces, and their imagination can be used in service of so much, whether this is problem-solving logistics, writing a movie or designing a new App – all require envisaging the end result through imagination. And what increases Pisces' possibility for success is when this creative trait combines with a practical approach; the inspiration and the graft is what yields results.

The other side of this can be such an inconclusive, dreamy approach, that nothing gets achieved and Pisces is misunderstood as lazy or ineffectual. This is when a choice of careers is important because nothing sets those necessary boundaries as comprehensively as having clarity of vision in the first place, and this can take time and possibly some false starts. But that's what Pisces at work has to focus on.

  ♓

PISCES AT HOME

Pisces can be delightful to live with not least because they are often so well attuned to those with whom they share their life and so willing to make it a happy place for everyone, that they're prepared to make the effort to ensure it's so. And when it comes to domestic chores, they are also responsive to the occasional reminder that the rubbish needs taking out or the washing-up needs to be done, and seldom have to be prompted more than once.

Pisces aren't particularly possessive about their personal space or their possessions; they find adaptation easier than many and also tend to live on a more spiritual plane. But they do like to know there's somewhere they can retire to, in order to refresh their body and mind. It's not that they need massive amounts of privacy but every now and then Pisces needs some time out, and likes to retreat to a sanctuary of their own making where they can refresh their spirit. This space could be their study or their bedroom, but it may also be a place outside in a garden or on the seashore, a 'spiritual home' where they can revive their energy. Most Pisces have this place and for some it's inside themselves and they take it with them. These free spirits are those capable of creating their own home, wherever they travel, and it may be that some Pisces always have a small bag of essentials packed, ready for that journey.

As long as Pisces isn't lost in the realms or their imagination, or absorbed in the latest creative project, they enjoy their home and enjoy sharing it. Pisces have a streak of kindness that will always accommodate others. They don't take offence easily either, although they also don't like being taken for granted (who does?), but with Pisces, it is generally pretty harmonious as they like to swim peacefully through life with whoever they share it with.

FREE THE
SPIRIT

Understanding your own sun sign astrology is only part of
the picture. It provides you with a template to examine and
reflect on your own life's journey but also the context for
this through your relationships with others, intimate or otherwise,
and within the culture and environment in which you live.

Throughout time, the Sun and planets of our universe have
kept to their paths and astrologers have used this ancient wisdom
to understand the pattern of the universe. In this way, astrology is
a tool to utilise these wisdoms, a way of helping make sense of the
energies we experience as the planets shift in our skies.

'A physician without a knowledge of astrology has no right to
call himself a physician,' said Hippocrates, the Greek physician born
in 460 BC, who understood better than anyone how these psychic
energies worked. As did Carl Jung, the 20th-century philosopher and
psychoanalyst, because he said, 'Astrology represents the summation
of all the psychological knowledge of antiquity.'

SUN

RULES THE ASTROLOGICAL SIGN OF LEO

Although the Sun is officially a star, for the purpose
of astrology it's considered a planet. It is also the
centre of our universe and gives us both light and
energy; our lives are dependent on it and it embodies
our creative life force. As a life giver, the Sun is
considered a masculine entity, the patriarch and
ruler of the skies. Our sun sign is where we start our
astrological journey whichever sign it falls in, and as
long as we know which day of which month we were
born, we have this primary knowledge.

MOON

RULES THE ASTROLOGICAL SIGN OF CANCER

We now know that the Moon is actually a natural satellite of the Earth (the third planet from the sun) rather than a planet but is considered such for the purposes of astrology. It's dependent on the Sun for its reflected light, and it is only through their celestial relationship that we can see it. In this way, the Moon in each of our birth charts depicts the feminine energy to balance the masculine sun's life force, the ying to its yang. It is not an impotent or subservient presence, particularly when you consider how it gives the world's oceans their tides, the relentless energy of the ebb and flow powering up the seas. The Moon's energy also helps illuminate our unconscious desires, helping to bring these to the service of our self-knowledge.

MERCURY

Mercury, messenger of the gods, has always been associated with speed and agility, whether in body or mind. Because of this, Mercury is considered to be the planet of quick wit and anything requiring verbal dexterity and the application of intelligence. Those with Mercury prominent in their chart love exchanging and debating ideas and telling stories (often with a tendency to embellish the truth of a situation), making them prominent in professions where these qualities are valuable.

Astronomically, Mercury is the closest planet to the sun and moves around a lot in our skies. What's also relevant is that several times a year Mercury appears to be retrograde (see page 99) which has the effect of slowing down or disrupting its influence.

VENUS

RULES THE ASTROLOGICAL SIGNS OF TAURUS AND LIBRA

The goddess of beauty, love and pleasure. Venus is
the second planet from the sun and benefits from
this proximity, having received its positive vibes.
Depending on which astrological sign Venus falls in
your chart will influence how you relate to art and
culture and the opposite sex. The characteristics of
this sign will tell you all you need to know about
what you aspire to, where you seek and how you
experience pleasure, along with the types of lover you
attract. Again, partly depending on where it's placed,
Venus can sometimes increase self-indulgence which
can be a less positive aspect of a hedonistic life.

MARS

RULES THE ASTROLOGICAL SIGN OF ARIES

This big, powerful planet is fourth from the sun
and exerts an energetic force, powering up the
characteristics of the astrological sign in which it
falls in your chart. This will tell you how you assert
yourself, whether your anger flares or smoulders,
what might stir your passion and how you express
your sexual desires. Mars will show you what works
best for you to turn ideas into action, the sort of
energy you might need to see something through
and how your independent spirit can be most
effectively engaged.

JUPITER

RULES THE ASTROLOGICAL SIGN OF SAGITTARIUS

Big, bountiful Jupiter is the largest planet in our solar
system and fifth from the sun. It heralds optimism,
generosity and general benevolence. Whichever sign
Jupiter falls in in your chart is where you will find
the characteristics for your particular experience of
luck, happiness and good fortune. Jupiter will show
you which areas to focus on to gain the most and
best from your life. Wherever Jupiter appears in your
chart it will bring a positive influence and when it's
prominent in our skies we all benefit.

SATURN

Saturn is considered akin to Old Father Time, with all the patience, realism and wisdom that archetype evokes. Sometimes called the taskmaster of the skies, its influence is all about how we handle responsibility and it requires that we graft and apply ourselves in order to learn life's lessons. The sixth planet from the sun, Saturn's 'return' (see page 100) to its place in an individual's birth chart occurs approximately every 28 years. How self-disciplined you are about overcoming opposition or adversity will be influenced by the characteristics of the sign in which this powerful planet falls in your chart.

URANUS

The seventh planet from the sun, Uranus is the planet of unpredictability, change and surprise, and whether you love or loathe the impact of Uranus will depend in part on which astrological sign it influences in your chart. How you respond to its influence is entirely up to the characteristics of the sign it occupies in your chart. Whether you see the change it heralds as a gift or a curse is up to you, but because it takes seven years to travel through a sign, its presence in a sign can influence a generation.

NEPTUNE

RULES THE ASTROLOGICAL SIGN OF PISCES

Neptune ruled the sea, and this planet is all about
deep waters of mystery, imagination and secrets.
It's also representative of our spiritual side so the
characteristics of whichever astrological sign it
occupies in your chart will influence how this
plays out in your life. Neptune is the eighth planet
from the sun and its influence can be subtle and
mysterious. The astrological sign in which it falls in
your chart will indicate how you realise your vision,
dream and goals. The only precaution is if it falls in
an equally watery sign, creating a potential difficulty
in distinguishing between fantasy and reality.

PLUTO

Pluto is the furthest planet from the sun and exerts a regenerative energy that transforms but often requires destruction to erase what's come before in order to begin again. Its energy often lies dormant and then erupts, so the astrological sign in which it falls will have a bearing on how this might play out in your chart. Transformation can be very positive but also very painful. When Pluto's influence is strong, change occurs and how you react or respond to this will be very individual. Don't fear it, but reflect on how to use its energy to your benefit.

YOUR SUN SIGN

Your sun or zodiac sign is the one in which you were born, determined by the date of your birth. Your sun sign is ruled by a specific planet. For example, Pisces is ruled by Neptune but Gemini by Mercury, so we already have the first piece of information and the first piece of our individual jigsaw puzzle.

The next piece of the jigsaw is understanding that the energy of a particular planet in your birth chart (see page 78) plays out via the characteristics of the astrological sign in which it's positioned, and this is hugely valuable in understanding some of the patterns of your life. You may have your Sun in Pisces, and a good insight into the characteristics of this sign, but what if you have Neptune in Leo? Or Venus in Aries? Uranus in Virgo? Understanding the impact of these influences can help you reflect on the way you react or respond and the choices you can make, helping to ensure more positive outcomes.

If, for example, with Uranus in Taurus you are resistant to change, remind yourself that change is inevitable and can be positive, allowing you to work with it rather than against its influence. If you have Neptune in Virgo, it will bring a more spiritual element to this practical earth sign, while Mercury in Aquarius will enhance the predictive element of your analysis and judgement. The scope and range and useful aspect of having this knowledge is just the beginning of how you can utilise astrology to live your best life.

PLANETS IN TRANSIT

In addition, the planets do not stay still. They are said to transit (move) through the course of an astrological year. Those closest to us, like Mercury, transit quite regularly (every 88 days), while those further away, like Pluto, take much longer, in this case 248 years to come full circle. So the effects of each planet can vary depending on their position and this is why we hear astrologers talk about someone's Saturn return (see page 100), Mercury retrograde (see page 99) or about Capricorn (or other sun sign) 'weather'. This is indicative of an influence that can be anticipated and worked with and is both universal and personal. The shifting positions of the planets bring an influence to bear on each of us, linked to the position of our own planetary influences and how these have a bearing on each other. If you understand the nature of these planetary influences you can begin to work with, rather than against, them and this information can be very much to your benefit. First, though, you need to take a look at the component parts of astrology, the pieces of your personal jigsaw, then you'll have the information you need to make sense of how your sun sign might be affected during the changing patterns of the planets.

YOUR BIRTH CHART

With the date, time and place of birth, you can easily find out where your (or anyone else's) planets are positioned from an online astrological chart programme (see page 110). This will give you an exact sun sign position, which you probably already know, but it can also be useful if you think you were born 'on the cusp' because it will give you an *exact* indication of what sign you were born in. In addition, this natal chart will tell you your Ascendant sign, which sign your Moon is in, along with the other planets specific to your personal and completely individual chart and the Houses (see page 81) in which the astrological signs are positioned.

A birth chart is divided into 12 sections, representing each of the 12 Houses (see pages 82–85) with your Ascendant or Rising sign always positioned in the 1st House, and the other 11 Houses running counter-clockwise from one to 12.

ASCENDANT OR RISING SIGN

Your Ascendant is a first, important part of the complexity of an individual birth chart. While your sun sign gives you an indication of the personality you will inhabit through the course of your life, it is your Ascendant or Rising sign – which is the sign rising at the break of dawn on the Eastern horizon at the time and on the date of your birth – that often gives a truer indication of how you will project your personality and consequently how the world sees you. So even though you were born a sun sign Pisces, whatever sign your Ascendant is in, for example Cancer, will be read through the characteristics of this astrological sign.

Your Ascendant is always in your 1st House, which is the House of the Self (see page 82) and the other houses always follow the same consecutive astrological order. So if, for example, your Ascendant is Leo, then your second house is in Virgo, your third house in Libra, and so on. Each house has its own characteristics but how these will play out in your individual chart will be influenced by the sign positioned in it.

Opposite your Ascendant is your Descendant sign, positioned in the 7th House (see page 84) and this shows what you look for in a partnership, your complementary 'other half' as it were. There's always something intriguing about what the Descendant can help us to understand, and it's worth knowing yours and being on the lookout for it when considering a long-term marital or business partnership.

THE 12 HOUSES

W hile each of the 12 Houses represent different aspects of our lives, they are also ruled by one of the 12 astrological signs, giving each house its specific characteristics.

When we discover, for example, that we have Capricorn in the 12th House, this might suggest a pragmatic or practical approach to spirituality. Or, if you had Gemini in your 6th House, this might suggest a rather airy approach to organisation.

1ST HOUSE

RULED BY ARIES

The first impression you give walking into
a room, how you like to be seen, your sense
of self and the energy with which you
approach life.

2ND HOUSE

RULED BY TAURUS

What you value, including what you own
that provides your material security; your
self-value and work ethic, how you earn
your income.

3RD HOUSE

RULED BY GEMINI

How you communicate through words,
deeds and gestures; also how you learn and
function in a group, including within your
own family.

4 TH HOUSE

RULED BY CANCER

This is about your home, your security
and how you take care of yourself and
your family; and also about those family
traditions you hold dear.

5 TH HOUSE

RULED BY LEO

Creativity in all its forms, including fun
and eroticism, intimate relationships and
procreation, self-expression
and positive fulfilment.

6 TH HOUSE

RULED BY VIRGO

How you organise your daily routine, your
health, your business affairs, and how you
are of service to others, from those
in your family to the workplace.

7 TH HOUSE

RULED BY LIBRA

This is about partnerships and shared
goals, whether marital or in business,
and what we look for in these to
complement ourselves.

8 TH HOUSE

RULED BY SCORPIO

Regeneration, through death and rebirth,
and also our legacy and how this might be
realised through sex, procreation
and progeny.

9 TH HOUSE

RULED BY SAGITTARIUS

Our world view, cultures outside our
own and the bigger picture beyond our
immediate horizon, to which we travel
either in body or mind.

10TH HOUSE

RULED BY CAPRICORN

Our aims and ambitions in life, what we aspire
to and what we're prepared to do to achieve it;
this is how we approach our working lives.

11TH HOUSE

RULED BY AQUARIUS

The house of humanity and our
friendships, our relationships with the
wider world, our tribe or group to which
we feel an affiliation.

12TH HOUSE

RULED BY PISCES

Our spiritual side resides here. Whether this
is religious or not, it embodies our inner life,
beliefs and the deeper connections we forge.

THE FOUR
ELEMENTS

The 12 astrological signs are divided into four groups, representing the four elements: fire, water, earth and air. This gives each of the three signs in each group additional characteristics.

FIRE

ARIES ☙ LEO ☙ SAGITTARIUS

Are fire signs, embodying warmth, spontaneity and enthusiasm.

PISCES

WATER

CANCER ∾ SCORPIO ∾ PISCES

Are water signs, and embody a more feeling, spiritual and intuitive side.

EARTH

TAURUS ✿ VIRGO ✿ CAPRICORN

Are earth signs, grounded and sure-footed and sometimes rather stubborn.

AIR

GEMINI ❧ LIBRA ❧ AQUARIUS

Are air signsflourishing in the world of vision, ideas and perception.

FIXED, CARDINAL OR MUTABLE?

The 12 signs are further divided into three groups of four, giving additional characteristics of being fixed, cardinal or mutable. These represent the way in which they respond to situations.

FIXED

TAURUS, LEO, SCORPIO AND AQUARIUS ARE FIXED SIGNS

Their energy tends to be steady and they are less reactive, more responsive, although they can have a tendency to be resistant to change and need encouragement.

CARDINAL

ARIES, CANCER, LIBRA AND CAPRICORN ARE CARDINAL SIGNS

Their energy is often instinctive and action-oriented, enabling them to get things started, although there's sometimes a tendency to fail to carry things through.

MUTABLE

GEMINI, VIRGO, SAGITTARIUS AND PISCES ARE MUTABLE SIGNS

The clue here is their adaptability and responsiveness to change, which they don't fear, and readiness to listen to and embrace new ideas.

MERCURY RETROGRADE

This occurs several times over the astrological year and lasts for around four weeks, with a shadow week either side (a quick Google search will tell you the forthcoming dates). It's important what sign Mercury is in while it's retrograde, because its impact will be affected by the characteristics of that sign. For example, if Mercury is retrograde in Gemini, the sign of communication that is ruled by Mercury, the effect will be keenly felt in all areas of communication. However, if Mercury is retrograde in Aquarius, which rules the house of friendships and relationships, this may keenly affect our communication with large groups, or if in Sagittarius, which rules the house of travel, it could affect travel itineraries and encourage us to check our documents carefully.

Mercury retrograde can also be seen as an opportunity to pause, review or reconsider ideas and plans, to regroup, recalibrate and recuperate, and generally to take stock of where we are and how we might proceed. In our fast-paced 24/7 lives, Mercury retrograde can often be a useful opportunity to slow down and allow ourselves space to restore some necessary equilibrium.

SATURN RETURN

When the planet Saturn returns to the place in your chart that it occupied at the time of your birth, it has an impact. This occurs roughly every 28 years, so we can see immediately that it correlates with ages that we consider representative of different life stages and when we might anticipate change or adjustment to a different era. At 28 we can be considered at full adult maturity, probably established in our careers and relationships, maybe with children; at 56 we have reached middle age and are possibly at another of life's crossroads; and at 84, we might be considered at the full height of our wisdom, our lives almost complete. If you know the time and place of your birth date, an online Saturn return calculator can give you the exact timing.

It will also be useful to identify in which astrological sign Saturn falls in your chart, which will help you reflect on its influence, as both influences can be very illuminating about how you will experience and manage the impact of its return. Often the time leading up to a personal Saturn return is a demanding one, but the lessons learnt help inform the decisions made about how to progress your own goals. Don't fear this period, but work with its influence: knowledge is power and Saturn has a powerful energy you can harness should you choose.

THE MINOR
PLANETS

Sun sign astrology seldom makes mention of these 'minor' planets that also orbit the sun, but increasingly their subtle influence is being referenced. If you have had your birth chart done (if you know your birth time and place you can do this online) you will have access to this additional information.

Like the 10 main planets on the previous pages, these 18 minor entities will also be positioned in an astrological sign, bringing their energy to bear on these characteristics. You may, for example, have Fortuna in Leo, or Diana in Sagittarius. Look to these for their subtle influences on your birth chart and life via the sign they inhabit, all of which will serve to animate and resonate further the information you can reference on your own personal journey.

AESCULAPIA

Jupiter's grandson and a powerful healer, Aesculapia was taught by Chiron and influences us in what could be life-saving action, realised through the characteristics of the sign in which it falls in our chart.

ACCHUS

Jupiter's son, acchus is similarly benevolent but can sometimes lack restraint in the pursuit of pleasure. How this plays out in your chart is dependent on the sign in which it falls.

APOLLO

Jupiter's son, gifted in art, music and healing, Apollo rides the Sun across the skies. His energy literally lights up the way in which you inspire others, characterised by the sign in which it falls in your chart.

CERES

Goddess of agriculture and mother of Proserpina, Ceres is associated with the seasons and how we manage cycles of change in our lives. This energy is influenced by the sign in which it falls in our chart

CHIRON

Teacher of the gods, Chiron knew
all about healing herbs and medical
practices and he lends his energy to
how we tackle the impossible or the
unthinkable, that which seems
difficult to do.

DIANA

Jupiter's independent daughter was
allowed to run free without the
shackles of marriage. Where this falls
in your birth chart will indicate what
you are not prepared to sacrifice in
order to conform.

CUPID

Son of Venus. The sign into which
Cupid falls will influence how you
inspire love and desire in others, not
always appropriately and sometimes
illogically but it can still be an
enduring passion.

FORTUNA

Jupiter's daughter, who is always
shown blindfolded, influences your
fated role in other people's lives, how
you show up for them without really
understanding why, and at the
right time.

HYGEIA

Daughter of Aesculapia and also associated with health, Hygeia is about how you anticipate risk and the avoidance of unwanted outcomes. The way you do this is characterised by the sign in which Hygeia falls.

MINERVA

Another of Jupiter's daughters, depicted by an owl, will show you via the energy given to a particular astrological sign in your chart how you show up at your most intelligent and smart. How you operate intellectually.

JUNO

Juno was the wife of Jupiter and her position in your chart will indicate where you will make a commitment in order to feel safe and secure. It's where you might seek protection in order to flourish.

OPS

The wife of Saturn, Ops saved the life of her son Jupiter by giving her husband a stone to eat instead of him. Her energy in our chart enables us to find positive solutions to life's demands and dilemmas.

PANACEA

Gifted with healing powers, Panacea
provides us with a remedy for all ills
and difficulties, and how this plays
out in your life will depend on the
characteristics of the astrological sign
in which her energy falls.

PSYCHE

Psyche, Venus' daughter-in-law, shows
us that part of ourselves that is easy to
love and endures through adversity,
and your soul that survives death and
flies free, like the butterfly that
depicts her.

PROSERPINA

Daughter of Ceres, abducted by Pluto,
Proserpina has to spend her life divided
between earth and the underworld and
she represents how we bridge the gulf
between different and difficult aspects
of our lives.

SALACIA

Neptune's wife, Salacia stands on
the seashore bridging land and sea,
happily bridging the two realities.
In your chart, she shows how you
can harmoniously bring two sides of
yourself together.

VESTA

Daughter of Saturn, Vesta's job was to protect Rome and in turn she was protected by vestal virgins. Her energy influences how we manage our relationships with competitive females and male authority figures.

VULCAN

Vulcan was a blacksmith who knew how to control fire and fashion metal into shape, and through the sign in which it falls in your chart will show you how you control your passion and make it work for you.

FURTHER READING

Jung's Studies in Astrology: Prophecies, Magic and the Qualities of Time,

Liz Greene, Routledge (2018)

Lunar Oracle: Harness the Power of the Moon,

Liberty Phi, OH Editions (2021)

Metaphysics of Astrology: Why Astrology Works,

Ivan Antic, Independently published (2020)

*Parkers' Astrology: The Definitive Guide to Using Astrology in Every Aspect
of Your Life*,

Julia and Derek Parker, Dorling Kindersley (2020)

USEFUL WEBSITES

Alicebellastrology.com
Astro.com
Astrology.com
Cafeastrology.com
Costarastrology.com
Jessicaadams.com

USEFUL APPS

Astro Future
Co-Star
Moon
Sanctuary
Time Nomad
Time Passages

ACKNOWLEDGEMENTS

Thanks are due to my Taurean publisher Kate Pollard for commissioning this Astrology Oracle series, to Piscean Matt Tomlinson for his careful editing, and to Evi O Studio for their beautiful design and illustrations.

ABOUT THE AUTHOR

As a sun sign Aquarius Liberty Phi loves to explore the world and has lived on three different continents, currently residing in North America. Their Gemini moon inspires them to communicate their love of astrology and other esoteric practices while Leo rising helps energise them. Their first publication, also released by OH Editions, is a box set of 36 oracle cards and accompanying guide, entitled *Lunar Oracle: Harness the Power of the Moon*.

Published in 2023 by OH Editions,
an imprint of Welbeck Non-Fiction Ltd,
part of the Welbeck Publishing Group.
Offices in London, 20 Mortimer Street, London, W1T 3JW,
and Sydney, 205 Commonwealth Street, Surry Hills, 2010.
www.welbeckpublishing.com

Design © 2023 OH Editions
Text © 2023 Liberty Phi
Illustrations © 2023 Evi O. Studio

A CIP catalogue record for this book is available from the British Library.

ISBN 978-1-80453-004-7

Publisher: Kate Pollard
Editor: Sophie Elletson
In-house editor: Matt Tomlinson
Designer: Evi O. Studio
Illustrator: Evi O. Studio
Production controller: Jess Brisley
Printed and bound by Leo Paper

10 9 8 7 6 5 4 3 2 1